The *Ultimate* GOLDEN RETRIEVER

Kipps.

**Edited by
Valerie Foss**

**HOWELL
BOOK HOUSE**

NEW YORK

Amanda Bulbeck.

HOWELL BOOK HOUSE
A Simon & Schuster / Macmillan Company
1633 Broadway
New York, NY 10019

MACMILLAN is a registered trademark of Macmillan, Inc.

Library of Congress Cataloging-in-Publication data
available on request.

ISBN 0 87605 196 4
Special Cover Edition   1 - 58245 - 035 - 8
Printed and bound in Singapore

10 9 8 7 6 5 4 3 2 1

CONTENTS

CONTRIBUTORS

VALERIE FOSS (Breed Consultant):
Valerie Foss has been involved with Golden Retrievers for over thirty years, and her Elswood kennel has an international reputation for producing top-quality stock. In 1996 Sh. Ch Elswood The Highlander won the CC at Crufts. Val is a highly respected Championship Show judge; she judged Golden Retrievers at Crufts in 1987; she officiated at the World Show in Switzerland in 1994 and has travelled to the USA, Australia, Sweden, Norway, Denmark and Belgium on judging assignments. Valerie is a well-known writer on gundogs; her books include *The Golden Retriever Book of Champions* and *Golden Retrievers Today. See Chapters 1 , 7, and 13.*

MARCIA R. SCHLEHR: Marcia and Golden Retrievers have been inseparable for more than forty years. Goldens of her Kyrie breeding have become Show Champions, Obedience (UDX to TDX), Hunting Test, and Agility title-holders. She is a Life Member of the Golden Retriever Club of America, and has served on its Board, and on the Breed Standard and Judges Education Committees. She has judged Goldens since 1981, including many Specialty shows throughout the US and Canada. Marcia is a well-known writer on the breed, and she has published two books: *A Study of the Golden Retriever*, and *The New Golden Retriever* (Howell Book House). A freelance artist specialising in canine illustration, Marcia has contributed the line drawings for this book, as well as for many other books and videos. *See Chapters 4, 6, 7, 8 and 14.*

JOAN GILL: Joan was given her first Golden Retriever, Simon of Brookshill, in 1936, as a birthday present, and she has been involved with the breed ever since. Her famous Westley affix is known and respected worldwide. To date, there have been 29 Westley title holders, including the breed's only International Dual Champion, and a Field Trial Champion. Joan has been a Championship Show judge of Goldens since 1953 and has judged in many European countries as well as in Australia, Canada and America. She is an A panel judge for Retriever Field Trials. *See Chapter 10.*

DAPHNE PHILPOTT Daphne owned her first Golden Retriever in 1963, and in 1970 she went into partnership with Joan Gill and her Westley Goldens. They enjoyed enormous success, both in the UK and overseas until Daphne's death in 1997. Daphne also owned the Standerwick prefix for her working-bred Goldens. She bred three Standerwick Field Trial Champions, plus a Standerwick Champion in the show ring. She made up a Field Trial Champion as well as winning many other awards in Trials with different dogs, including a diploma in the Retriever Championships. Daphne was an international Championship judge for Goldens, and an A Panel judge for Retriever Field Trials. *See Chapter 8*

PATRICK HOLDEN: Patrick has trained Retrievers for 25 years, and is an Obedience Competition judge. His present dog, Bramble, is the first Golden Retriever ever to qualify at the top level in both Working Trials (TD Ex) and Obedience (OC winner). Patrick and Bramble have competed successfully in

Zelia Bohsen.

Agility in the Super Dogs Final. They have been at Crufts for several years in the inter-regional Obedience competition. In 1996 Bramble was the only gundog in the UK to qualify for Crufts individual Obedience Championship. *See Chapter 4.*

VAL BIRKIN: Val has been involved with the Golden Retriever breed for over 30 years and has owned or bred 18 British title holders; 12 of these have qualified in the field to be full Champions. Sansue dogs have taken the Challenge Certificate at Crufts seven times, three of them going on to Best of Breed. Val has been awarded Top Breeder of the Year on

several occasions. She has judged the breed at Championship Show level since 1975, and has judged in twelve different countries. *See Chapter 11.*

ANNE WEEKS: The Beldonburn kennel was founded in 1974 in partnership with Anne's daughter, Fiona. They have maintained a small but very select kennel, and have owned two Show Champions and one full Champion. Their biggest success was winning Best in Show at a general Championship Show, achieved with a homebred dog. Anne is a strong advocate of dual-purpose Goldens. A number of her dogs have participated in

Working Tests, and one has also competed in Field Trials. Anne is an international Championship judge of the breed. *See Chapters 2 and 3.*

ANNE FALCONER: Anne's interest in dog showing started in childhood when she competed in junior handling classes. However, her first Golden Retriever was Mathias of Westley, an Obedience competitor, and his name lives on through her prefix Siatham – an anagram of his name. Anne's interest in training continued, and in the 1980s she competed with a Test C dog who was also a Championship show winner and the holder of a Show Gundog Working Certificate. Anne has owned two Champions, bred a bitch with two CCs, and three Junior warrant winners. She awards CCs in Golden Retrievers and has travelled abroad on judging appointments.

HILARY VOGEL: Although born and educated in Britain, Hilary has lived in Germany for over thirty years. She first became involved with Golden Retreivers in the late 1960s and started a breeding programme using her Baltic Golden prefix. She has now bred or owned nine Champions including the breed's record-holding bitch (3 Ch. titles and 3 Field Trial awards). She is an International Championship judge, and is responsible for training and examining judges for the German Kennel Club. *See Chapters 7 and 15.*

DICK LANE BSC FRAGS FRCVS: Dick has worked as a veterinary surgeon in practice for the last thirty-five years, and is a consultant to the Guide Dogs for the Blind Association. He was awarded the Fellowship of the Royal College of Veterinary Surgeons in 1968, and the Fellowship of the Royal Agricultural Societies in 1993. Other successes include the BSAVA's Dunkin Award in 1977 and the BSAVA's Melton Award in 1987. Dick's literary work includes joint authorship of the *A-Z of Dog Diseases and Health Problems* (published by Ringpress Books in the UK and Howell Book House in the USA), editing *Animal Nursing*, now in its fifth edition, and joint editor of *Veterinary Nursing*. He is an occasional contributor to the *New Scientist, Veterinary Times*, and *Veterinary Practice. See Chapters 16 and 17.*

ALISON JONES BVetMed MRCVS: Alison, an expert in canine nutrition, qualified from the Royal Veterinary College, London, in 1987. After a short period in research, she entered a mixed practice in Gloucestershire where she worked for seven years. She then joined Hill's Pet Nutrition Ltd as a veterinary advisor. *See Chapter 5.*

HAZEL M. HINKS: Hazel acquired her first Golden Retriever in the early 1950s and started the Styal kennel ten years later. All her dogs today are descended from her first champion, Styal Sibella. Styal Goldens have won over 100 Challenge Certificates, and Hazel bred both the breed record holders, Ch. Styal Scott of Glengilde (42 CCs), and the bitch, Ch. Styal Stephanie of Camrose (27 CCs). Her great brood/show bitch Susila, litter sister of Stephanie, was the dam of Scott and three further Champions. A highly-respected international judge of Golden Retrievers, Hazel has judged in 15 countries including Australia, as well as at Crufts and the World Show. *She is the author of Chapter 6.*

Other contributions include Henric Fryckstrand (Scandinavia), Sandra Patterson (Australia), Sandie Milne (New Zealand) and Di Phillipson (South Africa).

1 INTRODUCING THE GOLDEN RETRIEVER

There are many reasons why a person chooses a particular breed of dog, but is usually strongly linked to the breed's inherent temperament – and how this fits in with your own temperament and lifestyle. The Golden Retriever is a friendly, loving dog, devoted to its human family. Intelligent and easy to train, the Golden's kindly disposition means that it will mix in with other household pets. This is a breed that adores children, and will never retaliate, despite provocation. The Golden Retriever's aim is to please you, and to add sunshine to your family's life.

Bred as working dog, the Golden Retriever has no problems relating to strange dogs. If it has a fault, it is a slightly over-exuberant attitude towards life. However, this is easily controlled with a sensible training programme. The Golden has a positive temperament, never showing aggression, nor being timid or nervous. Although most Goldens will give a warning when strangers approach, you should not expect your dog to act as a guard. If you want a guard dog, you would be better advised looking for another breed.

The most important consideration when choosing a Golden to join your home is its temperament. A slight beauty fault, which might mean that it would not win top honours in the show ring, will not impair its most important role – as a super companion and pet. Temperament, intelligence, love and obedience take it to the top of the class – and these qualities are more important than all the successes the show ring can bring.

A ROLE FOR YOUR DOG
The Golden Retriever is a superb companion dog, but if you want to train your dog to a higher standard, you will find a willing pupil.

Ch. Hye Tyme's Clipper, UD, JH, WCX. Nancy Corbin wanted her first dog to be one she could work with in several areas. Clipper certainly proved capable, but the first requirement for such achievement is a versatile owner/trainer, without which little will be accomplished.

Evelyn Smith owned and trained these three Goldens: Centre, Am. Can. Ch. Gayhaven Daemon, Am. CDX WC, Can. CDX, bred by Betty Gay: Left, Can. Ch. Smithaven's Danae of Glendavis, Am. CDX, Can. UD, bred by June Smith. Right, Am. Can. Ch. Orion of Alderbrooke, Am. UD, Can. UDT, bred by Carole Kvamme. Breeders are always pleased to have someone devote this amount of effort to developing their dogs' capabilities.

Bred originally as a working gundog, retrieving game over land and water, the Golden Retriever is still widely used in the field. They are quick to learn and make excellent shooting companions. Whether you want a rough-shooting companion, a Field Trial specialist, or a working test competitor, the Golden Retriever will excel in all disciplines.

The breed has also made its mark in Competitive Obedience, and its athletic physique and enthusiastic temperament makes it a keen competitor in Agility. The wonderful combination of intelligence and gentleness also makes the Golden a first-class assistance dog, and they are widely used as guide dogs for the blind, hearing dogs for the deaf, dogs for the disabled, and as therapy dogs. An added bonus is the breed's tremendous sense of smell, and many do important work as 'sniffer dogs', detecting drugs, arms and explosives.

CARING FOR YOUR GOLDEN RETRIEVER
The Golden Retriever is a beautiful dog to look at, with no exaggerations in body. They are easy to look after, as long as you keep to a regular routine of brushing and combing, particularly in wet and muddy conditions.

A strongly-built dog of medium size, the Golden Retriever requires a balanced diet of good-quality food (see Chapter Five: Diet and Nutrition), but they are not fussy feeders.

When you are rearing a puppy, it is especially important to give the correct food in order to promote correct growth and development. With maturity, you have to watch your Golden's figure for they can run to fat, and obesity constitutes a major health hazard.

Goldens do not require hours of strenuous exercise, but they do need regular exercise every day, rain or shine. An adult Golden requires one short, brisk walk and one decent-sized walk a day. The longer walk should be of about an hour's duration, with the opportunity for free-running exercise. Resist the temptation of giving a puppy too much exercise too young. This can pose an undue strain on developing bones. However, we are fortunate that the Golden Retriever is a hardy, no-nonsense breed, and most will go through life with relatively few health problems.

All breeds have their enthusiasts, but with the Golden Retriever it can be said without fear of contradiction that once you have owned – or been owned by – a Golden, you will not be content to live without one.

Am Ch. Farm Fresh Twenty-four K Bunny SH, WCX owned by Leslie Dickerson.

HISTORY OF THE BREED
After a long period during which no new information was forthcoming on breed history, the last few years have seen some exciting new, discoveries. The desire to go back to our roots in Golden Retrievers has provided a very worthwhile hobby for many 'Goldenites', for there is more to a breed than just going to a show at the weekend.

RETRIEVING DOGS
Retrievers, as specific breeds, were not seen until the late 19th century. There were no standardised breeds, but all retrieving dogs were very much in a state of flux, and were mated for their working ability, not for their looks. In themselves, Golden Retrievers do not have the history of the English Setter, whose natural work has been described in literature since the 14th century. Setters were evolved over hundreds of years from Spaniels, who are described in Count Gaston de Foix's book *Livre de Chasse,* written in 1387. Setters lie in the background of the early evolution of

Golden Retrievers. It is true to say that guns made retrievers! In the days of the muzzle-loading gun, not many birds would be shot in a day. The owner of an estate would walk it with his Setter or Pointer, and shoot an average of ten birds daily. By the 1880s, the steel-barrelled breech-loading shotgun, with its single trigger, came into being. This led to the shooting of flying birds and the introduction of French partridges suited to driven shoots, that is the driving of the birds over standing guns, as opposed to the guns walking up to sitting birds. Better guns, such as the modern break-and-load shotgun, led to pheasants replacing partridges as the number one game bird on most estates. Their higher and faster flight provided more sport for what was becoming for many an all-absorbing hobby.

Many estates were developed with great emphasis placed on their sporting facilities. The game books of the period tell the stories. Lord de Grey, an excellent shot, worked out that between 1867 and 1923 he shot 250,000 pheasants, 150,000 grouse and 100,000 partridge. Shooting became linked with status, wealth and fashion. Sportsmen with improved

*Water Spaniel –
Canis familiaris
hirsutus aquatilis.
J.G. Wood, 1898.*

guns started to need a specialist retrieving dog during the 19th century because, before birds were shot in flight, there were few lost birds. Some started to train their Setters and Pointers to retrieve, but this meant they did not hold the point, and demand grew for a breed specifically for retrieving.

EARLY BREEDING
At this stage, breeding was for working ability as well as individual characteristics of favourite dogs. Gundog breeds were mated among themselves. Fanciers built up their strains and guarded them jealously, only letting friends, or owners they wanted a puppy from, use their dogs. Aristocrats had strains named after them, as we know from old books and word of mouth: Lord Lovat's Beaufort Setters; The Southesk Setters; The Earl of Seafield's own; The Earl of Derby's own; and Lord Ossulton's Black Setters.

Sportsmen soon found an element of competition entering their hobby. The first trial for Setters and Pointers took place on April 18th 1865, on the Bedfordshire estate of Samuel Whitebread MP. The dogs were judged for nose, pace and range, as well as temperament plus style. Retrievers were still in the melting pot, but, nevertheless, the first retriever trials were held at Stafford in 1867. This breed trial, for retrieving dogs only, required a dog with a good nose and a soft mouth, who was obedient, without the Setter's desire to range out. Sportsmen crossed their retrieving Setters with the smaller St John's Newfoundland Dog. These dogs were brought into Britain by the Newfoundland fishing

fleets which unloaded in Southern ports like Poole, and also up the North Eastern coasts of the British Isles.

The St John's Newfoundland was a much lighter-built dog than the heavier strain of Newfoundland, and was crossed with Setters. The cross was further augmented by the addition of English Water Spaniels and Collies, leading to the development of the wavy-coated retriever, forerunner of one part of our Golden Retriever jigsaw.

One very important point to remember is that those dogs with the name of Spaniel or Setter looked very different from the same breeds today. The Kennel Club was founded in 1873 by the great Flatcoat enthusiast S.E. Shirley MP. There is a woodcut illustration in Colonel Hutchinson's famous book on dog training which shows crosses between Water Spaniel and Newfoundland Dog, between Water Spaniel and Setter Dog, and between Setter and Newfoundland Dog. Depending on the cross, offspring could be black, liver, black and tan or brindled, with a height of about 24 inches. Yellow-coloured puppies from black parents were not unknown. Thus retrievers, as their name implies, were doing their retrieving job, but particular breed or varieties were soon to become a growing part of the shooting scene. A quotation from *The Badminton Library,* a series of books published in 1886, says: "A Retriever is to our mind the king of all sporting dogs. His mien is dignified, his actions show the height of animal intelligence and he is affectionate and companionable as is no other dog used for shooting."

THE TWEEDMOUTH CONNECTION

The man whose early breeding created the Golden Retriever was Sir Dudley Coutts Marjoribanks MP, later the first Lord Tweedmouth. He lived with his wife and family in Brook House, Park Lane, London, but, during the long parliamentary recess, he devoted his time to his great interest, which was anything to do with sporting pursuits in the Highlands of Scotland. He moved in the highest echelons of Victorian society. In 1854, he paid £52,000 for the Guisachan Estate, about 20,000 acres near Loch Ness. Its outstanding beauty is still intact today, and well worth a visit. Although the handsome mansion he built is now a ruin, one can realise why country pursuits were so important to him. There is a description of his kennels in the book *The Seeing Eye: The diary of a Scottish Naturalist* by Sir John Lister Kaye, who bought an estate cottage called The Kennels in the early 1970s. The author explains how the kennels were a concept ahead of their time.

In the second half of the 19th century, new sporting estates were developed in areas opened up by the growth of the railway system. The first Lord Tweedmouth created, in the Guisachan estate, a showpiece of aristocratic Victorian self-indulgence. The great Georgian mansion was set in magnificent parkland with exotic species of trees from all over the world. The farm had a unique dairy and the largest enclosed steading in Scotland. The village of Tomich, where the workers lived, is now a protected monument to estate architecture. Today, beneath the overgrown vegetation, ladies' walks and rides can still be detected, and paved remnants found up to a mile and a half away from the house, not to mention ornate little bridges over burns or beside crashing waterfalls. A prototype power plant beneath a waterfall was probably one of the first private hydro-electric installations in Britain. All is now in total decay, and the great house a roofless ruin. But the primary attraction of the Scottish Highlands for wealthy Victorian aristocrats and self-made millionaires was the sport.

Red deer and grouse were the top British sporting quarry, and both abounded at Guisachan. On every sporting estate, the gundog was as important as everything else. Golden Retriever enthusiasts are indebted to Elma Stonex, and her work as a breed historian in the 1940s and 50s. She discovered, through information written by the sixth Earl of Ilchester, a great-nephew of the first Lord Tweedmouth, that his great-uncle had kept a stud book/game book/inventory with notes from 1835 until 1889 and the last litter he bred. This book was in the possession of Lord Tweedmouth's grand-daughter Lady Pentland. She gave the book to the Kennel Club where it can be seen to this day. I have a copy, and it brings the first Lord Tweedmouth to life as a man with an abiding interest and great skill in his hobbies – shooting, working gundogs and conservation.

In 1960 the Kennel Club officially recognised this, and stated in its description of the Golden Retriever: "The origin of the Golden Retriever is less obscure than most of the Retriever varieties, as the breed was

Guisachan – home of the first Lord Tweedsmouth.

Photo: A. Weeks

Sinnhein Goldens visiting Guisachan – their ancestral home.   *Photo courtesy: V. Foss.*

definitely started by the first Lord Tweedmouth last century, as shown by his carefully kept private stud book and notes, first brought to life by his great-nephew, the Earl of Ilchester, in 1952."

The romantic story of the Golden's descent from a troupe of Russian circus dogs has no foundation in fact. If this version were correct, there was no reason for Lord Tweedmouth not to mention it. His account of the Golden's origins is as follows.

The first Lord Tweedmouth and his son were walking in Brighton in the 1860s when they met a cobbler with a handsome young yellow retriever. He had acquired the puppy from Obed Miles, the keeper at Stanmer (Lord Chichester's estate) in payment for a debt. Lord Tweedmouth liked the cobbler's dog, bought him and called him Nous (Gaelic for Wisdom). He was a single yellow in a litter of black wavy coats, quite a common occurrence.

Dr Bond Moore, who had a very influential retriever kennel in the 1870s, is recorded as having a litter from Ch. Midnight which included two pups of a pale liver colour. The term liver had a different meaning in those days, covering all of the sandy colour from yellow to brown. Major, a wavy coated retriever, is mentioned in the 1891 Kennel Club Stud Book as colour lemon. There were quite a few livers and reds in the early Stud Books.

Nous has his entry in the 1865 Stud Book of Lord Tweedmouth as follows: "Lord Chichester's Breed. Pupped June 1864. Purchased at Brighton." In 1868, Nous was mated to Belle, given to Lord Tweedmouth by a relative, David Robertson MP, who lived at Ladykirk on the River Tweed. The stud book entry says: "Belle – Ladykirk breed 1863 – bred at Ladykirk from D. Robertson."

THE FIRST GOLDEN LITTER

Belle was a Water Spaniel from the Tweed. In Thomas Bewick's *History of Quadrupeds* there is a woodcut of the Small Water Spaniel, showing the shape and size of a retriever. Included in the colours for these Water Spaniels is liver and black with brindle. Nous was mated to Belle in 1868, and the resulting litter of three yellow puppies was the foundation of Goldens as a distinct breed. One pup, Crocus, was given to Edward Marjoribanks (the second Lord Tweedmouth) while Cowslip and Primrose were kept in the home kennel. A second litter from Nous and Belle in 1872 included Ada, who was given to Lord Tweedmouth's nephew, the fifth Earl of Ilchester. He started the Ilchester strain of retrievers, whose later prefix was Melbury. Unlike Lord Tweedmouth's early careful breeding, obviously aimed at keeping the Golden colour, Ilchester used black dogs freely right from the beginning. A black dog and a yellow bitch invariably produced yellows, whereas both colours came from a yellow dog and a black bitch.

From the stud book, we can see how thoughtfully matings were planned from 1868 to the last litter in 1889-1890, before the death of the first Lord Tweedmouth in 1894. Cowslip was mated to Tweed (Tweed Water Spaniel) and then one of the puppies, Topsy, was put to Sambo, a wavy coat presumed to be black, belonging to Lord Tweedmouth's business partner Sir Henry Meux. A bitch, Zoe, was kept from the mating. In 1884, she was mated to Jack, the son of her grand-dam, Cowslip. Jack was sired by Sampson, an Irish Setter belonging to Edward, later the second Lord Tweedmouth. Setters in those days were much heavier than today's streamlined models, and also a shade thicker in head.

Two of the litter mates from the pairing of Zoe and Jack were Nous (N2) and Gill, born in 1884. A study of the stud book shows that Cowslip and Tweed appear three times in four generations. In 1887, an outcross mated Gill to Tracer, a full brother of the famous black wavy coated retriever Ch. Moonstone, and resulted in ten black puppies. One of these, Queenie, was mated to her dam's litter brother, Nous 2. The two yellow puppies, Prim and Rose, born in 1889, were the last ones recorded as bred by the first Lord Tweedmouth. In another line, Sweep, who was descended from the original Ada, was mated to Zoe. At some time during the 1890s, a sandy-coloured bloodhound was used as a cross (obviously to improve tracking and nose). This information was written in Lord Tweedmouth's hand, on a piece of paper kept in the stud book and seen by Lord Ilchester, but then lost.

When the first Lord Tweedmouth's youngest son, the Hon. Archie Marjoribanks, went to

LEFT: Henry 5th Earl of Ilchester with Ada. Painting by H. Graves 1875.

RIGHT: Cowslip or Primrose from the first litter, establishing the Golden Retriever as a distinct breed. Detail from a painting by Gourley Stell RSA, 1871.

Ada's gravestone at Melbury: Born 1872, died 1882.

Photo courtesy: L.M. Sawtell.

America to run the family ranch, he took with him a Golden Retriever called Lady. Pictures survive of Lady in America and Canada. Archie Marjoribanks married in America, and, after his death, his widow remarried. Her son, Lord Hailsham (the longest-serving Lord Chancellor of this country), wrote to me saying: "My mother mentioned the Tweedmouth connection, and that of Guisachan, with the then new breed of Golden Retrievers, and in particular a dog called Sol."

THE CULHAM PEDIGREES

As I explained initially, the last few years have been exciting for Golden enthusiasts. In 1995 came the wonderful find of the Culham Pedigrees in Lord Harcourt's papers at the Bodleian Library in Oxford. Due to the information they contain, we can now trace the line on from Rose, in Lord Tweedmouth's last recorded litter, to Lord Harcourt's Culhams – so there is written evidence providing the link behind today's Golden Retrievers.

It is important to bear in mind that, in those early days, the same names were used for dogs in different generations. We have documentary proof (Lord Hailsham's letter) of the first Lord Tweedmouth's preference for 'colour' names, e.g. Primrose and Sol, and this runs through the very early pedigrees with names such as Sun, Topaz, Amber, Ginger and Sulphur. At this time dogs were used at stud very late in life – sometimes as old as fifteen years – and bitches would be used for breeding for as long as they were capable of producing litters. The famous post-war dog Ch. Torrdale Happy was born when his dam was eleven years of age, and there are records of dams producing litters when they were even older. There are further research difficulties when it comes to deciphering the names on pedigrees, and often names will be spelt differently, although referring to the same dog.

Rose, from the first Lord Tweedmouth's last recorded litter, born in 1889, was mated to her sire Nous 2. They produced Zoy 2, who was mated to Sal. In the resulting litter was Flow, later to be the dam of Haddow (sired by Sol,

ABOVE: Culham Copper, owned by Lord Harcourt: This dog appears in the extended pedigree of virtually every Golden Retriever.

BELOW: St Huberts Peter, owned and bred by the Hon le Poer Trench. Presented to King George V in 1913.

Painting by Maud Earl.

who was by Saxon ex Lady). The family link comes through the first Lord Tweedmouth's youngest daughter. She became the Countess of Aberdeen, and the title of the eldest son of the Earls of Aberdeen was Lord Haddo. In pedigrees the name is spelt both as Haddo and Haddow.

The Golden Retriever breed was founded on Lord Tweedmouth's breeding via the Culham Kennel of Lord Harcourt, who started his Goldens in 1904, ten years after the first Lord Tweedmouth's death. Lord Harcourt went to Guisachan to shoot when the second Lord Tweedmouth lived there, and also when Lord Portsmouth bought the estate. Lady Pentland, grand-daughter of the first Lord Tweedmouth, had a letter from John McLennon, one of the family of Guisachan keepers, in which he says: "Mr Lewis Harcourt (later the first Viscount Harcourt) got the foundations of his breed from two puppies he bought from me when I was at Kerrow House. The mother of these pups was out of a bitch called Lady, belonging to your uncle, Archie Marjoribanks." One great problem with the very old pedigrees is the use of the same names over and over again, particularly the colour names, of which all early breeders, including Lord Tweedmouth, seemed especially fond.

GOLDENS IN NORTH AMERICA

All Golden Retrievers throughout the world are founded on British stock. North America, where Archie Marjoribanks took Lady and Sol, is mentioned in Lord Tweedmouth's Stud Book. Its author noted that Sol "died at Ranche, given to Archie". Did Lady have a litter in America? Did Sol mate wavy coat bitches? We shall never know. All we can say is that Goldens from the earliest strain lived in North America, and that Lady can be called an international ancestress.

The first kennel of importance was Gilnockie, founded by Bert Armstrong in Winnipeg, Canada, in 1918. The man who did most for the breed in its early years was Colonel S.S. Magoffin who founded the Rockhaven Kennel in British Columbia. On the death of Bert Armstrong, Gilnockie was combined with Rockhaven, which stayed in British Columbia, while Gilnockie went to Inglewood, Colorado. From Britain, Col. Magoffin imported the great founding sire, Am. and Can. Ch. Speedwell Pluto, born on May 26th 1929. He was the first Golden Retriever Champion in the USA. The Rockhaven bitch foundations from Britain were the sisters, Saffron Chipmonk and Penelope, by Ch. Haulstone Dan and Am. and Can. Ch. Wilderness Tangerine. In the early years of the breed in the USA, many important bloodlines were brought in from Britain. Gradually, the nucleus of American-bred Champions became larger, and the breed has now become one of the most popular in the USA.

WORLDWIDE POPULARITY

Australia imported its first Golden Retrievers from Britain before the Second World War. The first post-war Champions came from Kuldana, Arbrook and Tone. In 1954, a Boltby dog and a Halsham bitch laid important foundations. Over the years many British imports, and latterly a few dogs from USA, have given a strong hand to Australian breeders, and Goldens are among the most popular breeds in Australia and New Zealand.

Sweden has had a history of Goldens since 1927, but in the 1950s influential British imports, built up over the years, made it one of the strongest countries in the breed. The other Scandinavian countries have also built up lovely lines, with stock from Sweden and Britain. The rest of Europe has, once again, used British bloodlines to start off, then combined further imports with their own breeding programmes.

2 THE GOLDEN RETRIEVER PUPPY

Y ou have decided to share your life with a Golden Retriever. It is a wonderful choice! Temperament is the most important characteristic, and the great majority of Golden Retrievers display the kind, gentle nature for which the breed is noted.

IMPORTANT CONSIDERATIONS

Consider the effect that the acquisition of a dog will have on your life. Everyone involved should appreciate that you are taking on a commitment for the dog's lifetime. A dog is not a machine, replaceable by a new model when older and not working as well. At the very least, your Golden Retriever will need to be fed and exercised every day, plus given regular grooming. In return for all the work and the changes to your lifestyle, you will gain a warm, loving and trusting companion.

Spend some time considering the implications of ownership. During a dog's lifetime it will cost you money, initially for the purchase and injections, and regularly for food, boosters and insurance to cover third party risks (essential) and, perhaps, veterinary bills (read the policy to check that the benefits justify the outlay). Over the years, the services of a veterinary surgeon are likely to be required, thus incurring more expense. Hopefully, you will have a healthy dog, but you should be aware of the possibilities. If an emergency occurred and you were called away, would family or friends be able, or prepared, to look after the dog? It is costly, and perhaps disturbing, for your Golden to be kennelled on such occasions.

Introducing a new dog into any household disrupts the normal routine. Remember that the puppy you hope to acquire will grow into a medium/large dog. Is your home suitable and sufficiently large to accommodate a fully grown Golden Retriever? Have you considered where the dog is going to spend most of the time? Living in a flat or apartment, unless it is on the ground floor with an exercise area, could give rise to complications. There should be access to a fenced, safe area where a dog can be free to run and explore, although a huge garden is unnecessary, and more difficult to make puppy-proof. It may seem impossible for your Golden to wriggle through a small gap in the fence, or between the bars of a wrought-iron gate. But puppies can, and they do!

If you have a vehicle, is there enough space in it for your family and the dog to travel in comfort? Although your Golden can be left for short periods, it is totally unreasonable to leave any dog unattended in the house, or kennel, all day. By instinct, a dog is a pack animal needing affection and companionship and, particularly at the puppy stage, someone must be available for company and to attend to the youngster's needs.

During the first nights, the puppy may be lonely and cry, missing the warmth and closeness of mother and litter mates. Cosy in bed, but feeling compassionate, you will want to comfort the puppy and encourage sleep. In the early stages of house-training, be prepared to escort the puppy outside several times a day, whatever the weather. On getting older

The Golden Retriever makes an ideal family pet, but you must weigh up all the pros and cons of owning a medium-sized, lively dog, before buying a puppy.

Photo: Kipps.

and nearly house-trained, but not able to go right through every night, your puppy might bark and need to go out quickly. Even when it is cold and wet, you have to accompany and then dry the pup, before returning to your own bed. It seems a never-ending process, but the majority of Golden Retrievers are extremely clean, soon learning that outside is the correct place to satisfy the calls of nature, and then barking to be let out. Some accidents are inevitable. If you are extremely house-proud, is this dog really for you? Daily grooming does not prevent hairs on the carpet and, as your dog brushes past you, hairs on your clothing. If you do not clean paws when they are muddy, you know what the result will be!

After discussions, make sure that the whole family still agrees that buying a puppy is a good idea, and that everyone accepts the responsibilities of ownership.

FINDING A BREEDER

How do you set about getting the right dog? Responding to the first advertisement seen in the newspaper could be a mistake. Even though well-known kennels sometimes sell their puppies in this way, or a caring owner may be having a litter from a pet bitch, having taken every precaution to ensure healthy puppies, you must beware of the pitfalls. The litter could be from a bitch with an unknown pedigree, mated to the equally unknown dog down the road. These puppies may be attractive and appear sound, but nothing is known about the parents.

The same cautionary remarks also apply to pet shops. Some are reputable, others take surplus stock from the casual breeder or from puppy farms. *Never* consider buying from one of the latter establishments, which are reputed to breed indiscriminately with no thought for bitches, who become breeding machines, having a litter every season whatever their health, until they are too old to be bred from. There are reports of litters reared in deplorable conditions, the puppies often sickly and with poor temperaments. The latter fault may be inherited, due to careless choice of parents, or caused by the puppies' early removal from their mother and insufficient human contact at an early age. These problems can cause heartache and unnecessary expense to the new owner. Pedigrees may be promised and not materialise or, if produced, may be inaccurate.

Do you know a reputable breeder who can give advice? If not, contact your national Kennel Club asking for a list of regional Golden Retriever Breed Societies. Their secretaries usually know of breeders who have, or are expecting, litters. Only consider puppies whose parents have passed tests carried out by experts from the British Veterinary Association (BVA), or your national equivalent. These confirm that both

Take time to seek out a reputable breeder who is known for their good-quality stock.

Photo: Marilyn Hartman.

sire and dam were clear of the hereditary eye defects, Cataract (HC) and Central Progressive Retinal Atrophy (CPRA), within twelve months of the mating, and that their hips have been X-rayed and scored for hip dysplasia, which is also an inherited condition (see Chapter Sixteen: Breed Associated Diseases).

The Kennel Club may also supply lists of breeders who have registered puppies. Be aware that such registration does not guarantee that their parents have undergone any of the above tests. Your vet may also be able to suggest a suitable breeder, having dealt with this person and his or her stock for some time.

SHOW AND WORKING POTENTIAL
Before talking to breeders, think about your reasons for wishing to own a Golden Retriever. Does the idea of showing your dog appeal? You may say "No" at the moment, but, later, you might be tempted to try it and find it is an enjoyable pastime. Are you ever

likely to use your dog for the breed's original purpose of retrieving shot game? Do both options appeal? The answers to these questions will determine whether you approach a specialist show, working, or dual-purpose kennel. Look for those which have a consistent record of success in their speciality. Most show-bred Goldens can be trained to retrieve game but, in competitions, they may not be as fast as their working-bred cousins, who are generally finer-bodied and lighter-boned. However, the offspring of working parents may be too quick and lively for a novice handler. Golden Retrievers are very versatile, and can participate in obedience and agility events, or in working trials, which combine elements of the first two. All are regulated by the Kennel Club and specialist clubs cater for these interests. Refer to the appropriate chapter for further information.

Alternatively, you may simply wish to enjoy the company of a beautiful dog without taking

In most cases, working gundogs are bred from working bloodlines, and you will need to go to a kennel that specialises in this.

Photos: Graham Cox.

Baltic Golden Valentine: If you have ambitions to show your Golden Retriever, the breeder will help you pick out a puppy with show potential.

Photos: B. Simon.

part in any activities. It often happens, however, that your puppy brings you into contact with other enthusiasts, who widen your horizons. The more you study the breed, the more you will appreciate the differences. The majority of Goldens are highly intelligent, but all puppies need basic obedience training and careful handling to achieve their full potential. It may be helpful to attend some dog shows. Details of shows in the UK may be found in the canine press. At the bigger shows you can see many Golden Retrievers, and study the differences in type and colour. Buy a catalogue, note the number of any dogs you like, and talk to their owners (but avoid disturbing them while they are preparing their dogs for exhibition, or when about to enter the ring). At Championship Shows, when the dogs are not being exhibited, they will be found together in benched rows, to which the public has access. Each dog is allocated a space, numbered to correspond with the number displayed by their handler in the ring. The owners and/or breeders are usually found beside their dogs and you can ask their advice.

Generally, it is not possible to watch a working dog in a Field Trial, as spectators may disturb game and landowners are reluctant to allow strangers on to their land. Many of these dogs also participate in Cold Game and Working Tests where spectators are welcome, or they may be seen working at home, or while training, thus demonstrating some of their ability.

You may hear of a puppy instantly available, but this is not necessarily the one for you. Highly regarded kennels often have waiting lists, so be patient until the puppy nearest to your ideal is available. The choice becomes wider the further you are prepared to travel.

I have advocated going to a breeder with a good reputation, but this does not mean that I would never buy a puppy from someone who only has an occasional litter. The owner may wish to keep a puppy to ensure the continuation of a selected bloodline, and is therefore selling the rest of the litter. The bitch may be of impeccable breeding, mated to a carefully selected stud dog and, providing that they have both achieved satisfactory results in the BVA tests, this is perfectly acceptable. Such a litter may receive more individual attention than those in larger establishments, which is a positive advantage.

DOG OR BITCH?
Your search now begins, and you know more than when you first fancied a Golden. Is your pup to be male or female? Neither presents any problem, if handled in the correct way from the earliest days. As the male grows older, he may become more difficult when nearby bitches are in season, crying or trying to escape to visit them. Most male Goldens are honourable gentlemen and behave themselves. Some may be a trifle more headstrong than their sisters and require firm, consistent handling. If, in future, you wish to perpetuate the breed, a bitch is preferable, because a dog is unlikely to be used at stud unless he has been successful in some form of competition. Opinions vary as to whether dogs or bitches are easier to train, but training depends on the particular individual, as well as the relationship between handler and dog.

A bitch can present problems during her season/heat/oestrus, which can occur as early as six months. Her cycle may be twice a year, but the interval could be longer, as all bitches vary. Be vigilant, and watch for the reddish-brown discharge which signals the start of the season, and prepare to discourage unwelcome male suitors for three to four weeks. At this time, accompany your bitch when she is in the garden, and always have her on the lead during walks. Avoid laying a scent trail for neighbourhood dogs to follow, and take her by car to the start of her walk. The majority of bitches keep themselves clean, but, to prevent blood stains on carpeted areas, it is advisable to make her lie on washable bedding.

SELECTING A PUPPY
If you can visit possible litters at three to four weeks, you will see how the youngsters are being reared, make a preliminary assessment of them, and see their dam and the sire, if he also belongs to the breeder. If not, there may

ABOVE: The male Golden Retriever is a handsome dog, who may require firm handling.
Photo: Kipps.

BELOW: The female Golden Retriever is a gentle and loving companion.
Photo: Kipps.

be a photograph of him. Ask to see the pedigree, the eye certificates and the hip scores of the parents. The breeder can also assess the approach and behaviour of yourself, and your family, towards the litter and their mother.

Do not be surprised if you are asked to remove your shoes and wash your hands – both precautionary measures to protect the puppies against infection. If you rush in and cause a commotion, making a grab for the puppies, it may be that your journey will have been in vain. Although a preliminary assessment of you on the telephone may have been favourable, this type of behaviour is not acceptable to a reputable breeder. If you arrive in your Sunday best and are displeased when a puppy jumps all over you, the breeder may decide that your family and home will not be suitable. Never handle a puppy, or attempt to lift one, without permission.

Similarly, you must expect the interrogation that follows. This reassures the breeder that the puppy's new home will be a permanent and loving one, and that the youngster will not be returned in a few weeks or put into a rescue society. If it is agreed that you can have a puppy, confirm your position on the list of prospective purchasers, make a definite booking, specify the preferred sex, and ask for a diet sheet, so you can purchase food in advance. If possible, leave a blanket so that when you take your pup home the bedding will have a familiar smell, making your new arrival feel more at home in new surroundings. You may be asked for a deposit.

At eight weeks, your Golden puppy will be ready to collect. The litter has to be assessed and a decision taken. All puppies look absolutely gorgeous and totally irresistible. You might have pick of the litter, but, if not, others ahead of you on the list will have already chosen. Whatever your choice, the basic requirement is a dog with the true, gentle and biddable Golden Retriever temperament. The youngsters should be full of vitality, with nicely-rounded bodies (not pot-bellied) and displaying lots of individual character. If you have visited before, you will see significant

changes in them. All will meet the requirements of a family pet/companion. Take the advice of the breeder, or an experienced friend, on choosing the best puppy possible, in case you later decide to show or work the pup, but remember that not every litter contains a Champion. If this is your first visit, ask to see the dam who, although well cared for, may not be looking her best, having reared her family. Also see the sire, if possible.

With the Breed Standard in mind, assess the pups. Look for the desirable soft, gentle expression, with black-rimmed, dark brown eyes of medium size, set well apart and not round or protruding. Black pigmentation is desirable on mouth, lips, pads and nose, and a lack of pigmentation on the latter totally detracts from the Golden's appearance. At certain times of the year pigmentation may diminish, but, if absent at the puppy stage, it will not improve. The name Golden Retriever suggests a uniformity of colour, but, in practice, they come in a variety of shades. The Breed Standard specifies that any shade of gold or cream is acceptable, but red or mahogany are not. A few white hairs, only on the chest, are permissible. The choice of colour is entirely personal, and you may prefer one shade to another. The puppy's ears will be a darker shade than the rest of the body, and they give some indication of the dog's colour when adult. The adult coat can be flat or wavy with good feathering, and should have a dense, water-resisting undercoat.

The head should be well balanced, the breadth and length of the foreface being in the same proportion as the breadth and length of the skull. A well defined stop is desirable. This refers to the downward slope between the eyes, which joins the top of the head to the top of the muzzle when viewed in profile. From the front, the skull should be slightly rounded, not domed, and the muzzle powerful, wide and deep. The puppy's upper teeth will overlap the lower rather more than in the mature dog, who should have a correct scissor bite, the upper front teeth just overlapping the front teeth in the lower jaw. A few weeks after a pup's permanent teeth appear, one can assess

ABOVE: Temperament is all-important, so look for the bold, inquisitive puppy, who is keen to come up and greet you.
Photo: Marilyn Hartman.

RIGHT: Golden Retriever puppies are so appealing, it can be very hard to make a choice.
Photo: Amanda Bulbeck.

whether the mouth has a true scissor bite. Avoid any puppy obviously overshot or undershot. The ears should be set on neither too high nor too low. Their size, in relation to the head, varies as the puppy grows. They may appear too large at certain stages of development, but the pup will usually 'grow into them' when older. Reject any puppy with runny eyes, nose or ears.

ASSESSING SHOW POTENTIAL
For the show dog, good bone is essential, and the forelegs should be straight (avoid those which appear to come out of the same space, or which protrude at the elbows). Feet should be rounded and cat-like. If splayed, they are likely to remain so. To enable the shoulders to be well laid back, the shoulder blade (scapula) should slope, and the bone in the upper arm (humerus) be long, so that the forelegs appear well under the body. This construction must be complemented by a good length of neck to achieve balance. Even in a puppy of this age, a compact body with a level topline is desirable. Some puppies appear proud of their tails and carry them high, but, providing the

tail set is correct, it should be carried level with the back when mature. Hocks should turn neither in nor out. With broad hindquarters and well bent stifles, the desired overall picture is one of balance.

If the breeder exhibits at shows, the puppies may already be accustomed to being set into a show stance, which enables you to assess them from the side, front and rear. Most puppies can retrieve. If your Golden is from working parents, try testing the retrieving instinct by throwing some soft, small object for the puppy. The main thing, however, is for your pup to be active, bold and inquisitive. Remember that a working litter may be lighter-boned.

Most Golden Retrievers are highly sensitive, yet extremely outgoing. Occasionally, a quiet baby gets pushed out by boisterous siblings in the rush to greet you, and stays at the back. If the puppy is going to a family, the happy medium is best; the quiet one may be rather too shy, the extrovert too exuberant. My first Golden appeared very quiet, but, once home with us, his shyness disappeared.

The puppy will be wormed and weaned, and

you should receive information about the current diet, instructions for feeding in the coming weeks (if not supplied previously), and details of worming treatment to date.

BUYING EQUIPMENT

To comply with the law, every dog in a public place (which includes a car), must wear a collar giving details of ownership. A lead will also be required. Slip-chain collars can damage the coat – use one only if recommended at a training class and remove when off the lead. If caught on a projection, they can cause strangulation.

Feeding and water bowls will be required. Lightweight versions are not recommended, being easily overturned and thus creating a mess. Obtain supplies of food and milk as recommended by the breeder.

For bedding, proprietary brands of washable fleecy material, although costly, are a good investment as they are not easily destructible. Avoid newspapers, as the printing ink will make your puppy's coat dirty, but remember to save them for use in toilet training.

Grooming is an essential element of the daily routine. You will need: a metal comb (with two different spacings of teeth), a brush (not too stiff), and towels for drying after bathing or whenever wet. To keep occupied and prevent boredom, your puppy will need playthings such as a nylon bone (replace when well-chewed), a solid rubber ball or ring, a medium-sized hide chew and a hard squeaky toy, all large enough not to be swallowed. Apart from the nylon bone, only allow your pup these toys under supervision. Soft toys are soon damaged and small pieces are easily swallowed.

PREPARATIONS FOR YOUR PUPPY

The puppy will be joining a new pack, comprised of you and your family, and it is important to convey the message that you are the new leader. How are you to communicate with the new arrival? Dogs relate to each other through sounds (barking, whining), touch (pawing, nuzzling, mouthing) and smell. They can learn many human words and be conditioned to respond to these in a particular way (such as Sit, Stand, Stay, Come, Bed etc). They quickly learn to recognise their own name and know that, when used, it refers to them. Most importantly, they can interpret the meaning of different tones of voice – those which are kind and loving, and others which are not. Equally, some may decide that a softly-spoken command can be ignored, whereas a firm one should be obeyed. Animals are quick to recognise uncertainty and take advantage of it.

Choose your puppy's name in advance and decide on the commands to be used – short, single words are the easiest for a dog to learn and recognise, for example, use "Sit", rather than "Sit down." Consistency is essential, and all the family should agree to use the same words, with the same emphasis if possible.

Always talk in gentle tones, with frequent use of the name, so that the puppy gets used to it. As your Golden becomes confident with you, discourage anti-social behaviour by the word "No", spoken with varying degrees of severity. Always make sure you have your pup's attention before a command, by using the name, a touch, or, as a last resort, a handclap. When conditioning the puppy to respond to the command words, only use them when you can be reasonably sure they will be obeyed. Study Chapter Three on training carefully, as a well-trained dog is a joy to own. Remember to use touch to reinforce the bond of affection between you. Your pup will soon find a way of letting you know how much this contact is appreciated. A dog's sense of smell is remarkably sensitive, so try to avoid strong-smelling soaps, perfumes or smoking, when in your puppy's presence.

Decide whereabouts, outdoors, the pup's toilet is to be located. A grassed area is ideal, but it will become discoloured with many yellow circles, so choose a place where this will be least obvious. Male puppies squat like bitches until older, when they 'cock a leg' to mark their territory. Condition them to do this away from the house. If a hard area is to be used, it requires regular washing to avoid smells, so a drain will be required.

Colmar Summer Mist of Wheatcroft
FROM PUPPY TO SHOW CHAMPION

Photos: Kipps.

ABOVE LEFT: **Eight weeks.**
At this stage, Misty looks perfectly in proportion (very balanced, flowing lines, short coupled, level topline, correct angulation fore and aft, with excellent reach of neck). Patient observation of her movement showed that she moved very correctly and positively, with excellent head and tail carriage.

ABOVE RIGHT: **Four months.**
Suddenly we have a set of legs that seem to belong to another breed! At this stage, Misty's back legs overtook her front legs when she moved.

Two years.
Now boasting a lush coat, and learning to show herself. Her excellent construction cannot be denied. However, she is very tucked up, awaiting maturity when she will deepen. She gained her Junior Warrant at 14 months.

At three years.
A newly crowned
Champion and now in
her prime, showing
proof of the promise
she showed at eight
weeks.

At eight years.
Although lightly
shown, Misty still
loves the show scene
and has picked up
many veteran awards.

ACCOMMODATION: HOUSE OR KENNEL
A Golden Retriever is a friendly, affectionate creature. If yours is to be a single dog, it seems a great sadness to banish the puppy to live outside, alone in a kennel and maybe crying unheard. Neither you, nor your family, will have the pleasure of a growing dog's company in the house. You may have planned to kennel the pup, perhaps at night, or part of the day, but those pleading brown eyes might persuade you otherwise, which means you could waste money on adapting an existing

building or purchasing a new kennel. Make a sensible decision, and stick to it.

If your pup is to live in the house, or be indoors for part of the day, where is he to be allowed to roam? Until the puppy is house-trained, limit access to areas with non-absorbent flooring and to other rooms only under supervision. A baby gate is invaluable, in allowing one to see and talk to the pup from an adjoining room. Although sociable creatures, there are times when puppies prefer their own company and, to thrive, they must

Your puppy will start learning from the moment he arrives home, so make sure you teach him good habits.

Photo: Amanda Bulbeck.

have plenty of undisturbed sleep and relaxation. A pup's bed must be positioned somewhere draught-free. A puppy-sized, moulded plastic bed will soon be outgrown, and a cane basket can be a digestive hazard if chewed and swallowed. A cardboard box with a blanket is ideal, readily replaced when outgrown. Lower the front, so that the puppy can gain access easily and see the surroundings. Some adult dogs sleep stretched out (unless a few of them are cuddled together), so the expense of buying a large bed is unnecessary. The single dog may feel more snug in a box. Alternatively, you may prefer to use a crate (see section on crate training).

A kennel should be at least 6ft by 4ft, and high enough for you to enter to attend to the dog. It will need an opening window, covered with wire mesh, electricity for lighting and heating and should be lined and draughtproofed. When alone and bored, a pup cannot be checked from chewing the door frame etc. A raised bed is sometimes suggested to avoid draughts, but I believe the floor is warmer, provided a sleeping box is created with panelled sides (the front lower to allow access) and a roof, hinged to facilitate cleaning. A baby puppy, used to nestling up against litter mates for warmth, cannot be expected to settle alone in a kennel in cold weather. Warm the atmosphere safely, with a heat lamp.

Make a concrete run, joined to the kennel and surrounded by a wire mesh fence, at least six feet high, boarded halfway up on two adjacent sides as a windbreak. Concrete is easily hosed with water, and will also harden the pup's pads and keep nails trim. Consider protection from rain and sun while a puppy is in the run. A slightly-raised wooden platform provides an alternative to lying on cement, but your puppy may not use it. For convenience, and for you and the dog to see each other, have the kennel close to the house, approached by a concrete path rather than grass, which becomes muddy in bad weather. Padlocks for the kennel and the run are required, or an alarm system should be installed.

Newspaper or sawdust on some form of linoleum-type floor-covering absorbs urine until the puppy no longer soils the kennel. It is easily swept up, and the lino can be washed and disinfected. For bedding, washable fleecy material is recommended. Alternatives include white shredded paper, straw (prone to dust and parasites) or wood shavings. The last two, and sawdust, may cause coat discoloration if the pup wets them. Beware of chemicals which may have been used in the production of straw and wood products.

SAFETY FIRST
The following may sound like common sense. It is – but if you have not had a puppy before, you may not realise what mischief one can get into. Even if you have had dogs previously, it is easy to forget. Puppies are all inquisitive, and some are destructive. Keep small toys out of reach. Dangers lurk everywhere: electrical cables not quite hidden away could be chewed with catastrophic results; kitchens and bathrooms are potentially dangerous, soap

powder, bleach, disinfectants, medicines and tablets are easily devoured, if at puppy level. Aerosol cans are pressurised and hazardous if punctured by sharp teeth. On emptying your washing machine, immediately lift the clothes-basket out of reach, since minuscule underwear, socks and tights seem to be attractive to young dogs and are easily swallowed. Some pass through naturally, but others may necessitate surgery. Keep clothes-pegs out of reach, and be aware that spring action ones are most dangerous.

Lift house-plants out of harm's way. The garden holds a host of temptations. Some that are poisonous include slug pellets, laburnum seeds, daffodil and snowdrop bulbs, fungi and certain plants and berries. Heavily-spiked bushes such as pyracantha can cause eye damage. Sticks, twigs, stones and gravel seem irresistible. If chewed, they may lodge in teeth or jaws and, if swallowed, cause internal damage. Never allow your puppy to chew or play with them. Situate the shaded run, or pen, away from plants, which attract stinging insects. In the garage or garden shed, keep anti-freeze, insecticides, fungicides etc., well out of reach. One slip on a wet hosepipe left lying on damp grass could result in a skid and a pulled ligament. It has happened!

COLLECTING YOUR PUPPY
Preparations are complete and that magical, puppy-collection day has arrived. Though excited, listen carefully to any final advice and instructions from the breeder, who may find this parting emotional. Remember to collect the diet sheet, pedigree and registration documents, providing the Kennel Club have returned the latter. If not, make sure they have been applied for.

Registration is essential if you wish to participate in activities regulated by the Kennel Club, or to breed. The breeder may have arranged a puppy trial policy, covering the first four weeks in your care, which you have the option of extending. Hopefully, you will have a supply of appropriate food, but, if not, ask the breeder for sufficient to last until some can be obtained. You pay your money (if

The big day arrives when it is time to collect your puppy.

Photo: Amanda Bulbeck.

cash, remember to get a receipt) and the puppy is all yours. Hopefully, in the years ahead, this Golden Retriever puppy is going to give you an enormous amount of pleasure and fun, adding to your life's happiness.

Before setting off on the journey, with your puppy wrapped in a familiar-smelling blanket, attach a tiny collar complete with identity disc, which will enable you to be reunited if the pup escapes in the unlikely event of an accident. If travelling by car, take a companion, so that one of you can cuddle the puppy on the back seat. Speak in encouraging tones, as everything is new to your little charge, who may be bewildered by the motion of the car. If travelling alone, use a travelling box or crate/cage and talk to the puppy, who may not be able to see you. If you have to stop for any reason, the puppy must remain in the car until you reach home, to avoid infection. Be prepared, with plenty of paper tissues, newspapers, towels and baby wipes. Your Golden puppy may be an excellent traveller, but might still vomit and evacuate bladder and bowels. Give small amounts of water if the journey is long and hot, but avoid food. Its absence for a few hours will not be harmful.

ARRIVING HOME

The earlier you arrive home, the longer your puppy has to become accustomed to the new surroundings before bedtime. At the designated toilet area, encourage the pup to 'perform', which may or may not happen, but is worth a try. When indoors, remove the collar and gently introduce the puppy to the family. Try not to over-excite the new arrival. Under your watchful eye, allow the pup to explore, getting to know this new home without fear or stress. When offered food, your Golden may refuse, but bear in mind that the pup's tummy needs to settle. After all these new experiences, your puppy is bound to be tired, so place the youngster in the prepared sleeping quarters with a favourite blanket, loving the pup, saying his name and other terms of endearment. Remain for a while, then leave the puppy to rest.

If you have not had a dog before, remember, when the puppy awakens, resist the temptation to play, and take the pup straight outside. The first few times, carry your puppy to the toilet area and put him on the ground. You may be lucky if the pup is desperate to 'go' and performs immediately, but, in all probability, your youngster will run back towards the house and, before you can catch up, 'go' there. Your puppy does not yet know what is expected.

Puppies need to clean themselves every hour or so, and immediately after sleeping or feeding. Encourage your puppy to think of using only the chosen area outside, by making regular visits, some of which will, hopefully, coincide with the calls of nature. If an accident occurs in the house, do not scold or rub the puppy's nose in the puddle, because your Golden will not understand the reason for the harsh words. Clean it up, wiping the floor with deodoriser so the smell does not encourage the puppy to use the same spot again. If the puppy is accustomed to using newspaper, continue

with this. However, when left alone, a bored pup may tear the paper.

INTRODUCING THE LEAD

As early as possible, accustom your puppy to a collar and lead so that you are in control. At first, the youngster may sit down, or 'play up', try to rush off, jump up and lie on his back – anything to get rid of the constraint. In this event, spend time indoors getting the pup accustomed to this new experience. All my Golden puppies have taken to wearing a collar and lead quite quickly. With a little encouragement and perhaps a pat of the thigh to attract their attention, they have walked beside me reasonably well. When your puppy is familiar with the lead, walk to the toilet area, keeping the pup on your lefthand side. Then, using the lead, try to get the puppy to walk in small circles (as all puppies do naturally when seeking the right spot for elimination) and use your chosen command regularly (I find "Be clean" effective). Be patient, continue circling, letting your puppy choose a particular spot and, if success is achieved, praise enthusiastically. Do not be discouraged by the occasional failure, but persist and eventually it will work. Once the puppy has 'been', allow him off the lead to run and play. If your young Golden does not return when called, run towards the house and the puppy will probably follow.

Only when the pup knows where to toilet, and is obedient to the command "Come", take him to the appointed place off the lead. Eventually, with encouragement, your puppy will find the way there unaccompanied – but it will take time.

ACCEPTABLE BEHAVIOUR

The natural mother will have kept her pup in check until weaned. Since then, she will have spent less time with the litter and each puppy's life will have been mostly fun, chewing, crawling and playing with litter mates. Your pup enjoyed being fed and groomed and, hopefully, having games with the breeder. Now it is necessary to conform to a new set of rules. With kind and gentle understanding, you must let your Golden know what is acceptable behaviour. A young puppy will want to jump up at you, but you must firmly insist that all four feet are kept on the floor. Remember, this small puppy will soon grow into a large, powerful dog and few people enjoy having muddy paws on their clothes, together with the prospect of being overturned.

The puppy's first bedtime with you can be traumatic. A very young dog is pretty vulnerable, so expect your puppy to cry for the first few nights. If left indefinitely, the pup could become distressed, so go and give reassurance, then leave, speaking kindly, but firmly. Resist the temptation to take the puppy into your bedroom. Puppies must abide by human rules and stay in their beds. If your pup persists in crying or barking, do check that all is well but then, hard though it may be, ignore those puppy pleas.

When the puppy leaves the litter, he must learn to conform to a new set of rules.
Photo: Amanda Bulbeck.

3 *THE RIGHT START*

During a lifetime, your dog is going to meet people of varying age, sex, size, and appearance. The earlier puppies start, the more likely they are to enjoy the experience. Your popularity might rise now that you have a puppy, but crowds of people, too soon, may over-excite and bewilder this new member of your family. Your children, and any visitors, must understand and respect the pup's need for undisturbed sleep, to have meals in peace, and not to be treated as a plaything. A puppy loves a rough and tumble, but everybody must be gentle at all times and avoid lifting your Golden in case he struggles and falls. Children who are old enough can help with feeding and grooming. Check that they wash their hands after handling or feeding the pup. Contact with children outside your home is also important, so do your best to arrange for your puppy to meet some.

Introduce the pup to regular tradespeople, especially, the refuse collector with their noisy

The aim of every responsible dog owner is to have a well-adjusted, well-behaved pet.

Photo: Steve Nash.

machine. The window cleaner may appear to pose a threat if the pup is nearby when he is polishing the glass. The puppy will come to know these people and understand that they are allowed near your home without the need for excessive barking.

If you already have an older dog, introduce the new arrival carefully, restraining both until they are completely happy together. Do not allow the pup to worry an elder companion unduly. Older dogs may feel their territory is being usurped so, at first, feed the dogs well apart and supervise both to ensure that they do not invade each other's space. Continue these precautions until they are fully accustomed to being fed together. Cats require particular care, so discourage your pup from chasing, and look out for the quick paw which could catch a puppy's eyes. One day, you may find them lying together, the best of friends. Be sure that you do not neglect the established animals, thereby causing jealousy.

Once the puppy is vaccinated against infection, visit a shopping area, where your Golden will probably attract the attention of passers by, thus enlarging the social experience. Socialisation with other people's dogs in their homes, or out walking, can now be allowed. At a later date, a ringcraft or a puppy obedience class is an opportunity for your puppy to meet many dogs of all shapes and sizes. Your youngster may be a trifle overawed if a few dogs are excitable. If so, do not participate on the first occasion, just sit quietly with the pup, letting everything be taken in. Having attended these classes, you are under no obligation to take part in competitive events. Try introducing the pup to horses from the edge of a field, before meeting them at close quarters on a path or clattering along the road. As they approach, put the puppy on the lead, and make him sit as they pass.

FAMILIARISATION

Your Golden puppy may have been reared in a kennel, or with a family which has not familiarised the pup with the mechanical sounds we take for granted. Put yourself in the puppy's position – your bed is in the utility room or kitchen where many activities take place. Passed into the hands of strangers, you are a trifle apprehensive of your new surroundings. At breakfast time the toast jumps out of the toaster – burned – and the smoke alarm goes off. Later, the washing machine gurgles away and then empties, the tumble-drier is switched on and the food processor starts up. The worst monster of all comes roaring towards you, moves away and then approaches again. It vibrates the floor and appears as though it wants to gobble you up. Your sensitive hearing accentuates the noise. OK, you are supposed to be outgoing, but you have never encountered a vacuum cleaner before. You may take everything in your stride, but, if not, it might be a while before your confidence is restored.

To avoid the above scenario, try out each noise in turn, with the puppy at a distance, observing the reaction. If calm, move the puppy closer and try again until he is completely happy. If apprehensive, introduce the noise in small doses and reassure the puppy until familiarity is achieved. This may take several days.

Having spent the first few weeks sheltered from the traumas of life, being taken into the garden in darkness may seem eerie to your puppy. Be encouraging, and let the puppy see there is nothing to fear. If you do not have a floodlight, get your pup used to being guided by torchlight – stand quietly, getting him used to the sounds of the night, before returning inside.

When you collected your puppy, you may have travelled by train with all the associated noise and bustle, but it is more likely that your transport was a car. Hopefully, the youngster will not have been apprehensive, but it is a good idea to sit with your dog in the car on the drive or at the roadside where the puppy can see and hear traffic passing. A motorbike screaming past is bad enough for us, and we know the cause. If you hear one in the distance, reassure the puppy before the vehicle reaches you. Treat cars, buses, heavy lorries or low-flying aircraft similarly.

The more time you spend working with your dog when he is young and impressionable, the better the results will be.

Photo: Amanda Bulbeck.

For the first walks beside a busy road, find somewhere set back beyond the footpath to distance the puppy from traffic noise. Try to choose a dry day. Years ago, when walking my young dog, we were caught in a rainstorm, the spray from an overtaking lorry terrified him and he was scared of traffic for the rest of his life. Your pup could be upset by bicycles, creeping up silently from behind. Go out after dark with your young dog to experience vehicle headlights coming towards you both, and the shadows of street lights.

Many dogs, including trained gundogs, are afraid of thunderstorms, which they can detect earlier than humans. If possible, keep your dog company, whatever his age, and try to distract him. Equally, a dog may be startled by celebratory fireworks, or balloons bursting within earshot. Although your Golden Retriever is a gundog by heritage, this does not guarantee that your puppy will not be afraid of gunshot. Condition the puppy to it gradually, as with any new experience.

INOCULATIONS
If you do not know of a veterinarian, obtain a recommendation from another dog owner. Few vets make home visits, so choose one close at hand. The breeder may have arranged a temporary vaccination at six weeks, and two more are required at eight and twelve weeks. These protect against the potential killers: Canine Distemper (Hardpad), Hepatitis,

Leptospirosis and Canine Parvovirus. A further week must elapse after the final injection before your puppy can appear in public and meet other dogs. Ask the vet if Kennel Cough vaccination is recommended in your area.

When you know the date of collection, make an appointment for your puppy's inoculations as soon as possible after the age of eight weeks. For the journey to the surgery, do not forget your puppy's collar. To avoid infection, carry the pup at all times, do not allow contact with other patients and make sure he is not patted by all and sundry. Before inoculation, your Golden's general health will be checked, and you could enquire about further treatment for all types of worm.

TREATMENT FOR WORMS
(ENDOPARASITES)
Adverse publicity has been given to the subject of Toxocara Canis, but, provided sensible hygiene rules are observed by everyone in the family (especially children) and safe disposal of faeces is adopted, the risks are infinitesmal.

It can be presumed that a nursing bitch and her puppies carry the roundworm, Toxocara Canis. Dormant, roundworm larvae, activated by the release of hormones during pregnancy, pass into the developing puppies while in utero, and turn into adult worms two weeks after whelping. Larvae are also transferred via the bitch's milk. It is imperative that the worming programme, already commenced by the breeder, should be continued in accordance with veterinary advice, to safeguard the health of the pup and of any humans in contact with him. This entails further doses of precise quantities of medication, related to the puppy's body weight.

For the remainder of the puppy's life, regular worming will be necessary and is sometimes combined with booster inoculations. Modern treatment is administered without fasting. Digestive problems will arise if correct procedures are not adopted.

Roundworms usually disintegrate with treatment and may not be seen in the faeces. This does not mean that they have not been present in the dog. The worm eggs are not affected by the treatment so it is essential that faeces should not be dug into the garden, or composted, as the eggs can survive for years in the soil.

Tapeworms are segmented and, if present, sections may be visible around the anus, on the hindquarters or in the excrement. If your dog has fleas, tapeworms may also be present, as the two complement each other. Less common are hook, lung and whip worms.

FEEDING
Fresh water must always be available. Replenish regularly. Keep your pup's utensils separate from your own. Puppies require frequent meals, evenly spaced throughout the day and at regular times. It is best to keep to the breeder's original food for a while, but, if you later decide to change, do so gradually, introducing new products in small quantities over several days to avoid digestive problems.

Until the age of one year, specially formulated puppy milk is essential for continued development, as its ingredients are nearest to mother's milk. Other milks are unsuitable, being lower in fat and other solubles. Within a few weeks, your pup will enjoy chewing a beef marrow bone, but they can become smelly and encourage flies. Never give other bones as they disintegrate and, if

swallowed, can puncture the intestine. Large, hard dog biscuits assist in teething, keep teeth clean and exercise the jaws.

In the daily routine, meals are a highlight, so allow your puppy to eat undisturbed. Do not, however, allow your young dog to become over-protective about food, bones or toys. You must be able to touch and remove them at will, so get the pup used to this as soon as possible. If your puppy has been unwell, he may need tempting to eat. Do not pander to puppies, otherwise they will become finicky and only eat the delicacies they prefer. A slow starter may need a little encouragement. Breeders are usually willing to help with any problems you encounter.

A typical diet sheet is included as an illustration.

DIET SHEET
AT EIGHT WEEKS
Note: References to milk should be taken as puppy milk.

Breakfast: Half a pint of milk with two dessertspoons of baby porridge and one portion of wholewheat cereal.
Mid-morning: One third of a pint of milk.
Lunch: One third of a cup of soaked biscuit meal with one quarter of a tin of puppy meat. One third of a pint of milk after the meal.
Tea: As for breakfast, plus a scrambled egg.
Supper: As lunch.

Alternate meat with fish or grated cheese. Toasted wholemeal bread can be given instead of porridge or cereal. Increase amounts in each meal gradually and according to appetite. At three months, cut out the mid-morning drink, but continue to give one pint of special puppy milk per day until one year old. Reduce to three meals per day at four months old, and to two meals per day at six months old.

ADULT DIET (from six months)
Two meals or one to two cups of biscuit meal and a half tin of adult tinned meat, plus biscuits at bedtime. Occasionally substitute

eggs or fish in place of the meat. You may prefer to use a dry, complete food, containing both protein and carbohydrate, in place of the meat and biscuit meal shown above. If so, follow the supplier's instructions.

NOTE: With some diet sheets, calcium and vitamin supplements may be desirable. Seek the advice of your vet, as excess quantities are harmful.

GROOMING

Goldens are easily kept clean. Regular grooming is needed, daily until your puppy is used to it. Pups think it is great fun, and want to bite and gnaw. This is a bad habit and milk teeth are like needles, so discourage it. Accustom your Golden to being handled all over. It may be easier to have your puppy on your knee when small, but make him stand for part of the time. With increasing size and weight, insist that your Golden stands, either on the floor or on a non-slip mat on a steady table.

Brush softly, then use the more widely-spaced teeth of the comb to tease out tangles. It is also ideal for the tail and for feathering on legs, as the coat lengthens. The more closely-spaced teeth are for the final combing. If your pup's nails are too sharp or long, take care when cutting. Taking off too much exposes the quick, causing pain and bleeding. Scissors may be used at first when the nails are soft but, later, special guillotine clippers are needed. Seek advice before use.

Clean eyes and, if necessary, remove wax from the external parts of ears, but do not poke inside. Teeth should be cleaned occasionally. While the pup is teething, be particularly gentle around the mouth as it will be tender. When all the permanent teeth are in place, they should be cleaned regularly with a toothbrush and canine toothpaste.

As your Golden loses puppy coat, you will need a stiffer brush and a double-sided hound glove. Brush the coat sparingly, using the side with closely-spaced wires, then produce a shine with the corduroy side. Obtain good quality trimming, and single-sided thinning,

scissors, nail-clippers and a stripping knife. Even if you have no intention of showing your pup, his appearance will be enhanced by being correctly trimmed (see Chapter Seven: The Show Dog) but, before experimenting, seek advice from someone familiar with the correct trimming of Goldens, otherwise your pup's glamorous appearance may not be improved. For hands-on guidance, some clubs hold trimming demonstrations which are most helpful, and the pup's breeder may also be of assistance.

When grooming, check for any unaccountable lumps and abrasions. The most well-cared-for dog may be playing host to external parasites (ectoparasites), even if not persistently scratching. Ruffle the hair backwards to disclose unwanted visitors such as fast-moving fleas, sometimes indicated by the black specks of their faeces, or slow-moving brown insects, like lice. Insecticidal shampoos and sprays are available, but, before using them on the dog and other furry pets, check the instructions. A specially-formulated spray is available for canine bedding, your carpets and car. Intense irritation is caused to a dog by mange mites, invisible to the naked eye. If symptoms persist, seek professional advice.

Ticks look like a small bean. To release their grip, apply surgical spirit with cotton wool. Do not attempt to pull the body, as it can become detached, leaving the head with a vicious hook embedded in the dog's flesh, which could cause infection. Consult your vet about their removal if any difficulties are encountered.

Frequent bathing is not necessary for a Golden, unless your dog is to be shown. Brush off dried mud, or, if excessive, remove with warm water from a watering can or hosepipe connected to the hot and cold taps. Encourage the dog to shake, then towel dry. For quicker drying, use a hairdryer, but not too close at first to avoid frightening a puppy.

CRATE TRAINING

The mention of the word crate makes many new owners cringe, as they think it is an

It will not be long before your puppy looks on his crate as his own special, safe haven.

undesirable way to contain a puppy. Perhaps calling a crate a transportable folding kennel would make it more acceptable. Easily-assembled, and sturdily-constructed with strong wire sides and solid base, a crate can give you peace of mind when your Golden is in the car, hotel room, or staying with friends, because you know he cannot get up to mischief. While your puppy is small, the crate can double as an outside playpen.

The crate must be large enough to house an adult Golden, and should be placed somewhere the dog is happy to go. Place familiar bedding inside, and entice your puppy in with tidbits and toys. Let your pup go in and out many times before you close the gate. He may protest, so soothe and leave for a short time, gradually extending the periods until your puppy accepts being confined. A dog should not be locked in for long periods during the day, probably no more than an hour, and must be left with water. Your Golden will get to know the crate, properly introduced, as his domain where he can usually come and go as he pleases. Its use in the car is discussed under car travel. As a bedroom, it must be a pleasant place to retire to. The dog must never be put there after chastisement.

EXERCISE
Once allowed out, do not be tempted to take your Golden puppy for long walks. Apart from small trips for socialisation and

Woody enjoying Michigan's winter snows. Ch. Signature's Natural Wonder is a companion and "real dog" as well as a show winner. Owned by Judy and Kurt Macanley.

familiarisation, playing and running in the garden is sufficient until four months. Between then and twelve months, gradually increase the length of the walks from fifteen minutes to about an hour if taken at one time, or somewhat longer if spread over a number of outgoings, whichever suits your lifestyle. Choose a varied terrain, including roads, woods, pastures, and, as the pup's fitness increases, hills and dales to develop muscle. In hot weather, exercise in the early morning or evening.

Your Golden may be obedient at home, but, the first time you allow freedom on a walk, the puppy may become excited and disobey your command to come. If possible, take an assistant and choose a place where one of you can be sure of catching the pup. A narrow passage between walls or hedges is ideal. Call the puppy to you, and, if he obeys, give lots of praise and a tidbit, but do not make a habit of the latter. If the pup fails to return, do not chase, just walk towards him quietly until you can get a hand on him, then it is back on the lead and more training.

Once you are confident the puppy will return, vary the walk with a combination of walking to heel, on and off the lead, running freely ahead (but not beyond your control), perhaps a retrieve, then lead work again.

INTRODUCTION TO WATER

Most Goldens adore water, and the difficulty is usually getting them out. On the first occasion, pick a warm day, find a shallow stream for the pup to paddle in and join in, if necessary, to give confidence. A pond, or slow-moving water, is best for the first swimming lesson, when the pup is about six months old. Walk your Golden into the water and encourage the puppy in more deeply, perhaps throwing a ball, until the pup is out of his depth, when most will swim naturally. Be there to help if he panics.

If at the seaside, choose a pool for the first experience, then walk along the edge of the sea, gradually encouraging your puppy out of his depth. In the sea, or any large body of water, be cautious about removing the lead – your pup may set off for the horizon, oblivious of your calls to return. Sea water may affect a young dog's stomach, if swallowed. On returning home, a Golden's coat should be rinsed with fresh water to remove salt. Remember, after heavy rain a quiet stream may become a raging torrent, and a dog could be swept away. Thin ice is a death warrant.

SAFETY

Discourage your dog from rolling in offensive matter, and from eating the carcasses of wild animals which may have been poisoned or be riddled with disease. Also discourage the equally unpleasant habit of eating stools (coprophagy). If caught in these acts, speak extremely sternly to your young Golden. Keep

Even "super showdogs" can be real dogs, and take every chance to do what retrievers like to do. Meg hits the water with great enthusiasm. And no, it won't ruin the coat! Meg is Am. Ch. Brandymist QB Gal, winner of more than 20 Best in Shows.

clear of crops and verges sprayed with insecticide and weedkillers. Obey the rules of the countryside, keep your dog leashed when livestock are encountered, and avoid cultivated fields. However obedient, never allow your Golden off lead when walking along a road. Something may divert your attention, your puppy may chase after a moving object and you would never forgive yourself if he caused an accident, resulting in injury to himself or to anyone else. When about to cross a road, make the dog sit at the kerb, even when there is no traffic, so the pup is conditioned to do this when the road is busy. Before crossing, give a command, so your dog knows to go with you.

If your dog is correctly-trained, it is unnecessary to walk using a halter which fits over the head and muzzle, and is designed to prevent pulling. In the early stages of training, an extending lead enables you to encourage a difficult young dog to return, but discard it when the dog is trained.

Now to a delicate matter: never give anyone the chance to complain about your dog fouling in a public place, or risk a fine if by-laws exist. However well-trained to 'perform' at home, exercise might make your puppy want to 'go' again. Carry a supply of plastic bags. If the need arises, place your hand in the bag and lift the excreta, then pull the bag back, turning it inside out in the process. Finally, knot the open end and take home for disposal or place in a bin, authorised by the council for this purpose. When a dog is old enough to lift his leg to mark his territory, do not permit him to do so where it may cause offence.

CAR TRAVEL
Many puppies suffer from car sickness, which most, fortunately, outgrow. If not, medication is available. Feed well in advance of a journey, however short, or, if you plan an early start, let the pup travel on an empty stomach. The sooner a puppy gets used to the movement of the car, the better. Start brief journeys as soon as possible, a few miles along the road and back, not getting out, of course, until the pup is fully vaccinated.

Extend the distance daily, chat to distract your puppy from feeling sick and have fun afterwards so he will associate the car with something pleasurable.

To avoid damage to developing joints when young, always lift the puppy into, and out of, the car. In old age, give the same helping hand when those joints are no longer supple. A dog must never jump out of the car until given the appropriate command.

Never leave your Golden unattended in a car on a hot day. Even with the windows left partly open, the temperature rises rapidly and the vehicle quickly becomes an oven, causing great distress and, on occasion, death. Try to avoid leaving your puppy at any time, as the dog could be stolen, or become agitated if someone outside the car deliberately annoys him.

In what area of the car the pup travels will depend on the model. The important thing is to ensure that your puppy cannot interfere with the driver, or chew the interior. You may have room for your crate, but, if not, custom-built dog guards or cages are available. The latter may be too restricting for an adult dog on a long journey, but are preferred by some owners on safety grounds. Keep newspaper and plastic bags in the car for emergencies. A drinking bowl and a container of water never come amiss, either for drinking or removing mud, and towels are useful to dry the dog.

HOUSE RULES
Until your puppy's skeletal frame is more mature, and muscles and ligaments can take the strain, climbing stairs or high steps should be discouraged. Never leave a puppy alone in a room with a baby, young children or an unguarded fire. Stop him licking anyone's face and lips. Do not feed tidbits at the table, or your dog will become a nuisance at mealtimes.

You have bought a retriever, so expect to be brought presents – cushions, shoes, clothing, in fact anything that can be carried. Whatever your pup brings, never snatch it, but give praise. Your Golden must be taught to give readily with a suitable command. If you give old shoes and slippers to play with and your pup is allowed to chew them, you can hardly be cross if he decides to treat your best ones in the same way. It is better not to allow any in the first place. Move anything you value out of your puppy's reach. It is no good being wise after the event if he has gnawed, or knocked over, something precious.

Canine bedding gets dirty, covered with hairs and has a slightly doggy odour, however frequently it is washed. If your dog is allowed on to beds and furniture, they will be similarly affected. You may be quite happy about this, but your visitors may not. My own dogs are not allowed on beds or furniture, a rule they fully accept. Occasionally, this might be permitted, perhaps for a photograph, but they are decidedly uneasy because they know it is generally against the rules. When I want to cuddle them, I join them on the floor.

It is hard for a dog to resist food if left at eye level, so place it higher and cover it. Only disapprove of a dog's misdemeanour if caught in the act. Your puppy will keep you busy, so make time to have fun and then you can both relax, and you can slip on the lead and make your dog lie at your feet. A puppy must understand that you cannot play all the time.

If conditions are wet, avoid damp or muddy pawprints by wiping your dog's feet. A Golden is unlikely to bark a warning until older, and the majority of the breed are not prone to barking continuously. It is good for a dog to warn of strangers, but continuous barking is the surest way to antagonise neighbours, and irritate passers-by. Check all is well, then say "No" and persist in this until the barking stops. You will distinguish a different kind of bark when your dog recognises the visitor.

FINAL THOUGHTS
The breeder has laid the foundation stone on which you can build. Your pup's subsequent progress and the final outcome now depend on you, so do your best to make it as good as possible. A few weeks after collecting your Golden, you may feel that the puppy does not look quite as attractive as when you first brought him home. Do not be despondent, as all puppies go through this stage, which is part of the process of growing up. Even the most gorgeous pups have to suffer the indignity of becoming a bit of an ugly duckling before being transformed into a beautiful swan.

The breeder will always be pleased to receive news of your pup's further progress, together with confirmation that you are still thrilled with your Golden, and most will welcome the opportunity to offer guidance on any problems you may encounter.

The Golden Retriever is a slow-maturing breed, so enjoy puppyhood and be patient. Over many years, with such endearing ways, your dog will capture countless hearts and you will never regret your choice. Come rain or shine, your Golden will always be there to greet you with that expressive, smiling face and a happy, wagging tail.

4 TRAINING YOUR GOLDEN RETRIEVER

Your puppy must learn the good manners required to ensure that you, your family and your neighbours and friends enjoy your Golden Retriever. A puppy is a member of the family, and, as a pack animal, he must learn his place in the hierarchy, respect all members of the family, and fit in with the prescribed routine. To achieve this, your puppy must be taught basic house rules, and be socialised in order to take the outside world in his stride. Modern training emphasises 'shaping' behaviour positively by well-timed rewards for executed commands, rather than negatively by punishment. It is a good idea to join a dog training club to work out a training programme for your puppy, and to get him used to working alongside other dogs. Details of clubs in your area can be obtained from your vet or from your national Kennel Club.

For the purpose of this chapter, the term 'he' has been used when referring to the trainee dog, although, obviously, it applies to dogs and bitches alike!

COMMANDS AND REWARDS
Start basic training as soon as you bring the puppy home. Try to turn all training into a game that is pleasurable for you both. Remember that the handler is pack leader and that the puppy must be controlled by him or her. *Never* get cross with your puppy, as this only causes confusion for the dog and frustration for you. You must make the puppy want to please you by ensuring that whenever he is right you reward him. 'Rewards' are praise, patting, tidbits and/or a game with a favourite toy (which is brought out only in the training sessions). The 'aids' are the voice, the hands, the lead, tidbits and toy. When the puppy makes a mistake, keep silent, i.e. withhold the reward – do not use your voice to correct at this stage. Only if you are *certain* that the puppy is misbehaving wilfully should you punish. The correct punishment is to do as his mother would – to give a quick shake with both hands by the loose skin on the neck, while giving the "No" command in reinforcement. The moment the correction is over, forget it, as does his mother. Throughout training, always use the reward. Timing is essential.

There are specific exercises which must be taught at an early stage. These include:-

NOISE FAMILIARISATION
You must train your puppy positively to accept children visitors and others dogs, and you must also work at noise familiarisation. With the puppy close to you, make a deliberate noise by bringing together two objects. Reward with voice - "Good boy" – and the other aids. Rattle his dinner dish and progress to banging a tin tray. Introduce your puppy to the vacuum cleaner, the washing machine, etc. Outdoor training is equally important. Start with small noises close by and then progress to louder noises. Introduce your puppy positively to cars, aeroplanes, guns, etc. Do not rush – and reward each successful stage.

THE RECALL

The Recall is essential. Nothing is more annoying than a dog who will not come when called. At mealtimes, kneel down and call the pup's name and the word "Come", rattling his feed bowl at the same time, and he will almost certainly come to you at once. Praise excitedly with "Good dog", and give the food. Always do this 'shaping' as part of his training. You will quickly find that when you play with the puppy he comes running towards you. Do not waste this opportunity, but again call his name with the command "Come", and the appropriate reward, as soon as he responds. Do not call him at this stage for anything nasty like bedtime, as you will only encourage him to disobey. *Never* punish him when he comes to you after misdemeanours committed elsewhere, or you will very soon find that he will not respond. Later, call him in randomly, remembering the sequence of Name, Command, Reward. You will shape his behaviour to learn that coming really is pleasurable, and preferable to 'doing his own thing'.

COLLAR AND LEAD WALKING

The collar and lead should be introduced at an early stage (see Chapter Two). You may find that your puppy makes a huge fuss over the lead to begin with, but you must persevere. Start at home (indoors or in the garden). Walk in a wide lefthand circle with the puppy on your left side. Do not be surprised if, to begin with, he leaps around you. Quietly go on walking. When the puppy lands by your left leg (the position you eventually want him to take), and say the word "Close" firmly, followed by the reward "Good boy" in an excited voice. Do not keep the lead short at this stage, but rather let him learn the extent of his freedom. Once he is confident of the lead and no longer fighting it, you can incorporate a small flick of the lead when he starts to pull, so that he learns that this is not a good thing to do.

SIT, DOWN, AND SETTLE

It is also important to teach any pup to remain quietly in one place, both inside and outside.

At six weeks old, this puppy has learnt to recognise his name and come for a reward.

Photos: Steve Nash.

LEFT: When establishing basic control, look for a prompt response to your commands.

RIGHT: The "Down" command is taught using tidbits, then you can gradually extend the time your dog stays in position.

PhotoS: Steve Nash.

THE SIT: When you come to halt in your heelwork, gently place the puppy beside you and push him gently but firmly into a sit by pulling the lead up with your right hand and pressing gently on the pup's rump with your left hand. As you do this give the command "Sit" with the immediate reward of a tidbit in your right hand held up over his head before being given, and the spoken reward of "Good boy."

THE DOWN: Either have the pup on a table with a non-slip surface, or get down on the floor yourself. When he is attentive, give the command "Down", and firmly push the puppy downwards and backwards into the down position with your hands across the front of the dog's chest and round his shoulders. Do not force him down from above as this can damage his legs and back. Reward with a tidbit held under his head down between his feet. He has to go down to get his reward! Follow with immediate praise and then the quick release "Off."

SETTLE: Even the most senior competition dogs do no more than ten minutes of a formal Down Stay, yet I often want a pup to remain in one position for much longer periods. I use the command "Settle" for this general quietness. Teach the pup by putting him in his indoor crate or bed after his meal, after toilet training and after a game, so that he is tired. He should be commanded to "Settle" each time he is put in his crate. You may find that a chewy toy will help in the early stages. The dog will soon realise that the crate is his own territory, and associate it with relaxation.

BASIC COMMANDS
It is very important that you always use the same single words of command, praise etc. Dogs learn by repetition, and so, if your commands are even slightly different, you will cause great confusion and accomplish very little; e.g. always use "Sit", not "Sit down!" Ideally, a command should only be given once. If properly taught, a dog will wish to respond to his pack leader, and his correct response to the command must be reinforced by reward (praise, a tidbit, a favourite toy and or a game). Constant use of the command using all the aids (voice, lead, hands, reward) will shape correct behaviour.

Always use the dog's name to get his attention, then the single word command. Initially, his vocabulary will consist of "No", "Come", "Sit", "Down", "Settle", "Heel", and "Be Good". Other command words will be introduced in more advanced training: "Wait", "Stay", "Fetch", "Speak", "Quiet", "Back", "Away", "Find" etc.

Make a point of always telling him when you have finished and he can do his own thing, by giving the command "Off" or "Go free."

CORRECTING PROBLEM BEHAVIOUR
CHEWING
All puppies will chew. This is a natural way for them to deal with the teething problems that will occur in the first few months of their lives. The important thing is for them to learn what they are allowed to chew, and what is forbidden. When the pup is found chewing the handler's possessions, shape his behaviour by removing the article from the pup with a firm "No" and replacing it with one of the pup's own chew toys, with the command "Chew". After he has finished teething, teach "Hold". Never leave a pup to run around the house when you are absent or busy. Use the indoor kennel. It will be too late to correct him for chewing when you return.

BARKING
Puppies should be discouraged from unnecessary barking, from the start, with the command "Quiet", accompanied by the reward of a gentle stroke of the pup's head. In cases of older dogs who have already acquired the maddening habit of endless barking, the only solution which I have found to work is to squirt water suddenly from a plastic squeezy bottle, while saying very firmly "Quiet", with immediate praise once the command is obeyed.

PULLING
Pulling on the lead is a common problem. Do not pit your strength against the dog; he will only pull harder. Use the dog's own momentum, and thus put him at a loss. With the dog on the lead on the handler's left, hold the lead in the left hand with its handle (the end grip) over the thumb and half the lead looped in the left hand. When the dog pulls, release the loop from the left hand. The dog will surge forward because he is suddenly released. Call "Name", and simultaneously with both hands jerk the lead, spinning the dog

round towards the handler, and release lead tension. The dog is off-balance and is turned easily. Sometimes, the handler turns about and walks back. Timing is important, but it works!

JUMPING UP
A puppy should be pleased to see his people, and will often jump up to be closer to faces. Not everyone appreciates this loving gesture. Shape his behaviour against jumping, but be careful not to flatten natural exuberance. There are three tips for curing this problem: (a) get down on one knee before he arrives and only reward when the pup is on four feet; (b) Lift your knee in his chest with good timing when he jumps and say "No", then get down yourself to reward (play on the ground praising with "Good boy"); (c) Train your puppy by teaching the Present/ Front (see Obedience section later).

DOMINANCE
A submissive dog is seldom a problem. A dominant dog may well be, or become, one. Dominance is shown by rushing through doorways ahead of the handler, adopting a favourite piece of furniture, being insistent about food, rushing ahead in walks, and showing aggression towards other dogs and people. These traits must be countered by insisting that the dog follow the handler (pack leader) through doorways, by not allowing the dog to claim territory (e.g. taking over an armchair or corner of the room as his own), and by the pup being made to sleep in his own cage, in a different room from the handler. He must be fed at a different time to the family, either well before or after, and must not be allowed to beg while the family is eating. If there are small children in the house, the pup should be put in his crate during mealtimes. Games must only be played when the handler wants them, and not when the pup demands them.

SUMMARY OF BASIC TRAINING
Keep all training sessions short and simple. Always use the aid and rewards. Always use the same words of command and praise to

shape the puppy's behaviour. Make sure that you are always the boss. You control the pup, and not the other way round. Break each exercise into its elements, and train these separately. Make haste slowly. Never try to rush any teaching. The slow methods are always the best. It is very hard to re-teach an exercise which has been taught incorrectly in the first place.

Enjoy the time you spend with your pup. Look forward to your training sessions. Plan what you hope to achieve in each session. Do not practise everything in every session. It is far better to get one thing right than simply to run through the pup's repertoire without correction and constructive criticism. This will only reinforce error. Always end with something at which the pup can and will succeed, so that you can both feel positive and ready for the next session.

NEW CHALLENGES

The Golden Retriever is bred to be a working dog and will enjoy the physical and mental challenge of competitive training. If you do not want to train your Golden to work in the field, there are still plenty of sports available to you. The main areas of competition, apart from breed showing, are: Obedience, Agility and Working Trials or Working Tests. In North America, Tracking and Hunting Tests are also classified. Goldens are doing well at the topmost level in each sport.. The number at the top is a fair percentage of the total competing compared to other breeds. Do come and join us!

TRAINING IN NORTH AMERICA

Originally nearly all training of dogs for competition followed the military style of training, based largely on the use of physical and verbal correction. Praise and physical petting might be used to encourage a reluctant dog, and were considered sufficient reward for a good performance. Many good working dogs were created using these techniques, although success was largely dependent upon the skills of the trainer and the dog's degree of toughness or forgiveness. Some breeds of dog

Patrick Holden with Menola Bramble CDEx, UDEx, WDEx, TDEx: The first Golden Retriever to qualify at the top level in Working Trials (TDEx) and Obedience (OC winner).

Photo: Steve Nash.

simply did not respond well to this approach.

In the 1960s and 70s, pioneer dog trainers utilised the findings of scientists in working with the dog's natural characteristics and in developing better teaching methods. In the late 1980s applications of operant conditioning and behavioural modification were taken out of the laboratory and into the training of dolphins, horses – and dogs. A veritable explosion of dog-training books, seminars, and classes brought the concepts and applications directly to dog owners and trainers.

Old-style trainers derided the new as 'cookie-trainers', and it is true that many people never grasped the basics, and were doing no more than bribing the dog to perform. However, properly used, the use of aids and rewards (food, toys, or games) as positive reinforcement in 'motivational

Can. Ch. and OT Ch. Jonore's Courthill Timothy, Am. CDX, TD, JH; Can. UD, WCI, owned and trained by Cindi Olson. A handsome Golden successful in many areas of activity, in the best tradition of the breed.

training' is extremely useful, and makes training much less stressful and more fun for both dog and trainer.

Another school of training has developed, partly through Schutzhund trainers, partly through behaviourists, utilising the concept of 'drives'. This is another way of stating some of the natural canine characteristics of behaviour, such as the urge to pursue and catch a small moving object or live creature (the 'prey drive'), or the dog's inherent sociability and willingness to follow a leader ('pack drive').

The most successful trainers are able to utilise all these concepts to 'think like a dog' and to take fullest advantage of all the dog's natural characteristics. The best trainers use both 'motivational' methods and a certain amount of compulsion (negative reinforcement), so that the dog learns that certain actions/responses (the ones the trainer is aiming for) result in wonderful things, and other responses may bring about no result at all, or something that is preferably to be avoided. A great trainer makes the dog think it was all his own idea, and develops happy, willing, reliable workers.

No matter what terms may be used, or how the concepts are organised for the understanding of the trainer, the advantage of all the newer methods is that they attempt to work with and take advantage of the dog's natural characteristics, rather than merely subjugate the dog into performance.

GETTING STARTED
BASIC CONTROL: This is vital to all the competitive disciplines, and must be taught early. The first training club you join will, inevitably, be Obedience-based because few Working Trials or Agility clubs offer classes in control, since it is not possible to compete in these sports until pups are older – at around 12 months of age.
HELP: In addition to training at a club, it is possible to do well these days by self-training; each of the sports now has excellent training books and videos dealing either with the whole sport or individual aspects of it. At top level, as with most other sports, competitors also make use of a personal or group trainer.
EQUIPMENT: For Obedience you need a lead, collar (leather or nylon) and a dumbbell. Working Trials require these, plus a leather harness and 30ft line and poles. Agility needs a lead, a hoop, plus the equipment described below. Always remember your other aids: your voice, your hands and rewards.
ATTITUDE: Modern trainers refer frequently to 'attitude', meaning the keenness, fitness, appetite for work, attention span, and concentration of today's top dogs and handlers. There should be no problem with a Golden Retriever, who has most of these attributes and can be trained to have the others. Great care, however, must be taken to ensure that the Golden's natural exuberance is not flattened. He is an intelligent working dog. His liking and aptitude for games should be built on and encouraged.

OBEDIENCE

Obedience is a progressive sport with handlers
and dogs having to achieve a qualification to
progress upwards through the classes. These
competitions are run according to rules laid
down by the your national Kennel Club. Many
more Goldens than ever before are now
qualified to compete at the highest level, and
more are coming into the sport.

TEAMWORK

Dog and handler work as a team. There is no
point in having the best trained and presented
dog on the circuit if the handler is all arms and
legs in the wrong places. Handler faults and
extra commands are marked. Every handler
must, therefore, learn deportment. I advise
training and practice without the dog, so that
the dog is not thrown wide or out of position
by incorrect handling. As always, incorrect
teaching reinforces error, and is doubly
difficult since it has to be unlearnt before the
correct teaching can be given.

ELEMENTS – TRAINING AND PRACTICE

Modern training breaks each exercise into
component elements and trains each
individually. Only when mastered are they
trained together. Some exercises are then
incorporated into others (e.g. Recall into
Retrieve, Retrieve into Scent).

HEELWORK

BASIC POSITION AND "WATCH" COMMAND

The Basic position element is crucial. The dog
must be to the left of his handler, his shoulder
close to the handler's leg, ideally parallel with
the seam of the trousers. His feet should be
parallel, but a little behind the handler's toes.
The dog should look at his handler. When
stationary, the dog is in the Sit.

Guide the pup into this Basic position using
all the aids – the command "Sit", the hands,
and the lead to guide him round. Then
command "Watch". After initially very short
periods allow him to relax with the command
"Off" and give a reward (praise, tidbit and/or

HEELWORK

*Position your
dog at the left-
hand side. Make
sure you have
his full attention
using the
"Watch"
command.*

*The aim is for
the dog to
maintain the
correct position,
regardless of
turns, changes
of pace, and
changes of
direction.*

game). The period for the dog to concentrate
on his handler with eye contact should be
increased progressively. Eventually,
distractions may be employed with the dog
being reminded that he is still under "Watch"

and corrected when he inevitably looks away to see what else is happening.

TURNS AND SPOTWORK
I train turns initially in the stationary position on the spot (spotwork). For the turns themselves, see the diagrams under Deportment. Only when handler and dog are proficient with the elements of turns on the spot should they attempt to do them on the move, and then only a pace away. Ensure there is no confusion in the minds of either dog or handler. If any is exhibited, go back to the Basic position and spotwork. Do not attempt fast pace until turns are thoroughly mastered at slow and normal.

OTHER HEELWORK EXERCISES
To tighten basic position on the move, using the aids, do:
● Righthand circles to bring a lagging dog *up* to Basic position. Large circles, then smaller.
● Lefthand circles to bring a forward worker *back* to Basic.
● Dressage exercises to keep the dog thinking and using his feet correctly. These are: the Serpentine (lefthand semi-circle, then righthand, with the dog changing the leading leg); Sidestep (handler moves at right angles crossing left foot over right – ensure the dog is in the Basic position throughout); Backward (handler and dog move backwards against a wall); Figures of eight.

Always train at slow and normal paces, then fast only when secure. Do not build in any error!

OTHER SET TEST ELEMENTS
THE WAIT
With the dog in the Basic position, place him in the Sit, giving the command "Sit" firmly. Ensure that he is sitting tidily, with his feet neatly under him and his tail out straight behind him. Do not let him lean on to your leg. As in Heelwork, his front feet should be level with your instep and his bottom exactly parallel to your legs. Give the command "Sit" and, holding the lead in the left hand above his head, take a half-pace away from him to the

right, ensuring by use of the lead and your left hand that he does not move. Count to five in your head and return to him, praising him greatly but still ensuring that he does not move from the Sit position. Gradually increase the distance away from him to the side, the front and the back of him, keeping him on the lead at all times and making quite sure that he never changes position. It is better to keep the timing of this exercise short than to allow the dog to break his position.

THE PRESENT/FRONT
With your dog on a lead in front of you and your feet slightly apart, gently encourage the dog into your body and command "Come". Use tidbits held high and close to your body, ensuring that you urge him into a straight position. Once you are satisfied that he is in the right position, give the command "Sit" so that the dog ends up with his nose pointing up your body and his bottom in a straight line in front of you. If the dog does not come into a correct Present position, put your hands gently into his collar under his chin and gently draw him into the position, making quite sure that he is absolutely straight, and that your hands are returned to the 'V' position, before giving the "Sit" command. Reward with a tidbit, then Release and play.

PRESENT
The Present or Front position, with the dog sitting absolutely straight to the handler.

THE FINISH

With the dog on the lead in front of you and the lead in your left hand, give the command "Close". Encourage your dog round your right leg with the right hand on the lead, and take a step forward with the left leg at the same time bringing the dog round behind you into the Basic position and commanding him to "Sit". Reward. Repeat this several times until the dog is coming round your legs happily. At this stage you can drop the forward step and simply stand still. Do not, however, forget to encourage the dog both with your right hand with the signal to finish, your left hand on the lead and your voice encouraging him at all times. Reward, then Release and play.

THE COMPLETE SET TESTS

The exercises in Obedience competition vary slightly according to the rules of the different national Kennel Clubs. However, the basic elements and principles are shared.

DISTANT CONTROL

Modern teachers use Distant Control training from the early stages because DC provides elements for many other exercises.

   Use a table with a non-slip surface (also useful training for the vet's surgery for grooming, and one of the Agility exercises), or get down on the ground. There are three DC positions – the Sit, the Down and the Stand. Each is taken up from another. I use a tidbit (or a toy) and the other aids. Timing is essential.

SIT: Play, then command "Control". As the pup comes towards you, stop him with your hands cupped on his chest. Hold a tidbit *over* his nose, command "Sit", and press down on his rump with the other hand. Reward in the position before release.

STAND: I use the command "Back" as "Stand" is too similar in sound to "Sit". With the pup in the basic Sit, stand in front of him with one hand on his chest and give the command "Control". Hold the tidbit just *under* his nose against his chest. Use your hand and foot under his stomach to help him move backwards into the Stand. Command "Back"

FINISH

The Finish is an exercise to get the dog back to the handler's left-hand side. On the command "Close", Bramble sets off.

Hugging the back of the legs, Bramble reaches the left-hand side.

The exercise finishes with Bramble in the Sit.

DISTANT CONTROL

Distant Control training starts in easy stages, with the dog responding to a toy or a tidbit, with the verbal command.

The secret is to proceed slowly until your dog is confident to maintain his position at a distance and respond instantly to commands.

and reward while still in position.

DOWN: With your puppy in the Stand, command "Control". Hold the tidbit *on the floor* between and behind his front feet. Command "Down". Use gentle pressure on the shoulders first, then on the rump if necessary. Reward while in position.

CHANGES BETWEEN POSITIONS AND DISTANCE: Do not teach changes until each stationary element is mastered. Proceed slowly!

NOVICE RECALL

THE TEST: Handler leaves the dog in the Sit, proceeding forward until commanded to halt and face. Handler then calls the dog to Present and Finish, both on command.

THE ELEMENTS: Wait; Walkout/turn; Recall; Present; Finish.

If you have followed this book, you will already have a puppy who comes quickly and happily as soon as his name and "Come" are called. Simply add the elements! First the Wait and Come to Present position on the spot. Then short-distance Come to Present. Then extend in length. Train Finish ("Close") separately, and only include it with the full exercise when the other elements are mastered.

ADVANCED RECALL

THE TEST: Handler leaves the dog in Sit or Down (I prefer Down) and proceeds away until commanded to call the dog to heel on the move.

THE ELEMENTS: Wait; Walkout; Recall to Basic.

Proceed as for Novice Recall. The only difference is that when the dog joins his handler the handler is moving and the dog comes to heel in the Basic position. Then proceed as Heelwork until halt.

TEMPERAMENT TEST

THE TEST: The dog stands by the handler. The judge approaches from the front and runs his hand down the dog's back. The dog must not react adversely.

THE ELEMENTS: Stand; Wait.

The dog who has been socialised (see Basic Training) and trained to these elements will have no problems!

RETRIEVE
THE TEST: The handler has the dog stationary in Sit, and throws the dumb-bell (other articles in more advanced classes) on command. He then commands the dog to retrieve the dumb-bell. The dog retrieves and picks it up, recalls, and presents to handler, releases bell and finishes, both on command.
THE ELEMENTS: Sit/Wait; Recall; Present and Finish (all as above); plus Outrun, Pick-up/Hold and Release.

Outrun: Encourage this; most Goldens chase objects thrown – after all they are bred for it!

Pick-up: Train close to handler initially, and further away only when secure.

Hold: Ensure no mouthing during Recall; spot train close to handler, initially.

When the dog presents, take the dumb-bell with two hands using the command "Give". Ensure he releases it cleanly without mouthing. Then finish on command. Reward each successful element.

SCENT
THE TEST: Handler's scent on one cloth (6ins x 6ins) out of six in first test – the judge's scent is used in the more advanced classes. Dog to go out, reject any decoy, choose the cloth with the handler/judge's scent, and return and present it to handler. Handler to take and finish on command.

THE ELEMENTS: Wait; Outrun; Discrimination (rejection of blanks and decoys, choice of scented cloth); Pick-up; Recall; Present; Release; Finish.

The exercise is therefore a Retrieve, plus Discrimination, so train Retrieve with a placed cloth. Scent is often a problem area for handlers, usually due to unfortunate training. Every dog, particularly a Golden, can scent. The most junior dogs in Working Trials, who can find an article as small as a sparkplug, can certainly scent a huge white square! It is essential to train the dog (a) to use his nose

ADVANCED RECALL

Bramble is left in the Down.

On command, Bramble is in the move.

The exercise is competed when Bramble takes up the Heel position on the left-hand side.

THE RETRIEVE

1. The handler throws the dumb-bell, and bramble waits for the command to fetch.

2. Bramble runs out in a straight line to the dumb-bell.

3 and 4. Bramble picks up the dumb-bell cleanly, and returns directly to the handler.

5. Bramble presents the dumb-bell.

6. On command, Bramble lets go of the dumb-bell.

7 and 8. The exercise is finished when Bramble returns to the handler's left-hand side.

SCENT

*ABOVE: Bramble is given
the scent he has to go out
and find.*

*TOP RIGHT: Bramble sets
off and works his way round,
scenting the cloths.*

RIGHT: Found it!

rather than his eyes, and (b) to discriminate, i.e. reject unwanted cloths.

Train scenting by hiding toys both around the house and in long grass. Use the command "Find". Progress to one cloth under one of two or three plastic flowerpots. Train discrimination by using only two cloths, then progressively more; one with the handler's scent, the other affixed to a heavy board, tile or similar so that it cannot be moved. Use the word "No". Put table salt or Epsom salts on the reject cloths as a deterrent. As soon as the dog has the correct cloth, reward, then proceed as for a Retrieve. Only drop the use of the aids (voice, hands, lead, tidbit) when the dog is confident. Do not rush this exercise.

SENDAWAY

THE TEST: The handler has the dog by his side in Sit and sends the dog away on command. The dog continues forward at test until commanded to stop. He remains in position until commanded to rejoin the handler on the move. I recommend exactly the same training for Obedience Sendaways as for Working Trials. A dog who thoroughly understands Sendaways of 100 metres will have little problem in the much shorter Obedience ones. Refine for Obedience using a different set-up (the handler must stand up) and command "Away".

THE ELEMENTS: Wait; Outrun; Down; Advanced Recall.

1. Command "Wait". Train separate set up, turn his head towards the target and shield his eyes so the dog looks straight. I use the command "Away" in Obedience (and "Go" in Working Trials).

2. Train the common Sendaway targets: box; triangle; back marker; through markers. Goldens are bright enough to recognise the differences. I tell Bramble which one to go for during the set-up.

3. Train instant "Down".

4. Train for longer distance, to his Working Trials Sendaway spot, and through markers.

SENDAWAY

On command, Bramble is sent to the target area.

Without deviating, Bramble heads right for the spot.

Bramble goes into the Down, and must stay there until recalled.

Then when under Test at an Obedience Show, the exercise is shorter and easier!

STAYS
THE TEST: The handler leaves the dog in each Sit/Stand or Down position for a specified period. The handler returns to the dog after the expiry of period. The handler is in sight (out of sight in Senior classes).
THE ELEMENTS: Sit; Down; Stand.
Proceed as in Wait or DC. Use the command "Sit" ("Back"/"Down"), and "Stay" (to tell the dog that his handler will return to him). Train close to the handler at the beginning. Use the aids (voice, repeat "Stay", and lead). When secure by the handler, move to the end of the lead. Return and reward. Ensure the dog is absolutely solid first by the handler, then on the lead, then off, all in sight. Then have distractions (e.g. from other handlers). Only when the dog is secure, go out of sight and return after a short period. Release and reward. Gradually extend the periods, and return at random times.

OBEDIENCE TRIALS IN NORTH AMERICA
In the US and Canada there are hundreds of dog training clubs providing training classes open to both their members and to the general public. Many of these clubs also hold Obedience Trials and/or Tracking Tests. Most provide both basic training for pet dogs, and classes for those participating in formal obedience events. There are also many classes of various sorts and quality run by individuals or private training schools.

Throughout North America there are also numerous seminars or working clinics for every sort of training activity imaginable, featuring instructors of some achievement. These range from one-day lectures to "training camps" of a week or more of intensive instruction – there's no shortage of people willing to impart their knowledge.

North American Obedience Trials have some features in common with both British obedience tests and British working trials, utilizing jumping and retrieving exercises in the advanced classes. While some breeds, such as Border Collies and Golden Retrievers, are commonly in the top scorers, North American Obedience attracts an amazing variety of breeds, as it is the qualifying score that is essential in earning titles, not having to win a high placement in the class. It would not be unusual to see a Chihuahua, a Bulldog, or an Irish Wolfhound in the ring next to your Golden!

There have been several changes in the exercises and in the scoring over the years, and some titles have been added. Dogs who qualify in both Open B and Utility B at ten trials earn the title Utility Dog Excellent (UDX). UD Dogs who place first and second in Utility B and Open B at enough all-breed trials to earn 100 points (figured according to the number of dogs in competition in those classes) can earn the title Obedience Trial Champion (OTCh.). Given that aspirants for the OTCh. title have to compete directly against other UD, UDX and OTCh. dogs at most trials for the first and second placements, it is not an easy title to earn.

AGILITY

Agility is one of the most popular of the major dog sports. The sport is akin to show-jumping with the dog having to complete a course, clearing various obstacles against the clock. It is good fun for competitors, both the handlers and their dogs, and eminently watchable for the public.

While the handler does not touch the dog during the competition, it is a team exercise. Although a skilled handler, by choosing the right position, can reduce the amount he or she has to move, the competition is a time trial, and the handler has to be in the right spot to give the right command to the dog to ensure that he covers all the obstacles in as short as possible time. Both dog and handler must be fit! Agility is also dominated by working sheepdogs and Border Collies, principally because of their deft footwork and speed. However, Goldens can and do excel at the sport.

BASIC TRAINING AND CONTROL
Do not start Agility until you have mastered basic control. Your dog must be able to do the elements: Sit; Down; Wait; and Come (Recall) instantly on command. Sendaway (see Working Trials section) and Retrieve are also very helpful.

GENERAL PRINCIPLES
These are the same as for the other sports:
1) Break each exercise into its elements, then train each element separately. Only train the elements together when each has been mastered.
2) Use the aids: voice (command and praise); hands (to demonstrate and pat); lead (one or two together); tidbits and/or his toy (play).
3) Emphasise behaviour shaping by correct teaching and understanding.
4) Give reward rather than correction or compulsion.
5) Ensure both dog and handler are fit!

THE OBSTACLES
CONTACT POINTS: Teach the dog to touch each contact point (the yellow strip at each of the relevant obstacles). Three tips are:
1) Train the dog to go through a hand-held hoop. Hold the hoop before each point and call the dog through it (particularly the A-Frame and Walkway).
2) Instantly "Down" the dog on each contact (particularly the Seesaw).
3) Reward on each point touched.

CONTACT EQUIPMENT: Train in the order: A-frame, Seesaw, Walkway.
A-frame: Guide the dog up on lead. Use a toy as incentive (on double lead held over top and drawn upwards). Command "Walk on". Alternatively, the instructor holds the dog at the bottom, while the handler climbs up the other side and recalls. Try both.
Seesaw: Train before Walkway. Start with a plank, on the ground, then raised on one brick. Have your dog on a lead. Command "Walk on". Take your time – Goldens are less deft

JUMPS

These are of two main types: the Over jumps (clear hurdle, 'brick' wall and spread – long over elements) and the Through jumps (tyre/hoop and wishing well).

Over jumps: Start with a low pole and the dog on the lead. Walk over the pole and command "Over", then repeat at the run. Use the aids. Then raise the pole. Walk over, then run as before. Progress gradually. If your dog hesitates, goes through or knocks down a pole, go back a stage. Use a toy thrown over and your other aids.

Through jumps: Train with hoop and aids, both at ground level. Use the command "Through". Then raise the jumps. When the dog is proficient, increase the height.

TABLE

The dog has to jump on a table and go down for five seconds before proceeding. Initially I lift the pup, then have an intermediate box as a step, and finally encourage him to jump up. Command "Table". Use the aids, particularly his toy, first as an incentive, then as a reward for success. In the unlikely event of these tips not working, the handler must get on the table himself and recall the dog up to him. Use the "Down" and "Stay" elements.

WEAVE

Start with the weave poles placed in two lines, alternating, with the poles angled outwards. Walk the dog through on his short lead several times. Then place his toy at the end as an incentive. Command "weave", and gradually:
1) Steepen the angles of the poles until vertical.

than Collies. Continue until comfortable. Next, raise one end as a slope, teaching descent first, then reverse for the ascent.

Progress to seesaw, with the handler encouraging the dog on and the instructor holding level. When at the fulcrum, the instructor gently holds the rear end. The handler then encourages his dog to go down, with the aids.

Then go up, then level. Next reduce the balancing by the instructor, so the dog learns the fulcrum. Train contact points separately (see above).

Walkway: Train in full only after the Seesaw (otherwise your dog may 'freak' when high up). Break this obstacle up into elements and train each one separately: going up, along, going down, as for Seesaw. Use the command "Walk on", and only progress when dog thoroughly understands.

For all three of these obstacles, train contact points, and with handler on the left and then right. Build up speed gradually.

58

2) Reduce the space between the poles progressively until they are in a straight line. Continue the incentive, but vary the use of the lead. Reward when the dog is through. Thoroughly master weaving with the poles vertical, before increasing speed gradually.

TUNNELS
These are both fixed and collapsible. Train the hoop so the dog is proficient. The instructor holds the dog at the mouth of either tunnel while the handler holds open the other end, shows the toy, and recalls dog through. The command is "Through". Later reverse the instructor and handler, then use the "Wait" element at the tunnel mouth.

TURNS AND COURSE
Only when both handler and dog are proficient with individual obstacles (elements training), progress to pairs, then beyond. So a straight line first. Again, when proficient, introduce turns between obstacles. Teach handling with your dog on both left and right sides of the handler. Turn directions are the commands "Left" and "Right" (also useful for Working Trials Sendaway redirect). When a dog has arrived at this level, his handler is beyond the scope of this chapter!

WORKING TRIALS
Working Trials is derived from the training of Sheep, Police and Army and other service dogs who are being trained to track fugitives, retrieve missing objects and the like.

Working Trials are very rewarding both to the handler and the trained dog, who will be using his natural inbred instincts in a controlled fashion. All dogs, whatever their breed, have a good sense of smell, thousands of times superior to that of any human being. Goldens are certainly no exception. Indeed they were, of course, originally bred for retrieving. This means usually using not only their eyes, but in particular following scents with their nose.

THE SPORT
As with the other sports, dogs progress through stages which also act as a handicap system to encourage the less experienced dogs. Each completed stage entitles the dog to relevant title initials e.g. CDEx (Companion Dog Excellent) etc.

EXERCISES AND TESTS
The sport consists of three main parts: Nosework, Control and Agility.

NOSEWORK
This is the most important area of Working Trials. There are two parts:
1) The track, where the dog has to retrieve up to three articles on a man track left by a steward up to three hours before.
2) The square, where the dog has to recover up to four articles placed randomly in a 25-yard square. Each of these exercises is to be performed within a time limit.

TRACKING: The track will be up to 1,000 yards long, with left and right turns, acute and obtuse angles and may include curves. The dog will be ahead of his handler, and will need to follow the track accurately so that he can mark and recover the articles that have been dropped thereon. Tracks are aged progressively (up to three hours old) through the tests.

It is essential for a beginner to get the right start. There is nothing more frustrating for handler and dog than to have to un-learn bad faults, particularly as it is considerably more difficult than learning procedures correctly in the first place. Tracking is certainly no exception – I speak from bitter personal experience! As always, break the exercise into its component elements.

The main element is to train the dog to become fanatical about articles. The track is incidental to his finding articles. The other main principle to bear in mind is that tracking is a control exercise. While the majority of Goldens love it, their natural enthusiasm must be channelled to ensure that they do not overrun corners, or take the track at such a speed that they miss the articles, which will be

both small and hidden. Do not allow your pup to yaw wildly from side to side, or charge at the full extent of his 30-foot line so that he overshoots corners, leaving the beginner handler using the line like a wild west cowboy practising with a lariat.

***WORKING
TRIALS***
*Photos
Steve Nash.*

TRACKING

*TOP: Bramble
comes to the
start pole.*

*LEFT: On the
track.*

ARTICLES: For the 'mad about articles' element, the pup must be encouraged to find and then play with them. Show the article to him indoors, and then hide it about the house. When the pup successfully finds the article, reward him, preferably with vigorous play with the article as a toy. For this purpose, a length of thick rope, rubber hose or a ball on a rope are ideal. Extend the games to the garden, and then further afield.

Finding articles after a search is the foundation both of tracking and the search square. While the articles may themselves be as large as a hosepipe or ball, they must be hidden**.** The dog is being taught to use his nose on the ground, so that it is a scent and not a sight test.

EARLY TRACKING WITH THE DOG: It is helpful to have either another handler to hold the pup, or a post to which to tie him. First tracks are laid by having the toy – still the hose or the ball on the rope – at the end of a lead or a line. It should be shown to the pup, and the pup's attention kept on it all the way through until it is hidden. The handler will then rush back to the pup, affix a double lead and, later on, the harness to the pup, and then encourage him to "Find". When he does, reward him (with praise, a tidbit and a game with his toy). When he is 100 per cent certain with this game, it should be extended as regards length, going gradually from 20 yards up to 50.

*Returning with
the article.*

CORNERS AND CURVES: Only move to corners when both handler and dog are fully proficient with straight tracks of differing lengths working up to around 100 yards, and always recovering the articles.

Start with right angles. Lay a short 30-yard track up to a hedge or wall. Turn right for 25 yards. Triple lay (i.e. go back to the turn and back again). Hide the articles. Only progress to left angles, then acute and obtuse angles and, eventually, curves when proficient at the earlier stages.

SEARCH SQUARE: Here again, the elements training is similar, with the dog being shown articles which are then hidden, initially within the house or other area well-known to the pup, and later on in the great wide world, until at last he comes to the 25-yard square. Reward when found – play only when finding article elsewhere. Practise a formal square with the handler walking round the 25-yard square, hiding the articles then sending out the dog, with the command "Find".

CONTROL
Teaching some of these Control exercises (Heelwork, Stays, Sendaway, Retrieve, Recall, Gun and Speak) is covered in the section under Obedience.

WORKING TRIAL HEELWORK
WT Heelwork is similar to an Obedience 'B' round (no commands and slow, normal and fast paces), but differs from it in the following ways:
a) Emphasis is placed on a 'natural manner', so swing both arms.
b) Less precision is required (handlers are often stumbling round rough fields).

GUN: Steadiness to gunshot is covered in Basic Training (Noise Familiarisation).
SPEAK: The objective is to get the dog to bark on command and stop barking on command. The command "Speak" is not easy for a novice handler to teach. It is difficult to have a pup bark excitedly at a stranger at the door and to then have the pup told in front of the stranger that he is a good dog! Nevertheless, this is essential. When the dog is barking, either for his food or for attention, he must be encouraged with the command "Speak". He must also learn the other command of "Quiet". Start with the dog by the handler's side. Progress to on the move,

then away from the handler. Only progress when each stage is secure.

SENDAWAY: The objective is to train a dog to leave his handler's side on command, and proceed in the direction indicated by the handler until told by him to stop. He should stay in that designated spot until either recalled (in the lower classes) or redirected to another designated spot in the higher classes.

Modern trainers advocate that Sendaway training should be left until the handler has trained the elements of "Wait", and an instant "Down", but preliminary work should be done with a pup from the earliest stages.

Phase 1: We recommend that when the pup is about to be fed, put his dish at the end of a corridor. The pup, often wriggling, will be held at the other end while the handler lets him run with the command "Go" (move away from handler at the run). While the pup is, of course, intent on getting his food, this repetition of the command will nevertheless help 'shape' his future performance.
Extend this element by placing the food dish further away, for example in the garden.

Phase 2: For the next phase use a training companion. Each handler (but only one dog at a time) has one of the dog's toys. The first handler keeps the dog by his side while the dog's own handler goes initially ten paces, proceeding slowly to build up the distance. He exhibits the dog's toy and calls the dog. The first handler says "Go", the second handler says "Come". The dog runs between them. The second handler plays with the dog. The procedure is then reversed.
This will be of help in training Recall as well as Sendaway. It also has the distinct advantage for us older handlers of allowing the pup to take a lot of exercise pleasurable to him, without unduly tiring his handlers!

Phase 3: For the third, and more formal phase, the dog must be able to do the elements of Wait and instant Down (or Sit) at a distance, on the handler's command. In this

**THE
SCALE**

**THE
LONG JUMP**
(Below)
Photo courtesy:
Patrick Holden.

phase, we build on the behaviour shaped in the first two. The equipment required is two poles (a wooden broom handle with a nail at the bottom and a cup hook at the top is ideal). Here the handler places one pole in the ground. He downs the dog by that pole. He then runs some ten to twenty yards away and plants a second pole. He calls the dog to him as a Recall and then downs him at that pole. The handler then goes back to the first pole, attaching a toy to the hook on the pole. He goes back to the other pole and sets the dog up with the command "Go". As soon as the dog (following his own body scent down the now well-worn, well-scented path) gets to the pole he should be downed beside the pole. The handler must run after the dog, reward him instantly and play with the toy.

Phase 4: When the third phase has been thoroughly mastered, and the distance very gradually extended, the handler must then find a fence, hedge or other barrier against which to plant his pole in a particular spot. Use the Recall procedure as in Phase 3. Soon it should be possible for the dog to recognise his 'spot' without the aid of the pole. Here again, distance must be built up gradually with the dog. If there is any worry in the dog's mind (evidenced perhaps by looking around), the handler must go back a phase until the dog thoroughly understands.

Phase 5: is Redirection. A handler at this stage is beyond the scope of this book!

WORKING TRIALS AGILITY

Working Trials Agility consists of three jumps: the long jump of nine feet over five elements; the clear jump of three feet; and a scale of six feet. Your club will have this equipment. Beginner handlers must not train on these jumps without a competent instructor.

TRACKING IN NORTH AMERICA

Tracking people are a group unto themselves. As in the UK, it takes a particular sort to get out in all sorts of weather (often unpleasant) at some ungodly hour to trudge over and through all sorts of terrain behind a dog, following an invisible and (to the handler) incomprehensible trail. It is very difficult to force a dog to track; this is a subject the dog knows much more about than the handler!

Because of the limitations of time and land available, entries at Tests are very limited, and often there are a dozen candidates for the five to twelve slots available. Entrants are chosen by random draw.

The two judges plot the tracks the day before the Test, placing markers or flags in the field. On the day of the Test, a tracklayer follows the track, picking up all the markers except at the start, and leaving an article such as a glove at the end of the track. When the track has aged the required time, the dog is started on the track. The dog wears a harness and a long lead, 20 to 40 feet in length, and must work unaided by the handler. The judges follow and observe.

One 'pass' earns the title Tracking Dog (TD). Actually, the dog has passed under three judges, as a qualifying certificate signed by a tracking judge, attesting that the dog has successfully worked a track witnessed by the

Diva, Jingle, and Ganza were lovely housedogs and companions as well as being active in show, obedience, tracking and field work: Can. Ch. Ciadar Diva, Am. Can. CD, WC; Am. Can. Ch. & Can. OTCh. Ciadar Tintinabulation, UDT, WC, VCX, Can. UD; Am. Can. Ch. Ciadar Extravaganza CDX, TD, Can. CDX.

judge, is required for entry, then two judges do the actual Test. Tracking Tests are non-competitive; the dog will either pass or fail. The TDX Test has increased ageing, length, terrain, more articles, obstacles, and cross-tracks, which all give the dog more difficulty and more problems to solve.

The newest development is the Variable Surface Tracking Test. VST is intended to utilise more urban-type areas, including some paved surfaces, and is staged near buildings or other such obstacles. It is likely that success in VST will require somewhat different techniques from those routinely used for TD/TDX, where the dogs are worked in areas of vegetation, and are expected to follow the track very closely without utilising air scent. The urban tracker will need to make use of every talent available. So far, only a few VST Tests have been held, and these have been somewhat experimental.

Am. Can. Ch. Ciadar Extravaganza, CDX, TD, Can. CDX. Ganza was a third generation High Score in Trial winner for owner-breeder Pamela Ruddick. She completed her American show Championship when nearly 7 years of age.

5 DIET AND NUTRITION

Nutrition has never been the sole domain of the medical practitioner or of the veterinary surgeon. It is relatively recently that the medical profession has developed clinical nutrition to the point that there are professors in the subject, and that veterinary surgeons in companion animal practice have realised that they have an expertise to offer in this area of pet health care. This is curious because even the earliest medical and veterinary texts refer to the importance of correct diet, and for many years veterinary surgeons working with production animals such as cattle, pigs and sheep have been deluged with information about the most appropriate nutrition for those species.

Traditionally, of course, the breeder, neighbours, friends, relatives, the pet shop owner and even the local supermarket have been a main source of advice on feeding for many pet owners. Over the past fifteen years there has been a great increase in public awareness about the relationships between diet and disease, thanks mainly to media interest in the subject (which has at times bordered on hysteria), but also to marketing tactics by major manufacturing companies. Few people will not have heard about the alleged health benefits of 'high fibre', 'low fat', 'low cholesterol', 'high polyunsaturates', 'low saturates' and 'oat

bran' diets. While there are usually some data to support the use of these types of diets in certain situations, the benefits are frequently overstated, if they exist at all.

Breeders have always actively debated the best way to feed dogs. Most Golden Retriever owners are aware of the importance of good bone development and the role of nutrition in achieving optimal skeletal characteristics. However, as a veterinary surgeon in practice, I was constantly amazed and bewildered at the menus given to new puppy owners by breeders. These all too frequently consisted

Kerrien Churchill of Sansue: Feeding the correct diet is essential in developing good bone and optimum skeletal characteristics. Photo: Kipps.

of complex home-made recipes, usually based on large amounts of fresh meat, goat's milk, and a vast array of mineral supplements. These diets were often very imbalanced and could easily result in skeletal and other growth abnormalities.

Domesticated dogs usually have little opportunity to select their own diet, so it is important to realise that they are solely dependent upon their owners to provide all the nourishment that they need. In this chapter, I aim to explain what those needs are, in the process dispel a few myths, and hopefully give some guidance as to how to select the most appropriate diet for your dog.

ESSENTIAL NUTRITION

Dogs have a common ancestry with, and are still often classified as, carnivores, although from a nutritional point of view they are actually omnivores. This means that dogs can obtain all the essential nutrients that they need from dietary sources consisting of either animal or plant material. As far as we know, dogs can survive on food derived solely from plants – that is, they can be fed a 'vegetarian diet'. The same is not true for domesticated cats, which are still obligate carnivores, and whose nutritional needs cannot be met by an exclusively vegetarian diet.

ENERGY

All living cells require energy, and the more active they are the more energy they burn up. Individual dogs have their own energy needs, which can vary, even between dogs of the same breed, age, sex and activity level. Breeders will recognise the scenario in which some littermates develop differently, one tending towards obesity, another on the lean side, even when they are fed exactly the same amount of food. For adult maintenance, a Golden Retriever will need an energy intake of approximately 30 kcal/lb body weight (or 65 kcal/kg body weight). If you know the energy density of the food that you are giving, you can work out how much your dog needs; but you must remember that this is only an approximation, and you will need to adjust the amount you feed to suit each individual dog. This is best achieved by regular weighing of your dog and then maintaining an optimum body weight.

If you are feeding a commercially prepared food, you should be aware that the feeding guide recommended by the manufacturer is also based on average energy needs, and therefore you may need to increase or decrease the amount you give to meet your own individual dog's requirements. In some countries (such as those within the European Union) legislation may not allow the energy content to appear on the label of a prepared pet food; however, reputable manufacturing companies can and will provide this information upon request.

When considering different foods it is important to compare the metabolisable energy, which is the amount of energy in the food that is *available* to a dog. Some companies will provide you with figures for the 'gross energy', which is not as useful, because some of that energy (sometimes a substantial amount) will not be digested, absorbed and utilised.

There are many circumstances in which your dog's energy requirement may change from its basic adult maintenance energy requirement (MER):

WORK		**PREGNANCY**	**ENVIRONMENT**	
Light	1.1-1.5 x MER	First 6 weeks 1 x MER	Cold	1.25-1.75 x MER
Heavy	2-4 x MER	Last 3 weeks 1.1-1.3 MER	Heat	Up to 2.5 x MER
Inactivity	0.8 x MER	Peak lactation 2- 4 x MER		
		Growth 1.2- 2 x MER		

Light to moderate activity (work) barely increases energy needs, and it is only when dogs are doing heavy work, such as pulling sleds, that energy requirements are significantly increased. Note that there is no increased energy requirement during pregnancy, except in the last three weeks, and the main need for high energy intake is during the lactation period. If a bitch is getting sufficient energy, she should not lose weight or condition during pregnancy and lactation. Because the energy requirement is so great during lactation (up to 4 x MER), it can sometimes be impossible to meet this need by feeding conventional adult maintenance diets, because the bitch cannot physically eat enough food. As a result she will lose weight and condition. Switching to a high-energy diet is usually necessary to avoid this.

As dogs get older their energy needs usually decrease. This is due in large part to being less active caused by getting less exercise, e.g. if their owner is elderly, or enforced by locomotor problems such as arthritis, but there are also changes in the metabolism of older animals that reduce the amount of energy they need. The aim should be to maintain body weight throughout old age, and regular exercise can play an important part in this. If there is any tendency to decrease or increase weight, this should be countered by increasing or decreasing energy intake accordingly. If the body weight changes by more than ten per cent from usual, veterinary attention should be sought, in case there is a medical problem causing the weight change.

Changes in environmental conditions and all forms of stress (including showing), which particularly affects dogs with a nervous temperament, can increase energy needs. Some dogs when kennelled for long periods, lose weight due to a stress-related increase in energy requirements which cannot easily be met by a maintenance diet. A high-energy food containing at least 1,900 kcal of metabolisable energy/lb dry matter (4.2 kcal/gram) may be needed in order to maintain body weight under these circumstances. Excessive energy intake, on the other hand, results in obesity which can have very serious effects on health.

OVERWEIGHT DOGS

Orthopaedic problems such as rupture of the cruciate ligaments is more likely to occur in overweight dogs. This condition, which often requires surgical intervention, may present as a sudden-onset complete lameness, or a gradually worsening hind leg lameness. Dogs frequently develop heart disease in old age, and obesity puts significant extra demands on the cardiovascular system, with potentially serious consequences. Obesity is also a predisposing cause of non-insulin-dependent diabetes mellitus, and has many other detrimental effects on health, including reducing resistance to infection and increasing anaesthetic and surgical risks. Once obesity is present, activity tends to decrease and it becomes even more necessary to decrease energy intake; otherwise more body weight is gained and the situation is made worse. Prevention of obesity is vital in the Golden Retriever, since they are predisposed to the development of diabetes mellitus.

Energy is only available from the fat, carbohydrate and protein in a dog's diet. A gram of fat provides 2.25 times as much energy as a gram of carbohydrate or protein, and so high energy requirements are best met by feeding a relatively high fat diet. Dogs rarely develop the cardiovascular conditions, such as atherosclerosis and coronary artery disease, that have been associated with high fat intake in humans.

Owners may think that protein is the source of energy needed for exercise and performance, but this is not true. Protein is a relatively poor source of energy because a large amount of the energy theoretically available from it is lost in 'meal-induced heat'. Meal-induced heat is the metabolic heat 'wasted' in the digestion, absorption and utilisation of the protein. Fat and carbohydrates are better sources of energy for performance.

For obese or obesity-prone dogs, a low energy intake is indicated, and there are now specially prepared diets that have a very low energy density; those which are most effective have a high fibre content. Your veterinary surgeon will advise you about the most appropriate type of diet if you have such a problem dog. Incidentally, if you do have an overweight dog it is important to seek veterinary advice in case it is associated with some other medical condition.

CHOOSING A DIET

The first important consideration to make, when selecting a maintenance diet, is that it should meet the energy requirements of your dog. In some situations, specially formulated high-energy, or low-energy diets will be needed to achieve this. Other nutrients that must be provided in the diet include essential amino acids (from dietary protein), essential fatty acids (from dietary fat), minerals and vitamins. Carbohydrates are not an essential dietary component for dogs, because they can synthesise sufficient glucose from other sources.

Do not fall into the trap of thinking that if a diet is good for a human it must be good for a dog. There are many differences between a human's nutritional needs and those of the dog. For example, humans need a supply of vitamin C in the diet, but under normal circumstances a dog can synthesise its own vitamin C, and so a dietary source is not essential. The amount of nutrients that a dog needs will vary according to its stage of life, environment and activity level. For the rest of this section life-cycle feeding will be discussed.

FEEDING FOR GROWTH

Growing animals have tissues that are actively developing and growing in size, and so it is not surprising that they have a relatively higher requirement for energy, protein, vitamins and minerals than their adult counterparts (based on the daily intake of these nutrients per kg body weight).

Birth weight usually doubles in seven to ten days, and puppies should gain 1-2 ounces/day/lb (2-4 grams/day/kg) of anticipated adult weight. An important key to the successful rearing of neonates is to reduce the puppies' energy loss by maintaining their environmental temperature, as well as by ensuring sufficient energy intake. Bitch's milk is of particular importance to the puppy during the first few hours of life, as this early milk (called colostrum) provides some passive immunity to the puppy because of the maternal antibodies it contains. These will help to protect the puppy until it can produce its own immune response to challenge from infectious agents.

Survival rate is greatly decreased in puppies that do not get colostrum from their mother. Orphaned puppies are best fed a proprietary milk replacer, according to the manufacturer's recommendations, unless a foster mother can be found. Your veterinary surgeon will be able to help if you find yourself in such a situation.

Obesity must be avoided during puppyhood, as so-called juvenile obesity will increase the number of fat cells in the body, and so predispose the animal to obesity for the rest of its life. Overeating is most likely to occur when puppies are fed free choice (ad lib) throughout the day, particularly if there is competition between littermates. A better method is to feed a puppy a daily ration based on its body weight divided into two to four meals per day – the number decreasing as it gets older. Any food remaining after twenty minutes should be removed.

Limiting food intake in growing puppies has been associated with fewer signs of hip dysplasia. Proper growth and development is dependent upon a sufficient intake of essential nutrients, and if you consider how rapidly a puppy grows, usually achieving half its adult weight by four months of age, it is not surprising that nutritional deficiencies, excesses or imbalances can have disastrous results, especially in the larger breeds of dog. Deficiency diseases are rarely seen in veterinary practice nowadays, mainly because proprietary pet foods contain more than sufficient amounts of the essential nutrients. When a deficiency disease is diagnosed it is usually associated with an unbalanced home-made diet. A classic example of this is dogs fed on an all-meat diet. Meat is very low in calcium but high in phosphorus, and demineralisation of bones occurs on this type of diet. This leads to very thin bones that fracture easily, frequently resulting in folding fractures caused simply by weight-bearing.

BUILDING GOOD BONES
Development of a good skeleton results from an interaction of genetic, environmental, and nutritional influences. The genetic component can be influenced by the breeder in a desire to improve the breed. Environmental influences, including housing and activity level, can be controlled by the new puppy owner with good advice from the breeder. However, nutrition is one of the most important factors influencing correct development of the puppy's bones and muscles.

In growing puppies, it is particularly important to provide minerals, but in the correct proportions to each other. The calcium:phosphorus ratio should ideally be 1.2-1.4:1, and certainly within the wider range of 1-2:1. If there is more phosphorus than calcium in the diet (i.e. an inverse calcium:phosphorus ratio), normal bone development may be affected. Care also has to be taken to avoid feeding too much mineral. A diet for growing puppies should not contain more than two per cent calcium. Excessive calcium intake actually causes stunting of growth, and an intake of 3.3 per cent calcium has been shown to result in serious skeletal deformities, including deformities of the carpus, osteochondritis dissecans (OCD), wobbler syndrome and hip dysplasia. These are common diseases, and

while other factors such as genetic inheritance may also be involved, excessive mineral intake should be considered a risk factor in all cases.

Golden Retrievers are genetically predisposed to a form of OCD known as Ununited Anconeal Process, in which a small bone within the elbow joint fails to develop correctly. This leads to arthritis at a very young age. If diagnosed early enough, the condition can be surgically treated. However, normal joint function may not be possible in all cases.

If a diet already contains sufficient calcium, it is dangerously easy to increase the calcium content to well over three per cent if you give mineral supplements as well. Some commercially available treats and snacks are very high in salt, protein and calories. They can significantly upset a carefully-balanced diet, and it is advisable to ask your veterinary surgeon's opinion of the various treats available and to use them only very occasionally.

A growing puppy is best fed a specifically formulated diet to meet its nutritional needs. Those that are available both tinned and dry are especially suitable to rear even the youngest of puppies. Home-made diets may theoretically be adequate, but it is difficult to ensure that all the nutrients are provided in an available form. The only way to be sure about the adequacy of a diet is to have it analysed for its nutritional content *and* to put it through controlled feeding trials.

Supplements should only be used with rations that are known to be deficient, in order to provide whatever is missing from the diet. With a complete balanced diet *nothing* should be missing. If you use supplements with an already balanced diet, you could create an imbalance and/or provide excessive amounts of nutrients, particularly minerals.

Nutritional management alone is not sufficient to prevent developmental bone disease. However, we can prevent some skeletal disease by feeding appropriate amounts of a good-quality balanced diet.

Dietary deficiencies are of minimal concern with the ever-increasing range of commercial diets specifically prepared for young growing dogs. The potential for harm is in over-nutrition from excess consumption and supplementation.

PREGNANCY AND LACTATION

There is no need to increase the amount of food being fed to a bitch during early and mid-pregnancy, but there will be an increased demand for energy (i.e. carbohydrates and fats collectively), protein, minerals and vitamins during the *last* three weeks. A bitch's nutritional requirements will be maximum during lactation, particularly if she has a large litter to feed. Avoid giving calcium supplementation during pregnancy, as a high intake can frustrate calcium availability during milk production, and can increase the chances of eclampsia (also called 'milk fever' or puerperal tetany) occurring.

During pregnancy a bitch should maintain her body weight and condition. If she loses weight her energy intake needs to be increased. A specifically formulated growth-type diet is recommended to meet her nutritional needs at this time. If a bitch is on a diet formulated for this stage of her life, and she develops eclampsia, or has had previous episodes of the disease, your veterinary surgeon may advise calcium supplementation. If given during pregnancy, this is only advisable during the very last few days of pregnancy when milk let-down is occurring, and preferably is given only during lactation (i.e. *after* whelping).

MAINTENANCE AND OLD AGE

The objective of good nutrition is to provide all the energy and essential nutrients that a dog needs in sufficient amounts to avoid deficiency, and at the same time to limit their supply so as not to cause over-nutrition or toxicity. Some nutrients are known to play a role in disease processes, and it is prudent to avoid unnecessarily high intakes of these whenever possible. The veterinary

surgeons at Hill's Science and Technology Centre in Topeka, Kansas, are specialists in canine clinical nutrition and they are particularly concerned about the potential health risks associated with too high an intake of the following nutrients during a dog's adult life:

Protein
Sodium (salt)
Phosphorus

These nutrients are thought to have an important and serious impact once disease is present, particularly in heart and kidney diseases. Kidney failure and heart failure are very common in older dogs and it is believed to be important to avoid feeding diets high in these nutrients to such an 'at risk' group of dogs. Furthermore, these nutrients may be detrimental to dogs even before there is any evidence of disease. It is known that salt, for example, can be retained in dogs with subclinical heart disease, before there is any outward evidence of illness. Salt retention is an important contributing factor in the development of fluid retention (congestion), swelling of the limbs (oedema) and dropsy (ascites).

A leading veterinary cardiologist in the USA has claimed that 40 per cent of dogs over five years of age, and 80 per cent of dogs over ten years have some change in the heart – either endocardiosis and myocardial fibrosis (or both). Both of these lesions may reduce heart function. Phosphorus retention is an important consequence of advancing kidney disease which encourages mineral deposition in the soft tissues of the body, including the kidneys themselves, a condition known as nephrocalcinosis. Such deposits damage the kidneys even more, and hasten the onset of kidney failure.

As a dog ages, there are two major factors that determine its nutritional needs:

1. The dog's changing nutritional requirements due to the effects of age on organ function and metabolism

2. The increased likelihood of the presence of subclinical diseases, many of which have a protracted course, during which nutrient intake may influence progression of the condition.

Many Golden Retriever owners are aware of a condition called gastric dilatation and torsion, commonly known as 'bloat'. This potentially life-threatening condition was previously thought to be due to the ingestion of a high fat or carbohydrate meal. Current thinking is that bloat is due to aerophagia (the intake of large amounts of air with a meal), common in greedy individuals, and the predisposing factors may be:

Genetic make-up
Competitive feeding
Strenuous exercise around meal times
Excitement at feeding time

The last three factors encourage rapid eating.

Special highly-digestible diets are available from veterinary surgeons to feed to at-risk individuals.

Energy requirements usually decrease with increasing age, and food intake should be adjusted accordingly. Also the dietary intake of some nutrients needs to be minimised – in particular, protein, phosphorus, sodium and total energy intake. Dietary intake of other nutrients may need to be increased to meet the needs of some older dogs, notably essential fatty acids, some vitamins, some specific amino acids and zinc. Unlike humans, calcium and phosphorus do not need to be supplemented in ageing dogs – indeed to do so may prove detrimental.

INTERPRETATION OF LABELLING ON PET FOODS
Labelling laws differ from one country to the next. For example, pet foods sold in the USA must carry a Guaranteed Analysis, which states a maximum or a minimum amount for the various nutrients in the food. Pet foods sold in Europe must carry a Typical (as fed) Analysis, which is a declaration of the average amount of nutrients found from analysis of the product.

'COMPLETE' VERSUS 'COMPLEMENTARY'
In the UK, a pet food must declare whether it is 'complete' or 'complementary'. A 'complete' pet food must provide all the nutrients required to satisfy the needs of the group of pet animals for which it is recommended. At the time of writing there is no obligation for a manufacturer to submit such a diet to feeding trials to ensure that it is adequate.

In the USA, some manufacturers submit their pet foods to the feeding trials approved by the Association of American Feed Control Officials (AAFCO), to ensure that they meet the nutritional requirements of the National Research Council (e.g. the Hill's Pet Nutrition range of Science Diet products). A 'complementary' pet food needs to be fed with some other foodstuff in order to meet the needs of the animal. Anyone feeding a complementary food as a substantial part of a dog's ration is obliged to find out what it should be fed with, in order to balance the ration. Failure to do so could result in serious deficiency or imbalance of nutrients.

DRY MATTER
The water content of pet foods varies greatly, particularly in canned products. In the USA there is a legal maximum limit (78 per cent) which cannot be exceeded, but no such limit is in force in Europe and some European canned pet foods contain as much as 86 per cent water. Legislation now makes it compulsory for the water content to be declared on the label and this is important, because to compare one pet food with another, one should consider the percentage of a nutrient in the dry matter of food.

For example, two pet foods may declare the protein content to be 10 per cent in the

Typical Analysis printed on the label. If one product contains 75 per cent water, it has 25 per cent dry matter, so the protein content is actually 10/25 x 100 = 40 per cent. If the other product contains 85 per cent water, the protein content is 10/15 x 100 = 66.6 per cent. This type of calculation (called Dry Weight Analysis) becomes even more important when comparing canned with dry products, as the water content of dry food is usually only 7.5-12 per cent.

You can only effectively compare pet foods if you know:

1. The food's energy density
2. The dry weight analysis of the individual nutrients.

COST

The only valid way to compare the cost of one food against another is to compare the daily feeding costs to meet all the needs of your dog. A high-energy, nutritionally-concentrated type of diet might cost more to buy per kilogram of food, but it could be cheaper to feed on a cost per day basis. Conversely, a poor-quality, poorly-digestible diet may be cheaper per kilogram to buy, but actually cost more per day to feed, because you need to feed much more food to meet the dog's requirements. The only valid reason for feeding a food is that it meets the nutritional requirements of your dog. To do that, you need to read between the marketing strategies of the manufacturers and select a diet that you know provides your dog with what it needs.

HOME-MADE DIETS

What about home-made recipes? Well, theoretically it is possible to make a home-made diet that will meet all the nutritional requirements of a dog, and all foodstuffs have some nutritional value, *but* not all published recipes may actually achieve what they claim. The reason is that there is no strict quality control of ingredients, and the bioavailability of nutrients may vary from one ingredient source to another. If you feed a correctly-balanced home-made diet, meals are often time-consuming to prepare, usually need the addition of a vitamin/mineral supplement, and, if prepared accurately, can be expensive. Variations in raw ingredients will cause fluctuations in nutritional value.

The only way to be absolutely sure that a home-made diet has the nutritional profile that you want is to mix *all the* food ingredients plus supplements, treats, snacks, scraps etc. in a large pot, homogenise them and have a sample analysed chemically (this costs well over £100 – US$160 – for a partial analysis). Compare this analytical content with the published levels for nutrient requirements.

You may feel that feeding an existing home-made recipe passed on to you, or developed over a number of years, is adequate. But how do you know? What is the phosphorus level of the diet that you are feeding? An undesirably high level of intake may take a long time before it results in obvious problems.

Sometimes the condition of your dog(s) will give you an idea that all is not well with the diet you are feeding. One of the most common questions asked by breeders at dog shows is: "Can you recommend a diet that will keep weight on my dogs?" Unless there is a medical problem (and in such cases you should always seek veterinary attention first), the only reason dogs usually have difficulty maintaining their weight is simply that they have an inadequate energy intake. This does not mean that they are not eating well – they could be eating like a horse – but if the food is relatively low in energy content, and if it is poorly-digestible, your dog may be unable to eat sufficient food to meet its energy needs. Large bulky faeces are an indicator of low digestibility. A poor-looking, dull, dry or scurfy coat, poor skin and other external signs of unthriftiness may also be an indicator of poor nutrition. How many 'poor-doers' and dogs with recurrent infections are on a diet with a marginal nutritional level of adequacy?

SUMMARY

The importance of nutrition has been known for many years and yet, sadly, it is still surrounded by too many old wives' tales, myths and unsubstantiated claims. The emergence of clinical nutrition as a subject in its own right has set the stage for the future. Hopefully, in the future we shall hear about the benefits and dangers of different feeding practices from scientists who can base their statements on fact, not merely opinion. Already we know that an ill dog has different nutritional requirements to a healthy dog. In some cases, dietary management can even offer an alternative way to manage clinical cases. For example, we currently have the ability to dissolve struvite stones in the urinary bladder simply by manipulating dietary intake instead of having to resort to surgery.

But please note, dietary management is not 'alternative medicine'. Proper nutrition is the key to everything that a living animal has to do, be it work or repairing tissues after an injury. It is not an option; it is a crucial part of looking after an animal properly. If you own a dog, then you should at least ensure that the food you give supplies all his or her needs and avoids the excessive intake of energy or nutrients that may play a role in diseases which your pet could develop.

6 THE BREED STANDARDS

The Golden Retriever is an indigenous British dog. The breed was founded in this country just over 100 years ago, and it was here that the original Standard was formed. Over thousands of years, by selective breeding and crossing various strains, man has developed dogs to meet his particular needs; hence we have dogs designed to work, retrieve, point, hunt, herd, guard, etc. Once a breed has been established, a Breed Standard must follow, and from then on the Standard is the blueprint for that breed. The Kennel Club owns the copyright of all the Standards of registered breeds in this country.

The British Standard for the Golden Retriever has been accepted and is followed by countries governed by the Fédération Cynologique International (FCI), and so, at least in Europe, we are all guided by one Standard.

America originally had the same Standard as Europe, but over the years it has been changed. It describes, in much more detail, the characteristics of the Golden Retriever and, later on, I will be comparing these differentials. In order to do this, it has been necessary to re-arrange some of the points. The Kennel Club Breed Standard contains eighteen headings, while the American Breed Standard consists of eleven headings with sub-headings. However, all sections will be discussed in the following pages.

ORIGIN OF THE STANDARD
The Golden Retriever Club was formed in 1913, the same year in which the KC

recognised the breed as a retriever (golden, yellow). Prior to that, the dogs had been registered as flat or wavy coated retrievers. Enthusiastic and dedicated breeders, led by Winifred Maud Charlesworth, drew up the first Standard that same year, and today's version is still very much the same. In 1930, the Golden Retriever Club decided to include size and weight in the Standard, and these requirements were printed below the Breed Standard in the 1931 yearbook.

The ideal weight of adult dogs and bitches in good, hard condition was given as: dogs 65-68 lbs, bitches 55-60 lbs. Height at the shoulder: dogs 23-24 inches, bitches 20.5-22 inches. The weight was amended six years later in 1936 to 65-70 lbs for dogs and 55-60 lbs for bitches, and the height became 22-24 inches for dogs, and 20-22 inches for bitches. At the same time, the Standard was altered to include the colour cream. One cannot help feeling that, around 1936, someone of influence on the Golden Retriever Club committee must have been breeding smaller, paler and more cobby Goldens! It is interesting to note that the American Standard on height has not been changed from the original British Standard.

The early breeders preferred mid-golden to dark-golden coats and, although there were some pale to cream Golden Retrievers, they were not acceptable, nor indeed even recognised. Apart from one or two isolated cases, it took nearly twenty-five years before really pale dogs were regularly winning top honours in the show ring. Even then, they

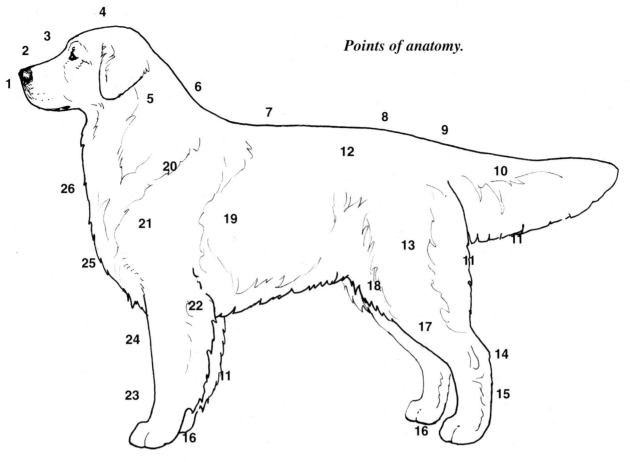

Points of anatomy.

1. Muzzle	10. Tail	19. Ribcage
2. Foreface	11. Feathering	20. Shoulder
3. Stop	12. Loin	21. Upper arm
4. Skull	13. Thigh	22. Elbow
5. Neck	14. Hock joint	23. Front pastern
6. Withers	15. Rear pastern	24. Forearm
7. Back	16. Foot	25. Forechest
8. Croup	17. Second thigh	26. Ruff
9. Tailset	18. Stifle	

were still being penalised by some judges. In 1986, the Standard was again revised and clarified. The 'ideal' weight of the dog was dropped, and temperament, characteristics and gait were added.

Tom Horner, in his book *Take Them Round Please* (an excellent guide for exhibitors and judges alike), states: "Some Standards are so poor that there is little wonder the breed they describe finds it hard to rise above the level of mediocrity."

This bears out my own opinion that the British Breed Standard is too concise, and is thus open to widely differing interpretations. Perhaps this is why, despite large entries at shows, we seldom see a Golden Retriever shortlisted in the Gundog Group. To the breeder, exhibitor and judge, the Breed Standard should describe the ideal specimen of that particular breed – in other words, the perfect dog. It should be a description written in such depth that it can enable the reader to mentally picture the ideal specimen. In a coated breed, such as the Golden, it is easy to be misled by a profuse coat. A sound knowledge is needed of general construction, the canine skeleton and the most important muscles that enable the dog to function. Also, one must never lose sight of the original purpose of the dog.

Ch. Styal Scott of Glenguilde: British breed record holder with 42CCs.

Photo courtesy: Hazel Hinks.

The breed's popularity as pets, due to the wonderful character and disposition of Goldens, has in some ways been detrimental to working ability. It would be a sad day if our Goldens were to lose the natural instinct to work and retrieve. Judges, breeders and exhibitors alike should all bear in mind the dog as a whole; construction, character and biddability are all of equal importance. As each dog is a living creature – each one will be different and unique – but all should conform to the Standard, and judges and breeders are required to interpret that Standard. But there will be some variation in the emphasis placed on faults and virtues, depending on each judge's interpretation.

COMPARISON OF BREED STANDARDS
I will now compare and discuss the two Breed Standards for the Golden Retriever, the American Kennel Club (AKC) Standard, approved in 1981 and reformated in 1990, and the British Kennel Club (BKC) Standard, approved in 1986. After quoting from the relevant sections in both, I will add some personal comments by way of interpretation of the two Standards and their implications for those who breed, own or show Golden Retrievers.

GENERAL APPEARANCE AND CHARACTERISTICS
AKC
GENERAL APPEARANCE: A symmetrical, powerful active dog, sound and well put together, not clumsy nor long in the leg, displaying a kindly expression and possessing a personality that is eager, alert and self-confident. Primarily a hunting dog, he should be shown in hard working condition. Overall appearance, balance, gait and purpose to be given more emphasis than any of his component parts. *Faults* – Any departure from the described ideal shall be considered faulty to the degree with which it interferes with the breed's purpose or is contrary to breed character.

BKC
**GENERAL APPEARANCE: Symmetrical, balanced, active, powerful, level mover; sound with kindly expression.
CHARACTERISTICS: Biddable, intelligent and possessing natural working ability.**

The two standards start very much on the same lines. If we analyse the terms "not clumsy nor long in the leg" and "primarily a hunting dog", we must remember that the American Standard gives a minimum height of 23 ins for males and 21.5 ins for females, which means their dogs will be taller and longer in the leg than the British counterparts. Emphasis is therefore given to them not becoming any taller. Perhaps the British Standard should put more emphasis on Goldens not becoming any shorter, and also on the condition necessary for them to work.

A well-balanced dog with a good topline, proper angulation, good body qualities, and a correct, practical coat.

A "working type" Golden, a little more wiry in build, in lean, hard condition, also a well-balanced, soundly-made dog capable of hard work.

Exaggerated "British show type". Good body, but short on leg, long in loin; lacking rear angulation; good topline. Exaggerated head with domed skull, short muzzle, throaty; over-trimmed on neck.

Exaggerated "American show type". Flashy but lacking balance: upright shoulders, over-angulated rear; poor topline with lumpy withers, sloping back. Exaggerated feathering. Plain head. Poor feet.

The American Standard stresses emphatically that the general overall fitness of the dog is of prime importance, and that the dog should be in hard working condition. This heading also encompasses the general characteristics of the breed, which are dealt with separately under the British Standard and will be incorporated under temperament.

SIZE, PROPORTION AND SUBSTANCE
AKC
SIZE, PROPORTION AND SUBSTANCE: Males 23-24 inches in height at withers; females 21.5 - 22.5 inches. Dogs of up to one inch above or below Standard size should be proportionately penalised. Deviation in height of more than one inch from the Standard shall disqualify. Length from breastbone to point of buttocks slightly greater than height at withers in ratio of 12:11. Weight for dogs 65-75 lbs; bitches 55-65 lbs.

BKC
SIZE: Height at withers: Dogs 56-61 cms (22-24 ins); Bitches 51-56 cms (20-22 ins).

As mentioned previously, the American dogs are slightly larger. Their Standard only allows variation of one inch. Any deviation from this in either direction, and the dog is disqualified. Also, by giving the proportions of length to height, the AKC Standard ensures the dog is balanced; equally, by stating the weight, more uniformity of bone and substance should result. I personally think this is very helpful for both breeders and judges.

HEAD AND SKULL; EYES, EARS, AND MOUTH

AKC

HEAD: Broad in skull, slightly arched laterally and longitudinally without prominence of frontal bones or occipital bones. Stop well defined but not abrupt. Foreface deep and wide, nearly as long as skull.

MUZZLE: Muzzle straight in profile, blending smoothly and strongly into skull; when viewed in profile or from above, slightly deeper and wider at stop than at tip. No heaviness in flews. Removal of whiskers is permitted but not preferred.

EYES: Friendly and intelligent in expression, medium size with dark, close-fitting rim, set well apart and reasonably deep in sockets. Color preferably dark brown, medium brown acceptable. Slant eyes and narrow, triangular eyes detract from correct expression and are to be faulted. No white or haw visible when looking straight ahead. Dogs showing function abnormality of eyelids or eyelashes (such as, but not limited to, trichiasis, entropion, ectropion or distichiasis) are to be excused from the ring.

EARS: Rather short, with front edge attached well behind and just above the eye and falling close to cheek. When pulled forward, tip of ear should just cover the eye. Low, hound-like ear-set to be faulted.

Nose: Black or brownish in color, though fading to a lighter shade in cold weather not serious. Pink nose or one seriously lacking in pigmentation to be faulted.

TEETH: Scissor bite, in which the outer side of the lower incisors touches inner side of upper incisors. Undershot or overshot bite is a disqualification. Misalignment of teeth (irregular placement of incisors) or level bite (incisors meet each other edge to edge) is undesirable, but not to be confused with undershot or overshot. Full dentition. Obvious gaps are serious faults.

BKC

HEAD AND SKULL: Balanced and well chiselled, skull broad without coarseness; well set on neck, muzzle powerful, wide and deep. Length of foreface approximately equals length from well-defined stop to occiput. Nose preferably black.

EYES: Dark brown, set well apart, dark rims.

EARS: Moderate size, set on approximate level with eyes.

MOUTH: Jaws strong, with perfect, regular and complete scissor bite, i.e. upper teeth closely overlapping lower teeth and set to the jaws.

Sh. Ch. Stanroph Sailor Boy: The Golden Retriever is typified by a gentle, endearing expression.

Photo: Kipps.

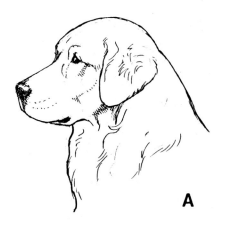

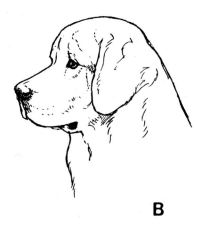

A

B

C

Attractive head, strong and cleanly made without extreme of any feature.

Overdone: Domed skull, excess skin making wrinkles on skull, flews, and throatiness. Large ears; round, loose eye.

Plain weak head, lacking distinction and nobility. No stop. Flat skull. Long pointed muzzle. Light eye. High-set ears.

Good head structure and expression. Ears carried well at attention. Note wide-set eyes, width/depth of muzzle, blending of muzzle into skull.

Overdone: Domed skull, excess skin making wrinkles on skull, flews, and throatiness. Large ears; round, loose eye.

Lacking distinction and breed character: Slanted eyes, snipey muzzle. Ears high-set and tending to fly away.

The Golden Retriever head, especially the eye and expression, is one of the breed's most endearing features. However, it should be remembered that this is a working dog, designed to retrieve game from pigeons to a large hare, and it should therefore have a gentle bite but a strong, well-formed muzzle. There should be no hint of coarseness – neither should it be weak or snipey. The British Standard states that the length of foreface should measure the same as from the stop to occiput. In my view, a balanced head should also have about the same width across the skull between the ears as the length of skull, again from stop to occiput.

The two Standards are, when analysed, very similar, but the British is more concise. It would appear from the American Standard that the result would be less strength in foreface. The British Standard gives more emphasis to chiselling. From this it would appear that the bone structure is more defined, i.e. at the occiput, but with a slightly broader head. The American Standard pays particular attention to "no heaviness in flews" and, as is often the case, this can lead to faults in the opposite direction, i.e. cutaway muzzles.

The British Standard requires a dark brown eye, while the American calls for "preferably dark brown, medium brown acceptable". However, we should all be cautious that a medium-brown eye does not become a light or amber eye, which would detract from the gentle expression we value so much in the breed. An amber eye should be penalised. The correct eye shape and expression are essential. Any eye abnormality is not accepted in either country. The British Standard does not stipulate this as the American does in detail, but it should be understood. The eye should be well-shaped, not triangular or slanted, and set well apart with dark rims and gentle expression.

I believe that the two Standards are similar with regard to ears, although what we would describe as moderate, the American Standard calls short. In both cases the requirement is for the ear to just cover the eye. There is, however, some deviation in the 'set on.' The British Standard calls for the ears to be level with the eyes, and the American for them to be set above the eye, which would slightly alter the expression, giving the appearance of a narrow skull. Low-set, hound-like ears should be faulted. This is stated in the American Standard, but not in the British.

Both standards prefer a black nose, but the American Standard states that pink should be penalised. A 'winter' nose (one that loses some pigmentation in colder weather) is acceptable under both Standards. However, for scenting and retrieving game, it is essential that the nostrils should be of good size to allow for the passage of air. A good width of muzzle would allow for this. Neither Standard refers to the size of the nose.

Both Standards require the same bite, but more detail of actual faults is given in the American Standard. If one is judging to either Standard, one should understand "a complete scissor bite". This means that the top teeth fit tightly over and in front of the bottom teeth. The American Standard calls for "full dentition" and obvious gaps are a serious fault. A dog should have 42 teeth. If any are missing, they are usually premolars and in certain lines this can be hereditary. As it is not in the British Standard, this fault is not considered important in the UK. It must be remembered that a whelping bitch needs these teeth to cut the umbilical cords. Although, as judges and breeders, we need to be aware of this, one should not become obsessed. Nevertheless, the point's importance should not be overlooked either, or it could cause problems for the future.

Although we have discussed each aspect of the head in detail, it should be remembered that the overall impression is more important than any one detail. This is understood by experienced breeders, but novices are not always to know.

NECK, TOPLINE AND BODY
AKC
NECK, TOPLINE AND BODY
NECK: Medium long, merging gradually into well laid-back shoulders, giving sturdy muscular appearance. No throatiness.
BACKLINE: Strong and level from withers to slightly sloping croup, whether standing or moving. Sloping backline, roach or sway back, flat or steep croup to be faulted.
BODY: Well balanced, short coupled, deep through chest.
Chest: Between forelegs at least as wide as a man's closed hand, including thumb, with well-developed forechest. Brisket extends to elbows.
RIBS: Long and well sprung but not barrel-shaped, extending well towards hindquarters.
LOIN: Short, muscular, wide and deep with very little tuck-up. Back line strong and level from withers to slightly sloping croup whether standing or moving. Slab-sidedness, narrow chest, lack of depth in brisket, sloping back line, roach or sway back, excessive tuck-up, flat or steep croup to be faulted.

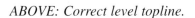

ABOVE: Correct level topline.

TOP RIGHT: Sloping topline.

RIGHT: Soft back, high rear.

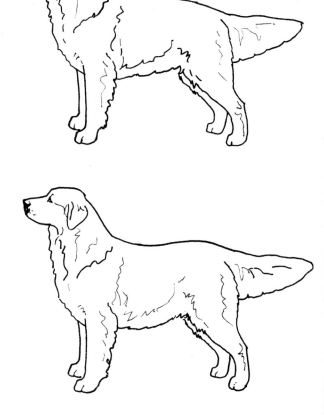

TAIL: Well set on, thick and muscular at the base, following the natural line of the croup. Tail bones extend to, but not below, the point of the hock. Carried with a merry action, level or with some moderate upward curve, never curled over back or between legs.

BKC
NECK: Good length, clean and muscular.
BODY: Balanced, short coupled, deep through heart. Ribs deep and well sprung. Level topline.
TAIL: Set on and carried level with back, reaching the hocks, without curl at tip.

The neck and shoulders are one of the most important parts of the construction of the working dog. The neck should be muscular and of good length, flowing into the withers. The American Standard states "medium long, merging gradually into well laid-back shoulders". This at once gives the reader the ideal picture of a well set on neck, which is so important in the overall make up of a Golden Retriever. "Clean" in the British Standard and "no throatiness" in the American means that

there that should be no excessive loose skin where the base of the lower jaw meets the neck.

The backline, or topline, is primarily the backbone of the dog taken from the withers, including the loin, to the croup, and both Standards call for this to be level. Where there appears to be a difference on first reading the Standards is that the American Standard calls for a slightly sloping croup. This refers to the angle of the pelvic bones in relation to the backbone, and is detailed later under the section on the hindquarters. The American Standard then goes on to point out faults in topline, so as to make it quite clear that the topline should be strong and level. ("Sloping backline, roach or sway back, flat or steep croup to be faulted.")

With regard to body, chest and ribs, both Standards start in a similar vein but, as usual, the American Standard gives a comprehensive description of the various parts of the body. The British Standard states that the ribs should be "deep and well sprung", whereas the American Standard says they should be "long and well sprung but not barrel-shaped, extending well towards the hindquarters". This is important – a Golden should be well-ribbed; it should not be barrel-shaped like a Labrador, nor should it be shallow or narrow in chest. It must have adequate room for lungs and heart to develop and function properly. Both Standards call for a well-balanced dog, in which each part of the anatomy is in proportion. The head, length of neck, body and hindquarters are all in proportion to the height of the dog and its length of leg. A dog with a long body and short legs is not balanced. Under the section on Size, Proportion and Substance, the American Standard describes the balance of a Golden Retriever as a 12:11 ratio.

The loin is mentioned as part of the back previously, and both Standards agree that the loin should be strong and muscular. However, the British Standard does not mention length of loin, though it is generally accepted that Goldens should be short-coupled. This is when the distance between the last rib and the commencement of the pelvic section is

relatively short, thereby giving strength of loin. There is a difference in stipulations for the tail. The ideal Golden Retriever in the British Standard has a well set on tail, carried level with the back. The Americans, however, required the same 'set on', but following the natural lines of the croup. This is a deviation from the original British Standard and, if exaggerated, would totally alter the outline of the Golden Retriever as we understand it.

FOREQUARTERS AND FEET
AKC
FOREQUARTERS: Muscular, well co-ordinated with hindquarters, and capable of free movement.
SHOULDER BLADES: Long and well laid back, with upper tips fairly close together at withers.
UPPER ARMS: Appear about the same length as the blades, setting the elbow back beneath the upper tip of the blades, close to the ribs without looseness.

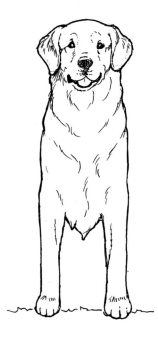

Correct front with good width and depth of chest, straight sound legs.

Faulty "fiddle-front", loose elbows, turned pasterns, feet pointing outwards.

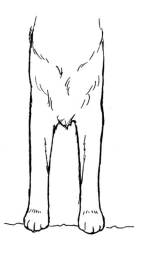

Straight, but far too narrow and lacking both depth and breadth of chest.

LEGS: Viewed from the front, straight with good bone but not to the point of coarseness.
PASTERNS: Short and strong, sloping slightly with no suggestion of weakness.
FEET: Medium size, round and compact and well knuckled with thick pads. Excess hair may be trimmed to show size and contour. Dewclaws on forelegs may be removed but are normally left on. Splay or hare feet to be faulted.

BKC
FOREQUARTERS: Forelegs straight with good bone, shoulders well laid back, long in blade with upper arm of equal length placing legs well under body. Elbows close fitting.
FEET: Round and cat-like.

This is the combined front assembly, from the shoulder-blade right down to the feet. The shoulder-blade (scapula) and the upper arm (humerus) make up the top section. The scapula is a fairly large triangular bone; its highest point forms the withers. The scapula is attached by muscles and ligaments to the first five ribs. As there is no connection by bone between the blade and the chest wall, it is absolutely essential that there should be strong muscular development in this area. If not, movement will suffer, shoulders become loose, the dog is inclined to stand 'out at elbow' and the back will tend to dip. The scapula's outside surface is divided by a spiny ridge. By feeling this ridge one can judge the 'lay back' of the shoulder. At the lower end of the shoulder blade there is a shallow cavity into which the humerus fits to form the shoulder joint or point of shoulder.

The humerus or upper arm is the largest bone in the front assembly, and is very strong. The angle formed by the scapula and humerus indicates the degree of shoulder angulation, and it is this angle that determines the extent of the forward reach of the dog on the move. As the angulation decreases, so the dog's reach is lessened, giving him a shorter stride and stilted front action. An upright is more or less 130 degrees, at which the dog will be unable to stretch out and which usually results in short, stilted steps. This is inefficient as the dog expends a lot of energy covering just a little ground, and may have to gallop to compensate.

The radius is the frontal bone of the foreleg and very strong. Set behind it is the ulna. These two bones are fused together, and run almost vertically down towards the carpus (wrist), forming the lower arm. The top section of the ulna flares out to form the olecranon, at the back of the elbow joint. This is known as the point of elbow. The region between the carpus and the foot is known as the pastern. The pastern should be as described in the American Standard. It is important to remember that the full weight of the dog when landing is taken on the front pasterns.

The American Standard places emphasis on the soundness of the dog in the first line of this section; "muscular, well co-ordinated with hindquarters and capable of free movement". As I have said previously, good front construction is essential for a working dog. Aesthetically, it is a lovely sight to see a Golden Retriever with a straight front, beautifully angulated shoulders, good reach of neck and head carriage – but these are also attributes essential for the dog to do the job of work it was bred for.

Both Standards say that the shoulder should be long in blade, well laid back with the upper arm of equal length, and legs placed well under the body. Elbows should be close-fitting with straight front legs. The American Standard states: "the elbows to be set back beneath the upper tip of the blades." This gives a picture of the dog with legs in position to take the weight of the body. Pasterns should be short and strong, sloping slightly, with no hint of weakness. The British Standard makes no mention of the pasterns.

Both Standards are similar, requiring the same type of foot. Although the British Standard is again more concise, the foot is not to be dismissed lightly! Large, untidy, or splayed feet give the whole dog an ungainly appearance, so although this section is small, it is not to be ignored. Neat, round feet, neither too small nor too large, are what is required. Sensible Golden feet are not hare, splayed or spread, but rather have well-arched toes and moderately thick pads as the ideal.

HINDQUARTERS
AKC

**HINDQUARTERS: Broad and strongly muscled. Profile of croup slopes slightly; the pelvic bone slopes at a slightly greater angle (approximately 30 degrees from the horizontal). In a natural stance, the femur joins the pelvis at approximately a 90 degree angle; stifles well bent; hocks well let down with short, strong rear pasterns. FEET: As in front.
LEGS: Straight when viewed from rear. Cow hocks, spread hocks and sickle hocks to be faulted.**

BKC

HINDQUARTERS: Loin and legs strong and muscular, good second thighs, well bent stifles. Hocks well let down, straight when viewed from rear, neither turning in nor out. Cow hocks highly undesirable.

Both Standards recognise the need for strong quarters, well muscled with well bent stifles. However, the British Standard goes on to point out the need for a good second thigh. The significant difference here is that the American Standard re-states that the croup should slope slightly but this has already been discussed under Backline/Topline in the section Neck, Topline and Body.

The importance of well bent stifles is to enable the dog to extend the rear leg on the move. The stifle, or knee joint, is made up from the lower end of the femur, the kneecap and the upper portions of the tibia and fibula. The femur or thigh bone is the longest single bone in the skeleton, the head of which lies in the acetabulum or hip socket. The extension of this joint is determined by the all-important stifle angulation. The stifle angulation is relevant to the width of thigh, and the muscles that cover it.

Hocks: The hock is a joint between the thigh and the back pastern. It is very important that the Golden Retriever has strong hocks. The dog drives from the hock, jumps from the hock and the whole rear drive hinges from the hock. Also, weak or inflexible hocks that do not give a strong vertical column of support to the rear leg will put stress on the other joints,

Correct rear: Good breadth, strong muscling, straight sound legs.

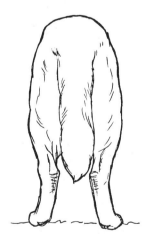

Faulty: Cowhocked, weak: hocks point in, feet outward.

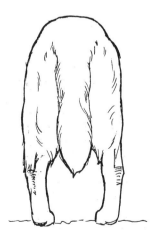

Faulty: Bowed rear is a different form of weakness.

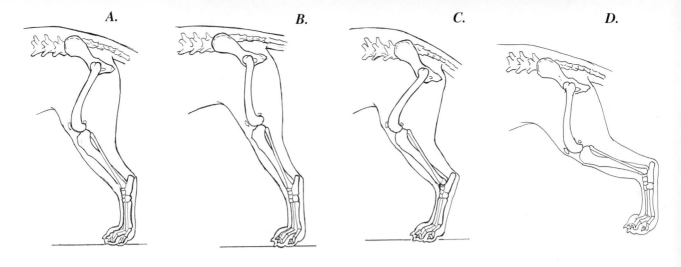

A. *Hindquarters: Correct.*
B. *Hindquarters: Too straight, lacking angulation at stifle and hock joint.*
C. *Hindquarters: Over-angulated; too much bend at stifle and hock joints; rear pasterns angling forward (sickle-hocks). Such extreme angulation lacks stability and strength.*
D. *The over-angulated hindquarter stretched into an extreme pose. The rear pastern appears to be correctly vertical but is placed much too far behind the dog. This is an extremely stressful position for the dog to maintain, and while it may be dramatic in the show ring, it is quite incorrect.*

e.g. the stifle; therefore strength and soundness of the hock is very important. The hock should be well let down and the rear pasterns should be nearly perpendicular to the ground. Both Standards penalise cow hocks. The American Standard also penalises spread and sickle hocks.

Feet: Hind feet should be as at the front. I dislike to see rear toes that turn up. This usually occurs when the dog is down on pastern. Movement is invariably stilted, with no drive.

COAT
AKC
COAT: Dense and water-repellent with good undercoat. Outer coat firm and resilient, neither coarse or silky, lying close to the body; may be straight or wavy. Untrimmed natural ruff; moderate feathering on back of forelegs and on underbody; heavier feathering on front of neck, back of thighs and underside of tail. Coat on head, paws and front of legs is short and even. Excessive length, open coats and limp, soft coats are very undesirable. Feet may be trimmed and stray hairs neatened, but the natural appearance of coat or outline should not be altered by cutting or clipping.
BKC
COAT: Flat or wavy with good feathering; dense, water-resisting undercoat.

It is very noticeable from the American Standard that trimming is undesirable. In the UK, no mention is made of trimming but it is generally understood that some trimming is carried out, mostly to tidy up the dog. In recent years, more trimming has become acceptable in the UK. Excessive trimming should be discouraged. The Golden Retriever is a coated breed, and nothing is more attractive than a Golden in full bloom, carrying full feathering as stated in the American Standard. The coat encompasses various shades and colours of gold, and all are attractive provided they are of good quality. There should be a dense, water-resisting undercoat with a good-quality flat or wavy top coat. The water-resisting undercoat is an advantage when the Golden is working, as it prevents cold water reaching the skin. The correct coat will also help prevent injuries

The Golden Retriever's coat must be dense and water-repellent, with a good undercoat.

Photo: B. Simon.

from bracken and thorns. Excessive stripping of chest feathering removes this protection.

It is quite clear that there are two different trains of thought in the American and British Standards on preparation of the coat and length of feathering. Another great divide is colour.

COLOUR
AKC
COLOR: Rich, lustrous golden of various shades. Feathering may be lighter than rest of coat. With the exception of greying or whitening of face or body due to age, any white marking, other than a few white hairs on the chest, should be penalised according to its extent. Allowable light shadings not to be confused with white marking. Predominant body color which is extremely pale or extremely dark is undesirable. Some latitude should be given to the light puppy whose coloring shows promise of deepening with maturity. Any noticeable area of black or other off-color hair is a serious fault.

BKC
***Colour:* Any shade of gold or cream, neither red nor mahogany. A few white hairs, on chest only, permissible.**

The British Standard allows for any shade of gold or cream, neither red nor mahogany. The American Standard states that any body colour that is extremely pale or extremely dark is undesirable. The two Standards agree with regard to the undesirability of very dark-coated dogs but, whereas the British Standard accepts pale or cream dogs, these are not readily accepted in the American Standard.

Colour has always been a most controversial

issue which has caused many heated arguments in the past and will, no doubt, in the future. The great Mrs Charlesworth, in her book, *The Book of the Golden Retriever* (published in 1993), said: "Those of us who drew up the standard of points in the early days realised that the foundation colour of the original Guisachan strain was cream and knew the difficulty, if not the impossibility, of completely eradicating this colour. I thought then, as I do now, that a mistake was made in forbidding the cream colour, but my views were in a minority." She also wrote: "Ripe cornfields of wheat, oats and barley are to be found in the range." One of the most appealing qualities of the Golden Retriever is the wide range in colour of coat. If we are to breed and judge to the Breed Standard, all shades of cream and gold should be acceptable and no judge should accept a judging appointment unless they can be completely unbiased when judging colour.

As Mrs Charlesworth stated, the original Guisachan goldens were cream. Early breeders tried to breed the colour out but, as always, nature and genetic make-up cannot be altered. In the end, the Standard had to reflect this fact. Unfortunately, even today, there are judges who are still biased towards either 'light' or 'dark' dogs in the ring but, either way, they are not judging to the Standard!

GAIT/MOVEMENT
AKC
GAIT: When trotting, gait is free, smooth, powerful and well co-ordinated, showing good reach. Viewed from any position legs turn neither in nor out, nor do feet cross or interfere with each other. As speed increases, feet tend to converge towards centre line of balance. It is recommended that dogs be shown on a loose lead to reflect true gait.

BKC
GAIT/MOVEMENT: Powerful with good drive. Straight and true in front and rear. Stride long and free with no sign of hackney action in front.

Sh. Ch. Elswood The Highlander, owned by Val Foss (left), and Sh. Ch. Stranroph Sailor Boy, owned by Anne Woodcock.
The British Standard allows any shade of gold or cream.

Photo: Kipps.

Ciadar Havoc CD, JH, TDX.
The American Standard requires a rich, lustrous golden of various shades. This dog is red-gold in colour.

Good front at the trot. Legs will tend to converge toward the centre line of travel, in order to stay under the centre of gravity, but remain straight from shoulder to foot, giving a sound straight line of support.

Faulty. Elbows out, loose shoulders, twisting pastern. Also called "winging".

Faulty. Foot turns inward as it takes the dog's weight. "Pin-toeing".

Good rear at the trot. Legs tend to converge toward the centre line of travel in order to stay under the centre of gravity, but remain straight from hip to foot giving a sound straight line of support.

Faulty. Cowhocks. Weakness allows hocks to flex/twist inward.

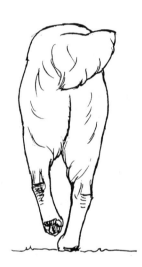

Faulty. Bowed rear. The straight line of support is lost, hocks flex outward.

If the dog is made in accordance with the Standards, as given previously, it should move correctly. However, condition and muscle tone can affect movement. Both Standards define movement as free, powerful, well co-ordinated with good drive, and call for the stride to be long with good reach. This cannot be over-emphasised. It is so important, both in the working dog and in the show ring. A Golden Retriever, moving correctly, covers the ground with ease; it stretches out in front and drives from the rear, fully extending the hocks. It is

efficient and does not waste energy. Hackney actions in front, or short, uneconomical steps, are not the correct action for a Golden. The American Standard differs from the British in that it goes on to describe the movement when viewed from any position, i.e. "legs turn neither in nor out, nor do feet cross or interfere with each other." It is a very valid point to mention that as speed increases, feet tend to converge towards the centre. It is only reasonable to expect to see the dog's legs move in a straight line when coming towards

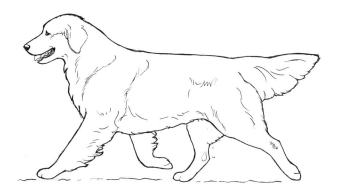

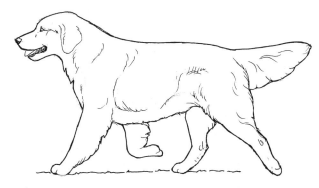

Good moving dog, balanced length of stride front and rear, good foot timing, strong level topline, good carriage of head and tail.

The short-strided dog lacks ease and efficiency. The right front pastern is flipping upward too far, indicating some weakness and/or lack of timing. This dog lacks proper angulation and balance and appears stilted and choppy.

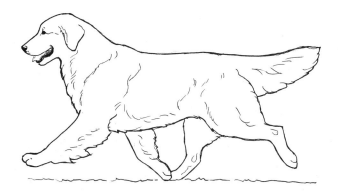

A showy but incorrect type of movement; the foot timing is poor. Note that diagonal pairs of legs are not co-ordinated properly; the trot should be a two-beat gait but this dog isn't doing it. The left front too high: the dog is over-reaching (right rear foot overtaking the right front), and kicking up behind with the left rear, which is not extending properly.

you at a steady trot. As speed increases, the laws of mechanics take over and the legs will have a tendency to converge under the body.

TEMPERAMENT
AKC
TEMPERAMENT: Friendly, reliable and trustworthy. Quarrelsomeness or hostility towards other dogs or people in normal situations, or an unwarranted show of timidity or nervousness, is not in keeping with the Golden Retriever character. Such actions should be penalised according to their significance.

BKC
TEMPERAMENT: Kindly, friendly and confident.
CHARACTERISTICS: Biddable, intelligent and possessing natural working ability.

The temperament of a Golden Retriever is the most important characteristic of the breed.

Both Standards stress that the Golden should be friendly, reliable and trustworthy. The American Standard makes mention that "quarrelsomeness or hostility towards other dogs or people in normal situations, or an unwarranted show of timidity or nervousness, is not in keeping with the Golden Retriever character." The British Standard summarises the above statement as "confident", and also includes natural working ability under the Standard's requirements.

This natural working ability should not be lost. It is part of the character of the Golden, even when not worked seriously, to search, find and retrieve. It is sad that this characteristic is disappearing in some cases. However, Goldens are used today in obedience and agility, as PAT (Pets As Therapy) dogs and guide dogs for the blind. One cannot help feeling that the enormous popularity of the breed in all fields is due to its superb temperament. As Goldens are so popular as family pets, it cannot be stressed too highly that, as breeders and judges, we

The Golden Retriever should be kind and trustworthy.

Photo: Kipps.

must ensure that maintaining the true Golden temperament is uppermost in our breeding programme. The American Standard is, therefore, wise to point out how very important it is that the Golden Retriever exhibits no nervousness or hostility.

FAULTS AND DISQUALIFICATIONS
AKC
DISQUALIFICATIONS: Deviation in height of more than one inch from standard either way. Undershot or overshot bite.

BKC
FAULTS: Any departure from the foregoing points should be considered a fault and the seriousness with which the fault should be regarded should be in exact proportion to its degree.
Note: Male animals should have two apparently normal testicles fully descended into the scrotum.

The British Standard appears to have avoided the issue of faults by a covering statement in all Breed Standards: "Any departure from the foregoing points should be considered a fault and the seriousness with which the fault should be regarded should be in exact proportion to its degree." This cleverly avoids the task of listing and grading faults and relying on the judge to weigh all faults in the dog against its virtues and then make a decision on his or her own knowledge of the dog. This would be hard even if we had a very comprehensive Breed Standard, but judges are left to decide themselves which are major faults and which lesser ones. There is no perfect dog, but judges should be extra-diligent when dealing with faults which could be perpetuated in future breeding stock to the long-term detriment of the breed; incorrect movement, wry mouths, very poor construction and any fault that would prevent the dog from doing the job it was originally bred for, including nervousness and unwillingness to be handled. These latter two faults indicate that the dog does not have the temperament we expect of a Golden Retriever.

It should be remembered when discussing faults that the dog must be taken as a whole and, as stated, each fault considered in relation to its severity and degree. Perhaps unsociable behaviour should be a disqualifying fault in the show ring.

The AKC approach is more all-embracing, and states that "any departure from the described ideal shall be considered faulty to the degree that it interferes with the breed's purpose or is contrary to the breed's character." The American Standard also disqualifies an exhibit on the grounds of incorrect height, or overshot or undershot bite.

The British Standard calls for two apparently normal testicles fully descended into the scrotum. As top stud dogs are vitally important to any breed, it is a little surprising that the American Standard makes no reference to the need for dogs to be entire.

CONCLUSION

The American Standard is much more precise and more detailed than the British equivalent, and it is certainly far easier to build up a mental picture of the dogs with the American Standard in mind, even if it is not quite the picture we in Britain would have of a Golden Retriever. Whether the Americans have altered their Standard to suit their dogs or have bred their dogs to their Standard I do not know, but the American Golden is a very different type of dog to its British counterpart. Nevertheless, the breed in the USA appears to conform much more closely to the AKC Standard's requirements. When we come to the British Standard, I reiterate the words of the late Tom Horner to the effect that the British Breed Standard is too brief and falls short in its explanation of the dog we are trying to assess. It is not easy to conjure up the ideal Golden from the Standard as it currently stands; so much is left to individual interpretation.

Both Standards require the true Golden Retriever temperament. Nearly all old photographs from the archives show Goldens as working gundogs, and this was the original aim of those pioneer breeders. Times have changed and so has the Golden Retriever's role in life, but, because of the breed's superb temperament, willingness to please and unique ability to communicate, Goldens today have diversified into all walks of life. They have become one of the most popular dogs worldwide; no longer used so much in sport, they have been found ideally suitable as family pets and for training as dogs for the blind, deaf and disabled people.

Today's breeder must remember that the original Golden Retriever was bred for work and to retrieve, and it is these characteristics that have made the dog so suitable to train in other fields. If we, as breeders, forget this and lose working ability in the Golden, we will lose the very special attribute that has made the Golden Retriever the much-loved and useful dog it is today.

Breeders and judges are the custodians of the breed, and it is up to us to use great care and thought in order to continue to breed sound, well-constructed and happy Golden Retrievers for the future.

7 THE JUDGE'S VIEW

When you have been involved in the dog showing world for a number of years, you may well feel ready to take on the task of judging. It may be that you have enjoyed a considerable degree of success, and you feel you have something to contribute. Or perhaps you have not been as lucky as you think you should have been, and you see judging as a way of redressing the balance. Whatever your reasons for wanting to judge, you will soon find out that it is not as easy as it looks! It is all too easy to criticise the judge's placings. It is quite another matter to stand in the centre of a busy ring and make calm, rational decisions, based on an in-depth knowledge of the breed, and, most importantly, on the ability to make a clear interpretation of the Breed Standard when assessing living specimens.

JUDGING IN THE UK

In the UK the judges have to be 'passed' by one of the Kennel Club's committees so that they can award the Kennel Club's Challenge Certificates, three of which make a dog a Champion or Show Champion. Prospective judges have to serve a judging apprenticeship acquiring experience in a breed and judging at Limited or Open Shows. At this level, Challenge Certificates are not on offer, and judges are not passed by the Kennel Club committee.

To quote from the Kennel Club's Guide for Judges: "Approval to award Kennel Club Challenge Certificates is the sole prerogative of the Kennel Club and is granted for each appointment."

The Kennel Club Committee bases its decision on:-

* A completed questionnaire.
* The opinion of the breed council clubs, if appropriate.
* The length and depth of judging experience. (Before considering a first appointment the committee will expect an overall judging experience of at least five years before the date of the proposed appointment, and will take into consideration whether the proposed judge has judged a breed club open or limited show for the breed concerned.)
* The dogs bred and/or owned by the proposed judge.

Judging is a learning process that never stops. It is comparing individual dogs to the Breed Standard, and then comparing the individual dogs to each other. The prospective judge must have served a meaningful apprenticeship, and have been objective with their own stock or stock related to theirs. A judge's task is to evaluate the dogs on the day – he is not assessing pedigrees or friends, or weighing up past or future glories. History judges the judges, so do not be found failing. Not only must you know your Standard by heart, you must know what it means – learning by discovery in depth. You must also know about what lies under the fur coat, the skeleton, etc.

The most important thing to bear in mind is the fundamental reason why the Golden

Retriever, as a breed, was developed. The Golden Retriever was evolved to do a specific job of work as a gundog. Therefore there should be no excesses in what is essentially a working dog. In temperament, the Golden should be kind, friendly and confident. In movement, he should be powerful with good drive: straight and true in front and rear. The stride should be long and free, with no sign of hackney action in front.

To judge is a great responsibility, because judges can change a breed, for it is the dog that wins in the show ring that is used for future breeding programmes.

JUDGING IN THE USA

In the USA, becoming an AKC licensed judge for any breed is a lengthy process. The AKC is constantly changing their stipulated requirements, seeking to improve the selection of judges with the implied intent of improving the quality of new judges.

An aspiring judge applying to AKC for the first time must meet the following minimum prerequisites: (1) have ten years' documented experience in the sport; (2) have owned or exhibited several dogs of the initial breed(s) requested; (3) have bred or raised at least four litters in any one breed; (4) have produced two champions out of a minimum of four litters;

The American show scene: Rory (Am. Can. Ch. Daystar's Tornado Warning), a son of Am. Can. Ch. Trowsnest Whirlwind UD WC, Can. CDX, was a very successful show dog and also an outstanding sire. Bred, owned and handled by Randy and Zelia Bohsen.

Golden Retrievers in Germany: Representatives of the Of Mill Lane kennel, bred by the late Pat Busch.

Photo: Birgit Simon.

(5) have five stewarding assignments at AKC Member or Licensed Shows; (6) have judged six Sanctioned matches, Sweepstakes or Futurities; (7) must meet the occupational eligibility requirements under AKC Rules; (8) must pass a comprehensive 'open book' examination demonstrating understanding of AKC Rules, Policies and Judging Procedures; (9) must pass a test on the Standard of each breed requested; (10) must be interviewed; (11) must provide two references. To satisfy these and additional requirements requires time, effort, and money on the part of the would-be judge. It is unnecessary to further detail all the convoluted arrangements whereby an applicant is finally approved to judge initially on a Provisional basis, and, after a specified number of assignments, to become a Regular Judge. The American Kennel Club publishes *Guidelines for Dog Show Judges,* which details the required judging procedures. All judges must physically examine each dog, i.e. must open the dog's mouth (or have the handler do so) to

check dentition and bite and must check that every male has two normally descended testicles. He/she must go over the dog to determine soundness of back, hocks and coat condition. The judge is required to individually gait each dog to determine soundness, always using the same ring pattern to ensure impartiality. The interpretation of the Standard is the sole responsibility of the judge. A judge can adjudicate only those dogs which are presented in the conformation ring on a particular day.

AMERICAN TYPE AND BRITISH TYPE

While the Golden Retriever is the same breed worldwide, trends in different areas have produced definite variations. The breed originated in Britain, but has been established much longer in North America than in other countries outside Britain; hence some of the differences in the breed here. Since most countries of the world have brought their foundation stock mostly from the UK, and mostly within the past 30 years or so, their populations tend more strongly to the British type of dog. In North America, the breed was founded upon the darker Goldens popular in England in the 1930s, and through the 1960s most American Goldens were of the deeper shades. The American foundation was very much based on working Goldens, contributing to early success at field trials and obedience trials. There were a number of British dogs imported fairly regularly; some made lasting contributions to the American lines, others found limited acceptance. Some were very successful: a good dog is a good dog wherever it may be shown. UK Am. Ch. Figaro of Yeo was one. His record included winning the GRCA National Specialty in 1963. Imports of working lines have left an indelible imprint upon American field and obedience competitors: the Holway lines crossed on to American working lines have been immensely successful.

American show dogs have gone through several trends in types of style. In the 1950s, it was the tall, Setter-like, dark-coated type, often with a narrow and tapering head. By the 1970s, a heavy-set dog with extreme substance and abundance of coat, was popular, sometimes reminding one of the Newfoundland. Now it is the very 'pretty', glamorous dog, spectacularly groomed and handled, often winning at a very young age but too often later coarsening, or else remaining a perennial puppy who never really matures. Field dogs have diverged considerably from show dogs. Present North American field trial bloodlines are very closely related and there are some real health problems, notably lymphoma and seizures. It is difficult to find an acceptable outcross that could be used without lessening the talent and style essential to field trial success.

Obedience trial dogs come from many different bloodlines: dogs from show, field, those purpose-bred for obedience, and nothing-in-particular bloodlines have all been quite successful over the years. Willingness, trainability, and a skilful trainer are the most important ingredients for success in obedience trials, which combine features of both the British Working Trials and obedience tests.

JUDGING IN GERMANY

The explosion in the popularity of the Golden Retriever during recent years is quite alarming. For example, entries in open bitch class at the Annual Club Championship Show have gone from 26 to 93 in just a few years. Obviously, in such a short space of time, it was not possible to find enough experienced breeders who were interested in judging, let alone for would-be judges to go through the lengthy process of training. To bridge the gap, many English breed judges are invited to Germany every year, as well as a few from Scandinavia and the neighbouring countries.

The Deutscher Retriever Club (which takes care of all the retriever breeds) and the Golden Retriever Club (founded in 1990) are members of the VDH (the German equivalent of the Kennel Club) and thus are also members of the FCI. At present these clubs have six breeder-judges, and the VDH has a further six judges of the FCI Group 8, who are permitted to judge Golden Retrievers.

The training system for judges is laid down by the VDH and only clubs which the VDH considers to have a representative and qualified judges committee are allowed to train and examine their own breed judges. In other cases specialist judges are trained by the Group 8 VDH judges. This is a fairly recent ruling, and the Deutscher Retriever Club was not officially authorised to take over this responsibility until 1993. The judges for the GRC are trained by the VDH, as at present this newly formed club only has one qualified judge.

The Germans like to have very clear stipulations in their regulations. The VDH booklet of regulations for judges contains twenty-four pages and fifty-four paragraphs. These serve as a guide line for the trainee and qualified judge. Perhaps it will suffice to mention the basic qualifications required for an applicant wishing to be accepted for training as a specialist breed judge:

● The applicant must be an absolutely reliable, trustworthy and responsible person in every respect, as the judge plays an extremely important role in the present-day standard and future development of pedigree dog breeding.

● He must be extremely knowledgeable, possess high intellectual and personal values and remember that at all times he represents his breed club, the VDH and the "Federation Cynologique Internationale" (FCI), both to exhibitors and to the public.

● He must have been a registered breeder with a VDH/FCI prefix for at least five years. During this period he must have bred at least three litters of the breed he wishes to judge, and have successfully exhibited dogs of his own breeding over a period of at least five years.

● The applicant must be at least 25 years old and no more than 50 years. He must have been member of a club affiliated to the VDH specialising in the breed concerned, for at least five years.

● He must have acted as ring secretary, ring steward or show manager at least five times during the course of a year, and on at least one occasion have managed a show.

● The attendance at two of the VDH annual show manager training courses is compulsory.

The lengthy and thorough training should be complete within two years, at the end of which a written and practical examination takes place. This includes a selection from approximately 200 questions covering the fields of anatomy, statics, dynamics, genetics and general behaviour of the dog. A knowledge of all the paragraphs in the VDH judging leaflet is required, as well as the rules and regulations regarding dog shows and breeding selection tests. The practical test entails the independent judging and placing of Golden Retrievers in different age groups and of both sexes.

A JUDGING EXERCISE

All Golden Retrievers must be judged by the Breed Standard which has been adopted in the country where the breed is being judged. This is the guide that all judges must follow, regardless of whether the type of Golden Retriever varies from country to country. The British and American Breed Standards vary slightly, particularly with regard to colour where the paler colour is faulted in the USA (see Chapter Six: the Breed Standards), and obviously, all judges form their own interpretation of the Standard.

As an academic exercise, three Championship judges, Marcia Schlehr (USA), Valerie Foss (UK) and Hilary Vogel (Germany), were asked to assess six Golden Retrievers – three dogs and three bitches – from a series of photographs, showing head, profile, forequarters, and hindquarters. The dogs were not named, the judges were merely told their ages.

Clearly, it is impossible to make an accurate evaluation of a dog from photographs alone, as the essential areas of temperament and movement cannot be brought into the balance. However, it is interesting to find out how the top judges approach each exhibit, and what is going through their minds when they are going over a dog.

Hilary Vogel (Germany) comments: "Fortunately judges are not normally required to pass their opinion on a dog just from photographs! However, it is an interesting exercise, although the picture is incomplete without being able to assess movement and temperament.

"As a judge of all six Retriever breeds, I consider good movement, resulting from correct conformation, to be of considerable importance in any gundog. The Golden Retriever, in particular, is a most versatile dog because of its wonderful temperament, and this is of the utmost importance. Finally, I consider that a good dog should be true to type. For the purpose of this exercise, I must assume that the featured dogs move satisfactorily, have the desired temperament, possess a correct bite, and have not been 'cleverly' trimmed to disguise the odd weakness."

A JUDGING EXERCISE

Photography: Carol Ann Johnson.

Golden Retriever A: Bitch (four years).

HEAD STUDY

Valerie Foss (UK): *"A good head with lovely eye-shape. The ears are a little large and high set. A 'snow nose' which will look better when it has turned black again."*

Marcia Schlehr (USA): *"A very attractive head, with a sweet expression which is not over-done. She has good width and depth of muzzle, a good skull and wide-set ears. The ears are acceptable. There is good strength under the eyes, with a nice blend of muzzle into the skull. Dark eyes with good pigment. A touch of 'snow nose', which should not be penalised."*

Hilary Vogel (Germany): *"This bitch has a feminine head and the gentle, melting expression that is typical of the breed. She has well-placed eyes, and her ears are set correctly. Pigment is good."*

PROFILE

Valerie Foss (UK): *"Attractive head shape in profile. A lovely neck with shoulders well laid back. Excellent upper arm, placing the legs well under the body. Good depth of brisket; a shade long in loin and maybe a little short on the leg. A good topline, and well-bent stifles."*

Marcia Schlehr (USA): *"Her head is very pleasing from the side, showing strength without being over-done. She has a level topline, strong loin, and a smooth croup and tail-set. The neck to the withers blend could be a little smoother, but it is not a major fault. The shoulder layback appears to be acceptable. The elbows are well under, and the rear angulation appears to be good. She is a bit long cast and slightly short on leg for optimum efficiency in action. her colour is a light, attractive golden, with some wave, and a nice texture. In all, she is a very pretty, very feminine bitch."*

Hilary Vogel (Germany): *"A quality show lady, displaying confidence and charm. She has a nicely-shaped head, a mature body, a super topline and tail-set, and excellent bone. She appears to be a little down in pasterns. Her hindquarters are placed well back which tends to make her appear too long. She has an attractive coat. I can imagine this bitch to be a steady mover, maintaining the good topline in action."*

FOREQUARTERS

Valerie Foss (UK): *"Correct bone for a bitch. She appears a shade narrow in front, but this could be the way she has been set up."*

Marcia Schlehr (USA): *"Stands rather narrow in front, and toeing out slightly. More than ample bone, verging on too much for usefulness. The chest looks to be of acceptable width and depth, and the elbows are tight."*

Hilary Vogel (Germany): *"This bitch is well-developed in the forechest. Perhaps it is the profuse feathering, but it looks to me as though she needs a little more height of foreleg. Strong bone. Again, there is a suspicion of weakness in the pasterns."*

HINDQUARTERS

Valerie Foss (UK): *It looks as though she is a little over-stretched behind, which tends to make her stand incorrectly."*

Marcia Schlehr (USA): *"Good breadth of rear, with plenty of substance. Unfortunately, the hocks incline inwards somewhat (cow-hocks). Her movement going away should reveal how serious this may be in action. The toe-out of the front is also obvious."*

Hilary Vogel (Germany): *"Well-developed quarters, nicely angulated with good bone and profuse feathering. She is not standing parallel, and she is turning her front feet slightly outwards."*

A JUDGING EXERCISE

Photography: Carol Ann Johnson.

Golden Retriever B: Bitch (three years).

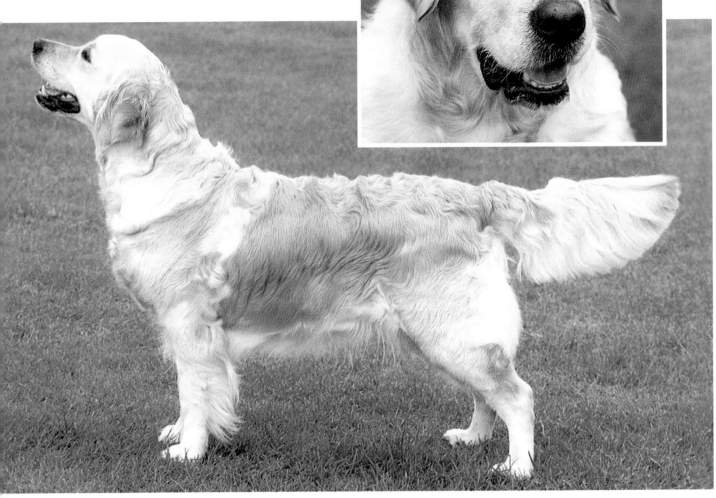

HEAD STUDY

Valerie Foss (UK): *An attractive head with good eyes. The ears are a little high-set and over moderate in size. The muzzle is a little narrow for perfect balance."*

Marcia Schlehr (USA): *"A bright, keen, alert expression. The ears are a little large, but they are nicely set and well-carried. Good pigment, and a good, dark eye. The eyes could be set a little closer together for optimum. She could use a little more strength under the eyes, where the muzzle blends into the skull – although this might be due to the open mouth."*

Hilary Vogel (Germany): *"At first glance, I found this bitch a bit plain in head, but it could be the angle of the photograph does not do her full justice. She has an alert expression. Her ears are set a little high. Her eyes are large and round: they may be positioned a shade close to each other. Good pigment."*

PROFILE

Valerie Foss (UK): *This bitch is very attractive in profile. She has the correct neck and shoulders, placing the legs well under the body. She has a good depth of brisket, a level topline and a perfect set-on of tail. The stifles are well-bent."*

Marcia Schlehr (USA) *"A lovely topline, with the reach of neck blending smoothly into the withers. Level back, with a nice croup and tail-set. She is well-coupled with strong loin, and her overall proportions are balanced with the correct length of leg. She is probably better in shoulder layback than Bitch A, and she is nearly as good in the upper arm. Although she has less forechest, she seems to 'fit together' better than Bitch A.*

"She has good feet, perhaps a bit upright in the front pastern. The rear angulation is very good, with excellent breadth of thigh. Lovely coat with some wave on top, and good, rich colouring. Her head is pleasant and feminine, but not as strong as Bitch A. Her overall structure, athletic look, reach of neck,

balanced with useful leg length and angulation, help to overcome her slightly weaker head."*

Hilary Vogel (Germany): *"This bitch is more compact than Bitch 1. She has quite a pleasing profile, with a good reach of neck flowing into a level topline. The shoulders are well laid back, but she appears to have a short upper arm. Reasonably angulated hindquarters, with good bone. Nice overall type."*

FOREQUARTERS

Valerie Foss (UK): *The forelegs are straight, with the correct bone for a bitch. She has good, tight elbows."*

Marica Schlehr (USA): *"Excellent straight legs and clean shoulders. The width of chest is good, although she could use a little more forechest. Substance is entirely sufficient."*

Hilary Vogel (Germany): *" From this angle, the bitch has a narrow appearance, lacking depth and indicating that she could do with more spring of rib. She appears to be a shade high on the forelegs; her hindlegs are not well positioned. I would guess that coming on, she may well move closely and pinning in."*

HINDQUARTERS

Valerie Foss (UK): *The hocks are not straight when viewed from the rear; this could look worse than it is because of the way she has been set up. The tail is the correct length, reaching to the hocks."*

Marcia Schlehr (USA): *"Poor stance as she is standing toed-out, the left hock, in particular, inclines inward. The short trim on the breeches emphasises this. Ribs well-sprung at top."*

Hilary Vogel (Germany): *"Rather wide behind, although the angulation is good and she is furnished with excellent feathering. in spite of the long grass, it appears here, and from the other angles, as though this young lady has flat feet."*

A JUDGING EXERCISE

Photography: Carol Ann Johnson.

Golden Retriever C: Bitch (18 months).

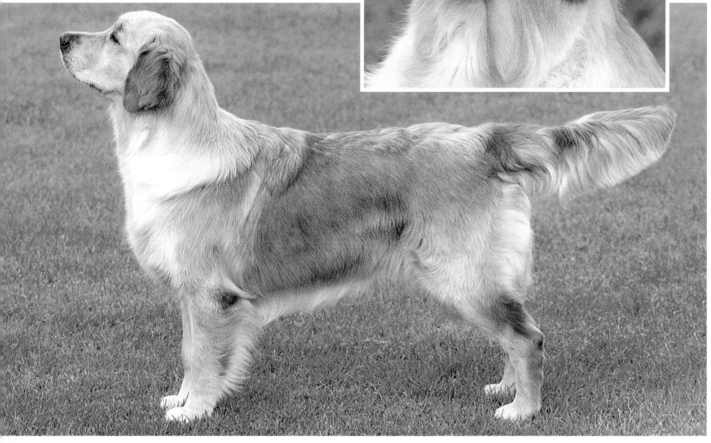

HEAD STUDY

Valerie Foss (UK): *A well-balanced and chiselled head. The ears are too big and thus, a little high-set. Lovely eyes and good expression."*

Marcia Schlehr (USA): *"Her very large ears, narrow muzzle pinched under the eyes, and a slightly dished face makes an entirely different and less pleasing head type. Her expression is somewhat reserved. The front of the muzzle is not deep, indicating that the apparent depth comes from hanging flews. Her deep, golden colouring makes the trimming of the ruff very obvious."*

Hilary Vogel (Germany): *"This bitch has an alert, but rather hard expression. She has large ears, dark eyes and excellent pigment. The lower jaw appears to be weak. The severely trimmed coat is not altogether complimentary to her general appearance."*

PROFILE

Valerie Foss (UK): *"From this angle, she appears to have a good head, but rather large ears. She could be cleaner in neck, and she is a shade straight in the upper arm. A good depth of brisket, short-coupled, and the topline is not level. Well-bent stifles. From the photograph, she appears to be in good feather with a good-quality coat."*

Marcia Schlehr (USA): *"Her topline is poor, with an upright neck stuck on to the shoulders (probably not well laid back), making an abrupt angle at the withers. The backline is slightly concave, the croup is short, possibly with a high tail-set. The loin appears somewhat long. The rear angulation appears to be better than the front. The pasterns and feet appear to be good. The shaded deep gold coat, with no wave, is acceptable. At only 18 months of age, she may not yet be in full furnishing. However, her head profile is still not pleasing: the stop is too deep, the short*

muzzle is cut away (lacking chin) and she is slightly throaty. the ears are large. Her overall proportions are acceptable, but she still lacks balance and harmony of structure."

FOREQUARTERS

Valerie Foss (UK): *"The correct bone for a bitch, but the forelegs tend to be weak at the pastern. It looks as though her elbows are nice and tight."*

Marcia Schlehr (USA): *"The legs are straight, although she is standing a bit close. A slight turn-out of feet may be due to close placement. The breadth and depth of chest appears to be adequate. She is maybe a little heavy in shoulder. From this angle, she is standing narrow in rear as well."*

Hilary Vogel (Germany): *"From this angle, she has a reasonable outline for her age. Again, the different layers of coat and shades of colouring can be misleading."*

HINDQUARTERS

Valerie Foss (UK): *"The hocks are well let down, but they are not straight when viewed from the rear, tending to turn in."*

Marcia Schlehr (USA): *"Fairly good rear. She has a slight turn-in of hocks, but she is at least as good as the other bitches. The light shading of the breeches is quite acceptable, and is attractive with the rich coat colouring."*

Hilary Vogel (Germany): *"Not quite muscled up yet – she needs time to fill out. This is recognisable in spite of the excellent feathering. A trifle high in the hocks."*

A JUDGING EXERCISE

Photography: Carol Ann Johnson.

Golden Retriever D: Dog (four years).

HEAD STUDY

Valerie Foss (UK): *"A well-shaped head, he could do with a little more depth of muzzle."*

Marcia Schlehr (USA): *"A good breadth and arch of skull. the ears are down and back in a relaxed position, but they appear to be acceptable. The expression could be a little softer. No excess flews; good pigmentation, dark eyes. The muzzle shape is not quite right – more breadth on top would help. Colour is good – a rich, shaded gold."*

Hilary Vogel (Germany): *"This dog has a masculine expression which appears to lack some of the softness required – this could be because he is not relaxed in this photograph. The ears seem to be a little low, and I would prefer a darker eye. The pigment is good. I believe that assessing the head from this angle probably does not do the dog justice."*

PROFILE

Valerie Foss (UK): *"An attractive outline with the correct balance of head, neck and shoulders. A shade straight in the upper arm. Correct depth of brisket, good topline and tail-set. Well bent stifles."*

Marcia Schlehr (USA): *"A strong neck and level topline. Croup and tail-set are good. Proper depth of body, although rather long-cast and possibly lacking spring of rib. A better trimming job would help the look of the forequarters – he is trimmed too low on the forechest which makes him look short in the upper arm and heavy in brisket. Examination with the hands is needed to determine the actual layback of shoulder, but it appears to be acceptable. Rear angulation is only moderate, but is reasonably balanced in front. Upright in pastern and somewhat short in second thigh, this dog would look better with a little more leg under him. With regard to his head, the stop is too concave, and there is a slight Roman finish to the top muzzle profile. The coat is an attractive shaded gold with some wave. He has adequate furnishings, and the coat appears to be of good texture."*

Hilary Vogel (Germany): *"A pleasing outline with good reach of neck, level topline and correct tail-set. he is rather long in body, but stands four-square and is relaxed. His head appeals to me more in profile."*

FOREQUARTERS

Valerie Foss (UK): *"Correct width of chest. I detect a slight weakness on the left pastern. Good bone."*

Marcia Schlehr (USA): *"The right leg looks very good, the left foot turns out (perhaps due to awkward posing?). Ample bone substance. It is hard to see the feet, but they appear to be acceptable. Chest width and depth is satisfactory."*

Hilary Vogel (Germany): *"Good width. The right leg is straight, the left one turns out. The pasterns appear to be weak. The feet are obscured by the grass, but they seem to be flat and could be tighter. Good bone. From this angle, as well as in profile, it looks as though this dog could do with a better spring of rib."*

HINDQUARTERS

Valerie Foss (UK): *"The hocks are well let down – they could be straighter."*

Marcia Schlehr (USA): Appears slightly lighter in substance than in front. Good width at croup and hip, with muscular appearance. The toes are out somewhat, but this could be the result of feet set widely apart. The coat is a bit rough; shaded colouring is acceptable. Toe-out of left front is again evident from this angle."*

Hilary Vogel (Germany): *"Strong legs, but the dog is standing unnaturally. A good, wide front. Good feathering. The back-end appears to be reasonably well-muscled."*

A JUDGING EXERCISE

Photography: Carol Ann Johnson.

Golden Retriever E: Dog (three years).

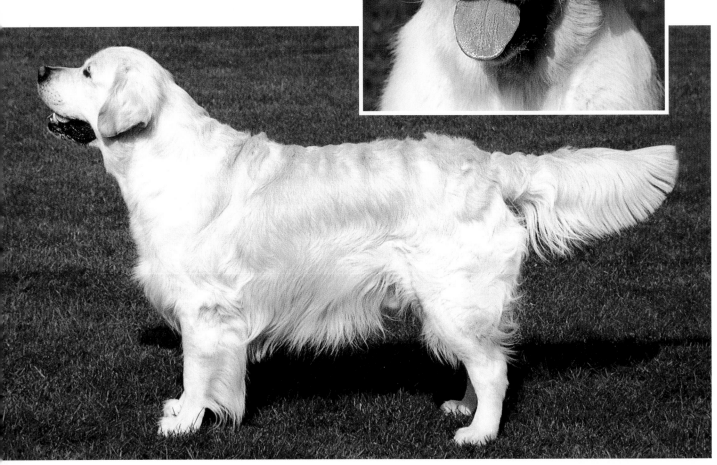

HEAD STUDY
Valerie Foss (UK): *"A well-balanced and well-chiselled head, with the correct eye shape. I would prefer a black nose, but this will change."*

Marcia Schlehr (USA): *"Pale gold dog with good pigment ('winter nose' or 'snow nose' is acceptable) and very dark eyes. The top of the skull might be a bit broader: if the ears were down in relaxed position, would the skull be domey? The impression of a very deep stop and a dished face should be verified in profile view. The ears are somewhat large and heavy. The ruff is over-trimmed, making the neck look stuck into the shoulders."*

Hilary Vogel (Germany): *"A pleasing head with a alert, though slightly feminine expression. Kind, dark eye; perhaps a little short in muzzle. the ears appear to be on the large side. This dog seems to possess the kindly, confident temperament which is typical of the breed."*

PROFILE
Valerie Foss (UK): *" An attractive type of dog who is standing all wrong. He tends to lean back, which is spoiling his topline and making his croup high. Good bone, head, neck and shoulders, and a good depth of chest. If he was stacked by his handler, he would have been 'pulled' into shape."*

Marcia Schlehr (USA): *"This dog appears short in foreleg, giving a low front/high rear look. Poor topline with short, steep croup (not helped by the rough patch of hair). The hindlegs seem too much under the dog, lacking angulation, short in both upper thigh and second thigh. The body depth is good – I suspect a long loin and a short ribcage. The neck is a bit stuffy in spite of zealous trimming. The shoulders might be OK, but they are likely to be short and upright in upper arm. Good feet and pasterns. the head is over-done: the skull is too sharply domed, and the muzzle is short and tipped forward (contrast with Dog C). Loose, wet flews and large ears. Overall, this dog is not well put together – he looks like a collection of spare parts. Better trimming might help with the general appearance, but it won't change the basic shape of the dog."*

Hilary Vogel (Germany): *"Rather a short neck, an adequate layback of shoulder and a short upper arm. This dog is slightly over-built and his tail-set is a shade low, which spoils his topline. The profile also suggests that he is a bit short in muzzle. He is well-developed in body, with only moderate angulation behind. A dog with an attractive coat, perhaps looking a shade too mature for his age and from this angle. Trimmed with care."*

FOREQUARTERS
Valerie Foss (UK): *"Well-boned. He could be stronger and thus straighter in pasterns."*

Marcia Schlehr (USA): *"Standing close in front; the right leg especially turns out. The shoulders appear rather heavy. This is emphasised by the trimming away of the ruff, which also reveals throatiness (and a wet mouth). Not the strong, sound front I would like to see."*

Hilary Vogel (Germany): *"He appears to be well-developed in forechest and has good bone, but he looks to be narrow in front and is probably a fraction down in pasterns."*

HINDQUARTERS
Valerie Foss (UK): *"Again, appearances may be deceptive due to the way this dog has been set up, but he looks a shade straight behind. The hocks are well let down."*

Marcia Schlehr (USA): *"The hocks turn inwards, and the toes and stifles turn out. Lack of angulation gives a stiff 'proppy' look. In general, not a strong rear. I suspect that this weakness, especially in the left hock, will be evident when the dog is moving away."*

Hilary Vogel (Germany): *"Rather disappointing from this angle, as even the attractive feathering cannot disguise the weak quarters. He stands close behind, the feet turning out."*

A JUDGING EXERCISE

Photography: Carol Ann Johnson.

Golden Retriever F: Dog (five years).

HEAD STUDY

Valerie Foss (UK): *"A well-chiselled head. I would like to see the mouth shut in order to check if the muzzle is deep enough. It is obviously powerful and wide."*

Marcia Schlehr (USA): *"I would like to see this smiling boy with his ears up. This view exaggerates the dome of skull, which looks better in the profile photo. The ears are OK, although they are hanging in the relaxed position. Very nice strong, full muzzle without excess flews or loose lips. Dark eyes, good pigment, no penalty for the fading on the nose. Enough ruff is left to help keep the soft expression."*

Hilary Vogel (Germany): *"This dog has a sweet expression. From this angle he appears to have a slightly domed head and rather low-set ears. There could be more work under the eyes, which seem to be a shade too small, possibly a reaction to the bright light. The stop could be more accentuated. The neck also looks rather short. In this photo, he appears to be an 'old' five years."*

PROFILE

Valerie Foss (UK): *"Attractive overall outline, with good outline of head, neck and shoulder. Correct upper arm which places the legs well under the body. Good depth of brisket. A well-balanced body with correct bend of stifle.*

Marcia Schlehr (USA): *"A strong, very masculine fellow. He has a good topline, and I would expect a good layback of shoulders. Clean fore-assembly, with good forechest and elbows nicely placed. Deep body, good length of rib, very short-coupled. Adequate rear angulation, good breadth of thigh, strong second thigh, and hocks well-placed. Good feet and pasterns. The neck is of the proper, moderate length, and is very muscular. He is nicely trimmed so as not to distort his good features. He has a lovely shaded gold colour, and an attractive coat with sufficient feathering, still keeping a clean outline. Unfortunately, the wind has blown his tail feathering askew. He has a very pleasing head profile with the proper shape and depth, a good balance of muzzle and skull, clean lips, and no throatiness. I would like to see a bit more length of foreleg, and I would hope that his very short loin does not interfere with suppleness and freedom of movement."*

Hilary Vogel (USA): *"A compact dog with a short neck, a good topline, excellent bone and a nice coat. It is a pity that his overall balance is spoilt by the lack of strength in the hindquarters."*

FOREQUARTERS

Valerie Foss (UK): *"He has the correct width of chest, but I would like to see a little more bone for a male. He has good, straight forelegs."*

Marcia Schlehr (USA): *"This dog has the best front of the three males. He is standing with more weight on the left; as a casual stance, this makes a very slight turn-out which is still acceptable. Ample bone. The feet are obscured. The breadth and depth of chest appear to be good, the elbows are nicely held – a happy, wagging tail as well!"*

Hilary Vogel (Germany): *"He is not standing quite parallel here. The right leg is straight, the left one turns out and possibly only needs correction of stance. Good bone, well-feathered coat."*

HINDQUARTERS

Valerie Foss (UK): *"I would like to see more muscular development. The hocks are well let down. From this pose, it looks as though they could be straighter, but this could be an optical illusion."*

Marcia Schlehr (USA): *"A good rear, with breadth of hip and evidence of muscling. The left leg toes out slightly – movement would reveal if this is just a momentary stance or an indication of weakness. It appears to be a minor fault."*

Hilary Vogel (Germany): *"Although the angulation is reasonable, the thighs are lacking in width and strength."*

8 THE COMPLETE GUNDOG

There are far fewer working Golden Retrievers competing in Field Trials than the ever-popular working Labrador Retrievers. However, over the years a number of Goldens have proved their worth, and the breed is still highly-prized as a working gundog.

TOP WORKING DOGS
BRITAIN
The most successful British working kennel in Goldens is June Atkinson's Holway kennel. She has made up sixteen Field Trial Champions, and her son Robert has made up five. This compares very favourably with the total of of 67 FT Champions made up since the Second World War. There are now several successful working kennels in Britain. Many Goldens have been in the awards at Retriever Championships. In 1952 Jean Lumsden (then Jean Train) won the Championships with FT Ch. Treunair Cala. June Atkinson won the 1954 Championships with FT Ch. Holway Mazurka, and her son Robert won it in 1982 with FT Ch. Little Marston Chorus of Holway.

The last Dual Champion was Int. Dual Ch. David of Westley, Ch. FT Ch. Irish Ch. and FT Ch. He was bred by Joan Gill, owned by Lucy Ross and trained and handled at trials by Jim Cranston. He was born in 1951 and completed his titles in 1956.

NORTH AMERICA
In 1941, the first National Championship Retriever Trial was held. Dogs had to qualify, in order to enter, by earning placements in Open Stakes held during the previous year. The winner in 1941, and the first NFT Champion, was the Golden FTC-NFTC King Midas of Woodend. Three other Goldens have

Pictured left to right: Strathcarron Seil of Standerwick (foundation of the famous Standerwick kennel) with her daughters Ch. Standerwick Thomasina and FT Ch. Standerwick Roberta of Abnalls.

Photo: Sally Anne Thompson.
Photo courtesy: Daphne Philpott.

NAFC-FC Topbrass Cotton (AFC Holway Barty x Ch. Sunstream Gypsy of Topbrass), born 7-6-78, is the winner of more points at retriever field trials than any other Golden Retriever. At the age of ten years, Cotton had earned nearly 200 Amateur points and at least 79 Open points; he qualified for the National Amateur Retriever trial for nine consecutive years, for the Open Championship 5 years, and in 1985 became the first (and only) Golden to win the title of National Amateur Field Champion. Cotton was bred by Jackie Mertens out of a show champion bitch (with field lines) and was first campaigned by Bev and Jeff Finley; in 1982 Jackie became a co-owner and took Cotton on to an unprecedented career. He also placed in the Field Trial (conformation) class at the GRCA National specialty in 1988 at age ten plus!

won the National Championship.

In 1985 the first Golden won the National Amateur Field Trial Championship – FC AFC Topbrass Cotton, bred and handled by Jackie Mertens, and owned by Jackie and Jeff Finley. Cotton, and his two titled siblings, were sired by the English import who has had such a strong influence on American field (and Obedience Trial) lines, AFC Holway Barty, owned by Barbara Howard.

The influence of Barty, and other imports, on working pedigrees has been tremendous. Crossing on to old American lines, such as Gunnerman, Kinike and Riverview, resulted in brilliant, intelligent, stylish workers, and these dogs now typify the winning Trial Goldens.

THE EARLY STAGES OF GUN TRAINING
If you wish to gun train your Golden, and maybe train to Field Trial standard, your first course of action is, perhaps, to go to watch a Working Test. Then go to a good working

kennel whose stock is consistently worked and appears in the awards at Field Trials. Even if you do not intend to go in for competitions, it is much more satisfactory to have a Golden puppy from working lines.

Unfortunately, there is a something of a split in the breed. Show dogs are bred for construction, type and quality, together with lovely temperaments and showmanship, and they usually lack the speed and biddability of the working-bred dog. Workers are bred for their biddability, speed, style, good noses, hunting and game-finding abilities, willingness to face thick cover and, of course, their equally lovely temperaments.

It is a good idea to watch other people work their dogs. This can be seen at Working Tests in the summer, and at Field Trials during the shooting season. There are many good videos on training now available, and these are very helpful. There are also books which cover the subject in great depth. Training classes, too, are held in most areas. However, I hope that this chapter will serve as an introduction to the early stages of gun training your Golden Retriever. For convenience I have referred to the puppy as he, though all the tips and techniques apply equally to both sexes.

CHOOSING YOUR PUPPY

In a litter, I look for the responsive puppy – one that wants to be with you, looking at you, tail wagging. Try and see the litter running around outside, and watch for style and tail action. An independent puppy is not usually the one to choose, although, of course, puppies can change considerably as they mature. It is enjoyable to watch them explore and be confident, and to hope they respond when you call them or clap your hands.

It is quite good fun to see whether very young puppies will retrieve. Some will manage a tennis ball, but a large hanky tied in a knot is usually the favourite article. I always put a hand in front of them to stop them running in straightaway, even at this early age. Obviously, you do not go on giving them lots of retrieves.

It is important to pick the puppy who most appeals to you, as this can vary from person to person, and it is a very personal thing. Bear in mind that you are the one to whom the puppy will have to respond. Next, you will have to get to know and understand your puppy's little ways. Remember, you and the puppy do not know each other, so the next few weeks will be spent getting acquainted and developing that very special bond.

PRAISE AND ROUTINE

Praise is very important. When a puppy does what he is asked, make a fuss, and let him really understand that he has done the right thing. The next six months are crucial for gun training, and so is routine. Routine is so important – the puppy must be fed at particular times, have his bed in the same place, and know exactly when you want him in it. A baby Golden can learn to sit, come when called, and 'heel' with you when outside. Call the puppy by using his name,

followed by the Recall whistle (see following paragraph), then squat down to the puppy's height to encourage him in. On arrival, give the puppy lots of praise. The best whistle to use is a black plastic one. Buy either size 210.5 or 211.5 so that, should you lose it, it can be replaced with one of the same tone.

It is a good idea, at the puppy's dinner time, to use the whistle as a signal to for him come. This is known as a Recall whistle, and consists of several pips. The other whistle is the Sit or Stop whistle, which is one long blast. Always remember that quiet handling is just as effective as noisy handling. A quiet whistle when the puppy is near you is all that is necessary. Then, when the puppy is at a distance, you have the louder noise to fall back on.

There is no need to give your puppy lots of retrieves. Encourage a puppy who happens to be carrying something around to bring the article to you. When you take it, say "Dead", and he should be happy to part with the find. At this early stage, give the toy back after praising the puppy.

USE OF HANDS

Your use of hands is very important, as all your signals in the future will involve them. The dog watches your hand signals. Let the puppy follow your hands. When you ask the puppy to sit, place the flat of your hand above him and, with the other hand, press gently on the hindquarters to put him in the position. Quite soon you will be able to raise your hand and the puppy will sit.

To teach your puppy to stay, sit him down and, with the flat of your hand above him, repeat the word "Stay" and just lean away from him. Soon you will find that you will be able to take one step away, then be able to walk right round him. Increase time and distance very slowly. Never overdo it. Your puppy must understand what the word means.

USE OF THE WHISTLE

To teach the Stop whistle, walk your puppy to heel, stop suddenly, blowing a quiet Stop whistle and gently pushing him into the Sit

TRAINING EXERCISES

Demonstrated by Daphne Philpott and Standerwick Ricarda.
Photos Graham Cox.

HEELWORK

ABOVE: Close heelwork is encouraged if you practise along the side of a fence.

ABOVE (RIGHT): By using the lead, your dog will learn to turn close to you.

position as described above. Do this several times and stop every few yards. Your puppy should soon learn to sit smartly. Do not forget to praise him when he does.

Most working-bred puppies will come automatically to the Recall whistle. If your puppy does not do this, use it when he is already coming towards you and praise him when he reaches you.

EDUCATION IN THE EARLY DAYS

On the puppy's short walks and playtimes, introduce him to everything possible; a small stream, a slope, long grass, etc. Find some bracken or fallen leaves in autumn. Walk among people, and carefully include a little traffic. Let your puppy meet friendly dogs, but teach him manners and do not let him jump all over them. Also, get him used to short rides in the car. Never let the puppy jump straight out of the car as soon as you open the door. There could be another vehicle passing, and he could be killed or cause an accident. You have taught the puppy to sit and stay, so make him stay in the car until you are ready to get him out. I always put a lead on my dogs first, so they learn to wait until this is done.

By six months of age, you should have a happy, confident puppy, who understands the basic commands you have taught him. He should know that the word "Come", or a succession of pips on the whistle, means that he should come to you, and that the command "Sit" (or a raised hand) means that he must sit immediately. Your puppy should be able to heel on your lefthand side, know that "Stay" means he must not move, and that "Give" or "Dead" means that he must release to you whatever he is carrying. Most of all, your Golden puppy should be full of confidence, anxious to please, becoming bold and wanting to explore. In fact, he will be ready to begin very basic training.

PROGRESSING TO A RETRIEVE

The next step is to teach your puppy to heel off a lead. To keep him close to your side, find a hedge or a fence, and walk him between you and it. If he is in the open and walks ahead of you, swing round and walk in the opposite direction, encouraging the puppy to come with you. Until he is about twelve months of age, all these little exercises can be increased in length and time and in different places.

Once he is steady, you can then give a retrieve. The first time, the best way is to sit

THE RETRIEVE

LEFT: A good delivery should be worked on from an early age.

RIGHT: The dog must give up the dummy/game on command.

LEARNING HAND SIGNALS

LEFT: The working dog must be finely attuned to hand signals. This is a clear left hand signal.

RIGHT: Sending a dog out.

LEFT: Teaching Stay.

RIGHT: In instant response to the Stop signal.

LEFT: "Go back"

RIGHT: Sending on a blind retrieve.

the dog facing you and throw the dummy over your head, so you are between the dog and the dummy and can stop him if he moves. Next, throw the dummy into light cover so the puppy can hunt and use his nose. Delivery is very important; never snatch a dummy from him. Encourage the puppy to sit, and stroke his chest, or the side of his head, before taking the dummy from him. Your aim is for the dog to raise his head and give you the retrieve. Taking it too quickly will encourage your Golden to drop the dummy, or spit it out, on reaching you. When throwing the dummy, see that the wind is blowing from it towards the puppy. This will carry the scent to him, making the retrieve easier to find.

When your puppy reaches the area where the retrieve is to be found, use the command "Hie Lost", or similar. Later on, when he is able to be handled on to a blind retrieve, he will realise this command means: "That is the right area, find it there."

MEMORY
Memory training is a great help. One good way is to walk along a path, or track, let the puppy see you throw a dummy behind you, and then walk on. After a few yards, turn round, sit the puppy up facing you and, with your hand high in the air above your head and the flat of your hand towards the puppy, push your hand back with the words "Go back" – a new command. This is an exercise puppies really enjoy, and the distances can be slowly increased until the puppy will be confident to go quite a long way back. It is also the start of your hand signals and taking directions.

The next signal is to sit your puppy in front of you, facing you, and throw one dummy in a straight line to the right, and one to the left. Raise one arm slowly and lean that way, saying your puppy's name. This is the introduction to the right and left signals. You must remember that all this takes time, and must be done gradually. To develop the natural hunting instinct, it is a good idea to find a patch of light cover, long grass, short bracken etc., and put out about five dummies, well apart to avoid swapping. Next, bring your

puppy and tell him to "Hie lost". He will be able to find a dummy quite easily with that number down, and this will give him confidence. Then send him back for a second one. With this one safely retrieved, pick up by hand those that are left.

Once this exercise has been learned well, send the puppy out to hunt on the next occasion without putting anything down. Keep him in the area, using your Recall whistle if he goes too far. After a few minutes hunting, place a dummy out while the dog is not looking, so that he eventually finds it. This will make your Golden realise that, if he keeps hunting the area, he will eventually be rewarded by a find. It also teaches him to 'hold an area', and not go tearing around in huge spaces.

BLIND RETRIEVES
Using a track on the side of a fence or hedge, get somebody to throw a mark in a straight line with the puppy. On your command "Go back", the puppy will retrieve it. While the puppy is returning with the dummy, put another one down in exactly the same place. Using the same command, "Go back", the puppy will usually go straight back, having remembered the previous mark.

A useful exercise for the use of the Stop whistle and control is the following. Send the puppy out in front of you with the "Go back" command. Blow your Stop whistle. The puppy should sit. Immediately, throw a dummy out to his side, about 25 yards away. Blow the Recall whistle for the puppy to return to you. Praise him, and then send him for the dummy. An alternative method is to throw a long mark, stop the dog half way, throw another dummy to the right or left, and, with the "Go back" signal, send him for the first mark thrown. Pick up the diversion by hand. This exercise must not be overdone, as you do not want the dog to stop on a normal, marked retrieve. However, it is good for control.

If your puppy fails to stop on the whistle, never be tempted to blow it again, but go out to him and take him back to the spot where he should have stopped. Sit him up, and blow your whistle firmly at him. It is very important that you always take the dog back to the place where he should have stopped when the whistle was first blown.

WATER TRAINING

The introduction to water needs to be done on a warm day. Find somewhere with an easy entrance and throw in the dummy (only paddling distance away). Encourage the puppy to paddle and, very gradually, increase the distance of the throw. Even when the puppy has had quite a lot of experience in water, always check the point at which he is going to enter it. See that there are no sharp branches on which he could get impaled. A lot of dogs leap into water and, although this looks good and stylish, it can be dangerous.

Once your Golden is a confident swimmer, try and find a river or small lake where the dummy can be thrown on to the other side. Use the command "Get over". It is not a good idea for puppies to have too many retrieves solely in the water, as this can lead to difficulties later when you want them to go across.

JUMPING

Always introduce the puppy to a low, firm jump to start with, and do not increase the height until he is fully confident. Again, use the command "Get over". I feel jumping should be left until the puppy is about 12 months of age, when he is stronger and more developed. As progress is made, puppies learn to clear obstacles easily, but never let them jump barbed wire, and always be aware of steep drops on the other side of the jump.

GUNFIRE

Gunfire must be introduced carefully. Always get someone to fire the gun at a good distance (150 yards away to start with), with the wind blowing away from the shot, thus taking some of the sound with it. Very gradually, bring the gun nearer, providing the puppy is not showing any signs of being worried. If he is worried, repeat the exercise another day and, as the gun is being fired, give him a retrieve he can see. A ball often makes the puppy forget the bang. Firing a shot a good distance away when giving the puppy his food often helps too. Never overdo it. A gun-nervous puppy is quite different from a gun-shy one. The gun-shy dog will run away and hide, and

When your Golden Retriever is a confident swimmer, you can try a retrieve in a river or a small lake.

The working dog must also learn to wait his turn. No matter how great the temptation, a dog must not join in unless he is commanded to do so.

this is more difficult to overcome.

Obedience is essential at all times, and it comes quite naturally if the basic training has been done correctly. The small puppy dummies are the most useful to start with, gradually proceeding to the 1lb canvas dummies, which are used when the puppy is older and carrying the puppy ones correctly.

WORKING TESTS
Many Working Tests are held during the summer months throughout Britain. These are great fun, and make a lovely day out which all the family can enjoy. Canvas dummies weighing 1lb are used, and various exercises are performed by each dog in turn. Usually these consist of a marked retrieve, a blind retrieve to see how your dog handles, a walk-up in line with other dogs, each of whom must retrieve a mark in turn, and maybe a retrieve from water. At higher levels, diversions are used, testing the control of the dog. A mark may be thrown, and the dog asked to get a retrieve he has not seen (a blind retrieve) in another area.

PICKING UP
When the basic training is completed, and your dog is steady to a thrown dummy, will stop on the whistle and take direction, you may wish to take him 'picking up'. It is advisable to introduce your Golden to a cold bird first and see whether he will retrieve it. It is better, if you are able, to get a freshly-shot bird (preferably a partridge or a small hen

pheasant) to start with. When he is picking this cleanly, introduce a cock bird. This is because a smaller bird is easier to retrieve. If you are unable to get a freshly-shot bird, one from the freezer is the next best thing, making sure it is properly thawed out and that it was frozen when fresh. Never re-freeze them. Two or three retrieves are the most one should do with the same bird, then dispose of it.

If your dog refuses to pick up a bird – and this can happen as he may not like feather to start with – try the following. Some trainers put the bird in a stocking, but I prefer to bind the centre of the bird with a crepe bandage or a piece of cotton material. This leaves the head and tail free. Your dog will then usually pick it up and hold it in the middle. Gradually reduce the size of the bandage, which is usually is enough to encourage him to pick up. If this strategy fails, the competition of another dog will often solve the problem.

If all is well and your first day of picking up has arrived, stand well back from the guns so the gunfire can be heard a long way off. At the end of the drive, walk forward and hunt for any birds that have been shot. It is a good thing, if possible, to have an experienced picker-up with you, so that his dog can retrieve any wounded birds to start with. A young dog should be introduced to dead game first.

FIELD TRIALS
If you feel your dog is good enough to enter a Field Trial, get advice from an experienced

*FT Ch. Rossmor of
Clancallum working
with Malcolm Stringer.*

Field Trialler first. He or she will be able to
tell you if your dog is under enough control,
and will make sure he has had experience on
all types of game, including runners, and
knows how to take a line on a wounded bird.
Eliminating faults at a trial are: hard mouths,
whining or barking, out-of-control dogs,
running in, chasing, failing to enter water and
changing game while retrieving. *Never* enter
with a dog who has any of these faults. Field
Trials are very much over-subscribed and, if
your dog is not good enough or has an
eliminating fault, you are possibly taking a
good dog's place.

Runs in trials are difficult to get in the first
place. One has to belong to a lot of societies to
stand a chance of being lucky in the draw. All
entries are taken and then drawn for the
number running in the actual trial.

CARE OF YOUR WORKING DOG

After a day's work, it is a good idea to comb
Goldens through to see that their coats are free
from burrs. Check feet for thorns, and also
look between the pads. If they are muddy,
wash the feet so that you can see more clearly.
Check ears and eyes for grass seeds, especially
in the early part of the season, and always
after training during the summer and autumn.
If Goldens have been in water it is always as
well to dry their ears. This can avoid ear
problems developing. Although you will take
liquid with you when working your dogs,
always offer them a drink on return. They will
then need a meal and a warm dry bed.

FIELD EVENTS IN NORTH AMERICA

Field Trials began in the USA in the early
1930s. Retriever fanciers in the Eastern US at
that time were wealthy men who had imported
their dogs directly from British field trainers
and were anxious to prove the dogs'
capabilities among their peers. However,
although such tests had been held in Britain
since the turn of the century, few Americans
had much, or any, experience with Field
Trials, and there was a definite lack of
experienced judges for the trials.

EARLY FIELD TRIALS

Trials in the USA were run along the lines of
British trials, with a number of competing
dogs in line waiting to work. Because of the
different style of hunting in this country there
were no driven shoots; rather, birds were
thrown for the gunners, usually at some
distance from the dogs. At some trials a dog
might only have the opportunity to work on
one or two birds, and it was the luck of the
draw whether the dog actually had a chance to
demonstrate his true capabilities. There were
very few blind retrieves, most being marking
tests. Dogs did not necessarily pinpoint the
marks, but were expected to mark the area,
and to hunt intelligently with perseverance and
bird-sense, following the track of a crippled
bird if necessary.

At this time, there was seldom any
'handling' (signals by the handler to the dog)
to direct the dog to a fallen bird. The dog was
expected to puzzle it out alone, and most

retrievers were very good in this natural facility. Dogs were often worked out of blinds, such as would be used in actual hunting of waterfowl.

FIRST CHAMPION

The first American Golden to earn the title of Field Trial Champion was Paul Bakewell's FT Ch. Rip, a big long-legged fellow with a white snip on his face. Rip was bred out of John K. Wallace's Ch. Speedwell Tango by Speedwell Reuben (both imported from England) in 1935. He was the last pup in the litter to be sold, for the magnificent sum of $35, but he blazed a trail for Goldens in retriever trial competition. In just three years of trials he earned 63 points (enough for six championships), and won the Country Life Trophy for Outstanding Retriever of the Year twice. His brilliant career was cut short at barely six years of age, when most retrievers are in their prime. He did leave a legacy in both field and show pedigrees, however: one of his grandsons was several times a Best in Show winner, and another was the first American Dual Champion.

TRAINERS

The wealthy Eastern retriever owners often imported, with the dogs, experienced British trainers to train and work the retrievers. In this way, such excellent dog men as Dave Elliott and James Cowie, among others, came to USA and were a great influence on retriever training. In the early years, as in Britain, dog trainers had the status of servants; however, it did not take long for the American spirit of democracy to greatly lessen such distinctions, and the trainers were seated at the same tables as the owners – particularly after they had demonstrated their worth in competition.

Dave Elliott was one of the first to utilize a whistle and hand signals to direct retrievers working at a distance. The technique was inspired by British shepherds' use of such signals in working their very clever sheepdogs. The ability to control the dog's work in such a way was at first scoffed at, but within a few years became not only accepted,

but expected. In later years, Dave Elliott expressed some regret at how this sort of handling came to dominate dog work at Retriever Trials. In the opinion of many, the dogs became little more than remote-controlled machines, following the handler's directions with no use of natural intelligence and bird-sense. Indeed, dogs who found the bird on their own, if they hunted too long or ignored the handler's whistle, were dropped from competition in favour of those who could be stopped 'on a dime' and sent in whichever direction the handler indicated.

POST-WAR TRIALS

During the post-war years, trials became more standardised. There were fewer tests such as the 'walk-up' which simulated two hunters, with their dogs at heel, flushing and shooting the birds; one dog 'honored', or stayed at heel, while the other retrieved. Though Puppy and Derby (dogs under two years) Stakes might still have single birds, double marks (two birds shot, then retrieved one at a time) and blinds (dog is sent to a 'planted' bird, an unseen fall) on both land and water were used. Distances increased. Trials were arranged so that all dogs would run the first 'series', as nearly as possible doing the identical test. After the first series, dogs still in competition were called back for the next test. Dogs would be dropped for serious errors, such as breaking (leaving the handler before the judge indicated), not finding the bird, showing hard-mouth or gun-shyness, refusing to enter water or wilfully disobeying the handler. As competition became stronger over the years, dogs would be eliminated for less serious errors. Having each dog run the same test and dropping the poorer ones made judging much easier, as it became largely an elimination contest. Unfortunately, it also meant that a dog who made a moderate error early on did not have any chance to make it up later in the day.

Marking ability also became extremely important. Dogs were required to mark, and remember accurately, each fall, usually two or three at a time, in order to complete the retrieves efficiently. Speed and style became important; two dogs might each work with equal skill and efficiency, but the one who displayed quickness and obvious zest and dash would invariably be placed ahead of the less brilliant one.

Included with handling ability is the ability to 'take a line', that is, to go away from the handler on the exact line indicated, and to stay on that line regardless of whatever obstacles or changes of terrain might be encountered. A good lining dog will enter any cover on land, or water, at any angle, going over or through anything in front of him until he reaches the fall, or until he is stopped by the handler's whistle. This talent is achieved only by careful training, as the dog's natural tendency would be to follow a shoreline, or to go from one land point to the next nearest the fall, since running on land is faster than swimming. However, the 'bank runner', or dog who detours around heavy going, often gets into difficulties by losing his mark or by encountering unexpected obstacles.

Alamo in field training, retrieving a plastic dummy from the water. Am. Can. Ch. Farm Fresh Apple Pie Ala Mode, CDX, MH, WCX, VCX, Can. CD, owned by Leslie Dickerson.

MODERN STAKES

By the 1970s, retriever training had advanced to the point where the Derby dogs were routinely doing work that Open dogs had been winning with 20 years earlier. There were more professional trainers, many of whom were apprenticed under such master trainers as Charles Morgan, Cotton Pershall and Billy Wunderlich, and had then gone on to set up their own training kennels. They trained many dogs as personal gundogs for hunters, but they showcased their talents at Field Trials with the best dogs brought to them by private owners. Many pros also worked with owner-trainers, those amateurs who truly enjoyed developing their own dogs and competing at trials. Competitors at trials also worked together in training, as it is impossible to train a trial dog single-handedly. In such ways, training techniques spread fairly rapidly.

Since the late 1930s amateur-handled stakes had been provided at trials (though often the dogs had been trained by professionals). These proved so popular and well supported that the title of Amateur Field Champion was

established, the first Golden achieving that award in 1952. The title of Field Trial Champion (later merely Field Champion) was earned by the dog winning a total of ten points at trials in the Open Stake. Points are awarded on the scale of five for first, three for second, one for third and half a point for fourth place. Judges' Awards of Merit (JAMs) are also awarded, at the discretion of the judges, to dogs who complete the trial satisfactorily but are not in the first four. The ten points required for FC must include a first at an all-breed retriever trial, open to all breeds of retriever (and Irish Water Spaniels, although it has been years since an IWS has competed). In order for championship points to be awarded, at least twelve qualified dogs must be in competition. A qualified dog is one who has placed or earned a JAM in a stake carrying championship points, or placed first or second in a Qualifying Stake. These dogs are often called 'three-star- dogs, and carry *** after the name. Dogs with lesser placements are entitled to two **s.

Am. Can. Ch. Heron Acres Sandcastle, Am. Can. UDTX***, WCX; Am. MH; GRCA VCX and Outstanding Dam; UKC UD and HR Ch; NAHRA MHR. Castle and Betty Drobac are shown with the Ch. Tonkahof Bang** Trophy which they won twice, for the show champion placing highest in the GRCA National Specialty Field Trial.

Robbee (Landican's Rite of Spring, Am. Can. CD, Am. WC) tenderly retrieves a mallard duck. The duck is carefully taped to hold the wings to the body; the Golden's soft mouth will not injure the bird at all.

Photo: Marilyn Hartman.

ABOVE: This 13-week old puppy knows exactly how to handle a full-grown mallard in field training. This is Farm Fresh Giddyap Go, owned by Leslie Dickerson of Colorado.

RIGHT: The Golden's "soft mouth" enables game to be carried without injury. Aureo Kyrie Touf Acto Follow, Am. Can. UD WC, Am. JH WCX delivers a duck to owner Neida Heusinkvelt.

The AFC (Amateur Field Champion), rather oddly, must earn 15 points in order to gain the title, but they may be earned in either the Amateur Stake, limited to dogs handled by bona-fide amateurs, or in the Open stake, if the dog is amateur-handled. So an amateur-handled dog placing in Open stake earns points towards both titles. Dogs competing in Open include those professionally trained and handled, and dogs who may have already completed their championships. The Open competition is intense, but it is often just as tight in the Amateur, as there are many extremely skilled and capable amateurs competing.

In North America, work on land and on water are given equal importance. The dog must get himself into the water unhesitatingly, since a dog with a stylish water entry and good swimming style and endurance is highly valued. Because of the size of the country and the different sorts of terrain and cover, retriever trials may be held in vastly disparate conditions. Weather may vary from dry desert heat to torrential rain to snowstorms and ice that must be broken as the dog swims. The well-travelled retriever might work in desert scrub and in 'water' that is "too thick to swim in and too thin to walk on"; grainfields, lakes, 'stick ponds'; hedgerows, pasturelands, woodlands, and rivers; and in parts of the South, lakes and swamps with alligators as an added difficulty!

WORKING CERTIFICATE TESTS

In 1964, the GRCA developed and established a basic field test for dogs to demonstrate that they possessed basic working attributes. Dogs were not expected to be highly-trained, but were expected to mark and retrieve a simple short double on land, and two single marks in water which were run 'back to back' in order to show that the dog did not hesitate to re-enter the water. Gun-shyness and hard-mouth were cause for failure. The dog may be held by the collar or a slip lead. Once the dog is sent for the retrieve, the handler must remain quiet and not assist the dog in any way. When the dog has picked up the bird, the handler

may call the dog in. The dog need not deliver to hand, but must deliver within a small area defined by the judges. The test was designed to demonstrate natural qualities rather than training, and should indicate that the dog has some inherent basic aptitude for field work. Dogs who pass this basic Working Certificate Test are entitled to carry the initials WC after their names in all GRCA records, although it is not an AKC title.

The Working Certificate Excellent test was added a few years later. The WCX title indicates that the dog has natural ability, plus the training to remain steady for a triple mark on land (including a shot live flyer) and a double mark on water; the dog must also honor the working dog by remaining at heel off lead during that dog's water test. The WCX dog must retrieve the triple and double marks without handling, and retrieve to hand. Again, the dog's natural aptitude is the primary focus.

In Canada the WC test was first held by the GRCC in 1971, and quickly adopted by other retriever clubs, and in the late 1980s the Canadian Kennel Club recognised the WC, WCI (Working Certificate Intermediate) and WCX titles officially. In Canada, the WC is two singles on land and two singles on water. The dog must retrieve to hand. WCI consists of a pair of double retrieves, land and water. The Canadian WCX is more complex than in the USA, and includes a walk-up and a blind retrieve. Standard Poodles are also entitled to run in retriever Working tests in Canada, as is the Nova Scotia Duck Tolling Retriever, a native Canadian breed.

In all Working Certificate tests the dog is marked either pass or fail. There is no scoring and no competition for placements, and the dog need pass just one complete test in order to achieve the title. It is a great way to introduce dogs (and handlers) to the basics of field work, as well as demonstrate that dogs who might otherwise have no opportunity in field work do indeed have the natural aptitudes we need to maintain in the breed. Some are primarily show dogs or pets, while some may be personal gundogs, but all have a

TOP LEFT: C-Vu's Barkentine, CD, MH, WCX, VC, owned and trained by Nancy Corbin. "Tina" won the class for bitches with a Hunting Retriever title at the 1995 GRCA National Specialty.

TOP RIGHT: Ritz exemplified the versatile Golden, willing to excel at whatever she was asked to do. Ch. Comstock Sunfire O'Hillcrest, UDT, MH, VCX, owned and trained by Kathy Eddy McCue DVM. Photo: Warren Cook.

place at Working tests. Quite a few who start here go on into Hunting Tests, and even Field Trials.

HUNTING TESTS

Hunting Tests were developed in answer to the sporting dog owners who, for years, had asked for a means of demonstrating and testing the qualities needed in a working gundog. Formal Field Trials were too intensely competitive and, many times, the tests were far from anything like a practical or true-to-life hunting situation. The North American Hunting Retriever Association (NAHRA) developed the first Hunting Tests, in co-operation with the AKC. Shortly thereafter NAHRA went its own way, and today holds its own tests, as do the AKC and UKC. All are non-competitive tests. They vary somewhat, but many retriever owners participate in, and enjoy, all of them.

There are three levels of tests: Junior, Senior and Master. The first AKC level is Junior, which is all single marked retrieves, at least four. Dogs may be held on line. Senior dogs must be steady; the tests include doubles on land and water, a simple blind, and a diversion bird. Master level dogs may be asked to do almost anything that might be encountered in

hunting, and dogs at this level are probably capable of work similar to that in a Qualifying stake. Canada has also implemented a Hunting Test Program which is very similar to the AKC's.

All the usual paraphernalia of hunting is used, including dark or camouflage clothing, decoys, duck/goose calls, blinds, etc. The handler is expected to carry a gun, although the official gunners will do the actual shooting. The dog may be asked to work from a boat or a dock, or any type of hunting situation. Part of the fun of the Hunting Tests is the ingenuity of the judges in planning interesting tests that do not require the intense and rigorous handling skills of field trial competition. Even those dogs who have achieved Master Hunter status can continue to participate in Hunting Tests, and, if they qualify enough times, they are eligible to enter the annual AKC Master National. This also is non-competitive, but all dogs who complete the tests at the Master National receive a special award, and their owners may be proud of having a dog who is a skilled retriever companion, useful in any sort of hunting situation.

TRAINING FOR THE FIELD

Prospective field workers receive the same basic or 'yard training' that is given to nearly all performance dogs: heel, sit, stay, and come when called. Many trainers start with the puppy as young as eight or nine weeks of age. Of course, this early training is done very gently and in a playful way, with no real corrections. It is important to encourage the dog's willingness and enjoyment, particularly in retrieving. At first the puppy is allowed to scamper after the training dummy as soon as it is thrown. 'Obedience' work is done in a positive way, often with food treats to encourage compliance. It is important never to overdo the work, though. Far better to have the puppy do a couple of nice sits, a few yards of heeling, and two or three happy retrieves, and stop while the pup is still eager. One or two short sessions daily is far better than a grim hour's drill once a week!

As the puppy grows, mild constraint is very gradually added; for instance, the pup is gently restrained until the bumper hits the ground. He must stay and mark the fall before being allowed to retrieve. He may be worked on a long line to insure prompt return and recall. Distances and difficulties, such as higher cover, are gradually increased.

Somewhere between seven months and a year, the young dog is ready for more serious training. He should have the basics well in mind and be under good control, but still eager to retrieve. Some trainers insist on more control than others; some like the fiery dog who is just 'on the edge'. Much also depends on the dog's own temperament, of course.

Most experienced field trainers insist that the young retriever be 'force trained' before getting into serious field work. Opinions and definitions of force training will vary from one person to another, but its proponents generally agree that it is a means of teaching the dog that he has no choice but to do as he is commanded, and that if he does so he can escape/avoid the unpleasant consequences of the 'force' being applied. The force used can vary from relatively mild pressure on the dog's collar to an ear pinch, or even to the use of the remote trainer or electronic collar. As in so many aspects of dog training, the question is not so much what, but how? We should be dealing not with the type of force used, but its application.

The subject of force training is covered in detail in several good American retriever training books, particularly Jim Spencer's. Since most types of physical force used are very easily misused, and can result in destroying the trust and rapport that one wishes to develop in the retriever companion, specific techniques will not be detailed here. An expert trainer can develop a happy, confident, reliable worker using force training, but without skilled guidance it is more likely to confuse or terrify the dog.

ELECTRONIC COLLARS

Another subject of much controversy is the use of the electronic collar. Properly used, the remote training device enables the handler to make the dog instantly aware of whether he is doing right or not. Improperly used, it can be an instrument of torture. One thing to keep in mind: it has been said that one does not teach the dog anything with the collar. The dog *must know the meaning of the commands* before the collar is ever used. The collar is only a means of enforcing commands. Using the collar on a dog who does not know the commands is completely wrong, because the dog does not understand why he is being corrected.

Unfortunately, because so many people simply do not understand the proper use of the electronic collar (and it is so very easy to misuse), the device too often carries with it a hazy picture of nasty people deliberately punishing the hapless dog. It is also possible to strangle a dog to death with an ordinary collar and lead, but, properly used, they are all useful training tools.

That said, it is also very true that many excellent retrievers have been developed without their ever having encountered an electronic collar. A clever trainer, with a thoughtful approach and positive reinforcement (praise, a few tidbits and the opportunity to be allowed to fulfil retriever instincts), can get results every bit as good as the 'techno-trainer', with much less chance of ruining a promising dog. The Golden's sensitivity, willingness and biddability make this dog an excellent candidate for positive training, and for handlers who prefer not to take the risk of severe techniques.

FURTHER TRAINING

Once the basics of training are well in hand, with the dog under control and believing that being allowed to retrieve is the very best thing there is, more advanced work is largely a matter of setting up various exercises and drills to extend the dog's experience. The dog is taught to go directly to the fall (where the bird, or training dummy has fallen), and return to the handler on the same line. Various obstacles are introduced, such as ditches, banks and changes of cover; the dog must go straight, regardless.

Whistle signals are taught early on; the whistle to sit is taught at first while working close at heel, so that the command can be enforced quickly. The "Come in" whistle is simply used whenever the dog is already coming to the handler. Later, the dog will stop and sit immediately on a single whistle blast, and come to the handler on a different whistle, usually a series of pips. (Clever handlers can carry on a virtual conversation with the dog using the whistle.)

'Patterns' are set up, with carefully placed dummies, so that the dog can build upon each successful experience, and develop reliance upon the handler's direction.

Handling is introduced. The dog is taught to take direction to the right, to the left, straight back away from the handler, or coming in toward the handler. At first this is done with dummies placed out in plain sight on bare ground to make the exercise as simple as possible. When the dog has learned to go in the direction indicated by the handler's signals, short cover is used so that the retrieves are not readily seen. All this experience is aimed at getting the dog to go as directed, whether or not he has seen a bird/dummy fall. Eventually, he will be going a hundred yards, or even two hundred, for unseen ('blind') retrieves.

Water work is done only after the dog is quite reliable on land. It is difficult for the dog to stop and take direction when swimming, and there are many more diversions and temptations to muddle up the training and confuse the dog. Also, once a dog is out in the water, the handler is at quite a disadvantage should the dog decide to go independent. Handlers have been known to take to the water themselves when an errant dog needed guidance or correction! Good, stylish water work is essential in American field trials.

A well-trained working field retriever is a breath-taking example of developing the dog's capabilities to the highest degree, and one of the ultimate examples of human/canine teamwork.

9 THE GOLDEN RETRIEVER AT WORK

When guide dog training was in its infancy, German Shepherd Dogs were the favoured breed. However, it was swiftly discovered that the Retriever breeds were supremely suited to this type of work. The Labrador Retriever proved to be the easiest breed to train, and its short coat, which is easy to care for, was an added advantage. However, the Golden Retriever has other assets which proved beneficial to many blind owners. The Golden Retriever, like the Labrador, is a suitable height for working in harness, it has the intelligence to respond to training without showing too much initiative, and it creates a good impression as it goes about its work. Added to this, the Golden Retriever is generally more sensitive in its approach to training, and although this can occasionally cause problems, the results are excellent when the right match is made between dog and owner.

As the demand for guide dogs has grown, the need to consistently produce dogs suitable for training has become paramount. A breeding programme was launched, and with skilful management, the best lines for each breed used were developed. Today the Guide Dogs for the Blind Association in the UK manages a breeding stock of some 250 dogs and raises 900 puppies each year. There is a total of 4,000 working guide dogs in the UK.

It is interesting to look at the success rates of the various breeds and cross-breeds that are used, as shown in the table at the foot of the page.

In the USA, the Seeing Eye also has its own breeding programme. As in the UK, German Shepherd Dogs were the first Seeing Eye Dogs, but in the 1970s the use of retriever breeds increased enormously. The breakdown of breeds used in successive years was:
Labrador Retrievers: 120
German Shepherd Dogs: 116
Golden Retrievers: 16.

The following year the figures were:
Labrador Retrievers: 136
German Shepherd Dogs: 92
Golden Retrievers:44.

The total success rate with dogs bred by The Seeing Eye is 65-70 per cent.

The high success rate among first crosses, which are the product of a mating of two pure,

BREED	SUCCESS RATE (percentage)	NUMBER IN SURVEY
Labrador Retriever	72	4640
Golden Retriever	73	1119
German Shepherd Dog	61	908
Border Collie	65	79
Lab/Golden Ret.	82	1927
Lab/Curly Coat Ret.	82	112
Golden Ret/Collie	79	96

The Golden Retriever is widely used as a guide dog, showing a willingness to work and sensitivity.

Photo courtesy: The Guide Dogs for the Blind Association.

but different, breeds was first noted when adult dogs were brought in through the approval system – dogs obtained from sources other than the Association's breeding programme. It was therefore decided to experiment with first crosses within the breeding programme. By crossing the Labrador Retriever with the Golden Retriever it was hoped to combine the best qualities of both breeds. The Golden Retriever's coat is slightly more difficult to care for, and it has been found that Goldens can become a little worried when working. This, coupled with a streak of stubbornness, which can even result in a refusal to work, makes the Golden a complex breed. Cross-breeding the Labrador Retriever with the Golden Retriever has proved enormously successful, producing dogs that combine the tolerance of the Labrador with some of the sensitivity of the Golden Retriever.

However, it was found that the success rate dropped when attempts were made to breed from two cross-breeds, i.e. a Lab/Golden crossed with a Lab/Golden, and so breeding is now restricted to first crosses.

The Association has found that the ideal dog should be –

* Stable
* Of a pleasing disposition
* Not neurotic, shy or frightened
* Reasonably energetic
* Not hyperactive
* Not aggressive (pure, apprehensive or protective)
* Of low chasing instinct
* Able to concentrate for long periods
* Not easily distracted
* Willing
* Confident with and tolerant of children
* Confident with and tolerant of other animals
* Responsive to the human voice
* Not sound-shy
* Able to show reasonable initiative
* Not too dominant or self-interested
* Able to change environment and/or handler without undue stress
* Within the limits of body sensitivity
* As free as possible from hereditary defects (physical).

In the USA, The Seeing Eye has recently started experimenting with German Shepherd Dog/Labrador Retriever crosses, but it is still too early to evaluate the results. Golden Retriever/Labrador crosses are also being used for Seeing Eye work but, again, it is too early to generalise about the success of this project.

THE TRAINING PROCESS
The puppy-walking scheme is an essential ingredient in producing successful guide dogs,

and both the Guide Dogs for the Blind Association and The Seeing Eye operate similar programmes. In the UK, puppies are taken from the litter at six weeks of age to be placed in a family home. In the USA, the Puppy Raising Program waits until the pups are eight weeks before they are placed in homes. The aim is for the puppy to grow up in a normal family environment and to become thoroughly socialised, encountering a variety of different situations. The puppy must get used to traffic of all kinds, and learn to walk slightly ahead, ignoring all distractions. Basic obedience exercises are also taught at this stage. The puppies are supervised throughout the time they are at walk, and then they are assessed for further training.

In the UK, the dogs are brought in for training when they are around twelve months of age, while The Seeing Eye prefers to wait until dogs are 16 months old. Both dogs and bitches accepted for guide dog training are neutered. With bitches, this is done after their first season (about 14 months) to ensure physical and mental maturity. Males are neutered at around twelve months, before the onset of dominant characteristics.

Training at one of the GDBA centres in the UK usually takes around seven months. The Seeing Eye training course takes around four months. As with all forms of dog training, the work is based on basic obedience and response to commands. The training programme consists of developing a dog's concentration, along with a willingness to work for a handler. The dog is exposed to a wide range of environmental conditions, with particular emphasis on the conditions it would meet as a working guide dog, whether in a busy city or in a rural environment. The dog must learn to walk at an acceptable pace for a blind owner, in a straight line down the centre of the pavement, stopping at down kerbs. The dog is taught to avoid obstacles on the pavement, including other pedestrians, and to negotiate obstacles that block the whole pavement, returning to the pavement once the problem is by-passed.

Training in traffic is a crucial aspect of the programme. The dog is trained to develop a 'critical' area. If a vehicle comes inside the critical area, the dog would disobey a command to proceed. The critical area varies in size depending on the speed of the approaching vehicle, i.e. the faster the vehicle, the greater the critical area, and the earlier the dog should make the decision to disobey any command to proceed.

The dog would also be trained to work under all environmental circumstances, such as public transport, car travel, supermarkets, shops, locating road-crossings, finding doors, going in lifts, etc.

THE PARTNERSHIP
Blind students are individually assessed to find the right dog to suit each individual. Golden Retrievers have been found to be among the most adaptable, suiting a wide variety of differing needs and circumstances.

In the first instance, the breed of dog is chosen and this is often influenced by physical circumstances, such as the age and height of the student, as well as any other physical disability they may have. The lifestyle of the student is taken into consideration, taking account of the family situation and the work environment. The personality of each student is also evaluated, with the aim of finding a dog with the most suitable temperament. For example, some students would work better with a more sensitive dog, while others would get on better with a more tolerant, laid-back animal.

Training with the student takes four weeks on a residential course, but this can depend on the aptitude and understanding of the owner and the dog's acceptance of its change of circumstances. The new blind owner experiences the same circumstances as a dog in training, but in a more condensed form. A gradual build-up from quiet to busy city conditions will take place during the training period. The owner is given instruction on training methods and understanding dog psychology, as well as practical advice on feeding, grooming and general care of the dog.

After the course has been completed, the

new blind owners are visited in their homes to check that the dog is working successfully in its new environment. These visits may vary depending on individual needs, and, if necessary, the dog and owner will undergo a further week of residential training. Thereafter, guide dog owners are visited on a six-monthly basis, but more frequents visits are made if necessary.

ANN AND SOPHIE – A WORKING FRIENDSHIP

Ann Fletcher, married with adult twin daughters, had never owned a dog before she got her guide dog, and she met with some opposition from her family when she first expressed an interest in having a dog.

"Since I lost my sight I have always used a long cane. I can quite honestly say that the cane was my right hand. I was happy using it, and it gave me a reasonable degree of independence. I think my family found it difficult to see how I would benefit from having a guide dog."

There was an additional problem for Ann. Her daughter, Rachel, had been knocked over by a Bulldog when she was a toddler, and due to the incident had developed a profound fear of dogs.

"We discussed things over a long period of time, and at last we decided that I should give it a go. I was assessed for suitability, and I thought I might have to wait as long as two years before a dog was available. But within six months they contacted me and told me they had a dog that might be suitable."

Sophie, a rich-coloured Golden Retriever, was brought down to Ann's home for an initial visit to assess compatibility.

"She explored the house and then we had a short walk, but I did not really get to know her," said Ann. "When I got to the centre I was very nervous about the course, and I did not know how things were going to work out."

For the guide dog, one of the most difficult problems to cope with is the constant changes of allegiance during the training period. To begin with, the dog responds to the puppy-

walker. When advanced training begins, the instructor becomes the focal person in the dog's life. Then, finally, the dog is matched with a student, and must learn to respond to its new owner. At the training course, the students are given a couple of days to settle in, and then the instructor brings each dog to the student's room and training begins.

"I have to admit it was love at first sight," said Ann. "Sophie is such a beautiful dog that no one could resist her. She came right up to me with her tail wagging. She seemed to settle straightaway. Right from the first morning, she heard my alarm clock go off and she would come up to the side of the bed to say hello. She has a very gentle disposition and is very responsive."

The students take over full responsibility for their dogs within a couple of days, and this obviously helps to form a bond. They feed and groom their dogs, and are responsible for taking them out to the grass runs.

"Because I had never owned a dog before I was really worried about looking after her," said Ann. "I had never even groomed a dog before. But Sophie is so easy-going she makes things easy for you. When I put on her harness, she comes and puts her head forward; it is as if she is trying to help me."

The training course becomes increasingly complex as the students gain confidence working with their dogs. To begin with, they go on short walks in fairly quiet areas, graduating to going into the city centre, going on a bus and a train, negotiating an obstacle course, and going on a night walk. The student must learn to give the correct commands so that the dog is given clear directions in a logical sequence. This is particularly important when negotiating complicated obstacles, where the dog may have to guide his owner off the kerb, around the obstacle and then back on to the kerb again. The dog also has to assess the height of the obstacle so that there is sufficient room for his owner to pass beneath. Ann found the training course very demanding and was surprised at how tiring she found it.

"The hardest thing for me was learning the

Ann Fletcher with Sophie, the dog who has changed her life.

Photo courtesy: Guide Dogs for the Blind Association.

commands to give, and then giving them in the right order. Although I was used to negotiating kerbs and obstacles with the long cane, I found it completely different working with a dog. I had to think in a new way and try to anticipate how Sophie was going to react. To begin with, I think I got her thoroughly confused but, with practice, I am getting better."

Ann had to give up her work in a hospital as her eyesight deteriorated, but she still lives a busy, active life.

"I go shopping and I go to the library to get talking books for the blind. I have lots of friends whom I would have liked to visit, but, because of the problems of travelling, I always found an excuse not to go. With a guide dog, I will have the incentive to go out more often, and that will make my life far fuller. My daughters and my husband go to work, so she will also be company for me."

Even in the early stages of their partnership, Sophie and Ann seem to have formed a real bond.

"I talk to her all the time," said Ann. "Even though I have only just started working with her, I cannot imagine life without her."

A couple of weeks into the training course, Ann's family came to visit her at the centre and to meet Sophie for the first time.

"Sophie went up to my husband, David, and made a big fuss of him," said Ann. "Then she went up to my daughter, Samantha, and made a fuss of her. Finally she went up to Rachel, who is terrified of dogs. Immediately Rachel started to panic, shouting at me to get Sophie away. But Sophie did not take any notice. She was very calm and very gentle, but it was clear that she would not go away until Rachel had made a fuss of her. Slowly, Rachel calmed down and the next thing I knew she was stroking Sophie. I could not believe it. In a matter of minutes, Sophie had succeeded in doing something that no human – or dog – had ever managed to do. Rachel's boyfriend has a dog, and she had never allowed that dog to go near her. But Sophie managed to show her that there was nothing to fear."

There is another reason why this transformation in Rachel's attitude meant so much to her mother.

"Both my daughters have the same eye condition as me. At the moment, they both have their full sight, but this will certainly diminish. If Rachel loses her sight altogether, I wanted her to have the opportunity of having a guide dog. That could never have happened without Sophie."

Ann is now looking forward to living a fuller, more independent life with her guide dog.

"If I only knew what a comfort Sophie was going to be to me, I would never have waited so long before getting a guide dog," she said.

ASSISTANCE DOGS

Perhaps one of the Golden's most unique adaptations is as an Assistance Dog. Assistance dog organisations train dogs to help people with physical disabilities other than blindness. Schemes to train dogs to alert people with hearing loss started in the USA, and by 1980 several programmes were operating, such as the American Humane Association in Colorado. As a result of close co-operation, Hearing Dogs for the Deaf was started in the UK. Hearing Dogs are generally of mixed breed and selected from animal shelters. They are trained to make physical contact with a paw to alert their deaf owners, and then lead them to the source of the sound such as a doorbell, telephone, smoke alarm – or even to tell a deaf mother when her baby is crying. Again, the Golden Retriever's willing and steady temperament has been ideally suited to this work.

In the UK, Dogs for the Disabled is becoming a growing force, working in close co-operation with the Guide Dogs for the Blind Association. Many of the dogs used are those who have been rejected from the guide dog training programme. This is usually due to a particular problem that makes them unsuitable for guiding work in stressful traffic situations, but such dogs, many of them Golden Retrievers, can happily adapt to working in a different situation.

Working partners: Cal and his assistance dog Sherlock. Sherlock earned CD and WC titles before becoming a service dog.

Photo: Cindy Beare.

THERAPY DOGS
RECOGNISING THE NEED

Early in 1974, B.M. Levinson, a professor of psychology from New York, bravely presented a paper at a symposium held in London. In it, he attempted to forecast how life would be by the year 2,000. Twenty-two years on and just short of the turn of the century, it is interesting to check his forecasts. Over-fanciful in some respects, the professor nevertheless clearly spotted the trend. He predicted that man will become aware of the importance of companion animals as a source of mental health and stability in increasingly strained and unhappy family relationships. He foresaw an animal-lending service on prescription for sick and disabled people, charged for with appropriate bills.

With no knowledge of this, but greatly influenced by an international conference on the bond between people and animals held in Philadelphia in 1981, the Pets As Therapy charity was started in England in 1983. This programme offers animals, mostly dogs, who have all been carefully tested for good temperament. The animals and their owners regularly visit hospices, hospitals and homes for children and elderly people. Golden Retrievers figure high on the list for suitability as therapy dogs, because of their friendly personalities and willingness to please. All dog owners are welcome to submit their dog for temperament testing with a view to selection as therapy dogs, but more Goldens are successful than any other breed. The mature, older dog is ideal for visiting and is very popular with people of all ages.

In the USA, pioneering work was started in 1980, by the American Humane Association, on the first bibliography of Pets Facilitated Therapy to assist societies with an interest in this new field. Subsequently, a Pet Partners programme was started by the Delta Society which has now spread to 45 states and has nearly 2,000 Pet Partner teams. Michael McCulloch of Oregon State and Sam Corson of Ohio State were just two of the early and influential exponents of the benefits which animals can bring to lonely and depressed

Kyrie Wisperwind Willoughby CD has worked as a therapy dog in Michigan for many years.
Photo courtesy: Marcia Schlehr.

people. Back in England, Pets As Therapy got off to a sticky start, with plenty of kindly dog-and-owner teams but no takers. The organisation had much work to do in raising the acceptability of dogs in such an environment, and in changing the perception of dogs as a danger to human health. Medical consultants agreed that the risk to patients was far greater from the humans accompanying the dog than from the dog itself. But after several years, the tide started to turn. The charity, which provides the visiting scheme free of charge thanks to willing dog owners, now has 9,000 friendly PAT Dogs registered. It has a considerable grateful following among many thousands of people who seriously miss contact with animals in their lives.

THERAPY IN ACTION

Hilda had not spoken an intelligible word to anyone for more than a year. But you could tell she was cross, and very unhappy. Hilda was distressed with a world which had shut her up in a care unit, away from her rather scruffy but familiar home of so many years,

133

and the dog and chickens she had loved. No one visited Hilda. If they had, they would either have been ignored or rebuffed. She would sit for hours muttering angrily or rocking backwards and forwards, her bony body hunched up, seeking solace and comfort. Hilda was a prisoner in a society which thought it knew better than Hilda herself what was good for her.

But then PAT Dogs were invited to the home. Hilda was sitting in her usual chair when a friendly, gentle PAT Golden Retriever bounced happily into the room. Residents looked interested at once and their faces lit up with pleasure. A lot of patting began. Suddenly the blank, unseeing expression seemed to melt away from Hilda's face. "I had a dog like that once," she said slowly and distinctly. "That is the first time I have ever been able to hear and understand what Hilda said," remarked a member of the nursing staff in amazement. "It is a little miracle."

The little miracle continued to work on Hilda as the visits progressed each week. Hilda talked to the dog, though she still ignored the kindly PAT Dog owner. But as she stroked and cuddled the Golden, everyone could see the therapy working. Hilda learned to become a person again through the animal contact which she had missed more than anyone had recognised.

A different kind of help was provided by a PAT Dog visiting a fretful three-year-old girl waiting for an operation in a Suffolk hospital. Nurses were having a difficult time in getting her to accept her treatment, but when the visiting PAT Dog was allowed on to the cot, the child's face changed to pure delight and she accepted injections calmly as she cuddled the dog.

There is also a demand for therapy dogs who can help both children and adults to overcome a phobia or fear of dogs. Golden Retrievers are particularly well-suited to this task, as their calm and gentle temperament poses no threat. Important work is now being carried out at many clinics with therapy dogs helping to desensitize people and reduce their terror.

AWARD-WINNING DOGS

Our understanding of the many ways in which dogs provide assistance and therapy for humans is growing all the time. There is no other animal so responsive, willing and able to please. To celebrate this, the British charity, PRO Dogs, rewards dogs who have given particular service to their owners or to the community. Golden Retrievers have featured twice in the awards, and nominations are regularly received for consideration for this breed.

Golden Retriever Tansy received the Pet of the Year medal in 1979 for being a canine blood donor and saving the life of a West Highland White Terrier. This was before an organised scheme of blood donor dogs was available. The Westie had suffered a haemorrhage following surgery. A supply of blood was taken from Tansy's leg, although it is now commonly taken from the neck. The purpose of the award was partly to give publicity to the need for contributions of this kind in an emergency, and Tansy proved not only a patient and gentle contributor, but also a very beautiful and photogenic candidate for the press photographers.

Another PRO Dog of the Year Gold Medal award for the Pet of the Year was given to the popular Golden Retriever, Goldie, from the BBC children's television programme *Blue Peter*. She was nominated by large numbers of children, typified by nine-year-old Jessica McConnell who wanted her to win "for all the children who have not got a dog, because she is our dog to share."

10 BREEDING GOLDEN RETRIEVERS

Breeding is a great responsibility, not only to the breed and to those who purchase your stock, but also to your reputation. The bitch you breed from must be of good quality, free from hereditary defects, and have the true Golden Retriever temperament. If your bitch is not good enough to be your foundation bitch, then it is better to start with a puppy from a kennel whose stock you admire. It is a good idea to go to several shows, so as to see as many different dogs as you can. When you have decided what you want, book a puppy as soon as possible, as most successful breeders have a waiting list. Sometimes it is possible to buy an older bitch, but not very often in Goldens.

If it is working Goldens you want to breed, then the shows will not help you, so try to attend some Field Trials or Working Tests, or go to someone who is well-known for breeding good working dogs. The same rule applies as to temperament and freedom from hereditary defects, but working ability takes precedence over looks.

Before breeding a litter, your bitch should have her eyes tested and her hips X-rayed and scored under the appropriate national scheme. Eyes must be tested for hereditary cataract and progressive retinal atrophy (See Chapter Sixteen: Breed Associated Diseases.)

A good brood bitch puts her stamp on her progeny. In front is Belvedere's Kyrie Angel, JH, Am. Can. CD WC. Sitting, her three JH titled offspring, Gale, Indy and Misha, bred by Mercedes Hitchcock and Marcia Schlehr.

Photo: M. Hitchcock.

Litter sisters: Ch. Westley Mabella and Ch. Westley Martha.
The Westley kennel is famous worldwide for producing top-quality dogs, sound in mind and
body. *Photo: Sally Ann Thompson.*

Am. Can. Ch. Hunt's Amberwood Yardley had a successful show career that included a Canadian National Specialty win and an American Group 1st, but her crowning achievement was as the dam of nine American show champions. Owned by Robin Donahey. Sired by Ch. Shargleam Ferryman, an English-bred import.

BREEDING TO TYPE AND LINE BREEDING

If your bitch is the type you like and wish to keep, choose a stud dog of the same type who carries a similar blood line. This is line breeding and is the way to fix the characteristics you want. It is not, of course, as simple as it sounds. No dog is perfect, so there will be faults as well as virtues. You must try not to double on a fault. For instance, if your bitch is straight in stifle, choose a dog with good hind angulation, or if she is weak in head, choose a stud dog with a correct head.

Do not make the mistake of using a dog with an overdone head in the hope the puppies' heads will be somewhere in between the two. Breeding does not work that way. Try to use a dog who not only has a good head himself, but who consistently sires the same sort of head. I have used the head as an example, but the same applies to any other point you wish to improve.

Successful line breeding does not mean just having several of the same dogs on both sides of the pedigree. You must line breed to a really good, sound dog, or dogs, or to a combination that has produced good offspring. We try to breed to a dog and bitch, who, when mated together, produced six title holders (three Champions and three Show Champions). If a mating is successful and the resulting offspring are good and sound and the type you want, then it is a good idea to repeat it, but do not be surprised if the litter is not as successful the second time, as this happens occasionally. If it happens to you, try another dog the next time. If, however, the second litter is as successful as the first, there is no point in changing the sire unless you want to introduce some fresh blood into your lines.

OUTCROSSING

Every so often, an outcross mating is a good idea. Outcrossing is when you use a dog of different lines to your own, preferably one who is good in the points in which your bitch is not. The offspring of this mating can then go back to a dog of your own line.

So far, I have assumed that your bitch is of the type you like and want to keep. If that is not the case, but you have good reasons for wanting a puppy from her, then outcrossing is the answer. This happened to me in my early days of breeding. Simon, my first Golden, was the apple of my eye and was exactly the type I liked. He had a beautiful head and good conformation, but was too big. Of course, I wanted a son of his, but he was born in 1936 and during the war I did not do any breeding as, naturally, I was otherwise occupied.

When Simon was ten, he sired a litter of ten bitches and one dog. I had the dog, but he was not any good and not in the least like Simon, so I let him go and was fortunate enough to buy one of the bitches. She was nice, but not really what I wanted. Simon had a completely outcross pedigree, so did not reproduce his own type. There were none of his lines anywhere, so I used a dog of different lines but who was himself closely line-bred and of a type I admired. That worked well, producing two Champions, and the next time use of that dog's son resulted in another Champion and a CC winner. The point of this story is to emphasize that, if you want to change your type to that of the stud dog you use, it is wise to choose one who is line-bred and reproduces his own type – in other words, a dominant sire.

Many years later, we used a very good Champion dog of a different type and entirely different bloodlines. We did not want to change our type, but we liked this dog very much, so we decided to try him with our bitch. The resulting litter was disappointing, though the puppies were very sound and had lovely temperaments. An outcross mating is usually a gamble, but one worth taking sometimes.

It is important to establish a good bitch line, one that consistently produces puppies with good temperaments, type, soundness and freedom from hereditary defects. Unfortunately, these defects sometimes appear after generations of clear dogs. If that happens, you would obviously not repeat that mating.

IN-BREEDING

This is the mating together of very close relations, such as father to daughter, mother to son, half-brother and sister, or even brother and sister. *This should only be undertaken by very experienced breeders, who know what is behind the dogs concerned.* The dogs must be sound in every respect, and of really good temperament. The kind and friendly nature of Goldens should be of prime importance to you, as well as soundness and freedom from hereditary defects.

BREEDING WORKERS

In working dogs, the same principles apply as to line breeding, in-breeding and outcrossing. You are looking for the same temperament and soundness, but you usually have to sacrifice looks for working ability. This does not mean that working dogs are not nice-looking, but they usually lack the points necessary for success in the show ring, and are also more lightly built. It is exciting to watch a really stylish Golden working and, contrary to a widely held belief (by people who have never owned them), they make equally delightful companions and house dogs as do show dogs.

Temperament is very important. Workers have to mix with other dogs on shoots and at trials. We sometimes have ten Goldens (not all belonging to us) together in the back of a vehicle, which would be impossible with bad-tempered dogs.

DUAL-PURPOSE

Dual-purpose dogs are those that win at both shows and Field Trials. When I first started they were not uncommon, and several of us had trial awards with our Champions. There were three post-war dual champions – that is Champion and Field Trial Champion. The last

Good temperament is essential in the working dog.

Photo: Graham Cox.

was one I bred in 1951, and in 1956 he became an International Dual Champion (Dual Champion both in this country and Ireland). Since then, a few Goldens have been near to attaining the dual title but never quite achieved it.

Unfortunately, as in most gundog breeds, the split between show and working Goldens became wider and wider. There are a few people valiantly trying to keep the dual-purpose flag flying, but with rare exceptions they do not win anything at shows except in field trial classes (which are confined to dogs with trial awards) and usually minor awards at field trials. It is sad that this situation has arisen, but I am afraid that we gave up the struggle years ago and now have two separate lines, one for show and the other for work. I would not want to discourage anyone aiming to breed dual-purpose Goldens, but only warn them that it is very difficult to reach the top in either sphere, though it is possible. Three champions gained Field Trial awards in the 1980s, including a bitch of all-working lines who had gained many field trial awards. So far, there is just one in the 90s.

STUD DOGS

Owning a stud dog carries a great responsibility. No dog should be used without a clear eye certificate and hips X-rayed and scored, which cannot be done until after twelve months of age in the UK and 24 months for permanent US certification. You

Am. Can. Ch., Can. OTCh. Ciadar Tintinabulation, UDT, WC, VCX, still wet from a field training session. "Jingle" was an outstanding sire, producing both show and obedience winners with good working aptitude. Bred and owned by Pam Ruddick.

must also make sure that any bitch mated to him has an up-to-date eye certificate and a hip score which is acceptable. It is also advisable for the bitch to have a swab taken as soon as she comes into season, to make sure she has no infection, and also to test your dog periodically. Both dogs and bitches can have a local infection, which will not make them ill, but will prevent them having puppies. A course of antibiotics will nearly always put things right. Make sure you have your own bitch swabbed before mating.

I have often been asked how often I use a stud dog, but it is impossible to give an exact answer. Usually several bitches will come into season over a short period of time and your dog will be very busy! Then there will be a break, with no bitches coming to be mated. It is not advisable to use a young dog too frequently, and, with a working dog, it is better to wait until he is trained before allowing him to mate a bitch. An older dog will usually be able to cope with as many bitches as will be brought to him, providing he is fit, healthy and not too fat.

THE RIGHT AGE FOR A LITTER

The Kennel Club will not register puppies from a bitch over eight years old, but allows a bitch to have six litters. I consider that is too many, and, as far as I am concerned, the maximum is four. We usually have three from our bitches, providing they whelp easily and there is no trouble. Sometimes we only have two litters and, on the one occasion when our bitch had primary inertia and needed a Caesarean, we had just the one. It was unfortunate that we could not breed from her again, as her only daughter became Ch. Westley Victoria, who was dam of eight title holders in this country (which is a breed record), as well as an Irish, a Canadian and an American Champion.

The ideal age for a bitch to have a first litter is probably between two and three years old, though, providing she is strong and healthy and in good condition, it can be later than that. I have known bitches have first litters at five,

or even six years old, without any trouble, but earlier than that is preferable. Never let your bitch get too fat at any age.

There should be at least one year between litters, and preferably more than that. We often leave it for two years. Although bitches invariably enjoy their puppies and are devoted to them, they need plenty of time before the next litter to live their normal life.

CARE OF YOUR BITCH

Do not make the mistake of giving your bitch extra food immediately she is mated. For the first five weeks, give her the same amount she usually has and then increase it by a very small amount and change to a complete food, manufactured especially for in-whelp and nursing bitches. If you feed meat and biscuit, add a vitamin-mineral supplement, but do not add anything extra to a complete food. When you are sure your bitch is in whelp you can increase her food a little more, but not by too much. It is after whelping, when she is nursing her litter, that she needs about three times her normal amount. For the last two weeks it is advisable to divide her food into three separate meals.

Exercise should be normal, including swimming, but not jumping. Naturally, in the later stages of pregnancy, your bitch should not be taken for long walks but rather have plenty of gentle exercise, preferably somewhere she can wander about at her own pace. Many bitches will decide for themselves how much exercise they need!

Opinions vary as to the best time to worm a bitch and to give booster vaccinations, so it is best to consult your veterinary surgeon about the matter.

Your aim should be to breed quality and not quantity. Try to establish a good sound bitch line, which is the strength of any kennel and which, eventually, becomes recognisable. Always love and care for your bitch, and never treat her as a breeding machine. Although there will be disappointments and some heartbreaks, you will find breeding a rewarding and enjoyable hobby.

11 MATING, WHELPING AND REARING

Having taken into account cost (to cover stud fee, veterinary bills, feeding, bedding, heating and advertising), space (not only to accommodate the whelping box, but also suitably safe indoor and outdoor play/exercise areas for a growing litter), time (an unlimited amount is necessary), and, most importantly, the need for a responsible, caring attitude towards the breed, the bitch, any resulting puppies and their new owners, you have made the decision to breed a litter. How do you proceed?

CONTACTING THE STUD DOG OWNER
The owner of the chosen stud dog should be approached well in advance for permission to use the dog, and will need to see your bitch's pedigree, hip and eye status information. He or she may ask to see the bitch to assess her suitability for that particular dog (and vice versa, of course) before giving approval. If the answer is positive, all that needs to be done is to ensure that her booster vaccinations are up to date and to administer a suitable worming preparation to ensure that she is free from internal parasites. I usually worm again in the first few days of the bitch's season, but prefer not to do so during pregnancy.

THE IN-SEASON BITCH
Watch carefully for the onset of the bitch's oestrus cycle (period of heat, or season), which is indicated by the swelling of the vulva and a bloodstained vaginal discharge. Some bitches give considerable warning that they are about to come into season, exhibiting the urge to cover (almost like a male) by urinating on any doggy scents they discover on the ground when out for a walk. Bitches are usually extremely attractive to males at this pre-season stage, but the feeling is not reciprocated.

The first show of blood is generally counted as day one, so it is important not to miss this. Dabbing the bitch's vulva each morning with a white piece of tissue or cotton wool before she goes out will help establish the start. Contact the owner of the stud dog so that preliminary arrangements can be made. Of course, you will not know at this stage on which day she will be ready for mating. The season generally lasts about 21 days, and she must be kept well away from unwanted suitors for the whole period. The majority of Goldens ovulate and are ready to mate somewhere between days ten and fifteen, although there are exceptions – I have known bitches conceive from matings as early as day six, and as late as day 20. The time bitches ovulate often runs in families, but not always, my Ch. Sansue Royal Fancy being a case in point. On two separate occasions, I mated her on the thirteenth day, using a different well-known stud each time. Both were perfectly good matings, but neither proved fruitful. Her sisters, Ch. Sansue Royal Flair and Sh. Ch. Sansue Spring Mist of Ramblyne, and their dam Rossbourne Party Piece of Sansue, all conceived to thirteenth day matings, but using the familial pattern as a guide did not work for Fancy. However, she subsequently produced two litters, to matings on the eighth and tenth days.

It is essential that your bitch is in top physical condition before planning a mating.

Sometimes the discharge is rather sparse at the beginning and somewhat intermittent, even perhaps drying up completely for a few days and then restarting (in which case count from the new start), so it is important to check the bitch daily. Otherwise any calculations as to the correct day could be way out. The chief reason for bitches missing is mating them on the wrong day, but there are several pointers to help you determine the best time: a) the red discharge has usually changed to a paler pink or straw colour; b) the vulva and area above it will feel much softer and puffier than at the start of her season; c) she will indicate her feelings by twitching her tail to one side when touched or groomed around the rear end. If she has the company of other bitches, she will often indulge in enthusiastic sexual play, mounting them and encouraging them to mount her in return, by standing stiffly with her rear end pushed towards them with her tail turned as described above. If you are still unable to ascertain the right time, your vet can help to pinpoint ovulation by means of a cytology test, or a pre-mate blood test. I have found the latter method (although it can prove expensive as more than one test may be required) to be quite reliably accurate. I therefore advise this if there is any uncertainty, or if the bitch has missed to previous matings.

CHECKING FOR INFECTION
Another reason for infertility is infection, so it is wise to have your vet take a vaginal swab to check for this, especially if the bitch has had irregular seasons, a patchy start to the current season, has missed previously or even given birth in the past. This swab is best taken on days two or three of the season, which should give ample time to treat the bitch with a correctly prescribed antibiotic, should the test prove positive. Some breeders dose their bitches with antibiotics each season as a preventative measure against infection. I consider this most unwise, as it is possible for an immunity against the drug to be developed, causing problems if any future treatment becomes necessary.

VISITING THE STUD DOG

Having determined that your bitch is 'ready', make final arrangements for your visit to the stud. On arrival, allow her to stretch her legs and relieve herself so that she is completely comfortable, before introducing her to the dog. An experienced stud will know his job and just be eager to get on with it, preferring to skip the courtship stage. This might be satisfactory from the handler's point of view, but can be off-putting to the bitch, especially if she is a maiden and not entirely sure of his intentions.

Patience is not only a virtue – I consider it to be an essential ingredient in the handling of mating dogs. They must not be rushed just for the handlers' convenience. Always allow the dogs to meet outdoors first, with both animals restrained on leashes, before taking them to the place where the deed is to be done. Tearing round a paddock or large garden with a keen stud in full pursuit may frighten the bitch, exhaust the stud unnecessarily and, when the dog mounts, mean that the handlers are too far away to give any assistance that might be needed. Ideally, therefore, a confined area such as a good-sized garage or dog run should be provided, with enough space to enable the two to flirt and move around easily, without getting too far out of the handlers' reach.

COURTSHIP PHASE

If the bitch is responsive to the dog's advances, she will indicate this by pinning her ears back and swishing her tail, adopting the pose described earlier. Let her off the leash to enable her to examine the male, and her surroundings, without feeling under pressure. Some bitches (and I have to admit most of mine fall into this category) go wild, dashing madly about and flirting with the stud dog. Some are aloof, yet prepared to stand and think of England, while others are noticeably afraid and want to hide behind their owners, totally against the assignation even to the point of growling or snapping. This type often say Yes with their rear end, and No with the biting end! Usually, a little more time and encouragement will see a change of heart.

If no amount of cajoling from the dog and entreaties by her owner will make her see reason, and providing it has been ascertained she is absolutely ready, a bandage or tape can be wound round her muzzle, crossed underneath her chin and tied behind the ears. This prevents the stud dog being bitten and gives the owner something to hold on to, but should only be practised as a last resort. The binding should be removed as soon as the tie is effected, not left on for the duration. If the bitch is scared, it is likely that her vaginal secretions will have dried up temporarily, making penetration more difficult. A good dollop of Vaseline should remedy this.

THE MATING

Once the bitch is settled after the initial courtship, no matter how willing she seems, she should be held gently at the head by her owner. The handler of the stud dog should support the bitch at the rear end with a hand under her hindquarters, to prevent any sitting down or pulling away at the last moment. A non-slip mat for the animals to stand on will help to avoid the dog's hind feet slipping when he mounts the bitch, which he will do quickly when given the chance. If there is a height difference, it may be necessary to adjust by raising or lowering the bitch's hindquarters accordingly, depending on whether he is working too high or too low. Sloping ground, or several rugs or blankets, suitably placed, will help. Some dogs are very efficient and instantly get themselves into the right position for the union, whatever the shape or size of the bitch. Others are slower and fiddle around, climbing on and off a number of times before making any real effort, and will almost always need assistance. The handler can help guide the dog into position by placing two fingers under, and extending from, the vulva.

When the dog connects successfully, he will quickly thrust, penetrate and ejaculate into the bitch. A bulb of erectile tissue at the root of his extended penis will be gripped inside the bitch by her strong vaginal muscle, and the two will be 'tied' together for a period of between ten and 30 minutes, on average. The dog will climb down from the bitch and stand, either by her side or turned back to back with her. Unless they demonstrate a natural instinct to turn, I do not encourage my studs to assume this position, as I find it so much easier to hold on to them in the side-by-side stance.

No effort should be made to break the tie since the two will come apart naturally. The length of the the tie is said to be governed by the bitch. However, this must depend on the individual dog. My Ch. Sansue Golden Ruler used to tie for 20-60 minutes until the age of nine years, when one of his testicles was removed due to a tumour. A year later he was fertile again, but only tied between 10 and 20 minutes thereafter. His sire, Ch. Gaineda Consolidator of Sansue, never tied for longer than 20 minutes, and was usually away in 10!

As the two come apart, I usually up-end the bitch (wheelbarrow style) briefly, to prevent the rapid expulsion of seminal fluid, although this is probably totally unnecessary if the tie has been of normal duration. It is more important if a tie has not been effected and the dog comes away fully-extended, in which case hold the bitch in this position until the dog subsides. Of course, under these circumstances, a second mating should always be attempted.

AFTER THE MATING
Do not give the bitch the opportunity to relieve herself after the mating. Put her quickly back in the car or take her indoors, offer her a drink, and allow her to rest quietly for at least half an hour before setting off for home. The stud dog should be allowed to clean himself up naturally before being taken back to his living quarters for a nap. My males live together in the house and, after one of them has mated a bitch, he can return to the others without a problem. I have never found it necessary to wipe studs down with disinfectant to prevent attention from other males, as some breeders do. Perhaps 'kennel' dogs are rather more territorial. If in doubt, it would probably be wise to take this

precaution, or at least to watch them carefully.

The handlers can now relax with a welcome cup of tea or coffee, and exchange pedigrees and copies of hip and eye status papers. A Kennel Club form (for registering the litter) is then signed and the fee is paid. Bear in mind that the stud fee is generally paid for the service, not the result. Most stud dog owners offer a free return service in the unlikely event of the bitch missing, so it is wise to establish this and any other terms of agreement before mating takes place.

If the day is correct and the dogs tie, then one service is usually sufficient. However, if you are in any doubt, then it is advisable to mate a second time within an interval of no more than 48 hours.

CONFIRMATION OF PREGNANCY
The period of gestation (fertilisation to whelping) is nine weeks, or 63 days, but four days either side of this calculation is perfectly within the bounds of normality. Use this time to prepare for the forthcoming litter, and to catch up on any outstanding jobs around the house and garden. There will be little time for that once the puppies arrive!

Early signs that the bitch has conceived are increased drinking of water, a quieter demeanour, the vulva remaining slightly enlarged with sometimes a slight secretion of mucus visible, and the gradual reddening and enlarging of the teats from about the third week. Appetite often decreases for a short time around the fourth week, and your bitch may become choosy over food or even be sick once or twice, bringing up bile. Try offering chicken, fish or eggs for a change, with wholemeal bread. From about the fifth week, the loins begin to fill out gradually. At first this is often only noticeable after feeding, but it becomes more and more obvious as time goes by.

A blood test done between 28 to 37 days after mating, and/or ultrasound scanning around the fourth week, can help determine pregnancy. However, the latter method is only as reliable as the operator's expertise or the sophistication of the equipment, so it does not always yield correct results. I have had reports of bitches 'confirmed' in whelp who have produced nothing – much to their owners' frustration – and know of other cases where the scans showed no foetus but the bitch went on to produce puppies. There was at least one empty Golden Retriever bench at Crufts this year whose intended occupant was at home nursing puppies that did not show up on the scanner!

Personally, I see no point in pregnancy testing, as there is little one can do about the result at this time. Nature lets me know soon enough, so I prefer to wait and see. The following method is quite useful though, and free. At four weeks, measure around the bitch's loin, midway between the hind leg and the last rib (before feeding), and write down the time of day and the measurement. Repeat the exercise a week later. If the measurement has increased, it is likely that she is whelp. Unless of course you have drastically increased her food ration in the interim period!

The ultimate sign is, of course, the movement of the puppies which can be felt from the seventh week and seen quite clearly from the eighth week.

CARE OF THE PREGNANT BITCH

Ensure your bitch is still kept away from other males until her season has completely finished. Otherwise, treat her normally, continue feeding her usual quality diet, and begin regular walks again at the end of the season. It is important that she is kept fit to help her cope with the labour ahead, so, although it is best to exercise her separately from any boisterous youngsters who may knock into her, do not be over-protective – just let common sense prevail. I find my bitches regulate themselves. They still gallop around freely in the first few weeks, but decline invitations to join in play.

As the pregnancy develops, they slow down, thus dictating pace and distance. Two or three short walks are better than one long one. Any normal jumping, such as into the back of the car, should not harm her, but as she gets heavier it will be easier for her to climb in

through the side door, should a short journey be needed. Swimming, which is an excellent form of exercise, should only be allowed if the water is not polluted, as an infection picked up in this way could jeopardise the pregnancy.

FEEDING

Golden bitches are frequently prolific mothers, and, although six-to-eight is the average number of puppies produced, litters of ten or eleven are not unusual. Therefore, once the pregnancy is obvious (around the fifth or sixth week), it is best to begin to increase her daily food ration in order that her own resources are not drained.

I am not an advocate of giving calcium and vitamin supplements in artificial additive form (tablets, liquid or powder) to either bitch or puppies. I have only once experienced the dreaded eclampsia, and that was when I was persuaded to use these additives. Instead, I prefer to ensure all nutritional requirements are given in food form to allow the dog's metabolism to fully assimilate them in a natural way. The following method works fine for me, and ensures my bitches look as well in weight and body after gestation, lactation and weaning as they did when mated.

I feed a complete diet in extruded form, and give the normal amount in two daily feeds during pregnancy, plus:

At five-six weeks – Egg custard (one egg whisked and cooked with half a pint of milk and a teaspoonful of sugar or honey). Eggs and milk cooked in this way give extra protein, iron, calcium, and vitamins in a palatable easy-to-digest form.

At six-seven weeks – Add two eggs to the milk, and half a tin of puppy food to her other two meals.

At seven-eight weeks – Milk can be increased to three quarters of a pint, cooked with eggs as before, and a whole tin of puppy food with each of the other two feeds.

In the last two weeks, she may refuse the complete food. Her digestive system may not be able to cope with the expansion if her abdomen is packed with rapidly growing foetuses. If this happens, offer the puppy version of this, or give more of the tinned puppy food to compensate. Otherwise, fish, chicken, or bread and milk may be accepted. Do not just assume she is not hungry. The egg custards never seem to be refused!

PREPARATION FOR WHELPING

I like to bath my bitches in a suitable medicated shampoo at the eight-week stage. Trim your bitch's feet (and nails if necessary) and tidy her tail and trouser feathering to minimise soiling at the birth. Breast cream (available from chemists), massaged into her teats daily during the last two weeks, will help prepare them for the onslaught of lactation. Wash feathering, tail and undercarriage again – in plain water – once she goes into the first stages of labour.

WHELPING BOX

Have everything ready well in advance of the expected date. The whelping box should be about four feet square, or three feet six inches by four feet at the least, with sides two feet or 18ins high, and the front divided into removable sections. A pig or guard rail, three or four inches from the sides, will help to prevent puppies being suffocated if they lie behind the bitch in the early days.

A heat lamp of the infra-red dull-emitter type, should be hung no lower than three feet over the box (an overall temperature of 75-80 degrees F. is required for the first ten days at least).

Buy at least three pieces of the vetbed type of synthetic fleecy bedding, which washes easily and dries quickly. Cut them to fit the whelping box. You will also need abundant supplies of clean newspaper, to be used initially in thick wads under the synthetic bedding.

Other essential items are:
1. Sterile solution.
2. Round-ended, fairly blunt scissors in case you have to sever cords.
3. Several absorbent towels to help dry the puppies quickly.
4. Liquid paraffin to act as a lubricant (I always have this ready but have only needed it on one occasion).
5. Hot-water bottle and a suitable cardboard box fitted with a piece of bedding, in case you need to move the puppies.
6. A notepad and pen to keep record of the progress, times of birth and sex of the puppies, and number of placentas present.
7. A couple of Thermos flasks which can be filled once whelping starts in earnest, one for the owner, and the other with a warm milk and glucose drink for the bitch.
8. Some large plastic sacks to hold any soiled paper.
9. A comfortable chair for yourself!

SIGNS OF IMMINENT WHELPING

Most bitches give adequate warning of the impending birth. Signs to watch for in your bitch are the refusal of all food, disinclination to leave her bed, restlessness, and a drop in temperature (to below 100 degrees Fahrenheit) twelve or more hours before whelping. Take her temperature daily during the last week and, once it drops, alert your vet and keep a close eye on her. One of my bitches, on her second litter, had the drop in temperature but no other signs whatsoever (her previous litter had a 24-hour first stage, with all the usual displays). This time, she ate breakfast, then curled up in an armchair snoring. I popped out for only half an hour, returning to find her still in the same position but nursing a healthy puppy!

THE FIRST STAGE

I take my bitches into the bedroom at night during the last week so that I lose as little sleep as possible until the last minute, as this stage can last from two to 24 hours. Some breeders use a baby alarm to help monitor the situation. During this first stage, the birth passages will be dilating, but any contractions are minor and irregular and seem to cause no great discomfort to the bitch. Nest-making urges may manifest themselves and, if not given newspaper and an old piece of clean bedding, she may attempt to dig up the carpet or make holes under bushes in the garden.

SECOND STAGE AND BIRTH

As the transition into the final, expulsive stage nears and the contractions become regular and powerful, your bitch will probably be restless, panting and shivering violently, and may be sick. She may also attempt to go outside, giving the impression that she needs to relieve herself. Be warned, if you let her out, go with her and take a torch if it is dark – plus a towel in case you have to bring a puppy back in. She may be confusing the need-to-push feelings with those of defecation. This has happened with my bitches on two occasions but, luckily, they were accompanied each time, so all was well.

This is the time I hate, as I am such a worrier. However, no matter how panic-stricken one feels on the inside, a facade of calm dependability is essential. Your bitch, especially if this is her first litter, needs the reassurance of your presence, not your version of the neighbourhood watch!

When contractions are rhythmic and closer together, she will begin straining to expel the whelps. Her efforts will usually be slight at first, gradually gathering in strength and momentum until the water bag breaks, releasing a clear fluid. Some bitches seem hardly to push at all before a puppy arrives, others strain quite vigorously. On average the first puppy will arrive thirty minutes to one hour after the first push, and thereafter at intervals of 15-45 minutes. If she is straining in earnest for over an hour with no sign of a puppy, call your vet immediately as this can indicate problems.

As the first puppy enters the birth canal, the bitch will lift her tail with each contraction and you should soon see a puppy protruding from the vulva, enclosed in a membranous sac. One or two good strains should then result in the puppy slithering out. The placenta, which is attached to the puppy via the umbilical cord, follows closely. The mother will quickly turn and tear off the membrane to release the puppy, bite through the umbilical cord, eat the placenta (I always allow this providing it looks fresh and red like a piece of liver – but not if it is going green and rather dry), and lick the puppy vigorously to stimulate and dry it.

If the bitch is very large and unable to turn enough to reach her first born, or if this is her first litter and she is unsure what to do, lift the puppy with placenta intact round to her front end, quickly breaking the membrane (just like tearing a thin plastic bag) round the puppy's head to allow it to breathe. Usually, once she begins licking the puppy, she realises instantly what to. If not, then you must sever the cord. I slide the cord between my first two fingers, so that any blood present is squeezed back towards the puppy, before cutting the cord about three inches long. Make sure there is no pulling on the abdomen. Be sure to wipe the scissors and put them back in the sterilising solution, as they may be needed again, and dispose of the placenta if your bitch shows no sign of wanting to eat it.

Take hold of the puppy in a warm towel and rub rather roughly, with the head supported but pointing downwards to help expel any birth fluid that may have been swallowed or inhaled. Providing the puppy is breathing well, and wriggling about, get the puppy on to one of mother's teats as quickly as possible. Even if she has shown no interest thus far, once the puppy is sucking, her maternal instincts will usually come to the fore.

Most puppies are born strong and lusty, with a keen sense of smell directing them to the milk bar. Some need to be helped by having their mouth opened with slight pressure from your thumb and forefinger either side of the muzzle, and put directly on to a teat which you can then milk gently to stimulate suckling. Puppies seldom need showing twice! Once two or three puppies are born and feeding, the bitch will usually settle down to the job in hand.

As each new puppy arrives, I draw the other puppies gently away to a corner of the whelping box to prevent them getting wet all over again while the mother attends to the newcomer. My bitches soon look to me for this help. After each puppy is born, I remove as much of the soiled paper as possible without disturbing the mother, add more dry

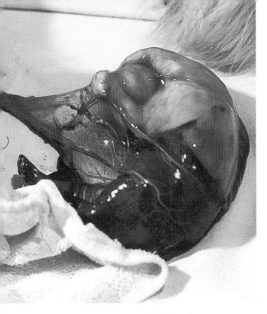

The arrival of the first puppy.
Photo: B. Simon.

The mother will clean the puppy, and will bite through the umbilical cord.   *Photo: B. Simon.*

paper and, if all is going well, offer her a drink of the warm milk mixture, which is usually accepted with relish.

Occasionally a weak, limp, lifeless-looking pup will arrive, perhaps half-drowned during a difficult, lengthy birth. Follow the directions above, and, in addition, give the puppy a few downward shakes. Remember to support the puppy's head, open the mouth and gently wipe away any mucus with a clean cloth, and carry on massaging by rubbing the wrong way of the coat along the back and ribs. Soon you may be rewarded with a gasp, followed by feeble cries. Continue working on the puppy until it is breathing normally, then keep it warm but not hot, and allow it to recover before joining the others at the milk bar. I never spend *too* long trying to revive puppies who are not breathing, as brain damage may have occurred which would only cause heartbreak later.

Puppies are often presented backwards (feet first) and, as this seldom causes problems, it is best not to interfere unless the bitch shows signs of distress. But if a puppy is stuck, perhaps through being prematurely separated from the placenta, and devoid of its lubricated sac, the birth will be 'dry' and may need your intervention. Squirting a little of the liquid paraffin around the vulva will help lubricate, and you can take careful hold of the puppy – a clean facecloth will help you get a better grip – and with downward movements, while the

bitch is straining, gently help to ease the puppy out.

Whelping time can vary between two and ten hours, and sometimes even longer. Puppies may arrive at regular, or irregular, intervals. Your bitch may deliver four or five puppies, and then have a rest of up to two hours before straining again and producing the rest of the litter. Once all the pups are born, the bitch should be given the chance to relieve herself. She will, no doubt, be reluctant to leave the nest, so place the puppies in the cardboard box which should be positioned inside the whelping box next to her. When she sees them snuggled up and content, she can be put on a leash and taken outside, but be prepared to be dragged back indoors at a rate of knots the second her toilet is completed!

I use absorbent chamois-type cloths to dry her bloodstained trousers and tail as much as possible, and quickly change the soiled bedding before returning the puppies to her. She will wash and check them all thoroughly, before having a good drink of the milk mixture and settling down for a well-earned nap.

WHEN TO CALL THE VET
Goldens, perhaps largely due to being what I term 'dog-shaped dogs' with no exaggerations, are generally easy whelpers and seldom need veterinary assistance for this natural occurrence. It is best to be aware, however, of

a few situations that *demand* professional veterinary attention or advice.

1. If the bitch has gone more than four days over the due date.
2. If she fails to have contractions at the start of the second stage, or if there is a green or bloody discharge present before contractions begin. This could signal primary inertia, or a dead puppy.
3. If she is straining earnestly for an hour without a sign of a puppy. It could signify a wrongly-placed puppy impossible to expel. If allowed to continue, the uterus may rupture and haemorrhage.
4. If she stops for more than two hours during whelping, when it is obvious there are more puppies. This could be secondary inertia due to an exhausted uterus.
5. If she appears at all unwell, and is off her food after the birth.
6. If she is unduly restless and panting a few days after the birth, or her walk is stiff or unsteady. It could be eclampsia, which is a serious condition requiring urgent treatment.

As a matter of course, I get my vet to visit in the 24 hours following the whelping, to check both mother and puppies over. Usually oxytocin and a long-acting antibiotic is given by injection to clear the bitch out, and to prevent infection.

CARE OF THE NURSING MOTHER
When the bitch next needs to go out for toilet purposes, wash all her soiled parts in warm water and dry her as much as possible before returning her to the whelping box. It may be necessary to do this daily for the first few days after the birth, as she is likely to be discharging quite a bit and, if left unwashed, the birth fluids will burn her skin causing soreness. Change the bedding daily.

Each time she goes out to relieve herself, wipe her milk glands with a clean, damp cotton wool pad and dry with clean kitchen roll, before putting the puppies back to her. Check at the same time that milk is flowing from all the teats and that none of the glands are hot, swollen or congested. If any feel hard to the touch, try applying warm flannel compresses to the area, express a little of the milk by hand, and encourage one of the pups to feed from the affected teat, then all should be well. If you cannot clear the teat by this method, veterinary attention will be required to prevent mastitis developing.

As far as litter size is concerned, the average (and ideal) for a Golden is six to eight pups. With this number, 'mum' (providing you are feeding her well) should be able to cope with their demands for the first three weeks. Be prepared to offer her food and drink in the whelping box for the first week, as she will not want to leave the puppies.

Normally, the bitch will have consumed a number of placentas during the birth so, for the first 48 hours, she will require only a light diet of boiled rice (which counteracts the laxative effect of the placentas), with white fish, chicken, or scrambled eggs, given three

At two weeks old, the litter is at its most demanding. so it is essential that your bitch is given adequate nutrition.

Photo courtesy: Val Birkin.

times daily. Half a pint of milk food can also be given three times daily. I use milk powder sold for lambs, reconstituted at half strength, for my nursing bitches and they seldom have diarrhoea. On the third day, introduce her normal food, as much as her appetite demands, half and half with the rice and fish etc. It should not be necessary to feed rice after the third day. Give milk feeds as before, increasing the amount gradually. It goes without saying that water should be freely available.

THE LACTATING BITCH
The puppies are born with eyelids tightly closed, and usually with pink pads and noses, which turn black within 24 hours. The first food they receive from their dam is colostrum, which is highly concentrated and contains antibodies to provide initial protection against infection, so it is vitally important they all get their share of this. From about day three, the milk proper begins to flow. The puppies should be feeding contentedly (their little tails sticking out like jug handles) and filling out considerably, so the demands on their dam increase daily. Her nutritional requirements are about doubled in the first week, and trebled in the second and third. A typical dietary regime for a Golden bitch on full milk production is five or six feeds daily. Two or three feeds should consist of her normal food, with tinned puppy food added. Also give two or three feeds of milk with egg and cereal added. My bitches take half a pint of milk with each milk feed during the first week, one pint with each feed in the second week, and a pint and a half with each feed by the third week. To each milk feed I add a handful of high-protein puppy cereal and a chopped hard-boiled egg.

If the litter is small, with five or less puppies, the bitch will not need such vast amounts of food, and the puppies must be watched in case they start to get too fat and crab-like, with flattened chests. Otherwise, they may develop into what are known as 'swimmers'.

Alternatively, if the litter is large with ten or more, the bitch will require her food intake increased accordingly, and the puppies may need supplementary feeding (topping-up) two-to-five times daily. Your vet can supply a milk powder specially designed for this purpose and some plastic syringes (minus the needles) to administer it. You will soon know if the puppies are not getting enough from their dam, as they will be continually trying to feed and giving protesting little squeaks. If I have to resort to supplementary feeding, I prefer to top up all the puppies so that each gets a fair share of everything. I begin two or three times a day with just five millilitres per pup per feed (the next day ten ml, the next probably 15 ml). My method is to dribble the milk from the syringe into the puppy's mouth, via a well-scrubbed finger which the puppies suck readily, until they are ready to take to a bottle.

CARE OF THE LITTER
When the puppies are about a week old, their nails will have grown into little hooked claws, so it is necessary to cut off the tips carefully (do not forget the tip of the dewclaws too) to

At two weeks old, the litter is at its most demanding, so it is essential that your bitch is given adequate nutrition.

Photo courtesy: Val Birkin.

prevent the bitch becoming scratched and torn. This exercise should be repeated at weekly intervals. At around ten days, the bitch sits up to feed her babies and may rest outside the box for a while, still keeping a watchful eye on them. Their eyes begin to open at this stage, but I doubt they see (or hear) much before three weeks of age. They start to stagger around the box, soon instinctively going to the edges of the bedding to empty. Toilet training has begun!

WORMING
There are many brands of worming remedy. Ask your vet for a suitable one. The one I use comes in easily administered paste form, and I dose the pups at two weeks, four weeks and six weeks, and recommend to puppy buyers that they continue at two-weekly intervals until vaccinations are completed. Continue worming at monthly intervals up to six months of age, and at six-monthly intervals thereafter. I worm the dam when the puppies are three weeks old, and again after they are completely weaned.

WEANING.
For more than 20 years, I followed a policy of rearing puppies on fresh meat, milk and cereals. But reliable supplies of fresh food are not so readily available now, and I have found the modern 'complete' dry or tinned puppy foods do the job just as well. I do not like putting all my eggs in one basket, so prefer to use both types of feed, feeling that this leads to a stronger canine digestive system in the long term. I also give specially-formulated puppy milk for a time. There is an enormous choice of these complete foods, so it is best to read the nutritional information and not just assume the most expensive is the best. However, I still give raw meat for the first

Weaning is a messy business, but it is not long before the puppies are feeding independently.

Photo: Weeks.

Even when they are eating solid food, the puppies will still be keen to feed from their mother.

Photo: Steve Nash.

week, using the following method.

At three weeks (slightly earlier for a big litter, slightly later for a small litter), the puppies will be ready for their first taste of solid food. They should still be getting plenty of milk from their dam, so I begin with about an ounce daily of lean, raw, minced meat for each pup, rolling the meat into little balls and letting them take it from my hand. They never seem to refuse it. The benefits are twofold, for not only is this food easy to digest but taking it from the human hand plays a valuable part in socialisation for the puppies. A few days later I introduce a second daily feed, of the dry, 'complete' type of puppy food, which can be made into a porridge at first with milk or water. Each puppy needs to be fed separately and to have the bowl held up to each individual's mouth until they all get the hang of feeding properly, which they should have

done by about four weeks of age.

At four weeks, if all the puppies' motions are correct, another of the complete meals can be added. At around this stage, I substitute tinned puppy food for the raw meat. Space the three daily puppy feeds well apart so their tummies do not become overloaded, for their dam should still have free access to them. She will stand to feed them now, but as their teeth will have erupted like sharp little needles, she may not wish to stay with them, preferring instead to rejoin her human family. She will still sleep with her litter at night, but she needs the provision of a bench or armchair so that she can occasionally escape their demands.

Incidentally, at this age the pups need more space to move around and play, so the front of the box should be removed and newspaper spread all over the surrounding floor area. Their dam is unable to keep pace with clearing

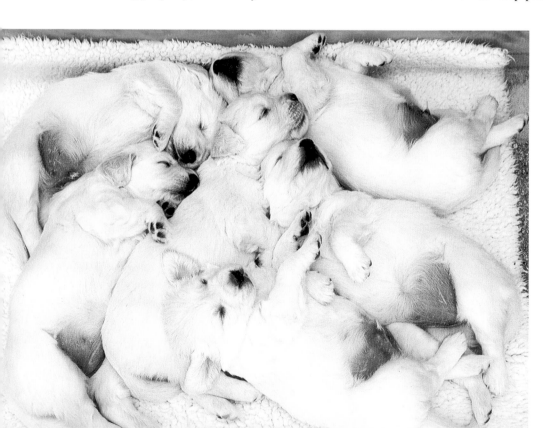

A litter at five weeks. At this age, puppies divide their time between sleeping, feeding and playing.

Photo: Kipps.

A beautifully reared litter of Sansue puppies.　　　　*Photo courtesy: Val Birkin.*

up after them once weaning begins, so the breeder must take over this chore. Wipe the pups' faces with a damp cloth after feeding so they do not become sticky with food. You will probably find that they usually help to clean each other's faces. I find that most puppies empty their bowels within half an hour of waking/being fed, so stay with them until they begin to fall asleep again and they should stay spotlessly clean. Once they are into a routine of using the newspaper, it can be confined to one or two areas, preferably near doors.

At five weeks, I add another daily feed, making three of complete puppy food, still made quite soft with puppy milk or water. Give the litter gradually increasing amounts (following the manufacturer's instructions) and one daily feed of tinned puppy food. There is no need for bitches to sleep with their pups after five weeks (very few show a desire to), and the new mother's daily intake of food should be gradually reduced now, cutting down one at a time on her milk feeds first. She may still wish to feed/visit her pups two to four times a day, but she must be watched after she has been fed, otherwise she may regurgitate her food for the puppies and they

do not need this. If any pups develop diarrhoea around this time, this is usually the cause, as their small stomachs become overloaded. At around this age, the puppies can be allowed outside for short play periods, which will further advance their toilet training. They must not be allowed to become cold or wet (nor be left out in hot sun), and should be taken back inside as soon as they begin to tire.

At six weeks and thereafter, continue the same routine of four feeds a day for the pups. Regular times are important, as they will have developed 'clocks' in their tummies by now and will become increasingly vocal if the food is late. The amount consumed will have increased considerably (I recommend increasing twice weekly), and should now be given in a firmer consistency. Their dam is perhaps still feeding them either late at night or early in the morning. Her food intake can be further decreased until she is back on her normal maintenance diet, and her visits to the pups further curtailed, allowing her milk supply to dry up naturally by the time the pups are ready to go. Once the bitch's milk has dried up, I give each pup a separate drink of puppy milk at bedtime.

PUPPIES' WEIGHT GAIN

Golden Retriever puppies grow rapidly from a birth weight of between ten and 20 oz (depending on size of litter) to between nine and 13 lbs at around seven weeks (depending on birth weight, activity etc.). Just as in humans (where two-pound babies sometimes grow into strapping six-footers), the finished size of an adult Golden is not reliant on birth weight. Heredity plays the biggest part in this. The point is that puppy weight is relatively unimportant. What is important is that by seven weeks the pups should be nicely-rounded, with a good covering of flesh, and solid and firm to the touch, with straight, strong, sturdy legs. They should be neither fat, soft and flabby, nor thin, bony and weedy.

SOCIALISATION

Golden Puppies are very friendly and inquisitive by nature, and especially from six weeks of age, by which time their play becomes quite exuberant. They need plenty of stimuli, in the form of suitable toys for chewing, carrying (but no tug of war toys, please), and the introduction of as many different everyday sights and sounds as possible. Introducing them to different locations within the premises is a good idea, to help prepare them for the move to a new home. It goes without saying that human contact plays a vital part in socialisation. It is said that puppies are great time-wasters, but few breeders would consider the time spent with their puppies to be wasted. From the earliest association of the gentle but firm, regular handling by the breeder during everyday care, including feeding, cleaning, grooming, play, and even weekly nail-cutting, the puppy learns to trust humans and find their attention pleasurable. This can be witnessed by the enthusiastic way a litter of Golden pups will greet visitors.

PLACING THE PUPPIES

Unfortunately, Goldens are almost too popular for their own good. Puppies are usually in demand, so great care must be taken to ensure that they are placed in suitable homes, where the new owner understands fully the responsibilities of Golden (or any dog) ownership and is able to continue the care that the breeder has begun.

12 RING TRAINING AND HANDLING

The aim of this chapter is to give help and advice so that your Golden Retriever enters the show ring correctly trimmed, well-presented and trained to stand to perfection.

Golden Retrievers are presented naturally in the show ring. They need only a small amount of trimming compared to many breeds, and with their happy, 'willing to please' disposition they have become popular show dogs and family pets. All this leads to strong competition in the show ring, and, to have a good chance of winning, your dog needs to be both well presented and nicely handled, in addition to being a correctly constructed, typical example of the breed.

THE SHOW STANCE
Golden Retrievers stand four-square, and are either 'stacked', or taught to stand free with a wagging tail. This training should start at a very young age, and your first show dog, if bought from a breeder, will almost certainly have been stood from a few weeks old to assess show potential. This early training is a great help if you are training a dog for the first time.

Training for the show ring starts as soon as possible. Puppies destined for the show ring should be stood every day, just for a minute or two. Remember that pet puppies will need to be examined on a table at a veterinary surgery at some time in their lives, so this early training is also good for them. Too long a time standing encourages boredom, and becomes an excuse for a puppy to wriggle about. A table covered with a rubber mat works well, as the puppy is stood on a level with you, which gives both encouragement to the puppy and prevents the handler from developing backache from having to stoop so low.

The puppy should be trained to stand four-square, with the front legs fairly close together, the elbows tucked in and the front legs set well back under the body. The back should be level and the hind legs stood slightly further apart than the front legs, with the hocks perpendicular to the ground. The handler should stand at the side of the dog, supporting the head in a natural position with the tail held at the end, level with the back. A dog that is stood 'free' needs to have the handler stood at the front, and the tail is not held but allowed to wag. Ensure that your dog becomes accustomed to you standing a little away from the head, so that the head is not pushed back into the shoulders.

Some judges in the show ring do not allow Golden Retrievers to be stacked, so it is advisable to teach your dog both methods of standing. At this stage, it is advisable to start using a lead so that your puppy becomes accustomed to the feel of it around the neck. A puppy by about ten to twelve weeks of age will be too big to stand on the table and will need to be stood on the ground. Lead training is now started.

SHOW LEADS
There are many types of show leads on the market, but the type that is most commonly used on Golden Retrievers is about 120cm

GROOMING AND TRIMMING
Photos: Steve Nash.
Demonstrated by Anne Falconer and Jonmere Jonathan of Siatham.

Gather all the trimming and grooming equipment together. A grooming table or rubber mat is useful as it teaches the dog that this is where they are trimmed. For the pet dog, all that is needed is a brush and comb, slicker brush, nail clippers and toothbrush and toothpaste. For the show dog add straight scissors, thinning scissors and a water spray to damp the dog down if the coat sticks up after bathing.

Brush all surfaces of the teeth moving the toothbrush up and down the tooth. The teeth should be brushed daily to avoid dental disease.

BELOW: Using a bristle brush, groom the dog all over before trimming, paying particular attention to the axilla where matts are often found in dogs that are not groomed correctly.

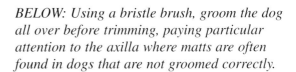

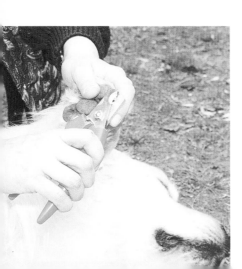

Guillotine nail-clippers are easier to use. Only take a very small amount off each time and clip the nails regularly.

long and 0.5cm wide, and consists of a metal ring at one end and a loop for the handler to hold at the other. This type can be loosened, when the dog is stood, to show the shoulder line to advantage. These leads are made of nylon (in a variety of colours), chain or leather.

INITIAL RING TRAINING

Puppies who are confident about standing can be taught to be examined, as they will be in the show ring. Starting with the mouth, keeping the jaws together, gently lift the top lip so that the bite is visible. It is advisable not to do this while a puppy is teething, as the mouth is likely to be sore at that time and it may cause problems later on if examination of the mouth is associated with pain. Check the length of the ears by gently pulling the pinna of the ear forwards so that it just touches the corner of the eye. Do not worry if the ears are not in proportion to the body at this stage.

Gently run your hands over the skull and down the neck feeling the shoulder placement. Keeping one hand on the point of the shoulder, gently run one hand down the shoulder-blade, then down the upper arm, and feel the amount of bone on the front leg. Check that the front legs are straight and that the front feet are not turning out. Then, using both hands, feel along the spring of rib, the couplings, and the quarters, and then feel for the second thigh.

Male dogs have to be examined to ensure that both testicles have descended into the scrotum, and it is a good idea to get a male puppy used to having this done from an early age.

Check the length of the tail, which should just reach the hock (again, this will probably not be in proportion in a young puppy), and stand behind the puppy to check that the hocks are straight. Once your puppy is confident about an examination by you, ask another person to go over the puppy. To start with, it is better to ask someone that the puppy knows to do this, but later get your puppy accustomed to being examined by strangers. One word of warning here. Ensure that people who

examine your puppy are very gentle and patient, and not unsure of a bouncy puppy. Many puppies are frightened both of people who are rough and of those who approach a dog hesitantly.

LEAD TRAINING

The dog now needs to be taught to move on a loose lead, on the lefthand side, in three ways: in a straight line away from the judge and back; in a triangle, away at an angle, straight across the line of the triangle and back to the beginning; and moving around in a circle. All this should be done at a trot, but the speed will depend on both the size and conformation of the dog. Your dog will eventually need to move in a circle with other dogs, so that will need to be practised at a ringcraft club.

RING TRAINING CLASSES

Ringcraft classes are organised in most areas, and these are a useful training ground for young puppies. Puppies socialise with other puppies of different breeds, meet new people and learn to behave in a confined space, away from the familiar surroundings of home. The trainers that take these classes are usually experienced handlers of different breeds, but your youngster will gain from their advice and experience in the show ring. However, you will still need to practise at home, remembering to keep these practice sessions short.

GROOMING

Golden Retrievers need to be in good physical condition, correctly trimmed and perfectly groomed, as well as being well-trained when they enter the show ring. Pet dogs also require dental care, grooming, nail-clipping and a small amount of trimming to keep them in good condition.

EQUIPMENT: Grooming for both pets and show dogs is basically the same. Start by obtaining the equipment needed: for the pet dog, a canine toothbrush and suitable toothpaste, nail clippers, a bristle brush and a steel comb. Add to that a seven-inch pair of

LEFT: A slicker brush is useful on a really thick coat. Teach the dog to stand and sit to be groomed.

ABOVE: Once the dog has been brushed, comb through all the coat using a steel comb.

straight-cutting scissors, and similar-sized thinning scissors (46 teeth) if you intend to trim your dog. For show dogs, a trimming knife and hound glove, as well as a smaller pair of straight scissors and one-sided thinning scissors, can be purchased. Buy the best scissors that you can afford as, with regular sharpening, they will last for many years. There are rubber grips available which fit into the finger-grips of scissors to prevent blisters on hands. These are a very worthwhile investment if you have several dogs to trim.

Grooming should start while the puppy is young, using a bristle brush and a comb. A puppy too young to be exercised on hard ground will probably need a nail trim. When the coat starts to grow, you will need to start trimming, in addition to brushing and combing.

TEETH: Get your dog used to having teeth brushed daily, as soon as the second teeth have erupted. Only use toothpaste produced for dogs, as human toothpaste contains a foaming agent that needs to be rinsed. Brush all surfaces of the teeth to prevent dental disease and reduce dental problems as your dog ages.

EYES: Wipe away any discharge from the eyes using a damp piece of cotton-wool (cotton). An eye that is constantly watering or

discharging needs veterinary treatment without delay.

EARS: Check the ears for any discharge, and wipe out the top of the ear using a proprietary ear-cleaner. Never use cotton buds in a dog's ear. If cleaning is needed, fill the ear canal with cleaner and massage any discharge to the top.

NAILS: Nail-clipping should be done regularly, to keep the nails short and the quick back. Take off only a very small amount at a time, taking great care not to cut into the quick. White nails are much easier to cut in this respect, as the quick can be clearly seen. The guillotine type of nail-clippers are the easiest to use.

COAT: Brush the coat in the direction that it grows, and be prepared to brush for about ten minutes daily to keep the coat shining and remove all the dead hairs. Comb all through afterwards with a steel comb. Teach your dog to lie on his back to ensure that all the coat underneath is combed through. The most common place for matts to occur is in the axilla and behind the ears. Trimming can then begin. Remember that the dog is simply tidied to show the outline to advantage, not heavily trimmed as in some breeds.

TRIMMING

British and continental dogs are trimmed differently from dogs in the USA. The ruff is left untrimmed in the USA, and tidied in dogs shown to the British Standard.

FEET AND HOCKS: The feet are usually trimmed first. All the hair is removed level with the pads, and the hair is then trimmed to the outline of the pad. Trim the hair that grows between the toes by pulling the hair through to the back of the pad and trimming off level. On the front feet, trim with straight scissors up as far as the stopper pad. Trim the hind feet in the same way, leaving the hocks at present, then stand the dog up. Carefully trim around the feet to show a neat catlike foot. Do not trim the feet so far back that the nails show.

Keep the dog standing while the hocks are trimmed. These are most easily trimmed using double-sided thinning scissors. In a downward direction, comb the coat between each cut until the hocks are smooth with no hair sticking out, then trim around the bottom of the hind pastern using straight scissors. It is often easier to use a smaller pair of scissors for the feet. Remove any feathering that hangs over the hock, using thinning scissors across the direction that the hair grows. Removing this hair gives a cleaner outline when the dog is being shown.

TAIL: Once the feet are trimmed, trim the tail. Follow the direction that the hair grows, starting about one cm from the end of the tail and curving round to about eight to ten cms at the base. The actual length of the tail depends on the size and balance of the dog. A very short-coupled small dog would look unbalanced with a very long tail, and likewise a dog that is longer in body needs a tail left a little longer.

There are two ways of positioning the dog to trim the tail. The first is to lie the dog on one side, comb out the tail and carefully trim it, following the natural growth, with straight scissors, then comb through again and trim off any long pieces. Turn the dog over and trim the other side. Some people use thinning scissors to trim the tail, which can give a more natural look, but personally I prefer to use sharp scissors. The second method of trimming the tail is to stand the dog up, comb the tail through and then cut it to shape. I use the method of having the dog lying down, which I find easier since my dogs always manage to wag their tail at an inappropriate time.

NECK AND SHOULDERS: Once the feet and the tail are trimmed, turn your attention to the neck and shoulders, except if you are exhibiting in the USA. This always seems the most difficult part to trim for many people. The neck and shoulders should be tidied, not sculpted, and the trimming should follow the natural line of the dog. Many dogs that are shown at the moment are trimmed as far as the breastbone leaving a large amount of hair protruding. This is incorrect, as it gives a Setter-like outline.

Starting with the ears, comb out the hair and, using double-sided thinning scissors, cut upwards close to the skin, then comb again. A stripping knife can be used on the soft hair on the ears, if preferred. Continue to do this until the ears look neat but not shaven, and shape around the ear using thinning scissors not straight scissors, which give a harder and less natural look.

Comb the hair on the front downwards and, again using thinning scissors and an upward action, cut close to the skin and then comb through again. Make just one cut, and then comb out the hair that has been removed, thus ensuring that you do not take too much out and leave some areas with very little hair. Continue to do this until the front is neatened, going down just below the breastbone and shaping back towards the front legs, so that the front looks natural. Do not take off so much hair that only the white undercoat is showing. The aim is to neaten the front only and remove undercoat, not topcoat.

Many dogs, particularly males, grow a large mane over their shoulders, and this will need to be thinned to allow the judge to see the set-in of neck and shoulder placement. Again,

LEFT: Trim off all the hair that grows between the pads so that the hair is level with the pad.

RIGHT: On the front feet, trim up as far as the stopper pad.

LEFT: Trim around the pad so that the hair is level with the pad up to the nail.

RIGHT: Then put the foot down and trim off any hair that is sticking up between the toes. The aim is to acheive a round, cat-like foot.

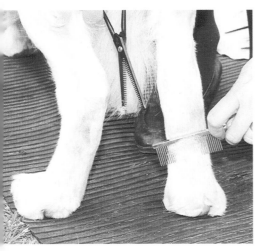

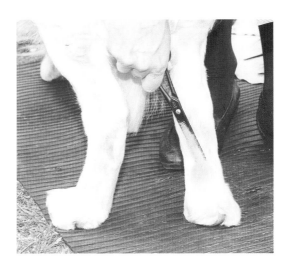

LEFT: Start by combing the hair through on the pastern.

RIGHT: Then using thinning scissors trim away the excess hair. Continue to do this until the pastern is smooth.

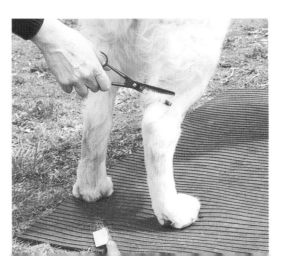

LEFT: Trim around the bottom of the pastern with straight scissors.

RIGHT: Trim about 2.5cm (1 inch) above the hock to give a clear view of the hock.

TOP LEFT: With the dog lying down comb through the hair on the tail.

ABOVE: Starting about 1cm from the tip of the tail and using straight scissors, shape around the tail following the natural growth.

LEFT: Having done this, stand the dog up and tidy any long hairs.

BOTTOM LEFT: With the dog in the sitting position, comb all the hair on the front and start to thin and tidy the front. To start, I would suggest that you use the scissors in an upward direction, combing the coat through after every cut. Once the front has been thinned, trim off any long hairs using the scissors in a downward direction.

BELOW: Continue to below the breastbone to avoid a "Setter-like" outline.

Comb the hair on the neck and shoulders downwards before starting to trim.

It is much easier to pull the pinna of the ear forward – and then the neckline can be seen easily.

A male dog grows a really heavy mane around the shoulders and this needs to be thinned out to show the outline. Use thinning scissors in an upward direction. Cut close to the skin and take great care in dark-coloured dogs, as it is easy to get a pale mark if you just leave the undercoat showing.

Trim away any hair that sticks out in front of the ear, using thinning scissors in a downward direction.

Trim the hair from the edges of the ear using thinning scissors, never straight scissors.

Then pull the earflap upwards and trim away hair underneath the ear.

Comb out the hair on the pinna ready to trim off the long hair that many dogs grow.

Trim off this excess hair using thinning scissors in an upward direction.

Trim off any long hair that grows over the edge of the ear, again using thinning scissors.

Trimmed but still wet from a bath, ready for the final touches.

using the thinning scissors in an upward movement against the direction that the hair grows, make one cut and then comb the hair through. To check that the correct amount of hair has been removed, stand behind the dog and you will be able to see if the shoulders are clean and the ridge of hair has been removed. Be extra cautious if you are trimming a very dark-coloured dog as, if you remove too much topcoat, you will be left with pale undercoat showing through. Never cut the coat on the top of the neck or shoulders. Any hair that sticks up can be flattened after bathing.

Many pet animals are neutered, and this alters both the texture and growth of the coat in Goldens. Long guard hairs that grow on the side of the dog can be carefully removed using either double-sided or single-sided thinning scissors in a downward direction. Once removed, these hairs often do not grow again and with careful attention to grooming, the coat of a neutered animal can be kept manageable and in show condition.

Once trimmed, bath your dog before checking the trimming and removing any more hair. Many people prefer to bath the dog before trimming, but it is probably easier to basically trim the dog before bathing and finish once the coat is completely dry. Coat types vary in Golden Retrievers. Some are straight and have no wave at all, other have gentle waves down their backs, while some curl from the top of their heads to the end of their tails. The easiest to prepare for the show ring are those with straight coats, but a dog with a wavy coat always looks really attractive when properly prepared. All the waves should be flat and the coat should not curl. It is often easier to comb the coat into the waves, rather than try to comb the waves flat.

BATHING

Nearly all dogs need bathing at some time in their lives, be it for veterinary treatment, preparation for a show, or to remove some awful substance that they have managed to roll in! The easiest way to bath a dog is to put them in a shower or bath, as bathing with buckets of water in the garden is time-consuming, and it is difficult to ensure that the coat has been rinsed adequately. The ideal solution is a tiled shower area downstairs. Special dog baths are available, but these tend to be quite expensive. It is possible to convert a cold water tank into a dog bath by putting a plug hole in the bottom and making a frame for the tank under an electric shower.

Use a shampoo made specially for dogs, as the ones made for humans are not suitable. Wet the dog thoroughly and then apply the shampoo. It is probably better to dilute the shampoo before putting any on the dog, and then rub until it foams. Make sure that all the coat is thoroughly wet, as Goldens have a waterproof coat and it can take quite a while to wet all the undercoat. Many shampoos for veterinary use have very specific instructions, and these should be followed accurately.

Kennel Club rules forbid any substance to be used in preparing a dog for exhibition that alters the natural texture of the coat, so conditioner cannot be used. However, if the dog is in really good physical condition, the coat will also be in good condition, unless your Golden has lost coat (for example after pregnancy), when it is probably best not to show in any case.

Roughly dry with a towel or water-absorbing cloth as the dog comes out of the bath, and allow your Golden to shake off excess water in an appropriate place. Continue to dry with a towel until the dog is reasonably dry and then comb the coat into place. Many people blow-dry the coat, which gives a very good finish, but a good result can also be

achieved by continually combing the coat into place until it is dry.

Sometimes it is not possible to continually comb the drying coat, so, to keep the coat flat, a towel can be fastened around the neck and placed over the back of the dog and then tied or pinned underneath to prevent the coat rolling upwards. It is better if possible to bath the dog early in the day, so that the coat is completely dry before bedtime. Damp coat has a tendency to curl, and, if the dog lies on it damp overnight, all your hard work will be wasted. When the coat is really dry, just check the trimming again as bathing often shows up one or two long hairs that need to be trimmed.

Beware of sending a show dog to a professional groomer unless they are experienced in preparing a Golden for the show ring. They often trim off the feathering on the hindlegs, and leave the ruff on.

PREPARATIONS FOR THE SHOW

So now you have a bathed, trimmed and trained dog ready to enter the ring. What else do you need to know?

Firstly, wear appropriate dress in the ring. The show ring is not the place for torn jeans, any more than it is for designer evening wear. Dark-coloured clothes allow a light-coloured dog to show up, and, similarly, wear a lighter colour if showing a dark dog. Do not wear jewellery that jangles or have loose change in your pocket. The handler should look smart, wear comfortable clothes, preferably something that does not show the dog hairs or muddy footprints. A pocket is useful to hold tidbits, otherwise buy a small bag that you can tie around your waist for this purpose. Several layers of clothes is a good idea, and always take waterproof clothing and wellington boots with you. A tube of sun protection cream is sometimes useful!

Use an appropriately coloured show lead. A pale dog looks better with a lead that matches the coat, and a white lead can easily be dyed with tea to become cream. Darker-coloured dogs look good with brown or leather leads, although many people use a particular colour for their kennel.

Starting to show a dog is a daunting procedure, and many people are unsure of what is expected of them. Basically, the dog is entered for a show a little while in advance, so you have several weeks to practise. Try and visit a show before going to one with your own dog so that you get an idea of what is required. On entering the ring, you will collect your number, and handlers, with their dogs stood in a show stance, stand in a circle around the ring. The judge usually walks around the ring and then often asks for the dogs to be moved in a circle all together. Then each dog is stood, examined and moved individually. Afterwards, the dogs are stood again and the judge will either short-list or place the first four or five dogs.

BASIC RULES

There are several basic rules to remember when showing a dog. Firstly, never stand between the dog and the judge, and be careful always to position yourself on the far side of your moving dog. Do not engage the judge in conversation in the ring. Do not obstruct or distract another exhibitor's dog.

Always stand your dog on a level piece of ground if possible, and do not crowd out other people or stand your dog forward of the line. When showing a dog for the first time, try and stand towards the back of the class so you can get an idea of what is required. Listen carefully to the instructions that the judge gives you, obey the stewards and remember how old your dog is, as many judges ask the age – particularly in the age classes!

HANDLING

The way in which a dog is handled can affect the amount of winning done in the ring. A really outstanding dog that is shown really badly will not reach full potential, whereas a dog of lesser quality, really well-handled and presented, often wins well. That is not due to bad judging. It is merely that the judge may never have seen the dog stood or moved properly so that the conformation and movement can be assessed.

To get the best out of our dog you must be aware of both faults and virtues. The perfect show dog has not yet been born, but every dog has some virtues and it is up to the handler to show off these virtues, while trying to disguise the faults.

Bad handling affects your dog's chances in the ring, but, fortunately, is something that can be improved. Start by standing the dog in front of a mirror. That way you can see how the dog stands in the show ring. Try altering the position of the legs slightly and see if this improves the outline. Then stand the dog facing the mirror to see whether the front is straight. By doing this, you can also check whether the dog stands with front feet straight, or whether you stand the dog too wide in front so that the elbows stick out. Then turn the dog around so that you see it from the rear view, and check that the stance is not cow-hocked or sickle-hocked.

COMMUNICATION

Once you have your dog standing correctly, it is time to ensure that you handle your Golden in the show ring to the best of your ability. To be able to handle well, you need to be able to control and communicate with your Golden, and to keep the dog's attention at all times, regardless of what else is going on. This is where a greedy dog has an advantage. If you keep one hand in the pocket where the tidbits are kept, those eyes never leave you.

A dog who does not respond to tidbits should be taught a command that means attention must be on you, and no one and nothing else. This can be achieved by insisting that the dog looks at you and nothing else when this command is given. This is best taught when there are no other distractions around, and the dog is rewarded for paying attention.

RING PROCEDURE

Make sure that you are in the ring at the correct time, in the correct class and wearing the number allotted to your dog. Once your Golden is standing correctly, do not fiddle or move the dog when the judge is looking, unless out of position. Do not come into the

SHOWING YOUR DOG
Photos: Steve Nash.
Demonstrated by Anne Falconer and Siatham Symposia

Standing the dog for the judge. Supporting the dog around the neck and under the chest, gently lower the dog so that the front legs drop under the body.

Once the front legs are dropped into position adjust the legs if necessary.

Once the front legs are correct, position the hindlegs by lifting the dog between the hind legs and lowering into place. Never lift the dog under the abdomen as the dog may then roach its back.

Once the hind legs have been dropped into position adjust the legs as necessary.

LEFT: Move the dog away from the judge in a straight line on a loose lead. The dog should not move too closely to the handler. Note the loose lead. Golden Retrievers should never be moved on a tight lead.

RIGHT: Move the dog across the top of the triangle.

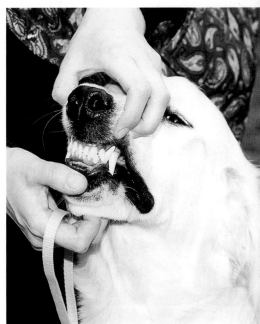

LEFT: Move the dog in a straight line back towards the judge.

RIGHT: This is the correct way to show the bite of the dog to the judge. Gently lift the top lip away and push down the lower lip to expose the bite. Practise this on a puppy before allowing other people to examine the mouth.

ring wearing rosettes which have been won in a previous class or, even worse, a previous show. Do not bring any bags or handbags into the ring with you, although it is a good idea to take a comb, to comb through hair just before the dog is judged, and again before the judge takes a final look round.

PROBLEMS

Many of the problems that arise in the show ring occur because the early training has been hurried, or missed. One of the most common is that of the puppy who will not stand but consistently sits down. The only way to cure this is to start again at the beginning, by giving a reward when the dog is stood and removing the reward as soon as sitting down occurs.

Some dogs insist on galloping around the ring, in which case try and move the dog at a fast walk, rather than a trot, as this will often stop this problem.

One word of warning here. Do not expect your puppy to behave perfectly every time. Those who behave well in the ring as puppies are often over-trained and lose enthusiasm later on, by which time a happy, enthusiastic show dog can have the edge over bored rivals.

Some dogs show little enthusiasm for showing and are much harder to show than

HANDLING FAULTS
Photos: Steve Nash.

This dog is stood correctly, but the handler's hands are obstructing the dog's head.

Once again, the dog is stood correctly but Kennel Club rules are being broken because the handler has let go of the lead.

The dog is stood correctly, but the handler's hands are obscuring the head; the lead is placed too far forward on the neck.

The dog is free-standing, but the handler is standing much too close. The dog's neck has been pushed back into her shoulders so that her long neck and correct shoulder placement are hidden from the judge. The lead is also in the wrong place again, adding to the illusion of a shorter neck.

The dog's feet are correctly placed here, but the tail is being held too low and the lead is placed too high around the neck, spoiling the outline.

Again the feet are correctly placed, but both head and tail are being held too high, spoiling the outline. The lead is incorrectly placed.

The dog is too stretched out and neither front or hind feet are under the body. The head is also too high and the lead incorrectly placed.

dogs who are a little naughty. The main thing to remember with such dogs is that you must make the show ring as pleasant a place as possible for them. Much reward, praise and enthusiasm from the handler helps, and never be afraid to play with your dog. However, if your Golden is really frightened and unhappy, it may be best to withdraw from the ring for a while and concentrate on training at home and ringcraft.

Movement in the show ring can also produce problems. The aim is to have a happy, sound-moving dog, moving at a steady trot in a straight line, not distracted by anything or anyone. A dog who pulls the owner around the ring, gallops instead of trots, or constantly pulls to one side does not enable the judge to assess the movement.

Firstly, teach the dog to walk on a loose lead, by your side at a steady trot. This can be achieved by starting to walk the dog or puppy at a fairly slow walk, checking the dog every time your Golden pulls ahead or to one side, and talking quietly and praising every time your dog is in the correct place. Use one word to tell the dog what behaviour or action is required. Usually "Heel" or "Close" are the commands used.

When your Golden is not in the correct position, check the dog back into position using the appropriate command. Gradually increase the speed until the dog is trotting at a steady trot. To correct pulling sideways, walk the dog against a fence or wall, and, to prevent distractions, try training in a crowded place once the dog has learnt what is expected. A dog who constantly crabs can be taught to walk correctly by walking in fairly small left-hand circles.

Another problem that occurs occasionally in the ring is that of a dog who has been frightened when being handled. This can be one of the most difficult things to cure. The best idea is to boost the dog's confidence by taking your Golden out and about with you, and asking people you meet to talk to the dog and perhaps offer a tidbit. Once the dog accepts that most people are harmless, start back at ringcraft or Obedience classes.

SUMMARY
Golden Retrievers are an easy breed to train and very few problems ever arise, provided that the initial training has been carried out carefully and that the dog has the typical temperament of the breed.

Remember that the dog you take to a show is the same dog that you take home, regardless of whether you win first place or nothing at all. Be a good sport and, most of all, ensure that both you and your dog enjoy the show ring.

13 BEST OF BRITISH

To write a chapter on British breeders who have made the Golden Retriever such a popular breed, we need to go back to the early years of the 20th century. In Chapter One we examined the early history of the Golden Retriever. Now let us concentrate on those breeders who combined all the early threads into a weave, creating the dog we know today.

THE CULHAM KENNEL

Lewis Harcourt, the first Viscount Harcourt (prefix Culham) was very friendly with the Tweedmouth family due to their political involvements. Lord Harcourt often shot at Guisachan where he saw the yellow retrievers working. He founded his kennel on John MacLennan's stock, who was one of the Guisachan keepers.

After the discovery of the Culham Pedigrees in the Harcourt papers in Oxford's Bodleian Library in 1995, a murky period in history became clear. From the second Lord Tweedmouth came Luna, born in 1898, Glen, born in 1902, and Haddow, a grandson of the Hon. Archie Majoribank's Lady (who lived in the USA and Canada with Archie) and also the great grandson of Rose, bred in the first Lord Tweedmouth's last litter in 1889. Other Culhams came from the Earl of Portsmouth (who bought Guisachan), and from other people who had yellow, wavy-coated retrievers: Mr Wareham, B. Haworth-Booth, Mr Pope, Mr Beechgrove, and the Earl of Ilchester. Lord Harcourt bought Culham Lassie, who was registered as 'a Flat Coated Retriever, colour Golden'. A great grand-daughter of the black Ch. Wimpole Peter, Lassie, was grand-dam of the influential sire Dual Champion, Balcombe Boy.

Lord Harcourt was one of the first to show his dogs, and in 1908 and 1909 he exhibited at Crufts and the Crystal Palace. There were about 20 dogs kept at Nuneham Park, Oxfordshire, the Harcourt country seat. Golden Retrievers had no classes of their own in those days. Lord Harcourt, in one of his last registered litters, bred Dual Ch. Balcombe Boy (the first Dual Champion) whom he gave as a present to Mr R. Herman. Lord Harcourt died in February 1922.

The Golden Retriever is now one of the most popular breeds in the UK, often attracting the biggest entries at all breed Championship shows. Photo: Kipps.

INGESTRE

Dogs of the era were still kept mainly for shooting; showing was a sideline. Shows were rare, and travel around the country was not easy. The Earl of Shrewsbury (prefix Ingestre), who was connected by marriage to the Earl of Ilchester, shot over yellow retrievers, and his head keeper Donald MacDonald was very involved in shooting and showing. Glen, belonging to Lady Tweedmouth, was used at stud in 1905. Glen's sister Corrie 2, born in 1902, was the dam of Ingestre Tyne, who is behind everything in the breed through her mating to Ingestre Scamp.

Ingestre made up two of the earliest Show Champions, Klip and Top Twig. They also bred the great brood Sh. Ch. Noranby Dandelion. The last official litter bred by Donald MacDonald was in March 1924.

NORANBY

Winifred Maud Charlsworth was the greatest force in developing the Golden Retriever in the UK. Her involvement spanned 50 years, and there are some people still involved in the breed who knew her well. Her first bitch was of unknown parentage, registered as Normanby Beauty. Through Beauty's matings with the Culham sires, and the buying in of Ingestre breeding (Sh. Ch. Noranby Dandelion), the breed took off. Mrs Charlsworth's prefix had initially been Normanby, after Normanby Hall where she was born, but after a mistake in writing the word, she changed the prefix and kept it as Noranby. She bred the first Champion in the breed, Ch. Noranby Campfire, and bred or owned a further six title-holders. After the 1939-45 war, she showed and trialled Dual Ch. Noranby Destiny to both titles. The great progress made in establishing a uniform type during the 1920s and 30s is largely due to her. She died in 1953.

IMPORTANT KENNELS AND STUD DOGS

The following British kennels all had important stud dogs as their main claim to fame, as well as bitch Champions.

KENTFORD: The Hon. Mrs E. Grigg owned the bitch Ch. Bess of Kentford (the first Champion bitch), the important stud dog Ch. & Indian Ch. Flight of Kentford, Sh. Ch. Noranby Dandelion, Champions Kib, Mischief Rip, all of Kentford, plus Field Trial Ch. Eredine Rufus.

WOOLLEY: Mrs J. Cottingham had influential dogs including Ch. Cubbington Diver, Ch. Reine, Ch. Banner, Ch. Vic, Ch. & Am. Ch. Vesta, Ch. Diver, Ch. Marine, Ch. Merry Rose, Ch. Mist, Ch. Bachelor, and Sh. Ch. Lancer, all of Woolley.

HEYDOWN: Lt. Col. The Hon. Douglas Carnegie's influential kennel was well-known for its lovely-headed dogs and many important stud dogs. Heydown Champions were H. Gunner, Grip, Guider, Gillyflower and Goody Two Shoes.

HAULSTONE: Pre-1939, Mr and Mrs Eccles showed and worked their dogs, who included Ch. Haulstone Dan, Ch. Haulstone Dusty, Ch. Haulstone Marker and Ch. Haulstone Sprig, and Field Trial Chs. Haulstone Larry and Brock. Post-war they only worked their dogs and made up FT Champions.

MORETON: Moreton was the prefix of Mr and Mrs R. Kirk, whose best-known dog, the sire of many title-holders, was Ch. Michael of Moreton. He won 17 CCs, a large number in those days when there were far fewer Championship shows. The Kirks also made up Ch. Haulstone Dusty, Ch. Abbots Winkle, Ch. Mary of Moreton and Ch. Abbots Trust.

SPEEDWELL: The Evans-Swindells started in 1921. They bought a puppy of Noranby/ Ingestre breeding and registered him Cornelius. He was a good winner and worker, and became a Champion and a great sire. They also had a good bitch line (Sh. Ch. Speedwell Emerald, Ch. Speedwell Beryl, Ch. Speedwell Brandy, Ch. Speedwell Molly, Sh. Ch. Speedwell Dainty), and bred a dog much used in the north, Ch. Kelso Of Aldgrove, and Ch. Joseph of Housesteads.

SUCCESSFUL BLOODLINES
The following breeders achieved success, both pre-and post-war.

ANNINGSLEY
Mr and Mrs Venables-Kyrke had one of the few kennels to have a Dual Champion, with Anningsley Stingo. Other Champions were Anningsley Fox, Beatrice (also an Am. Ch.), and FT Ch. Anningsley Crackers. Mr Venables-Kyrke was a very good trainer, and handled FT Ch. Avishays Lulu and her son FT Ch. Avishays Brush. Anningsley bloodlines played an important part in the breed after the Second World War, mainly through Ch. Masterpiece of Yeo, Ch. Dorcas Glorious of Slat, and Ch. Colin of Rosecott.

STUBBINGS
In the late 1920s, Nancy Nairn, living at the vicarage in Stubbings near Maidenhead, decided to acquire a larger breed than the dogs she had kept in the past. The result was Stubbings Lorelei, by Ch. Michael of Moreton ex a working-bred bitch. Mrs Nairn's large kennel at one time contained about 50 Goldens. The only homebred pre-war Champion was Ch. Stubbings Golden Gloria, but others were unlucky not to gain their titles. Stubbings also bought Ch. Birling James of Somersby after he had gained his title. He sired many winners. Mrs Nairn died in 1942, and the kennel was carried on by her daughter, Sylvia Winston. Many dogs were born during the war and thus unshown (no Championship shows were held during the war period), and with the return of shows several were too old to compete.

However, Stubbings Golden Timothy, Golden Lalage, Golden Nicholas (a winner of the G.R. Club Stud dog trophy and said by Elma Stonex to be a lovely dog and, except for the war, a certain Champion), Dandylyon and Daemen were all bred on, providing a very important link into the 1940s. Dual Ch. Stubblesdown Golden Lass, born 24.12.44, was by Stubbings Golden Garry ex Stubbings Golden Olympia, which would have thrilled Mrs Nairn, a great supporter of the dual-

purpose Golden. Lass founded a dynasty herself, as did Sunar (behind many Yelme Champions) who was all Stubbings breeding.

YELME
In 1926, Mr H. Wentworth-Smith and Mrs M.K. Wentworth-Smith (who for a short time had the prefix Skroy) bought their first Golden, Culnoran Bess. They always insisted on dual-purpose and would show and trial quite a few dogs, rather than concentrating on just one. In about 1933, Mr Wentworth-Smith bought an adult who became the outstanding stud dog of the time. Gilder, was an unfashionably pale colour for those days. He won many show awards and trial awards, and sired eight Champions. Pre-war, Yelme had Ch. Cubstone Bess, Ch. Gaiety Girl of Yelme, Ch. Chief of Yelme, Ch. Kandyd of Skroy, and Ch. & Am. Ch. Bingo of Yelme.

ABBOTS
Mr H.L. Jenner started in 1917 with a present – a two-year-old dog, Rory of Bentley, by Normanby Balfour ex a grand-daughter of Yellow Nell. It was not until 1921 that Mr Jenner bought a bitch, called Aurora. Abbots built up to become one of the greatest kennels of its day, and provided the foundation for other kennels, especially Torrdale. Torrdale, in turn, become one of the greatest kennels of the late 40s and 50s, and provided much foundation stock for kennels in the 70s and 80s. Mr Jenner was one of the kindest and most helpful breeders. He was never one for wearing rose-tinted spectacles, for he knew that it was only by seeing the faults that you could breed to improve the next generation.

Unlike most other well-known breeders at that time, who were mostly wealthy, Mr Jenner went to one of his first Championship shows (Birmingham National in 1924) travelling in a coal lorry. Lacking unlimited resources, he carefully controlled how many Goldens he kept, and often had to sell what he would have wished to keep. He bred or owned: Ch. Noble of Quinton, Ch. Michael of Moreton, Sh. Ch. Sewardstone Tess, Sh. Ch. Abbots Ann, Ch. Haulstone Marker, Sh. Ch.

Abbots Wisdom, Ch. Goldgleam of Aldgrove, Ch. Abbots Winkle, Ch. Abbots Music, Ch. Tickencote Jenny, Ch. Davie of Yelme, Sh. Ch. Leonder, Ch. Abbots Daisy, Ch. Dukeries Dancing Lady, and Ch. Abbots Trust. Mr Jenner gave up in 1937, but after the war he showed his lovely Sprig of Yelme to two Challenge Certificates. When he first exhibited, he liked to present his dogs on a loose lead, showing themselves naturally, very like the famous Cocker breeder H.S. Lloyd, whose skill earned him the nickname the 'Wizard of Ware'.

DORCAS

Elma Stonex was not only a brilliant breeder – her famous 'war baby' Dorcas Bruin spanned the war years with his important bloodlines – but she was also the first breed historian. Elma started her kennel in 1931 with Sally of Perrott, whose parents Ch. Haulstone Marker and Noranby Daphne were half-brother and sister by Ch. Michael of Moreton. Mated to Ch. Davie of Yelme, Sally's litter included Dorcas Bruin, the first gundog (except for Cockers) to gain a Junior Warrant, and who also won a Reserve CC. The Second World War stopped him becoming a Champion, but he sired the important stud dogs, Champion Dorcas Glorious of Slat, and Dorcas Timberscombe Topper (this winner of two CCs was a difficult dog to condition, so he never achieved the magic third CC, but instead made his mark as a sire). After the war, Ch. Dorcas Gardenia was made up.

In the late 1940s the Dorcas kennel provided the foundation bitches for some influential kennels: Dorcas Clorinda for Rosecott; Dorcas Leola for Beauchasse; through Beauchasse (who bred Boltby Kymba), the founding sire of Boltby; Dorcas Aurora for Deerflite, and the many kennels founded on Deerflite bloodlines.

TORRDALE

Fred and Rene Parsons (prefix Torrdale) were the owners of a kennel whose influence on the breed has been most important, especially through certain other kennels. Torrdale's first serious acquisition was a puppy from Mr Jenner, Dukeries Dancing Lady, who became a Champion in 1936. Sadly, none of the photographs we have of Paula, as she was known, do her justice. She was a cream bitch of great quality who left a tremendous amount of winning descendants. Ch. Torrdale Betty won 14 CCs, a record that stood for many years, and Sh. Ch. Torrdale Judy was also successful.

In 1936, Donkelve Rusty was bought from Mr Jenner, who had acquired him from his breeder Mrs Vernon-Wentworth. In 1937 Rusty became a Champion. He was much used at stud, and lies behind many Champions of the time. Three non-titled dogs who also had quite an influence were Torrdale Tinker, Torrdale Merry Michael and Torrdale Laddie. When shows restarted in 1946 and 1947, the Parsons won two CCs with Torrdale Don Juan. In 1947, they produced Torrdale Happy Lad out of Ch. Dukeries Dancing Lady (who was eleven when he was born), and sired by her grandson.

Happy Lad became the first post-war Champion, and sired many winners. Sh. Ch. Torrdale Kim of Stenbury, brother to Torrdale Don Juan, was made up by Mrs Enid Minter. Mrs Woods made up Ch. Torrdale Faithful, and Mrs J. Murray made up Sh. Ch. Torrdale Maida. Torrdale Suella and Torrdale Highland Gunner won at Field Trials. Most of the pre-war kennels were dual-purpose, and Goldens won consistently at trials. The same breeding was for both show and work At Championship shows after 1946, the dominance of Torrdale as breeders became obvious and many satellite breeders emerged, using Torrdale lines.

ELSIVILLE

Elsie Ford had started in 1944, breeding Ch. Alexander of Elsiville by Torrdale Tinker. He won ten CCs, and is important as the sire of Ch, Alresford Advertiser. The Fords had a lot of dogs and, in a short time, made up Sh. Ch. Nyda of Elsiville, a grand-daughter of Torrdale Laddie; Ch. Nicolai of Elsiville, a lovely dog who made a great impression on those who saw him – a grandson of Torrdale Merry Michael; Sh. Ch. Ophelia of Elsiville, a lovely-looking bitch – a Torrdale Laddie grand-daughter who was sold to Mrs Minter but never shown again; Sh. Ch. Major of Elsiville, a Torrdale Tinker grandson; and Sh. Ch. Shula of Elsiville, also a Torrdale Laddie grand-daughter. Amazingly after such success in the early 1950s, the family seemed to give up their interest in the breed and never showed again. They must have had the canine equivalent of green fingers, for they also bred an English Setter Show Champion and some winning Pointers.

STENBURY

Another kennel which started with a Torrdale foundation was that of Enid Minter. She started pre-war, and took quite a time deciding which lines she wanted, finally buying as a puppy Sh. Ch. Torrdale Kim of Stenbury, made up in 1947.

From the beginning she was great advocate of line breeding, which she soon put into practice when Torrdale Happy of Stenbury was mated to her uncle, Torrdale Tinker. Laughter of Stenbury was kept who, when mated to her half-brother Torrdale Don Juan (by Torrdale Tinker ex Torrdale Tip Toes who was sister to Torrdale Happy of Stenbury), produced the first of many beautiful bitches in Ch. Charming of Stenbury. When mated to Don Juan's full brother, Sh. Ch. Torrdale Kim of Stenbury, Laughter produced Ch. Gaiety Girl of Stenbury. That mating also produced a CC winner, Delightful of Stenbury, who, when mated to a son of Torrdale Tinker, produced

Bewitching of Stenbury, and, when mated to the Torrdale-bred Ch. Boltby Skylon, produced the Championship Show Best In Show winner, Sh. Ch. Waterwitch of Stenbury. When Waterwitch was mated to the Torrdale-bred Ch. Boltby Moonraker, she produced another Championship Show BIS winner, Sh. Ch. Watersprite of Stenbury. Sh. Ch. Waterwitch mated back to her sire Skylon, produced Sh. Ch. Waterwitchery of Stenbury. The inbred Waterwitchery was mated to her half-brother Waterboy, and produced Sh. Ch. Watersonnet of Stenbury and Sh. Ch. Glennessa Waterwisp of Stenbury. Sh. Ch. Watersonnet was mated to the Ch. Boltby Skylon son, Glennessa Crofter of Empshott, and produced Ch. Glenessa Seasprite of Stenbury. Sh. Ch. Watersprite, mated to her son Waterwizard, produced Waterminx, who, mated to the Skylon son, Crofter, produced Ch. Glenessa Seashanta.

In the early 1970s, Enid Minter acquired Nomis Portia of Stenbury whom she made into a full Champion. Her sire was out of Searose of Stenbury, who went back to the mother/son mating of Waterwizard and Sh. Ch. Watersprite. Portia's dam, Nomis Nina was mostly Boltby breeding. Portia, mated to the great sire Ch. Camrose Cabus Christopher, who had one Boltby line through his dam Cabus Boltby Charmer, produced Sh. Ch. Stenbury Seasonnet, Sh. Ch. Stenbury Sea Laughter, Sh. Ch. Stenbury Sea O'Dreams, and Ch. Stenbury Sea Tristram of Camrose. Sh. Ch. Stenbury Seasonnet, mated to her half-brother Ch. Camrose Fabius Tarquin, produced Sh. Ch. Stenbury Sealace.

Sh. Ch. Stenbury Sealace.

A group of Stenbury Golden Retrievers in Sweden.   *Photo courtesy: Marie Lore.*

In the mid-1980s, Enid took as a partner in her prefix, Anne Nerell, a Swedish Golden Retriever breeder. Stenbury dogs were henceforth not shown much in England, but more Champions were made up in Scandinavia. Enid Minter died in 1995, but is remembered for her magnificent bitch line, which produced the same lovely type from 1946 up to the present day.

BOLTBY
In the late 1940s, Mrs R. Harrison started to do a lot of winning. Founded before the war, Boltby had little success, then obtained B. Kymba, bred by Davie Barwise by Sh. Ch. Torrdale Kim of Stenbury ex Dorcas Leola, who won two CCs. This lovely dog should have been a Champion. However, with Enid Minter's help, Mrs Harrison bought the Torrdale-bred Boltby Sweet Melody. Mated to Kymba, she produced Ch. Boltby Skylon, a winner of CCs into double figures and a very influential sire. Sweet Melody was mated to Mrs Harrison's other influential stud dog, Ch. Boltby Moonraker, who was again by Kymba ex an all-Torrdale bred bitch. Melody produced Ch. & Am. Ch. Boltby Annabel. Other Boltby winners were Ch. Boltby Mistral Sh. Ch. Boltby Sugar Bush, and her brother Sh. Ch. Boltby Syrian. The last two Boltby Champions were born in 1962 – Ch. Boltby Felicity of Briarford and her brother Ch. Cabus Boltby Combine.

Mrs Harrison died in the 1960s and the great northern kennel was no more. Mrs Harrison was very proud of the fact she had one of the few road signs on the A1. The sign saying Boltby has long gone, but whenever I drive on that part of the A1, I imagine the great Skylon as Mrs Harrison used to advertise him – The Cock of the North.

YEO
We go from the north-east down to the south-west for one of the most important kennels, and the source of many others - Mrs Lucille Sawtell's Yeo. Other than Westley, Yeo is the only post-war kennel that has bred Field Trial Champions and Bench Champions. Mrs Sawtell's first Ch. Masterpiece of Yeo, by Ch. Anningsley Fox, was born in 1942 and became a Champion at nine years of age in 1952. His daughter was FT Ch. Musicmaker of Yeo. Mrs Sawtell bought Pandown Poppet of Yeo and made her a Show Champion. Poppet was by Ch. Torrdale Faithful ex Ch. Fiona of Maidafield, who was three-quarters Torrdale breeding. She was mated to Lottie Pilkington's sire, Ch. Alresford Advertiser, a winner of 35 CCs. Poppet's mating to Advertiser produced a good sire in Ringmaster of Yeo who, mated to his half-sister Alresford Badminton, fathered the lovely Ch. Figaro of Yeo, also an American Champion.

Poppet, mated to her grandson, produced Sh. Ch. Halsham Hifi of Yeo. Lucille Sawtell's working lines gave June Atkinson FT Ch. Holway Flush of Yeo. The first time I awarded Challenge Certificates in Golden Retrievers in the 1960s, I gave the dog CC to a dog owned in partnership with Mrs Sawtell and Mrs Eva Harkness from Ireland – Ch. & Irish Ch.

Mandingo Buidhe Colum. Colum's half-brother Mandingo Beau Geste of Yeo, sired one of the loveliest of bitches in Ch. Deerflite Endeavour of Yeo. Her son was Sh. Ch. Concord of Yeo, sire of Sh. Ch. Trident of Yeo Colbar.

Other Champions for this kennel were Ch. Toddytavern Kummel of Yeo and Ch. Challenger of Yeo Glengilde. Concord's sister Caprice was dam of another well-known stud dog, Ch. Moorquest Mugwump. In 1995, with a five-generation Yeo bitch line, Sh. Ch. Yeo Gold Medallion was made up. Yeo was the foundation for many south-western kennels, and the beautiful Ch. Deerflite Endeavour of Yeo is to be found in many pedigrees.

ALRESFORD
The Alresford kennel was started in 1931 and a number of good winners were bred. In 1948, Alresford Last Laugh won the CC at Crufts. In 1950, Lottie Pilkington made up his daughter, Ch. Alresford Mall. His son, Alresford Will Laugh, was a good winner at Trials. Mall, mated to Ch. Alexander of Elsiville, produced Ch. Advertiser, who won many CCs and sired the lovely Ch. Alresford Atom. The same mating produced Sh. Ch. Alresford Harringay, also an American Champion. The last Alresford to be made up was Sh. Ch. Alresford Purgold Tartan, born 17.2.62.

DEERFLITE
Liz Borrow's foundation bitch was Dorcas Aurora and when she was mated to Ch. Torrdale Happy Lad, the result was the very typical Sh. Ch. Sonnet. Sonnet, when mated to Celia of Stenbury, produced Ch. Deerflite Delilah, and was also the sire of the home kennel's Ch. Avondale Brandy. Brandy and Delilah produced Ch. Deerflite Headline who, when mated to Dorcas Aurora's daughter, Deerflite Flirt, produced Deerflite Highlight, the dam of Sh. Ch. Deerflite Rainfall. Rainfall, when mated to Mandingo Beau Geste of Yeo, gave us Ch. Deerflite Endeavour of Yeo and Sh. Ch. Deerflite Paragon. Rainfall was also mated to one of the last Boltby's in Nimble, and produced Deerflite Tradition of Janville,

sire of Ch. Moorquest Mugwump and Sh. Ch. Janville Tempestuous at Linchael. The same consistent type is still shown today under the Deerflite prefix.

GLENNESSA
This kennel which has, over the years, had a big influence on the breed, is owned by Wing Cm. 'Jimmy' Iles and his wife Muriel, and later also their daughter Julia. Their foundation bitch was Glennessa Alexa, who was mated to Ch. Boltby Skylon, a dog the Iles family admired very much. Alexa's son, Glennessa Crofter of Empshott sired some very nice stock. The kennel achieved titles with Alexa's grand-daughters Ch. Glennessa Seasprite of Stenbury and Ch. Glennessa Seashanta, and Alexa's great grandson Sh. Ch. Glennessa Leaderman. Crofter's great grand-daughter was Sh. Ch. Glennessa Emma of Fivewinds, and Emma's daughter was Sh. Ch. Glennessa Petrushka. Petrushka, mated to the northern-bred Sh. Ch. Rossbourne Timothy, produced Sh. Ch. Glennessa Clare. They also made up Sh. Ch. Glennessa Waterwisp of Stenbury. Glennessa Escapade, a lovely type of dog, sired one of the great sires of the late 80s and 90s, Ch. Gaineda Consolidator of Sansue.

ROSSBOURNE
Rossbourne, owned by Mr and Mrs Raymond and Jean Burnett, started as two kennels. Jean Burnett, formerly Jean Brison (Fordvale) before her marriage, made up the lovely Ch. Beauchasse Gaiety. The partnership kept Raymonds' Rossbourne prefix, although Jean had bred Ch. Fordvale Gay Moonlynn. Successes include Sh. Ch. Rossbourne Timothy, Sh. Ch. Rossbourne Harvest Gold, Sh. Ch. Rossbourne Abbotsford Hope, Sh. Ch. Rossbourne In Love and Sh. Ch. Melfricka Kudos of Rossbourne. Rossbourne Quality Miss won her third CC in 1996.

LINDYS
Lindy Anderson started in the 1950s and produced very good Goldens. She bred and campaigned Ch. Lindys Olivia whom I gave a

Sh. Ch. Rossbourne Quality Miss.

Photo: Kipps.

third CC to in 1969. She bred the Hathaways' Sh. Ch. Lindys Butterscotch of Melfricka and Mrs Tudor's Ch. Camrose Tamarisk.

STOLFORD

Peggy Robertson's Stolford is a very influential kennel with rare Brecklands bloodlines. Sh. Ch. Stolford Joy was born 12.8.56. Then, in the 1960s, came brother and sister Sh. Ch. Stolford Samala and Sh. Ch. Samdor Stolford Samarkand out of Stolford Samantha. There followed a further seven title holders, including the influential stud, Ch. Stolford Happy Lad.

MOORQUEST

The Moorquest kennel of Shirley Crick was founded on Deerflite and Stolford bloodlines. Ch. Moorquest Mugwump, an influential sire in the 1970s, produced his son Ch. Meant To Be at Moorquest, his daughter Ch. Make Haste to Moorquest and Penny Beauchamp's Sh. Ch. Moorquest Minervois of Bolberry.

WESTLEY

The two most important kennels of the last forty years, whose stud dogs and brood bitches have made a lasting impression on the breed, are Westley and Camrose. Joan Gill started Westley in 1936 with Simon of Brookshill, a beautifully-headed dog, given to her as a birthday present. Major Wentworth-Smith used him on Lively of Yelme and their daughter, Westley Frolic of Yelme, joined Westley. She was the dam, and Ch. Camrose Fantango the sire, of the influential stud Ch.

Simon of Westley, winner of 21 CCs and many Field Trial Awards. Other winners included Ch. Sally of Westley, a truly lovely bitch, and Ch. Kolahoi Willow of Westley.

A Ch. Hazelgilt grand-daughter was bought, who became Ch. Susan of Westley, and, mated to Spar of Yelme, produced Ch. William of Westley, an important sire. Mated again to Ch. Dorcas Glorious of Slat, she produced the last Dual Champion in the breed, born 6.6.51, the English Dual Ch. & Irish Dual Ch. David of Westley. William, mated to Ch. Camrose Jessica, produced another most influential stud dog, Ch. Camrose Nicolas of Westley, who gained 20 CCs, was a Field Trial winner and went BIS at a General Championship Show. David's sister Drusilla, mated to Ch. Simon, produced Echo of Westley, who was dam of a FT Ch. Holway Teal of Westley and Ch. Pippa of Westley, winners of 17 CCs.

Then Joan Gill and Daphne Philpott went into partnership, with the help of Daphne's husband Mervyn. At eleven years of age, Ch. Camrose Nicolas of Westley sired Ch. Sansue Saracan of Westley. Ch. Pippa mated to Ch. Sansue Camrose Phoenix, produced the superb Ch. Clarissa of Westley. Next a Ch. Pippa grand-daughter, Ch. Westley Jacquetta, was mated to Ch. Sansue Camrose Phoenix and produced Ch. Westley Victoria, top brood bitch in the breed and dam of eight UK title holders: Sh. Ch. Westley Tartan of Buidhe, Ch. Westley Topic of Sansue, Sh. Ch. Westley Munro of Nortonwood, Ch. Westley Mabella (22 CCs), Ch. Westley Martha, Sh. Ch. Westley Simone (12 CCs), Ch. Westley

ABOVE: Ch Simon of Westley: Winner of 21 CCs, Group and Reserve best in Show, and first prize in Field Trials.   Photo courtesy: Joan Gill.

RIGHT: Sh. Ch. Westley Jacob.
*   Photo: Sally Anne Thompson.*

BELOW: Ch. Camrose Nicolas of Westley: A Field Trial winner, Best in Show at an all breeds Championship show and winner of 20 CCs.
*   Photo: Sally Anne Thompson.*

Samuel and Sh. Ch. Westley Sophia of Papeta. Mabella produced Ch. Westley Felicia of Siatham and Sh. Ch. Westley Jacob. Martha was the dam of Ch. Westley Ramona, and Jacob's sister Julianna produced Sh. Chs. Westley Clementina and Christina, W. Glenn of Highguild and Ch. W. Gabriella of Siatham.

Daphne Philpott, who died in 1997, had the Standerwick prefix for the working lines, and bred Ch. Standerwick Thomasina (11 Field Trial Awards), FT Ch. Standerwick Rumbustuous of Catcombe, FT. Ch. Standerwick Roberta of Abnalls, and FT Ch. Standerwick Donna of Deadcraft, and owned FT Ch. Abnalls Hilary of Standerwick.

CATCOMBE
Wendy Andrews of Catcombe made up a FT. Ch. in Standerwick Rumbustuous, and also made up Ch. Royal Pal of Catcombe; she also bred Ch. Catcombe Charm.

CAMROSE
Joan Tudor's Camrose Golden Retrievers started with Golden Camrose Tess, born in 1946. Her dam was sister to Ch. Dorcas Glorious of Slat and Tess won a CC, but it is as the foundation of Camrose that she is remembered. Tess was the dam of Ch. Camrose Anthea and then of Ch. Camrose Fantango, an influential stud dog and the first in a chain of great studs. Fantango sired for his home kennel Ch. Camrose Tantara, Sh. Ch. Broadwater Camrose Tangay and Ch. Camrose Jessica, who was the dam, by Ch. William of Westley, of Ch. Camrose Nicolas of Westley. Tantara was the dam of Chs. Camrose Lucius and Loretta. A daughter of Lucius became Ch. Camrose Tamerisk. Another important stud dog for Camrose was the Fantango son, Ch. Camrose Tallyrand of Anbria. Margaret Barron's Anbria was a carefully-thought-out line, starting with Ch. Briar of Arbrook as a foundation. Briar, mated to Ch. William of Westley, produced Ch. Jane of Anbria. Jane, mated to Ch. Camrose Fantango, produced Ch. Camrose Tallyrand of Anbria who, through his outstanding son Ch. Camrose Cabus Christopher, is in most pedigrees today.

In all there were ten Anbria UK title holders.

The lovely Ch. Camrose Loretta, mated to Tallyrand, produced another lovely bitch in Ch. Camrose Wistura, and her sister Wistansy was a very influential brood bitch. Loretta had three outstanding grandchildren: Ch. Sansue Camrose Phoenix, Ch. Camrose Pruella of Davern, and Sh. Ch. Camrose Psyche of Vementry. When owned in partnership with Rosemary Wilcox, Camrose produced Ch. Camrose Matilda and Ch. Styal Stefanie of Camrose, the bitch CC record holder with 27 CCs. Other top dogs from the kennel include Sh. Ch. Camrose Hardangerfjord of Beldonburn (the Weeks family), a top stud Ch. Camrose Fabius Tarquin (20 CCs), Ch. Stenbury Sea Tristram of Camrose, Sh. Ch. Gyrima Wystonia of Camrose, Ch. Camrose Waterlyric of Beldonburn and Sh. Ch. Camrose Frangipani of Beldonburn.

In latter years, in sole ownership again, Camrose has seen Sh. Ch. Camrose Tulfes Intirol. A much-travelled dog was UK Can. and Bermudan Ch. Camrose Even Patrol (Johnson). The CC winner, Mjaerumhogda's Thor to Camrose, was born by artificial insemination many years after his famous sire's (Christopher's) death. Ch. Camrose Cabus Christopher is to date the top sire ever in Golden Retrievers, and was the leading sire of all breeds for a time in the UK. Sire of 26 UK title holders, this very interestingly bred dog was by the all southern-bred Ch. Camrose Tallyrand of Anbria ex Cabus Boltby Charmer (all northern Boltby bloodlines). This makes him almost an outcross, though both parents were line bred on different lines. He won 41 CCs, and held that record for quite a time. He won many Groups and BIS at Championship Shows, worked well on shoots as a picking up dog, and was a loving companion and also a pioneer of artificial insemination. The Golden Retriever story has been carried on by kennels who are really a combination of Westley and Camrose.

DAVERN
Chas and Brenda Lowe's first Davern Champion was Sutton Rudy in the 1960s.

ABOVE: Ch. Davern Figaro (aged ten years) with his daughter.

LEFT: Sh. Ch. Davern Josephine: a big winner in the late 1970s.

Photos courtesy: Mr and Mrs C.R. Lowe.

They had two Camrose bitches. One made up into Ch. Camrose Pruella of Davern, who, mated to Ch. Camrose Tallyrand of Anbria, produced one of my great favourites, and an influential sire, in Ch. Davern Figaro. The second Camrose bitch was Flavella, grandmother of Davern Gabriella, who, when mated to Figaro, produced the big winner, Sh. Ch. Davern Josephine (18 CCs). Other Champions of Davern have been Sh. Ch. Rosabella, Sh. Ch. Verdayne Dandini of Davern, Sh. Ch. Davern Alpine Rose of Lacons and Sh. Ch. Amirene King Eider of Davern, bred in the north-east by Margaret Woods.

TEECON
John Tiranti and Pat Holmes founded Teecon on Camrose/Westley/Anbria lines, and the dogs lie behind many of today's Goldens, through Sh. Ch. Gambird Debonair of Teecon. Other winners were Sh. Ch. Peatling Stella of Teecon, Ch. Teecon Ambassador, and Sh. Ch. Teecon Knight Errant. John and Janet Tiranti had Sh. Ch. Pitcote Arcadian of Garthfield and Pat and Bill Holmes had Sh. Ch. Elzac Amber of Beaconholme, both from Teecon bloodlines.

STYAL
Hazel Hinks runs this important kennel, with numbers always kept to a minimum. The foundation bitch, Styal Camrose Gilda, was mated to Ch. Camrose Nicholas of Westley, producing Ch. Styal Sibella who, mated to Ch. Camrose Cabus Christopher, gave Hazel the important brood and show bitch Ch. Styal Susila. She was the dam of the CC record holder, Ch. Styal Scott of Glengilde – sire of Champions and winner of 42 CCs. Hazel also bred Sh. Ch. Styal Shakespeare, Sh. Ch. Styal Shelley of Maundale and Sh. Ch. Styal Symetrya. Sibella, when mated to Christopher, produced Ch. Styal Stefanie of Camrose, Bitch CC record holder. Susila's great grand-daughter is the latest to gain her title. Sh. Ch. Styal Snowflake of Remington was the foundation for the Remington Golden Retrievers.

CABUS
Zilpha Morgan, formerly Moriarty, died in 1996 after showing for many years. She and her first husband, Maurice, started in the 1950s with a dog, Beauchasse Jason, who was beautifully bred with all the old Beauchasse and Torrdale lines. His son, Ch. & Irish Ch. Cabus Cadet, started a kennel of important stud dogs: Ch. & Ir. Ch. Cabus Boltby Combine, Ch. Cabus Janville Defender, Ch. Camrose Cabus Christopher (the greatest sire of them all), Ch. Cabus Caruso and Ch. Hughenden Cabus Columba.

BRYANSTOWN
This is very much a dual-purpose kennel for Michael and Cynthia Twist, now joined by their daughter Diana Ewings, although not so much showing is done nowadays. The 1960s saw Ch. & Irish Ch. Bryanstown Gale Warning, followed in the early 1980s by his grandson, the big-winning Ch. Bryanstown Gaucho.

LACONS
John and Kath Siminster's lovely Sh. Ch. Lacons Enterprise is in many pedigrees. They also had his sister, Sh. Ch. Lacons Candy Floss, and Enterprise's daughter, Sh. Ch. Davern Alpine Rose Of Lacons.

GYRIMA
Marigold Timson started Gyrima with two bitches as her foundation, which gave her two lines. They were Sh. Ch. Romside Raffeena of Gyrima from Ian Ferris' old-established kennel, and Styal Sonnet of Gyrima. Both were mated to Ch. Camrose Cabus Christopher, and Sonnet produced three Champions but, very sadly, died soon after the litter was born. The litter were magnificently hand-reared. The three Champions were Gyrima Pippaline, Pipparanda and Pipparetta.

Pippaline founded the Ninell kennel of Viv Jones and also now her daughter Briony Jones, who have bred and owned Ch. Ninell Crusade of Dabess (Rosemary Wilson), Sh. Ch. Ninell Charade of Nortonwood, Ch. Ninell Francheska, Ch. Ninell Morwenna, and Ch.

Ninell Rambruen. Ch. Gyrima Pipparanda founded Dr and Mrs A. Morris' Sandusky kennel. Sandusky, in partnership with Mrs Day of Darris, had Sh. Ch. Sandusky Brigitta of Darris and her son Ch. Darris Double Diamond (Gray). The BOB at Crufts 1996 was Sh. Ch. Sandusky Khamsin at Trewater (Clarke).

Sh. Ch. Pipparetta was the dam of Sh. Ch. Gyrima Moonstone, who was herself dam of Sh. Ch. Gyrima Wystonia of Camrose. The other Gyrima foundation bitch produced Sh. Ch. Gyrima Ariadne, and Gyrima Genevieve who was the dam of Sh. Ch. Gyrima Oliver, the sire of Sh. Ch. Portcullis Greeting of Gyrima. Sadly, Marigold Timson died young, but the Morrises made up Gyrima Solitaire, a daughter of Sh. Ch. Portcullis Greeting of Gyrima. Solly died, at over ten years of age, the last of Marigold Timson's titled Gyrimas.

SANSUE

Many kennels are known for stud dogs or bitches who go on to found other lines. The third kennel, after Westley and Camrose, which has been of such importance, not only for its stud dogs but also for its bitches, is Val Birkin's Sansue, now in partnership with her daughter Sandra. All at Sansue are mainly house dogs, like many from Westley and Camrose. These three great kennels put a lot of time into housing, exercising, conditioning and loving their dogs.

Sansue's first title holder was the outstanding Ch. Sansue Camrose Phoenix. Mrs Birkin built up a bitch line from her first bitch, Tingel Concorde, a Daniel of Westley daughter whose grand-daughter, Sansue Latisha, mated to Ch. Camrose Nicolas of Westley, produced Ch. Sansue Saracan of Westley. A Phoenix daughter produced a useful stud dog in Ch. Sansue Tobias, whose daughter Sansue Gillian, mated to Gyrima Moonlord of Rockwin, produced Sansue Wanda of Stirchley, dam of an influential stud in Sh. Ch. Stirchley Saxon and also Sh. Ch. Sansue Wrainbow. Wrainbow, when mated to her kennel mate Ch. Gaineda Consolidator of Sansue (an important stud dog, bringing in through his sire Glennessa Escapade, Stenbury and Glennessa lines), produced the influential show and stud dog Ch. Sansue Golden Ruler (32 CCs) and his sister Sh. Ch. Sansue Phoebe.

Ruler, mated to his owner's Rossbourne Party Piece of Sansue, daughter of Ch. Westley Topic of Sansue, produced the lovely Ch. Sansue Royal Fancy, who died before her time, her sister Ch. Sansue Royal Flair, her daughter Sh. Ch. Sansue Flairs Opal, and another sister Sh. Ch. Sansue Spring Mist of Rambleyne. Ruler's sister, Ch. Sansue Pepper of Lovehayne, is one of the foundations for Richard and Paula Edwards' Lovehayne Goldens. 1995 saw Sh. Ch. Sansue Water Lily, another Ruler daughter, gain her title, and to

Sh. Ch. Sansue Golden Ruler: A great show winner and an influential stud dog, pictured at 12 years of age.

Photo: Kipps.

Sh. Ch. Sansue Waterlily: A daughter of Sh. Ch. Sansue Golden Ruler.

Photo: Kipps.

date there have been 18 UK title holders owned or bred at Sansue.

NORTONWOOD

Ron and Madge Bradbury of Nortonwood have had a lot of important stud dogs. Ch. Nortonwood Faunus, the result of a Phoenix daughter mated to Christopher, sired 19 UK title holders and won 13 CCs. Other influential sires were Sh. Ch. Westley Munro of Nortonwood and Sh. Ch. Nortonwood Checkmate, out of Sh. Ch. Nortonwood Canella. Checkmate sired Sh. Ch. Nortonwood Silvanus, who sired the two Sh. Chs. Jobeka Jasper of Nortonwood and Jobeka Just James. Bitches made up include Sh. Ch. Ninell Charade of Nortonwood and Sh. Ch. Nortonwood Canella.

Ch. Nortonwood Faunus: Sire of 19 UK title holders.

Photo courtesy: M. Bradbury.

LYNCHAEL

Lyn Anderson started her kennel in the 1960s. Her first title holder was the dog Sh. Ch. Janville Tempestuous At Lynchael. Lyn mated her Deerflite Destiny of Linchael to Tempestuous and produced the lovely Sh. Ch. Linchael Heritage. Destiny mated to Ch. Bryanstown Gaucho produced Sh. Ch. Linchael Excelsior (Coopland). Her Rossbourne Angelene at Linchael, mated to Ch. Camrose Fabius Tarquin, produced Sh.

Ch. Linchael Delmoss, who was the dam of Sh. Ch. Linchael Cartier Of Gloi (founding sire of Lyn Walker's and Larry Roberts' Gloi kennel).

Delmoss, mated to Ch. Styal Scott of Glengilde, not only produced Cartier but also Sh. Ch. Linchael Conspiracy of Chevanne (Scragg's) and Ch. Linchael Wild Silk for the home kennel. Angeline mated to Fabius Tarquin also gave Lyn Sh. Ch. Linchael Freya of Gloi (Walker and Roberts). For two years Lyn had the Norwegian Ch. Mjaerumhogdas Crusader at stud in the UK. He sired Sh. Ch. Linchael Gulviva.

OKUS

Carol Gilbert has produced at Okus a lovely type, especially Ch. Okus Buccaneer, Ch. Okus Jallina of Kerrien, Sh. Ch. Okus Watersprite, Sh. Ch. Okus Songbird of Crowood, Sh. Ch. Okus Dancing Melody, (Wendy Gunner) and Sh. Ch. Okus Destiny of Carasan.

OTHER IMPORTANT KENNELS

* The latter two Okus dogs are both owned by Wendy Gunner (CROWOOD), who also has the big-winning Songbird's grandson Sh. Ch. Crowood Butch Cassidy.
* Sue and Peter Jolly own the KERRIEN kennel, whose Ch. Okus Jallina of Kerrien's grandson is Ch. Paudell Easter Plantagenet at Kerrien. Jallina's grand-daughter is Sh. Ch.

Telkaro Royal Romance of Colbar: A CC winner of the late 1990s.

Photo: Kipps.

Sh. Ch. Gaineda Imperial Ice: One of many Gaineda title holders.

Photo: Kipps.

Kerrien C'est La Vie. Barbara Keighley (COLBAR) had a big winner in Sh. Ch. Trident Of Yeo Colbar in the 1960s. After A long gap she came back with Sh. Ch. Rachenco Barbarella of Colbar and many more winning Colbars, including her latest Sh. Ch. Telkaro Royal Romance of Colbar.

* Lyn Kipps made up Sh. Ch. Ranchenco Barbarella of Colbar's grand-daughter into Sh. Ch. Colbar Summer Mist of Wheatcroft.

* Sylvia Cochrane of RACHENCO also produced Maureen Anderson's Sh. Ch. Ranchenco Charnez of Gaineda and Sh. Ch. Ranchenco Boomergang. Gaineda, as well as producing top sire Consolidator, also produced Sh. Ch. Gaineda Lost Heritage of Tarnbrook. Sylvia owned Ch. Gainspa Fanfare, and bred Sh. Ch. Gaineda Imperial Ice.

* Mr and Mrs Metcalfe of GAINSPA bred Ch. Gainspa Fanfare, Sh. Ch. Gainspa Fiona, Sh. Ch. Gainspa Florette of Shiremoor and Sh. Ch. Gainspa Oonah.

* Fred and Merial Hathaway MELFRICKA kennel started with a Sansue foundation and a dog from the old-established Lindys Golden Retrievers. Their dogs included Sh. Ch. Lindys Butterscotch of Melfricka, Sh. Ch. Melfricka Echo, Sh. Ch. Melfricka Kudos of Rossbourne, Sh. Ch. Melfricka Limelight and Sh. Chs. Melfricka Love Story and Zed.

* Hilary Lambshead (MUSKAN) had Sh. Ch. Hingstondown Notoriety of Muskan and bred Sh. Ch. Muskan Miss Dior; Mr and Mrs Comers' Sh. Ch. Muskan Most Charming of Cracksavon, who is the dam of Mr and Mrs

May's Ch. Cracksavon Charmed I'm Sure of Suregold, and Sh. Ch. Cracksavon Most Faithfull.

* Cheryl Bawden (DARTHILL) made up Sh. Ch. Darthill Lavender Lady, Sh. Ch. Darthill Wind in the Willows, Sh. Ch. Darthill Lavender and Lace, and Sh. Ch. Darthill Lily of the Valley.

* Mr and Mrs Sillence of CANINA first had Ch. Canina Winter Berry, then his son Sh. Ch. Fenwood Jagger of Canina and his daughter Sh. Ch. Fromeside O' So Sharp of Canina.

* Some lovely GARBANK Goldens for Mr and Mrs Crosbie were Ch. Bethrob Bracken, Sh. Ch. Garbank Charming Cindy, Mrs K. Crossbie-Black's Ch. and Irish Ch. Garbank Special Edition of Lislone and Mrs J. Sparrow's Sh. Ch. Oi Oi Garbank.

* A well-known Scottish kennel, John and Jess Clark's SINNHEIN, featured Sh. Ch. Sinnhein Minutemaid and her sons Sh. Ch. Sinnhein Sebastian and Sh. Ch. Sinnhein Toerag of Kilgraston.

* Mr and Mrs P. Nowell's TOKEIDA was started in the 1960s and made up the Stolford-bred Ch. Tranquillity Token of Regina, followed by Ch. Stolford Merienda. Next came Tranquillity Token's grandson Sh. Ch. Tokeida Starstealer. Synspur Briar of Tokeida has produced Sh. Ch. Tokeida Outlaws Treasure and Ch. Tokeida Outlaws Hussy at DIKEADAZE for Angela Cooper, and Starstealer's daughter, Ch. Tokeida Temptress of Mossburn, for Sue Pounds-Longhurst (Mossburn).

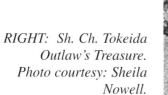

ABOVE: The Melfricka Goldens. Photo: Diane Pearce.

TOP RIGHT: Representatives of the Sinnhein kennel, based in Holland.

RIGHT: Sh. Ch. Tokeida Outlaw's Treasure. Photo courtesy: Sheila Nowell.

BOTTOM RIGHT: Four Stanroph title holders (left to right): Sh. Ch. Stanroph Spring Fantasy, Sh. Ch. Stanroph Soldier Boy, Ch. Stanroph Sailor Boy, (in front) Ch. Stanroph Steal A Glance.

Photo: Kipps.

Ch. Ritzilyn Cockney Robin.

Photo: Kipps.

Sh. Ch. Camrose Frangipani of Beldonburn. *Photo: Weeks.*

Ch. Westley Ramona: Foundation bitch of the Standfast kennel.
Photo courtesy: Eileen Caisley.

World Ch. Standfast Angus.

* The foundation lines of Mrs Ann Woodcock (STANROPH) were Rossbourne/Janville mated to Moorquest, producing Ch. Stanroph Steal A Glance. Then Clevarly Claire of Stanroph's grandson became Sh. Ch. Stanroph Soldier Boy (with Mr J. Brownlie), and her great great grand-daughter was Sh. Ch. Stanroph Spring Fantasy. The dam of Spring Fantasy produced Ch. Stanroph Sailor Boy, and Stanroph Silent Tears produced Sh. Ch. Stanroph Shoe Shine Boy At Lindjan for Janet Buckingham.

* George and Lynn Hennessy of RITZILYN started with a Sandusky bitch whose daughter, Heidi Hi, produced Sh. Ch. Ritzilyn Red Knicks who produced Sh. Ch. Ritzilyn Vivacity, and Ritzilyn Tickled Pink produced Ch. Ritzilyn Cockney Robin. Cockney Robin's son is Ch. Ritzilyn Barrow Boy for Messano (SEAMONS).
* Still very much involved in the breed even though nowadays most of their dogs are veterans, Anne Frank and Fiona Weeks (BELDONBURN) who in the 1980s made up

Sh. Ch. Skymaster of Jamescroft.

Photo: Kipps.

Sh. Ch. Starlance Baritone.

Sh. Ch. Camrose Hardangerfjord Of Beldonburn, Ch. Camrose Waterlyric Of Beldonburn, and Sh. Ch. Camrose Frangipani Of Beldonburn.

Ray and Sonia Scholes (GLENGILDE) owned and campaigned the breed CC record holder Ch. Styal Scott Of Glengilde (42 Challenge Certificates).

* Lyn Walker and Larry Roberts (GLOI) have made up Sh. Ch. Linchael Cartier of Gloi, Sh. Ch. Linchael Freya of Gloi and Sh. Ch. Gloi Bewitched.

* Joe and Beryl Stokes (JOBEKA) have been involved in Goldens since the late 1970s. They have bred Sh. Ch. Jobeka Jasper of Nortonwood and Sh. Ch. Jobeka Just James,

the dam of the two boys Stirchley Sugar Bush of Jobeka, bred by Graham and Brenda Ball (Stirchley) sister to their important sire Sh. Ch. Stirchley Saxon, and his brother Stirchley Solomen (1 CC).

* Sandy and Bob Lane (KULAWAND) have bred and shown typical Goldens since 1972 – Sh. Ch. Kulawand San Piper, her great granddaughter Sh. Ch. Kulawand Krystal (winner of 19 Challenge Certificates). San Catrina Krystal's dam is also dam of the CC winning Kulawand Keltic Sun.

* June and Tony Axe (TUGWOOD) started in 1954, with many winners over the years including Ch. Tugwood Viking and Sh. Ch. Tugwood Pirate, also World Ch. Tugwood

*Ch. Cracksavon Charmed
I'm Sure of Suregold.*

*Eng. Sh. Ch. Aust. Ch. Tasvane
Charles Henry.
Photo courtesy: Dave and Viv
Sterrett.*

Sh. Ch. Elswood The Highlander.

Photo: Kipps.

Maxim brother to Tugwood Ingvar who has 2 Challenge Certificates.

* Mrs Sue Almey (ARBUTUS) began in 1970 and bred Ch. Arbutus Kinsella Later on came Sh. Ch. Arbutus Coquihalla, two full Arbutus Swedish Champions, and Sue is now showing her sixth generation.

* Margaret and Bill Woods (AMIRENE) have stock that goes back to Stalyhills Miss Avenger Of Amirene born 27.8.1977. Darris Double Dutch At Amirene was a lovely bitch and most unlucky not to gain her title. She won 2 Challenge Certificates including one at Crufts. They also bred Amirene Egretta Of Nortonwood (2 CCs), Amirene Diver (2 CCs), Amirene Pacifique (1 CC).

* Dr J. and Mrs Eileen Caisley (STANDFAST) whose foundation bitch was Ch. Westley Ramona, dam of the outstanding show and stud dog in Europe World Ch. Standfast Angus. In England Ch. Standfast Augustus and Gordon Graham's Sh. Ch. Standfast Louisa, George and Anne Scragg (CHEVANNE) with Sh. Ch. Chevanne Sugar

'N' Spice and Sh. Ch. Linchael Conspiracy of Chevanne who is proving himself as the sire of many good winners.

* Val and Roy Burns (ABNALLS) is one of those rare kennels that has top class workers with Field Trial bloodlines. Roy's domain is the Field with Ft Ch. Standerwick Roberta Of Abnalls and Ft Ch. Abnalls Hilary Of Standerwick (Philpott). Val's part is the CC show winning Abnalls.

* Michael and Mary Gaffney (TYROL) from Cork have travelled more distances than most. The two best-known of their dogs are Ch. and Irish Ch. Papeta Philosopher and Ch. and Irish Ch. Galalith Crown Prince of Tyrol.

* Mrs Heather Avis (GLENAVIS) bred and made into a Sh. Ch. Glenavis Barman who then went to Sweden, did a lot of winning and sired a lot of winners. She also made up Ch. Mytonvale Jessica of Glenavis.

* The Pickards (PAPETA) owned Sh. Ch. Styal Shakespeare and Sh. Ch. Westley Sophie of Papeta, and bred Ch. and Irish Ch. Papeta Philosopher.

* Mrs E. Melville (CROUCHERS) has produced some lovely dual-purpose dogs – Ch. Crouchers Bambina, Ch. Crouchers Leo, Ch. Crouchers Pinecrest Melissa, Ch. Stradcot Simon of Crouchers.

* Richard and Paula Edwards (LOVEHAYNE) have always been interested in working their dogs as well as showing, and their Ch. Sansue Pepper of Lovehayne was a good worker. They also bred and owned Ch. Lovehayne Beteazle who is the dam of Jane Clark's Ch. Lovehayne Elisha of Trewater.

* Pauline Bevis (STARLANCE) has produced a fine line starting with Sh. Ch. Starlance Moonstone Meg, who was by Amberland Black Sabre, a dog who sired many winners. His sire was from Margaret and David Balamm's PINECREST kennel whose winners included Ch. Pinecrest Salvador, Ch. Pinecrest Topper, Ch. Pinecrest Susannah, Ch. Crouchers Pinecrest Melissa. After Sh. Ch. Starlance Moonstone Meg came Sh. Ch. Starlance Wizard of Oz at Revelsgold (for the McDonald Woods), who is out of Starlance Evita of Revelsgold. Wizard's sister bred Ch. Revelsgold Sargeant Pepper. Then followed Sh. Ch. Starlance Baritone; and Sh. Ch. Starlance Crystal Maze is the latest for Pauline Bevis.

* Hilda James (JAMESCROFT) has consistently bred good dogs. Ch. Jamescroft Mary Jayne at Bramlyedge, Sh. Ch. Jamescroft Flaxen Girl and Sh. Ch. Skymaster Of Jamescroft are the title holders to date.

* Gillian Hill is another breeder who has turned out a consistent type for many years. These include: Ch. Bramhills Pied Piper at Almerak for Seker and Betty King (ALMERAK), and Sh. Ch. Bramhills Tamarisk Of Darrochonna for Jim and Audrey Richardson (DARROCHONNA).

* Anne Falconer is Mervyn and Daphne Philpott's daughter, and under her SIATHAM prefix she has bred a consistent type. She owned Ch. Westley Felicia of Siatham, bred Siatham Virginnia (2 CCs) and, more recently has shown Ch. Westley Gabriella of Siatham.

* Pauline and Tom Comer (CRACKSAVON) first made up Sh. Ch. Muskan Most Charming Of Cracksavon. They bred the Mays' Ch. Cracksavon Charmed I'm Sure Of Suregold, their own Sh.Ch. Cracksavon Most Faithfull, and the CC winner Cracksavon Most Sincere of Willowlawn.

* Dave and Viv Sterrett (TASVANE) have had Goldens for many years. They campaigned the lovely Sh. Ch. Orchis Cherylee Of Tasvane, and made up her great grandson, Sh. Ch. Tasvane Charles Henry. When they went to Australia, Charles Henry became an Australian Champion.

* There have always been Elswood Golden Retrievers, bred by Valerie Foss, with the famous Elswood English Setters. The Goldens have fielded three English title holders. These were Sh. Ch. Westley Simone (12 CCs) who died after an operation for pyometra at only six years, Sh. Ch. Westley Clementina, and her son Sh. Ch. Elswood the Highlander, winner of the CC at Crufts 1996 and a Gundog group winner at Championship Shows. They are all much-loved house pets as well as show dogs.

Since the 1950s, Golden Retriever entries at shows have increased dramatically, often having the top entry over all breeds at Championship shows. This means that to win consistently is no easy matter – and this also applies to those who work their Golden Retrievers in Field Trials, Working Tests, and Obedience competitions.

WORKING KENNELS
In 1946 there were still many dual-purpose show/work kennels. One of the most famous was STUBBLESDOWN, owned by Bill and Olive Hickmott, whose dogs included Dual Ch. Stubblesdown Golden Lass, Ch. Braconlee Gaiety, FT Ch. Stubblesdown Larry, Ch. Stubblesdown Jester of Steddles, and FT Ch. Westhyde Stubblesdown Major.

The late Eric Baldwin had the PALGRAVE prefix. Eric, a brilliant trainer, either bred or owned FT Chs. Holway Teal of Westley, Palgrave Holway Harmony, Palgrave Holway Folly, Palgrave Fern of Ardyle and Volvo of Palgrave. The Trials success of Westley in the 1970s came with the STANDERWICK prefix. The Westleys had been dual-purpose and bred the last Dual Champion in David of Westley. But the Standerwick strain of Daphne Philpott and Joan Gill is pure working lines. Successes included FT Ch. Standerwick Rumbustuous of Catcombe (Mrs Wendy Andrews), Mr Roy Burns' FT Ch. Standerwick Roberta of Abnalls, FT Ch. Standerwick Donna of Deadcraft (Judy Hendry) and FT Ch. Abnalls Hilary of Standerwick.

But the Golden Retriever Field Trial world has been dominated by one kennel – Mrs June Atkinson's HOLWAY, with 29 FT Champions and a great Field Trial sire in FT Ch. Holway Corbiere. That record will take some beating, as will that of Westley/Standerwick in the show and Field Trial world.

14 THE GOLDEN RETRIEVER IN NORTH AMERICA

Bart Armstrong of Winnipeg, Manitoba, established his Gilnockie kennel of sporting dogs as early as 1916 and, by 1927, had exhibited to a Championship the imported Noranby Eventide. Armstrong was a bit irked when Eventide's title was published by the Canadian Kennel Club, or CKC, as a Retriever (Wavy-Coated), and it was only by dint of diligent correspondence that recognition was achieved for the Golden as a separate variety of retriever. The American Kennel Club recognised the Golden Retriever in 1932.

In 1930, Armstrong's friend, Samuel S. Magoffin, of Vancouver, British Columbia, imported Speedwell Pluto, a great gundog, who became the first American Champion Golden and the first to win a Best in Show. Within a few years, Pluto headed an array of quality imported bitches at Magoffin's Rockhaven Kennels; in addition, Magoffin's brother managed a kennel in Colorado under the Gilnockie name bequeathed by Bart Armstrong.

Early on, Goldens spread through the upper Midwest of the USA. They were used for work, retrieving ducks and geese during the great migrations along the Central Flyway, or the gaudy ringneck pheasant of the broad grainfields of the central states. In the off-season, they demonstrated their skills at the new sport of retriever field trials, and on occasion were brushed and polished to be exhibited at dog shows.

Other imports were scattered in the East, along the West Coast, and in Canada. With distances as great as they are in North America, and given the lack of easy transportation at the time, it took quite a while for the Golden Retriever to become established as something more than an uncommon breed. In Canada, numbers were considerably smaller. The 1950s saw a swing upwards in registrations, and Goldens became notable in their achievements. By the 1970s, registrations were climbing at an astonishing rate: Goldens were dominating obedience trials and were regularly taking Group and Best in Show wins at all-breed shows. While the number of field trials had increased, just as shows and obedience trials had, there were relatively fewer Goldens placing; the Labrador had become the pre-eminent field trial dog. In the mid 1980s, Hunting Tests were established and rapidly became very popular with those who wanted to work their dogs at a more realistic level than was the case at field trials.

The Golden has now been in the top ten of registrations for all breeds with the AKC for some time, holding steady at fourth or fifth for several years. In 1996, some 68,000 Goldens will have been registered with the AKC; and that is likely to be half the number whelped, since many owners never bother to send in the registration application. Registration figures for Canada are not readily available, but may not exceed a tenth of the USA numbers. Goldens are now one of the 'common' breeds, and one of America's most popular and recognisable.

Such popularity is often more a curse than a blessing. Goldens are bought and sold like so many market lambs, by producers ranging from casual backyard breeders to commercial puppy mills that sell to brokers and pet store outlets. While conscientious breeders have their animals examined against hereditary problems such as hip dysplasia and eye and heart defects, and try to breed towards better structure and temperament, the same is rarely true of those in it purely for profit.

THE GOLDEN RETRIEVER CLUB OF AMERICA

The GRCA was formally incorporated in 1938. In 1940, the GRCA held its first field trial, a two-day event, with a bench (conformation) show held the evening before. In 1950, obedience trials were added, and later, Tracking Tests and other events. Entries at the National have increased from a few dozen in 1940 to 1,500 or more in a carnival of Golden activity over a seven-to-ten day period in the 1990s.

The GRCA is one of the largest and most active breed clubs in the USA, with about 5,000 current members. It is the parent club for the Golden Retriever, representing the breed with the AKC. A national board of twelve directors, with dozens of committees and volunteer members, are responsible for a myriad of activities from rescue through to judges' education. The GRCA publishes a bi-monthly magazine of some 200-plus pages, which is a primary means of communication between members. There are about 48 local specialty clubs throughout the country, many holding their own specialty shows and other events.

The Golden Retriever Club of Canada was formed in the early 1960s. At first it was based in the Ontario area, but now has members and local clubs from British Columbia to the Maritime provinces, and a National Specialty that, like the GRCA's, rotates throughout various areas of the country annually. Many Golden fanciers belong to both the GRCA and the GRCC, and there have always been strong ties across the border.

INFLUENTIAL BREEDERS 1932–1962
THE MIDWEST

In the early years of the Golden in the USA, it was perhaps providential that Samuel S. Magoffin's two brothers-in-law were Ralph Boalt (STILROVIN, Minnesota) and Ben Boalt (BEAVERTAIL and GUNNERMAN, Wisconsin), and his sister-in-law was Mrs Henry B. Christiansen (GOLDWOOD, Minnesota). These names are solidly behind major American lines, especially working lines. Also in the Minnesota area were: the DES LACS kennel of Bartlett W. Foster; TONKAHOF (Henry Norton) produced a Best in Show winner and the first Dual Champion bitch; and BEAUTYWOOD (Dr L.M. Evans) had two National Field Trial Champions. KINGSWERE and GOLDEN VALLEY were well-known for working Goldens.

THE EAST

In the East, Reinhard Bischoff's LORELEI kennels were based on Midwest lines, and produced foundation stock for many Eastern breeders. Ch. and AFTCh. Lorelei's Golden Rockbottom UD (whelped 1949) bore a unique assortment of titles, and the distinction of winning first in Sporting Group at a show the day before placing in a Field Trial Stake. His son Ch. Little Joe of Tigathoe***, owned by Mrs George ('Torch') Flinn, was also a major contributor to Eastern lines. Little Joe's dam was a champion, field-placing daughter of FTCh. Stilrovin Katherine. One of the most notable later TIGATHOE litters was the combination of AFC Bonnie Brooks Elmer and Tigathoe's Chickasaw***, which produced no less then four field title holders, including the last Dual Champion, DCh. AFC Tigathoe's Funky Farquar. Mrs Flinn is still active in field trials, having had Champions in both Goldens and Labradors.

Other Eastern kennels such as FEATHERQUEST (Mrs Mark D. Elliot) and HIGH FARMS (Mr and Mrs Josiah Semans) contributed heavily to the foundations of Eastern bloodlines, and may still be found in pedigrees today. The GOLDEN PINES name has been transferred to Nancy B. Kelly in

California and is still very active. Mrs Elliot, who owned and trained the first Golden to earn a UD title (1941), is well-known world-wide as an historian of the Golden Retriever. She has also made an important contribution to understanding canine structure and movement through her lecture series 'Dogsteps', and the subsequent books and videos based on her cineography of dogs. She was honoured in 1993 by the GRCA, for her lifetime of contribution to the Golden world, by having the entire National Specialty dedicated to her.

THE WEST

In the West, Goldens were much more scattered, but there were pockets of activity along the West Coast. OAKWOOD (Charles Snell, Oregon) had a strong kennel of field trial Goldens. WILDWOOD (Eric Johnson, California) came from the Midwest, and strongly influenced Western lines through the Best in Show winning Ch. Czar of Wildwood, a grandson of the first Field Champion, FT Ch. Rip. Mr Johnson also imported Gilder of Elsiville, who was sold to Bart Foster. He completed the dog's Championship, and used Gilder on his Des Lacs bitches to produce a number of Champions. Mrs Donovan D. Fischer of California based her FLAREWIN bloodline on a Des Lacs bitch, and some dogs of this line were the first Goldens used by Guide Dogs for the Blind. Mrs Fischer was the GRCA's long-time correspondent for the AKC Gazette, writing a monthly column on Goldens for many, many years, and even in her later years could still be seen at Golden Retriever specialties. Many people still have a vivid picture of Gertrude zipping around the show grounds in a golf cart at the National Specialty in 1986.

THE MODERN ERA

Since the late 1960s, there has been a major change in the Golden world. As the breed entered a time of increasing popularity in all areas, so numbers increased dramatically. More people had the time, and the discretionary income, to become interested

and active in such areas as dog showing, obedience training, field work, and so on. Yet, rather than enjoying the fun of participating in activities and demonstrating the dogs' talents, people became more and more fixated upon winning. With increased numbers, better training, more shows and trials and more competition, it seemed necessary to concentrate on one area in order to be successful. The Golden became more of a specialist (or rather, the Goldens' owners did), with much less demand or opportunity to demonstrate inborn versatility. Winning was the wedge that split the Golden world into separate field, show, and obedience segments.

MODERN LINES

One of the most influential dogs of the 1970s, and later, was the sire Ch. Sunset's Happy Duke. His son Ch. Misty Morn's Sunset CD TD WC, better known as 'Sam', and owned by Peter and Rose Lewesky, accounted for more than 130 Champions and UD title holders, sired on bitches from all over the country. Another son of Duke, Ch. Cummings Gold-Rush Charlie, and Sam's son Ch. Wochica's Okeechobee Jake, between them accounted for more than 100 additional Champions. Charlie was the foundation of Ann Johnson's well-known large GOLD-RUSH kennel in New Jersey, which is still quite active. Jake was bred by Janet Bunce (WOCHICA) and owned by Susan Taylor (OKEECHOBEE), and was the first to win Best of Breed at the National Specialty show three times. Many kennels in the East and elsewhere now carry very heavy concentrations of lines based on the above dogs.Leslie Dove's GOLDWING line (Virginia) carries a strong Gold-Rush background. Ch. Goldwing Rhythm-n-Blue, and her son Ch. Goldwing True Bear (by Ch. Gold-Rush Great Teddy Bear), were prolific producers, having many notable descendants. Other Eastern kennels based on similar lines include SUNSHINEHILL (Elaine Fraze), TWIN-BEAU-D (Nancy Dallaire) and CLOVERDALE (Mr and Mrs Richard Zimmerman).

One aim of a successful kennel is consistency of type. This is a group from the Liberator/Synergold bloodlines: from left to right: Synergold Cicely, Featherquest Liberator Lara, Synergold Alder Liberator, Ch. Liberator Synergold Jubilee, Synergold Commotion, Synergold Alban Liberator, and Ch. Liberator Larkspur CD.

Bucking the trend towards strictly show purposes was a dog of exceptional quality, both individually and as a sire, Am. Can. Ch. Trowsnest Whirlwind UD WC Can. CDX. 'Whirly', whelped in 1978 and living past his sixteenth birthday, was bred by Marjorie Trowbridge (TROWSNEST, Connecticut) out of her Am. Can. Ch. Valhalla's Trowsnest Folly UDT WCX bred to the field trial dog, Bainin of Caernac CD*** (a sire of Ch., AFC, and UD title holders). The combination carried both American and English lines. Whirly's offspring include not only many Champions, but also field workers, guide dogs for the blind, and assistance dogs. Many people remember this great dog competing for several years in the Veterans Class at the National Specialty, and his beautifully co-ordinated, strong, fluent movement even at thirteen years of age.

Nancy Garrison's LIBERATOR Goldens in Massachusetts were a combination of American and English lines, Nancy having imported Deremar Ameche Liberator, a son of outstanding English Champions. 'Toffee', and other English dogs, also contributed strongly to Ed and Susan Brown-Leger's SYNERGOLD kennel. The Brown-Legers' Ch. Toryglen Idling Jerome UD*** was a triple-purpose Golden.

In the Midwest, bloodlines were varied. The old Midwestern lines were used with outcrosses to imports and to dogs from both East and West. Increasingly easy transport by air made cross-country breedings much more expedient, and breeders took advantage of the opportunity.

Barbara Dismukes (HUNT'S), based in western Pennsylvania, utilised Midwestern

lines as a foundation, producing three Show Dog Hall of Fame dogs, including Ch. Hunt's Copperfield Daemon CD TD. Barbara imported the English dog, Ch. Shargleam Ferryman, who proved to be a very successful sire on American bitches, imparting improvements to head structure and forequarter assembly, as well as a lovely personality.

Dick and Ludell Beckwith (BECKWITH'S) started in Duluth, Minnesota (later moving to Washington State on the West Coast), with their multiple-titled dog, Am. Can. Mex. Bda. Ch. Beckwith's Copper Coin CD, homebred from old American lines. A puppy bitch from Betty Gay, Beckwith's Gayhaven Fancy, was bred to Copper Coin, and produced the outstanding sire, Am. Can. Mex. Ch. Beckwith's Copper Ingot. Beckwith's also imported the lovely bitch Am. Can. Ch. Beckwith's Frolic of Yeo CDX. Bred to Ingot several times, Frolic produced a number of notable Goldens. The Beckwiths have incorporated a number of bloodlines into their breeding programme, and are also well-known as judges of sporting breeds.

Among the Ingot-Frolic offspring was Carole Kvamme's Am. Can. Ch. Beckwith's Malagold Flash, Am. Can. UD, Am. WC. 'Robbie' was Carole's once-in-a-lifetime dog: she handled him to Best of Breed at the National Specialty from the American-bred class, and also to both Best in Show and Highest Scoring Dog in Trial at one show in Canada. Robbie can be found in the pedigree of all of Carole's ALDERBROOKE Goldens in Washington.

Marilyn Hartman (Wisconsin) based her LANDICAN line on another of the Ingot-

Four generations of outstanding veterans gather for a family celebration in 1992. In front, the dowager queen, Reddigold's Landican Destiny, Am. Can. CD, WC (15 years). Left to right: Am. Can. Ch. Landican's Shining Sirius, CDX, WCX, JH, U-CD (7). Can. OTCh. Landican's Irish Contessa Am. Can. UD, WC (13). Am. Can. Ch. Landican's Streak of Lightning, WC, Am. Can. CDX, U-CDX (13). Ch. Landican's Dazzl'n Sir Brandon, CD, JH, WC (7). Landican's Second Chance, UD, Am. Can. WC, U-CDX (9). Am. Can. Ch. Landican's Lord Whiskers, Am. Can. CDX, WC, OS (11). Am. Can. Ch. Landican's Lady Diana, Am. Can. CD, WC, OD (11).
Photo: M. Hartman.

Frolic offspring, Ch. Beckwith Malagold Om K Ivan. Ivan was a dedicated hunting dog, and the Landican Goldens are titled in working as well as show areas. Am. Can. Ch. Landican's Shining Sirius, Am. Can. CDX WCX Am. JH, is a daughter of Ch. Landican's Lady Diana CDX WCX.

Connie Gerstner's MALAGOLD (Wisconsin) kennels also started in the early 1960s. Her first in the Show Dog Hall of Fame was Ch. Malagold Beckwith Big Buff CD, Best of Breed at the 1970 National Specialty. Malagold has produced an exceptionally consistent line, combining both American and English titles. Connie's Ch. Libra Malagold Coriander, a Best in Show dog, won first in Sporting Group at the AKC's Centennial Show in 1984, and Best of Breed at the 1988 GRCA National Veterans' Class. The latest Hall of Fame dog from Malagold is Am. Can. Ch. Malagold Storm Warning. His sister, Am. Can. Ch. Malagold Starheart Tory-Adore, has the unique distinction of having completed her Canadian title entirely at Specialty shows – including two GRCC Nationals.

No longer active as a breeder, but now a

What a way to finish a Championship! Malagold Starheart's Tory-Adore went to 3 shows in Canada and won at all three Specialties, including two Nationals. Adi is owned by Teri Kocher and Connie Gerstner; now Am. Can. Ch.

Am. Can. Ch. Signature's Natural Wonder, owned by Judy and Kurt MacCauley, is an American Best in Show winner. Sired by Sunshinehill's National Cowboy.

respected judge, Betty Gay (GAYHAVEN, Michigan) produced some excellent foundation stock during the 1960s and 1970s. Ch. Gayhaven Harmony CDX and her sons, Am. Can. Ch. Kyrie Daemon CDX WC and Am. Can. Ch. Gayhaven Lldiel Am. Can. CDX, Am. WC were all Outstanding Producers and can be found back behind many current pedigrees. Harmony was co-owned with Marcia Schlehr (KYRIE, Michigan), who owned and showed 'Diel' to his titles and some nice show wins, including becoming the youngest-ever Winners Dog at a National.

Cherie Berger's MEADOWPOND (Michigan) kennel was based on two males, Ch. Bardfield Boomer UDT and Ch. Laurell's Especial Jason UDT. Their descendants bred together, and later outcrossed to several imports brought from England, Ireland, and Australia, as well as to other American dogs, produced a very strong line of Obedience trial winners and show titles as well. OTCh. Meadowpond Stardust Reggie, owned by Alfred Einhorn, and Ch. OTCh. Meadowpond

Dust Commander, owned by Bernie Brown, both set exceptional records at Obedience trials.

Laura Ellis Kling's LAURELL name has been seen on many winning show dogs. Laura started, as a teenager, with a bitch from obedience background, bred to High Farms stud dogs. Ch. Duckdown's Unpredictable became one of Laurell's first notable sires. He produced another Outstanding Sire in Ch. Freedom's Celebration, whose close descendants are seen in many current pedigrees.

Bill Worley's foundation for the SUN DANCE kennel in Indiana was Ch. Indian Knoll's Roc Cloud UD. From him descended Ch. Sun Dance's Bronze CD, twice BB at the GRCA National, and Ch. Sun Dance's Contessa, who could hold her own against the male Champions. The Sun Dance name is being carried on by Bill's step-daughter, Lisa Halcomb, in Illinois. A Sun Dance dog, Ch. Faera's Sun Dance Raisen Cain, started Rhonda Hovan's present-day very successful

FAERA line (Ohio) of show winners and producers of show dogs.

Ellen Manke's AMBERAC kennels (Winconsin) has been producing winning show dogs for more than 20 years, including the Outstanding Producers Ch. Amberac's Aristocrat CD and Ch. Amberac's Asterling Aruba, owned by Mary Burke. Aruba was the foundation dam for Mary's ASTERLING bloodline. In her five litters she produced some 30 or so Champions, including the top-winning bitch, Ch. Asterling's Tahiti Sweetie (owned by Sylvia Donahey, BIRNAM WOOD). Concentrated line breeding and inbreeding on Aruba has produced a consistent line of dogs bred for show-winning achievement, including the Golden with the most Best in Show wins (43), Mary's own Ch. Asterling's Wild Blue Yonder. The SIGNATURE dogs of Robin and John Stirrat in Missouri are of similar background; Ch. Signature's Sound Barrier has sired many winners, including Wild Blue Yonder. Many other contemporary kennels also draw heavily upon these bloodlines.

Western Goldens include the aforementioned Beckwith and Alderbrooke kennels. A number of the Alderbrooke Champions also carried CDX and UD titles. One of Alderbrooke's successful products was Am. Can. Ch. Alderbrooke's Rush Hill Rebel CD, owned and shown quite successfully by Tonya Struble (RUSH HILL), based first in Alaska and then in Washington state. Rebel was a National Specialty Show winner and a productive sire. Mr and Mrs Paul Scoggins (PEPPERCREEK) are also successful in the Northwest, as is

Bernadette Cox's KAZAK kennels, formerly in California.

California has always had active Golden fanciers. Sylvia Donahey-Feeney started in the Midwest, moving to California with the very successful Birnam Wood Goldens.

Few will forget the vision of Sylvia in formal tuxedo outfit showing 'Brooke', Ch. Asterling's Tahiti Sweetie, to a Group placing at the Westminster Kennel Club show. Ch. Asterling's Buster Keaton ('Ace') and Ch. Birnam Wood's Douglas Furr ('DJ') were both Outstanding Sires of show dogs for the Birnam Wood kennel, and have had a strong influence on modern Goldens.

The VANREEL Goldens are a co-operative venture between Gretchen Vandenburg and Denise Reel, and have produced many well-known West Coast show dogs, including Ch. VanReel's Magnum of Stonecrest UD.

Nancy Kelly started as a teenager in the Junior Showmanship classes. Her first outstanding dog was Ch. Golden Pines Courvoisier CDX, a son of Ch. Misty Morn's Sunset, bred by Marilu Semans. 'Cognac' was a handsome dog who sired good workers as well, and was the grandsire of Canadian Dual Ch. Carolee's Something Special CDX. Marilu Semans has transferred the Golden Pines kennel name, active since the 1950s, to Nancy, so it should be around for many years more.

In the Southwest, Gloria Kerr's KRISHNA lines were built on the extremely successful combination of Ch. Lark Mill Genevive CD bred to Ch. Autumn Lodge's Mr Zap CD**, a son of Ch. Misty Morn's Sunset CD TD WC. Genevive was a daughter of 'Adolph', Ch.

Success doesn't mean you need a kennel operation. Evelyn Smith's Goldens are all house dogs first and foremost. Left to right: Am. Can. Ch. Orion of Alderbrooke, Am. Can. UD, Can. TD at 11 years. Can. OTCh. Smithaven Danae of Glendavis, at 7 . Can. Ch. Gayhaven Skye's the Limit, Can. CD, WC, the "baby" at 3 years.

ABOVE: *Quality in Goldens lasts: Tessa Ann was still sound and solid at nine years of age here, and having great fun. At seven she was BOS at the GRCA National Specialty over hundreds of younger dogs. Am. Can. Ch. Beaumaris Timberee Tessa Ann, UDT, Can. CDX., owned and shown by Sandy Fisher.*

RIGHT:*Am. Ch. Elysian's Li'l Leica Reprint, UDT, MH, WCX, VCX.*

Photo: Jean von Barby.

Cal-Vo's Happy Ambassador, a son of Ch. Footprint of Yeo CD. Adolph put his stamp on Goldens throughout the USA.

Colorado has been a special area of Golden activity ever since John Rogers Magoffin established the Gilnockie kennels there. Later, the Gilnockie name was carried on by Mrs Eleisa Enloe. She used both Gilnockie and GOLDENLOE as affixes. A Goldenloe bitch was one of Jackie Merten's foundation bitches for the TOPBRASS kennels, and Ch. Goldenloe's Tawny Samson UD, owned by Anne Couttet Shannon, was a well-known Obedience winner. Mrs Enloe was fondly known to the Colorado fanciers as 'Grandma Golden'. More than 40 years of her Golden activity came to an end with her death in 1995.

The BEAUMARIS kennel of John and Anne Bissette contributed many dogs of lovely type through several English imports, notably from Deerflite and Raynesgold background, with a contribution from Pam Ruddick's well-known sire Ch. Ciadar Tintinabulation UD WC. After John's death the kennel became inactive,

though Anne is still very much interested in Goldens.

Colorado seems to support a dedicated band of Golden devotees who still make full use of the breed's versatile capabilities. Among them, Jean von Barby's ELYSIAN prefix graces a number of capable performers, including the littermates Ch. Elysian's L'il Leica Reprint UDT MH (with a Best in Show, too!); Ch. Elysian Sky-Hi Dub'l Exposure UD MH** (Sandy Whicker) and Ch. Elysian's Image of Oak Shadows UDTX (Gail Burkett, Ohio), all of whom are proving to be producers of widely talented offspring. Anne Shannon's homebred KINSALE dogs, notably Ch. Kinsale Clipper and Ch. Kinsale She's The Boss, are also contributing worthy offspring.

DOG SHOWS IN NORTH AMERICA
There are both all-breed and specialty shows where points towards the title of Champion may be won. At every show the regular classes are Puppy (which may be divided into six-to-nine months and nine-to-twelve months), twelve to 18 months, Novice (except in

198

Canada), Bred by Exhibitor, American-Bred, and Open. Certain shows, usually specialties, may also offer non-regular classes, such as Veterans (over eight years of age for Goldens), Field Trial (for dogs having placed in field trial competition), Brace (two of same ownership, shown as a pair), Stud Dog (sires with two get) and Brood Bitch (dams with two progeny). Veterans and Field Trial class winners are eligible to compete for Best of Breed, but not for points.

Championship titles are earned by winning a total of 15 points in competition: points are awarded to the Winners Dog (best male in the classes) and the Winners Bitch (best female in the classes), which are chosen from the first-place winners of the seven regular classes. From one to five points are assigned to the WD and WB depending upon how many of each sex are in competition. Various regions of the country have differing point scales. For instance, in my area of the country where there are quite a few shows and an abundance of Golden entries, it takes 22 males or bitches in competition for three points or 52 dogs and 53 bitches for five points.

In order to be awarded a Championship, the dog must earn 15 points under at least three different judges, and at least two of the wins must be 'majors', that is, of three or more points. The remainder may be won at lesser shows. With entries often running at 50 to 80 in many shows – and into the 100s at Specialty shows – acquiring those points is not an easy task.

After the Winners Dog has been chosen, a Reserve Winner is picked from the remainder, all that have been defeated only by the WD. Then the bitch classes, WB, and Reserve are judged. The WD and WB then go into the Best of Breed competition, against any Champions who may be entered. These may be one or two at a small show, often more than a hundred at a national Specialty show. A Best of Breed (BB) is chosen, a Best of Opposite Sex to Best of Breed (BOS) and a Best of Winners (BW), this last being either the WD or WB. Best of Winners gives an opportunity for additional points in many cases; for instance, if the entry

Spring in Colorado. Ch. Elysian's Li'l Leica Reprint, UDT, MH, WCX, VCX. (by Ch. Wingwatcher Reddi to Rally CDX, WC out of Ch. Beaulieu's Akacia O'Darnley UDTX, JH). Owner, Jean von Barby.

in males was small, of only one or two points, but there are more points in bitches, the male awarded Best of Winners will receive the same number of points that the winning bitch did. And, if the WD is fortunate enough to go Best of Breed over a number of Champions, the Champions are added to the number of class entries defeated.

The Best of Breed winners are eligible to compete in the Group judging at all-breed shows. Four placements are made in each of the seven groups (Sporting; Hound; Working; Terrier; Toy; Non-sporting; Herding), and the first-place winners compete for Best in Show. Group and Best in Show are very hotly contested in the USA, and various rating systems in the dog magazines are followed quite closely by major competitors. Often dogs are sent on a whirlwind of air travel to get to as many shows under favourable judges as is possible in the quest for standing in the ratings, and very extensive advertising campaigns are carried on in those same dog magazines. This has contributed to the often cut-throat seriousness of competition in this country. Those exhibitors more interested in real quality rightly consider the competition within the breed to be of more importance than the Group judging, where it is often the handler's skill and the dog's showmanship and grooming ('presentation') that account for awards, rather than intrinisic quality.

There are, quite literally, hundreds of dog shows held under AKC rules throughout the country, and often 'clusters' of two to four shows at the same site, or 'circuits' of up to ten or twelve shows, where exhibitors caravan from one site to the next. Often the parking lots at a fair-sized show look like a mammoth holiday encampment, with accommodation ranging from huge motor-homes down through customised vans, trailers, and even tents.

Professional handlers may carry a string of 20 to 30 dogs, sometimes more, in custom-fitted vehicles, and the dash to the showgrounds to set up in the most advantageous position in the grooming area is one of the more amusing sidelights of showing (if you are not one of those trying to find space for your own equipment!). Of the hundreds of shows put on, only six all-breed shows are 'benched', where stalls or benches are provided and the dog must be on display during certain hours of the show. All the others are 'unbenched', meaning exhibitors may come in time for their judging and leave immediately thereafter if they wish. Generally, exhibitors will have a travelling crate for the dog, and often a grooming table, tack box, folding chair, and possibly a cooler with lunch and drinks (the quality of food at dog shows is another subject of wry comment). Shows may be held indoors, or outdoors, usually with tenting for the grooming areas, but still subject to the vagaries of the weather.

As well as shows where Championship points may be awarded, many clubs hold sanctioned matches, informal events where no points are given, but puppies as young as three months may be exhibited. Matches are used as training grounds for exhibitors and for potential show dogs, and also provide an opportunity for aspiring judges to gain

m. Can. Ch. Smithaven's Benchmark Caper, CD (9 years of age), shown "American style". Caper was a member of the GRCA's Show Dog Hall of Fame, and an Outstanding Sire as well. Owner, Debbie Kahla.

experience. They are very informal affairs, as are the fun matches held by non-AKC clubs.

WORKING LINES
In field trials, the TOPBRASS name of Jackie Mertens is well-known. Topbrass has also accounted for number of show titles and some exceptional obedience trial records. Jackie made good use of the English import AFC Holway Barty in her breeding programme, as well as the best American lines.

FC/AFC/NAFC Topbrass Cotton was one of three field title holders by Barty out of a show champion dam, and the first Golden to win the National Amateur Retriever Trial (1985). Barty also sired OTCh. Topbrass Ric O'Shay Barty, holder of an amazing number of High in Trial wins. Jackie's bitch FC/AFC Windbreaker's Smokin' Zigzag is famed as a producer of field trial winners. Ziggy was one of the winning combination of AFC Yankee's Smokin' Red Devil x FC Windbreakers

FC-AFC Tigathoe's Kiowa II (FC-AFC Bonnie Brooks Elmer x Tigathoe's Chickasaw***, born 1971) at nine years of age. Owned and trained by Pat Sadler, Ki sired both field and show champions, and was the grandsire of NAFC-FC Topbrass Cotton. A dog of rare character and intelligence.

Not started in field training until four years of age, 'Brenna' earned her Master Hunter title at five!

Am. FC-AFC Topbrass Dustbuster, owned by Barbara Howard, carries some of the most outstanding bloodlines in Field Trials. Willingness, trainability, and zest in performance are brought to high art in retriever field work.

The last Dual Champion in North America; Can. Dual Champion Carolee's Something Special, Can. CDX. 'Bumper' completed his Dual title in 1979, and also won a 5-point major at a Specialty show in the USA.

FC-AFC Windbreaker's Smoke'n Zig Zag, owned and trained by Jackie & Joe Mertens. From the famous breeding of AFC Yankee's Smoke'n Red Devil to FC Windbreaker's Razzmatazz which produced multiple field titelist, Ziggy qualified for 8 Nationals and produced four field titelists herself.

Headstudy of Belvedere's Gale Wind JH, expressive of Golden character.

Razzmatazz, bred by Pat DeNardo, which has been very influential in current field trial lines.

BONNIE BROOK (Dick Kerns, Illinois) is no longer active, although the influence of Bonnie Brook dogs on field trials is still strong. Dick started with bitches of Midwestern breeding bred to his 'Tuffy', Jolly Again of Ouilmette CD***, a son of the imported Holway Stubblesdown Jolly*** and a Gunnerman bitch. AFC Bonnie Brook's Elmer, owned by Torch Flinn, was the sire of at least five field title holders, and other Bonnie Brook dogs have done very well at trials.

RIVERVIEW (Sally Venerable), KINIKE (Philip K. Uehling) and HANDJEM (Henry Lardy) are no longer active, but their contribution to field lines is immeasurable; those names still indicate strong field qualities in a pedigree. MIOAKS, CHANCES R, SUNFIRE and HIGH TIMES are also working lines.

Field lines in the West of the USA include Val Walker's SUNGOLD, based on FC/AFC Misty's Sungold Lad CDX, son of the imported Sherrydan Tag*. As a teenager, Val handled Lad quite successfully to his titles, and the Sungold kennels now hold some outstanding field trial Labradors as well. Lad crossed very well with bitches descended from Holway Leo***. TANGELO (Terry Giffen-Woods) produced the very good-looking AFC Tangelo's Side Kick and others. The RONAKERS kennels (Ronald Akers) in California produced Dual Ch. Ronaker's Novato Cain CD, as well as versatile show Champions and UD title holders.

In Texas, Mercedes Hitchcock concentrates primarily on good gundogs at BELVEDERE, and the kennel is led by the imported dogs Holway Vodka MH*** and Midas Belvedere Houston MH***. Vodka, better known as 'Brit', has also sired a top winning Obedience Trial Champion. Kaye and Roger Fuller, also in Texas, have done well with the KC dogs, also strongly based on Holway lines.

In Colorado, Barbara Howard (TARTAN) owned and trained the memorable AFC Holway Barty, a dog of quality both individually and as a sire. Barty, born in 1971, carried the most impeccable English field trial breeding, and proved an extraordinary sire of both field and obedience talented Goldens. Carma Futhey's field competitors included Holway Joyful***, of similar pedigree.

THE GOLDEN RETRIEVER IN CANADA
Although Goldens arrived in Canada perhaps even earlier than in the US, the relatively smaller population meant a slower growth of activity. Early on there were pockets of activity in spots across the southern spread of Canada, such as the Gilnockie kennels in Winnipeg, Rockhaven kennels in Vancouver, and a few others. S.F.D. Roe of Red Deer, Alberta, supplied hunting dogs and breeding stock with the Roedare prefix as early as before 1940; Jack Reid, Goldrange prefix, in British Columbia started with Canadian stock, and imported from England in the 1960s.

In Ontario, Cliff MacDonald's Shadywell kennels was a strong force for many years, and George Mehlenbacker's Mel-Bach Goldens were well known. John McNicol imported several influential British dogs from Janville and Boltby. Starting with Mel-Bach stock, dogs bred by McNicol and further British imports, the well-known Chrys-haefen and Skylon kennels, still active, were developed by the twin sisters Jennifer McCauley and Judy Taylor.

In the Maritimes, Alex Wilson's Dual Champion Lady Bess was the first Canadian Dual Ch. bitch; the Wilsonia kennel name is carried on today by his son. There were four other Duals, all males:- the last, Canadian Dual Ch. Carolee's Something Special, CDX, bred by Shirley and Al Goodman and owned by George Stewart.

In the 1960s Golden activity began to increase. The first Golden Retriever club, formed in Ontario, eventually became the Golden Retriever Club of Canada and is now a strong, truly national club. The National Specialty now rotates through all areas of the Canada and includes sweepstakes, obedience trials, and Working Certificate Tests. There are well-established Golden breeders throughout Canada, some based on American stock, some on British, some combining both, and quality is high throughout the country.

Field trials in Canada are very similar to those in the USA, although entries are somewhat smaller in number. Hunting Tests are new north of the border, with the first official tests held in 1996. Working Certificate, Working Certificate Intermediate, and Working Certificate Excellent are now also official CKC-recognized titles, although the first WC tests for Goldens were held by the Golden Retriever Club in 1972. In Canada, these tests are open to all retriever breeds, including the Nova Scotia Duck Tolling Retriever, and the Irish Water Spaniel and the Standard Poodle.

Field training in Minnesota. Pam Ruddick's Can. Ch. Ciadar Gloucester CDX, TD, JH, WC, VC Can. CDX.

Midas Belvedere Houston, MH*** is a field worker of international pedigree. He was whelped in Canada, sired by a Texas dog out of an English imported bitch (by Sky-Lab Argus of Belvedere*** x Holway Dinar). Owned by Mercedes Hitchcock, Texas.

Dog shows in Canada are on the USA pattern except for the point schedules. At present 10 points are required for a championship title, under at least 3 different judges. No majors are required, although the topic of points and majors has been proposed, discussed (and cussed!) several times. As entries are smaller and shows fewer, the point schedule is less demanding; however, the competition in Goldens is often of very high quality and of good numbers. Canadian shows are smaller, often with less cut-throat competitiveness than in the States, and usually more fun overall, much like US shows of years ago (as we old fossils like to remember them!).

SUMMARY
The United States and Canada are very large countries, and with such a great deal of participation in all areas of activity, it is not possible to do more than barely skim the surface in a short chapter such as this.

Golden Retriever entries in conformation showing are among the highest of all breeds at many shows, and completing a title is not easy. Goldens have been a very strong force in obedience trials for years, with literally hundreds of titles annually. In field trials, there is a relatively small, but very determined, contingent of Goldens placing regularly. The popular Hunting Tests, and the GRCA's Working Certificate Tests, have opened up field work to greater numbers of Golden owners who do not have the resources for licensed trials. Registrations with the AKC seem to have levelled off, but are still far too high for the best interests of the breed.

Goldens also serve as Guide Dogs and as Assistance Dogs, in law enforcement for detection of narcotics, explosives and other materials. They work as Search and Rescue (SAR) dogs and as Therapy Dogs. And of course the Golden is an unparalleled companion dog. There seems no end to the talents of the Golden Retriever.

GERMANY
HISTORY OF THE BREED

Golden Retrievers were not introduced into Germany until the late 1950s. It seems that German gundog enthusiasts were for many years convinced that their native breeds would do all that was required of a satisfactory gundog. The long-wired and short-haired Pointer, the Dachshund, Dachsbracke and the Weimaraner covered their needs in the hunting world.

It was not until the late 50s and early 60s that business associates were invited to enjoy the sport in England, where they became aware of the popular retriever breeds and indeed their superb qualities.

A few retrievers were imported into Germany from England and Denmark. The first few enthusiasts showed perhaps most interest in the working qualities of their dogs, while others were kept as family pets. Eight different Goldens competed in All-Breed Gundog Working Trials, and the outstanding results enabled the German Retriever Club to be not only founded but officially recognised by the German Kennel Club (Verband fur das Deutsche Hundewesen – VDH) in 1963. This club still takes care of all the retriever breeds today. The German Labrador Club was founded in 1984 and the Golden Retriever Club in 1990. Both were also recognised by the VDH. The VDH is, in turn, affiliated to the Fédération Cynologique Internationale (FCI).

EARLY LITTERS

The first litter of Golden Retrievers was born on April 4th 1962, and was registered by the VDH one year before the Retriever Club was recognised. The dam, Linnet of Essendene, was bred in England by Mrs M. Woodbridge, and the sire was Bull of John v.d. Harstenbock, a Dutch dog descended from Ch. Masterstroke of Yeo.

Later in the same year a second litter was born. The bitch Cragmounts Tessa (born 24.10.1959) came from the Engelhards' kennels in New Jersey, USA, and was given as a present to Dr Wilhelm Hereaus in Hanau, Germany. She had Dorcas, Westley and Camrose lines in her pedigree and was mated to an English dog imported as a pet, with Noranby, Stenbury and Stubbings breeding behind him.

Many of the Goldens which were imported during the following years came from renowned kennels, but were primarily bought as pets. Most of these came from England, but some also came from Denmark, Holland, Belgium, Switzerland and Ireland and, latterly, from the other Scandinavian countries.

Very strict breeding regulations in the early days had, of course, an adverse effect on breeding, especially considering the breeding potential available at that time. For example, Goldens could only be bred from if they had been successful in a Field Trial and had a complete bite! During the following years, only a few litters were registered. Furthermore, a German Kennel Club rule prevented more than six puppies per litter being raised, a rule which held good until 1976.

Although a few good stud dogs in neighbouring countries were available for use, there were very few breeders sufficiently keen to travel as far as one thousand kilometres to have a bitch mated. Although even today such journeys are not unknown, the situation has improved considerably and a total of 70 different stud dogs were used in 1995.

With the steady increase in the popularity of the breed and their central position in Europe, German breeders now have a selection of quality stud dogs available in Holland, Belgium, Denmark and Switzerland. Due to recent amendments in quarantine regulations, borders have also been opened to the other Scandinavian countries.

The development of the breed is reflected in the number of Goldens registered during the last twenty-five years:

Pre-1970:   100
1970 to 1980:   1,130
1980 to 1990:   3,942
1990 to 1995:   6,832.

The numbers of *non-registered* puppies bred or imported during recent years is estimated at a similar figure.

At the same time there was a rapidly growing interest in all aspects of the breed, and an increasing demand for more shows, field trials, dummy and working tests. The main problem has been the lack of qualified and experienced judges and stewards to officiate at events organised by the clubs.

BREEDING TODAY
Breeding regulations continue to be strict. Nowadays, all breeding stock has to be X-rayed for hip dysplasia, and eye examinations are carried out either annually or before mating. During recent years, conscientious breeders and owners have, on a voluntary basis, also had other joints X-rayed to check for signs of osteochondritis dissecans. Discerning breeders are planning matings mindful of genetic problems associated with the breed.

Goldens used for breeding must also pass a selection test to ensure that in every respect they are typical representatives of the breed. Only breed judges who have passed through the German Kennel Club training scheme are recognised. The long-time compulsory, and somewhat controversial, temperament test is no longer a relevant factor for breeding. However, care is taken to eliminate Goldens from breeding who show obvious traits indicating extreme deviation from the truly desirable temperament set down in the Breed Standard.

The FCI member countries have, where required, their own translation of the Standard for each particular breed from the country of origin. Fine differences can be found, depending on the accuracy of the translation. For example, the nose of the Golden Retriever is described in the British Kennel Club Standard as "nose preferably black", whereas the German translation says "nose black" – implying that it *must* be black.

All available information is recorded and, since the beginning of 1990, all dogs registered through the German Retriever Club are being given a computer score based on the hip and eye results of parents, siblings, offspring etc. This score may be of interest as soon as the other clubs are included.

These results are all published in the club magazine, which appears six times annually. Together with all the show and field trial reports, breeders are provided with a valuable source of information when planning future matings.

SHOWING GOLDEN RETRIEVERS
Until 1980, a Golden Retriever in Germany could only get the show title of International Champion or Club Winner.

At the All-Breed International Championship Shows it is possible to get a certificate (CACIB) towards the title International Champion. To gain the full title, it is necessary to get one CACIB at one of the above-mentioned shows at home and one abroad, combined with a satisfactory result at a Working Test or Field Trial. The FCI requires all gundogs to gain at least 75 per cent of the maximum points obtainable before the title International Champion is confirmed.

The title Club Winner (Clubsieger) was given to the best of each sex at the annual Club Show. This award is still given to the best dog and bitch, who now must also have a working certificate or have passed an obedience test, and have successfully participated in the tests required for breeding.

In order to make up a German Champion, it was necessary, between 1980 and 1990, to gain three CACs under a minimum of two different judges and to have competed successfully in one of the working tests run by the German Retriever Club, as with the International Champion title.

These conditions were altered at the beginning of 1990. A junior CAC was introduced, three of these being required to win the title of Junior Champion. It also became necessary to win four CACs under at least three different judges, with not less than one year between the first and last of these. The working test is no longer obligatory. Similar conditions pertain for the title German Champion VDH (German Kennel Club Champion).

Nowadays, there are approximately twelve All-Breed International Championship shows annually, and a further thirteen Championship Shows run by the clubs in different regions. Exhibitors have to be very enthusiastic to travel often vast distances to the shows, not to mention pay very high entry fees and considerable costs for travel and overnight expenses. Fortunately, it was agreed that it was vital to invite well-known judges from England and, in recent years, from other countries, to ensure that typical representatives of the breed were being placed. This has resulted in a good number of entries at shows in most areas in the country. Exhibitors have come not only from Germany, but also from neighbouring countries and recently even a few from Scandinavia. At the Club Show in 1990 there was an entry of 26 in the open bitch class; three years later there were 40, and in 1996 a total of 92 at the Club Show in the same class.

Although we do not have all the intermediate classes as they are known in England, this expansion does reflect Germany's increasing interest in the breeding and showing of Goldens in recent years.

INFLUENTIAL BRITISH BLOODLINES
As Britain is the Golden Retriever's country of origin, it is natural that a fair number of imports over the years have Kennel Club registration numbers. Sadly, few of these were purchased for breeding purposes, although they came from good lines and would have helped considerably in getting the breed established in this country. Three kennels stand out for their efforts to breed on from promising puppies imported from England.

OF MILL LANE
In 1976 Ch. Camrose Mellowmist (Ch. Davern Figaro – Camrose Fillipa Thisbe) was imported by the "of Mill Lane" kennel. She won a number of show titles herself and is behind several Champions.

Mated to Swiss Ch. Camrose Listrender she produced Ch. Biscuit of Mill Lane. Ch. Esther of Mill Lane (by Norw. Ch. Camillo) was successful in the show ring and at Field Trials, and from a litter by Dutch Ch. Westley Floyd her breeder, Pat Busch, retained Ch. Guinevere of Mill Lane for her breeding programme. This bitch produced a number of winners including Ch. Miss Mellow of Mill Lane (by Dutch Ch. Noravon Amos), Ch. Ptarmigan of Mill Lane (by Ritzilyn Top Gun), and Ch. Raggle Taggle of Mill Lane (by Linchael Star of Africa).

Ritzilyn Top Gun joined this kennel from the UK and sired some winners of good type and temperament. Pat took great care to place the most promising offspring from Guinevere into good hands in the hope that others would breed on from her line. She started breeding Golden Retrievers in 1974 and bred nineteen litters in all, until her death in 1994. Although she did not train her own dogs for competitive work, she always endeavoured to breed typical, intelligent Goldens with particular emphasis on temperament.

Study of four Goldens. Breeder: the late Pat Busch. Kennel: "of Mill Lane".

BALTIC GOLDEN

Ch. Pennard Golden Mango was imported from Marjorie Thomsen's well-known, dual-purpose kennel by the Baltic Golden kennel in 1971. He was used at stud and sired several of the first litters in kennels which are still active today. These are vom Geesthang (this kennel later produced Ch. Donna v. Geesthang and Ch. Frederic v. Geesthang), vom Forsthaus Weyhausen, and vom Wacholderpark. With a Ch. and FT. Ch. in his pedigree, he not only passed on type but also his splendid temperament and working qualities, he himself having excelled in Obedience competitions. Several of the top Field Trial Goldens of that time were sired by him.

Int. Ch. Master Melody (Int. DK S Ch. Byxfield Cedar – DK Ch. Glenavis Bellagirl) proved to be a successful foundation bitch for the same kennel, winning several show titles and qualifying in the field. She was Europasieger, Clubsieger and three times Bundessieger.

Mated to Swiss Ch. Camrose Listrender she produced four different title winners in her first litter. Baltic Golden Arno was Clubseiger and also a successful Field Trial dog. His show career ended abrubtly owing to an injury. Her son Ch. Baltic Golden Echo (by Ch. Lawnwoods Nimrod) qualified in the field, and from a mating to Nor Ch. Camillo she produced Ch. Baltic Golden Foster and his

Ch. Nunsbrook Baltic Baron. Breeders: B. &. J Liggins. Owner: Hilary Vogel. Kennel: "Baltic Golden".

Ch. Baltic Golden Rhapsody. Breeder & Owner: Hilary Vogel. Kennel: "Baltic Golden".

sister Filippa. Mated to Ch. Lawnwoods Nimrod, Filippa had Ch. Baltic Golden Gwendy, who became the record winning bitch with the most show titles and field awards. Mated to NL Ch. Westley Floyd a further title and a CC winner were produced. Ch. Papeta Primrose (Sh. Ch. Lacons Enterprise ex Sh. Ch. Westley Sophia of Papeta) joined the Baltic kennel in 1983. Mated to Nortonwood Telstar, two winning daughters, Baltic Golden Hayley and Highness were produced. Hayley produced the show winning bitch, Baltic Golden Octavia and her sister Olivia, who was not only a CC winner, but also had four firsts in Field Trial events. Various title holders and different CC winners have been produced in this line, and in the fifth generation Ch. Baltic Golden Rhapsody, Club and Nordic Winner 1996, Brussels Winner 1995, 9 CCs (Linchael Star of Africa ex Baltic Golden Melinda) is winning well today. Ch. Nunsbrook Baltic Baron (Sh. Ch. Jobeka Jasper of Nortonwood – Cardrona Brontelle of Nunsbrook), born 1993, joined the Baltic Goldens, quickly gaining four show titles, and is siring some very promising youngsters.

FOURWIND COTTAGE
The first Golden Retriever owned by the Fourwind Cottage kennel was the English import Ch. Talmah Blake (Ch. Nortonwood Faununs ex Westley Larissa) born in 1983. In

1985 he was joined by the influential stud dog Ch. Styal Solar (Sh. Ch. Nortonwood Checkmate – Styal Solacea) who won several titles and proved his working ability in tests and trials. He passed his type and temperament on to many of his offpsring. In 1987 Ch. Styal Stargleam (Brambletyne Peppermint – Styal Symetra) was imported and was the foundation bitch for this kennel. Mated to Ch. Styal Solar she produced three Champions – Int. Ch. Fourwind Cottage Aramis, Ch. Fourwind Cottage April Love and Ch. Fourwind Cottage Bali, all of which were successful in the field. Aramis was mated to Ch. Garbank Golden Style producing Ch. Bentley of Baltic Lane, and to A Wise Decision of Lesmona producing Ch. Amirene the Queen of Quaxus. Ch. Styal Solar also sired three International Champions.

Ch. Fourwind Cottage Bali was the foundation bitch for the Stargleam kennel. She passed on her excellent type to her daughter, Amazing Grace Stargleam, and her winning granddaughter, Broken Silence Stargleam.

Ch. Lawnwoods Pickwick (Dabess Lindley of Honeyford – Lawnwood's Naughty Nancy) was imported from England in 1944. He qualified as a rescue dog and was sire of Ch. Annette vom Giesebrink. Edgeley Editor (Sh. Ch. Nortonwood Sylvanus – Edgeley Elstar) came to Germany in 1988 and both of these dogs were used extensively at stud producing good hips and clear eyes.

Ch. Styal Solar. Breeder: Hazel Hinks. Owner: Dagmar Winter. Kennel: "Fourwind Cottage".

SCANDINAVIAN INFLUENCE

The following kennels started with a foundation bitch from Denmark. Using dominant sires they have bred on producing Goldens which have been successful in the show ring as well as on the working side.

VOM MOHNFELD (1980): Foundation bitch was Sussi Birke (Banworth Man in the Moon – DK Ch. Masterlady). This kennel bred some winners including Ch. Goldfalter vom Mohnfeld and litter sisters Ghirali and Georgia (sired by Tallygold Tobi Dog, DK).

OF REDPINE (1983): Foundation bitch here was Birka (DK Ch. Chiko ex Dienesmindes Diana). Many winners have been bred in this kennel including Int. Ch. Alice of Redpine, and Ch. Baika of Redpine (by Int. Ch. Lawnwood's Nimrod). She was mated to Zodiak, DK (Int. Ch. Moviestar's Buster Keaton – Dainty's Taste of Honey), and produced Ch. Dandylion of Redpine.

GOLDEN DAYDREAMS (1985): Foundation bitch was Ch. Dear Darenca of Redpine. Mated to Westley Cumgen, Ch. Mack Lobell of the Hellacious Acres and Ch. Nunsbrook Baltic Baron, quality offspring have been produced.

OF GRACEFUL DELIGHT (1984): With Danish and Swedish lines behind the breeding, this kennel has a show line as well as a strictly working line, and is achieving promising results in both directions.

The future of the Golden Retriever in Germany rests on the shoulders of those breeders who started in a small but serious way. They imported promising puppies from long-established, renowned kennels, taking advice regarding the correct combinations of breeding. Although at the start the gene pool was extremely limited, borders have now been opened to almost all European and Scandinavian countries. Furthermore, if a bitch has produced a litter under normal circumstances, artificial insemination with fresh or frozen sperm is allowed for subsequent litters. However, even being given promising offpsring from the best bloodlines available will not ensure a successful breeding career. A considerable amount of time and energy must be spent on acquiring a basic knowledge of dog breeding. Some young enthusiasts who have made a good start would do well to fall back on the knowledge and experience of older breeders. Without this support these lines, however successful they may have been in the past, cannot be proliferated.

THE WORKING GOLDEN RETRIEVER

Now that the breed is becoming more popular in Germany, the club activities are spreading

ABOVE: Ch. Dear Darenca of Redpine. Photo: Simon.

TOP RIGHT: Ch. Goldfather Vom Mohnfeld. Breeder: Renate Burgman. Owner: Kennel: "Vom Mohnfeld".

RIGHT: Ch. Dandylion of Redpine. Breeder: Sylvia Sponholz. Owner: W. Hoffmeister. Kennel: "of Redpine".

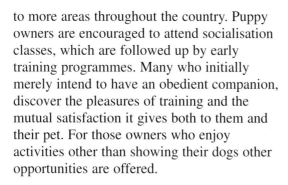

to more areas throughout the country. Puppy owners are encouraged to attend socialisation classes, which are followed up by early training programmes. Many who initially merely intend to have an obedient companion, discover the pleasures of training and the mutual satisfaction it gives both to them and their pet. For those owners who enjoy activities other than showing their dogs other opportunities are offered.

FIELD TRIALS AND WORKING TESTS
In the early days it was assumed that more advanced training would automatically be directed towards work in the field, the job of work for which the breed was evolved. The more intelligent Golden Retrievers even competed successfully against the all-round German gundog breeds. Latterly, it is becoming increasingly difficult to find suitable countryside where gundog trainers are welcome for regular training and for running

Field Trials using live game. Furthermore, the German National Gundog Association (Jagdgebrauchshundeverband – JGHV) prevents the breed clubs from running official trials for handlers not in possession of a shooting licence. To obtain a licence nowadays entails attending regular classes to acquire a considerable amount of theoretical knowledge for the final examination, plus a high standard of practical competence, not to mention the time required for this costly affair. An exception to this rule is only made in the first test, if the dog entered has been selected for breeding.

The German Retriever Club runs approximately 18 events in the late summer and autumn. Two of these trials are using cold game, and the more advanced event with cold and live game. An annual event has been introduced, The German Cup, which enables working test enthusiasts to compete in teams on a national basis. This work with dummies is becoming more and more popular, and the most successful participants are eligible to compete in the International Working Test. The latter is held in a different European Country each year and at the most recent event there were twenty-one teams from seven countries competing.

Since 1993 the Federation Cynologique Internationale (FCI) has organised the Coupe d'Europe every two years. This is a Field Trial run very closely to an actual day's shooting. A maximum of four retrievers from each European country can take part in this event, and these are selected on a national basis to represent their own country. In 1995 there were teams from Austria, Belgium, Denmark, Finland, France, Germany, Holland and Italy.

As in many other countries, the versatile Golden Retriever is trained and used for a variety of other exercises. In recent years Golden Retrievers are becoming increasingly popular as Guide Dogs for the Blind.

They also take an active part in qualified Rescue Work and have become very popular in this field. They work in connection with recognised organisations such as the Red Cross. The dogs are trained to search under all conditions and over every kind of surface. This includes areas and buildings where there have been explosions and earthquakes. Often they find victims that have been buried under several metres of debris. Frequently they are called out to search for old, ill, disturbed and suicidal persons as well as children. Their enthusiasm for work, good nose and will to please make them predestined for such demanding exercises. Dog and handler become a recognised team after a three-year training period, and refresher courses are compulsory to maintain the standard of this voluntary work.

Qualified dogs are registered with the ministry in Bonn and can be called up for international catastrophes such as the earthquake in Mexico City in 1985. On this occasion four teams were flown out and they found 27 living and over 100 dead under the debris.

Equally satisfying is the work which has

been started fairly recently training Golden Retrievers as companions for the handicapped (Hunde fur Handicaps). The founder of the training centre, herself confined to a wheeled chair, was inspired by the achievements of qualified retrievers she saw on a visit to America, and with her supporters is recognised for her work in this direction.

Golden Retrievers have also proved very successful as drug-sniffers. As well as supporting regular checks of luggage and lockers at airports and railways, a number are in service at various borders of the country. One of these was actually nominated as "sniffer" of the year

Agility will surely gain more popularity in the future as the ideal hobby to keep active owners fit and their dogs occupied and happy.

Surely there are few other breeds of dog which are capable of serving mankind so loyally in such a variety of ways, as well as being the most perfect companion.

AUSTRALIA

Golden Retrievers are these days one of the most popular breeds in Australia and New Zealand, and are to be found taking part in all aspects of canine competition with great success. Their popularity is evident in the continuing trend of using our beautiful dogs in advertising everything from dog food to cars, thus assuring they remain firm favourites as family pets and companions, for which they have a talent perhaps unequalled. In line with the rest of the world, Goldens have recently become an important part of aid organisations in both our countries and are used by the Guide Dog Associations. They are a common sight as visitors to hospitals, children's homes and homes for the aged, where their soft beauty and gentle natures make them an invaluable element of therapy.

To date, and contrary to the belief of many, American bloodlines do not feature in breeding programmes in Australia or New Zealand. Both ruling bodies adopt the English Kennel Club Breed Standard. It has taken many years of painstaking dedication by Australasian breeders, who have diligently bred to English guidelines, to produce the dogs we have today. They are to be congratulated for their efforts. During the breed's infancy in both countries, Goldens did not account for many 'in group' or 'in show' wins. These days, they are a force to contend with at all levels of all-breeds competition, regularly winning Best Exhibit in Show awards, and are praised by many overseas specialist judges.

The first documented information on Golden Retrievers in Australia can be found in Victoria, with the registration of Grakle of Tone (Noranby General x Silence of Tone), bred by Miss F. Newton-Deakin of Dorset, UK, and owned by Miss E Grice. Miss Grice also imported the bitch Temeraire (Stubbings Golden Hidalgo x Stubbings Golden Calypso), and, in 1938, her first Golden Retriever litter was bred from these imports under the RAHWEEN prefix. Gipsy of Rahween from this litter was sent to New Zealand and, later, stock from New Zealand arrived in Victoria.

This early exchange of bloodlines across the Tasman Sea was a forerunner of what has, to this day, remained as a healthy camaraderie between the breeders in Australia and those in New Zealand.

During the 1950s, some early imports into Australia included Alexander of Arbrook and Kristine of Kuldana. However, it was perhaps the importation from the UK in 1954 of Boltby Comet (UK Ch. Boltby Skylon x Goldawn Brandy) and Halsham Hazel (UK Sh. Ch. Major of Elsiville x Halsham Merrie Maid) by Mr and Mrs Spencer that founded the BONSPIEL kennel and had the most impact. Comet and Hazel both gained their Championships and were bred extensively by the Spencers. Following the death of Mr Spencer, they were acquired by Mr and Mrs W. Davis and bred under the EDMAY prefix. The Bonspiel and Edmay prefixes were to feature predominantly in the early founding years of the breed in Australia. A dog who had a great influence on the breed in this country was Benedict of Golconda (imported from the UK, Dorcas Quicksilver x Jyntee of

Golconda). Although not in Australia long, he was most influential through Mr Philp's homebred Ch. Kyvalley Kyva, whose dam was Ch. Bonspiel Gold Glint. Kyva is believed to have sired in excess of 70 Champions and the bitches from the KYVALLEY prefix were to spread to all states of Australia and found many a top and influential kennel. At one stage, there were few Goldens in Australia who did not contain Kyva in their pedigrees.

Another early UK import to feature predominantly in the breed's early foundation was Ch. Glennessa Seahawk of Stenbury (Glennessa Crofter of Empshot x Waterminx of Stenbury). He provided the much-needed outcross after the Kyva years and sired many Champions.

CLUBS AND SHOWS

In 1964, a Golden Retriever Club was formed in New South Wales and other states were to follow suit in subsequent years. Today there are five Golden Retriever Clubs in Australia, boasting a total membership well in excess of the 1,000 mark, and moves are under way to form a club in Tasmania. Throughout Australia's states, Championship and Open Shows, Parades, Member Competitions and Obedience Trials are held during the year, and all clubs promote the dual-purpose function of the Golden Retriever club through field trial activities, although this facet is not as popular as the conformation and obedience rings.

The popularity of the Golden Retriever has increased substantially since its introduction. In 1964, Golden Retriever Championship shows drew less than 55 dogs. Since then, entries have steadily increased yearly until entries at the New South Wales Golden Retriever Club September Championship show in 1995 exceeded 270. This show was judged by Margaret Somerton (UK), and Best in Show was Jim and Jan Mackendar's home-bred, Ch. Uneek Robin Hood. On many occasions at all-breed shows, Goldens are the largest breed entry in the Gundog group, as well as at most of the 'Royal' shows, which are held yearly in each state. One dog worthy

Ch. Buffalo Kingpin.

Robyn Ramsay's home-bred Ch. Ramgold Rhyme 'N' Reason.

To become a Champion in Australia a dog must gain 100 points. CCs are awarded (at the discretion of the judge) to the best dog and bitch on the day. The challenge winner earns five points, plus one point for every Golden of its sex entered and exhibited. As the maximum points per challenge is 25, the minimum challenge certificates possible is four, and no one judge can award more than 50 points.

If the entrant is the only representative of its sex exhibited, and the judge feels that the dog is an outstanding representative of the breed and worthy of the title of Australian Champion, he or she can award a CC and six points is gained. The onus is on the judge to ensure that quality is maintained at all times, and to refuse a CC if such action is warranted. Should the dog win Best Gundog Exhibit, then further points are awarded – one point for every dog exhibited in the Group and, once again, up to a maximum of 25 (if they have already obtained 25 points at breed level, then no further points are attainable), and the same principle applies should the dog win Best Exhibit in Show.

Puppies can be exhibited from three months, with CCs awarded only to dogs or bitches over the age of six months. It is possible for a title to be gained before the age of twelve

of mention here is Ch. Balandra Delta Darius UD, bred by Mrs J. Bridges and owned by Mrs J. Trout (Karrell). In 1981, Darius won Best in Show at the prestigious Sydney Royal show. Darius (Stolford Sheriff (imp UK) x Ch. Cambronze Melody) sired many Champion progeny, including Ch. and NZ Ch. Brygolden Oatly Tyrone, the current breed record-holder for challenge winning points. Best of Breed at the 1995 Sydney Royal Show was Mike and

Ch. & NZ Ch. Brygolden Oatly Tyrone.

months. There is no Grand Champion award in Australia at the present time. However, the breed's top dogs usually continue in the ring long after they have achieved their titles and accumulate challenge points, thus earning their titles many times over.

TOP WINNING GOLDENS

Ch. Buffalo Kingpin, a multi Best in Show winner, sire of eleven Australian Champions and Sydney Royal Best of Breed winner himself, finished with over 2,000 points. Vicorian bred dogs to have achieved the magic 1,000 points or more include Ch. Ferngold Commodore (Mrs J McAdam) and, more recently, Ch. Tahmero Gay Cavalier (Tahmero kennels).

Bitches excelling in the show ring include Ch. Talltree Tradition (L. Broom, Vic), Ch. Queenlee Lady Lion (N. Bolton, NSW), Ch. Buffalo Luvmelots (Tahmero Kennels, Victoria), Ch. Ramgold Rhyme 'N' Reason (M. and R. Ramsay, NSW) and Ch. Coombehill Brae Roshen (D. and M. McKittrick, Qld), all of whom have over 1,300 points. Ch. and NZ Ch. Brygolden Oatly Tyrone, owned by Mick and Pauline O'Sheehy (NSW), is the current breed record holder for challenge points with 3,586 points, surpassing the long-standing record of over 3,200 points held by Ch. Queenlee Debonair OC (whelped in 1970 and owned by N. Bolton).

Debonair OC remains the current breed record-holder for Best in Show wins, with 21 to his credit as well as 16 times runner-up BIS. Not only was Debonair a top show dog in his day, he also attained the title of Obedience Champion (OC). His progeny have performed well in the show, obedience and field areas, with many gaining both show and Obedience titles.

OBEDIENCE WINNERS

Golden Retrievers remain a force to contend with in the Australian obedience ring, and often win Best of Winners at major trials throughout the country. Gary Somerville is a well-known competitor, and his dogs, Karrell Impact UD, Nunkeri Sonny Gold UD and Ch.

Dykinta Star Commotion UD, are famous for their success over the years. Kerry and Ann Upton's Buffalo Regal Charm CDX was a top obedience trial winner, and her sons, Jukeran Chyzanta Ariki CDX, owned and bred by the Uptons, and Jukeran Future Impact CDX (Somerville) have followed suit.

The road to an obedience Championship is very time-consuming and much dedication is required. The dog must attain the titles of Companion Dog, Companion Dog Excellent, Utility Dog, Tracking Dog and Tracking Dog Excellent. A recent Golden to achieve this title is Tiptree Timbarra OC, owned by Ruth Nicholls (Vic).

DUAL CHAMPIONS

The QUEENLEE kennel in NSW was well-known for producing dual-purpose stock. A more recent dual-purpose advocate in NSW is Wendy Atkins with her Dykinta Goldens. John Lawton (Ferntip) is among those who promote field trial activities in Victoria, having owned and trained Dual Ch. (FT) Tiptree Timothy CD (a descendant of Ch. Queenlea Debonair OC), bred by Barbara Moore (SA).

A Dual Champion in Australia is made up when a dog obtains a Championship in the breed ring as well as a Championship in the

Ch. Ramgold Rhyme & Reason.

field. Few Goldens boast this highly-coveted award. The most recent, in Victoria, was Steve and Kim Burke's Dual Ch. Allanora Xmas Holly CD NRD.

IMPORTANT DOGS

Other imports to have a strong influence on breed development include Byxfield Lindys Golden Gleam (imp UK), Ch. Noravon Otto Goldtreve (imp UK), Ch. Lawnwoods Love a Lot (imp UK) and Ch. Arnell of Rustledene (imp NZ). Further imports from the UK to Australia over the years have included dogs from Camrose, Glennessa, Yeo, Westley, Gaylon, Sansue, Bournehouse, Nortonwood, Styal, Stolford, Rossbourne, Amblaire and Garbank.

In 1993, David and Viv Sterrett of the UK Tasvane kennel emigrated, bringing with them their UK Sh. Ch. Tasvane Charles Henry. Before departing for Australia, Henry was a multi CC winner and successful sire in England. He gained his Australian Championship and, in 1994, won Best Exhibit in Show at the GRC of Victoria's Championship show, and was Runner-up the following year. In 1996 he won Best Exhibit in Show at the New South Wales Championship Show, just one week before his untimely death. This was a tragic loss to the breed in Australia. Fortunately, Henry sired many quality offspring and Champion, thus enabling breeders to obtain the benefitis of his bloodline for many years to come. The Sterretts also brought with them Henry's son, Tasvane Indiana. Indiana is also proving himself the sire of some quality progeny.

In 1995, Jan and Louise Patterson (Euraidd) imported the four-year-old UK-bred Sandusky Klammer from Sweden (UK Sh. Ch. Linchael Conspiracy of Chevanne x Sansue Golden Gloria of Sandusky). 'Frasse' gained his Australian title that same year, and has produced promising youngsters to date. No doubt his bloodline will be a valuable addition to the gene pool in Australia, as will that of the youngster, Dewmist Silverado, imported from Sweden by Kim Handley, Janelle Salvestrain and Robyn Peirce.

ARTIFICIAL INSEMINATION

In Australia there are no restrictions on the use of frozen semen from deceased and/or live dogs, and this gives breeders the opportunity to obtain bloodlines from the best dogs the world has to offer.

Towards the end of the 1970s, two litters were successfully obtained from the frozen semen of the great UK Ch. Camrose Cabus Christopher.

A first for the breed in Australia was a litter of four puppies bred by Mr and Mrs E.J. Phillipson, of Ferngold. The dam of this historic litter was Ch. Nayr Melodymaker. Soon to follow were Fred and Beryl Hession (Goldtreve) whose Ch. Gaewynd Tapestry produced six puppies. Progeny from this litter went on to produce many Champions, their Ch. Goldtreve Cameron (AI) being a prolific sire. Later, their Ch. Goldtreve Tosca was to produce a bitch puppy from Christopher semen.

Other NSW breeders successful with the use of frozen semen have been Denece Hutcheson (Briden) through Glennessa bloodlines, Robyn Palazzi (Azzigold) with UK Ch. Sansue Golden Ruler, and Claire and Andre Kaspura (Taransay) with semen from UK Sh. Ch. Nortonwood Silvanus.

In Victoria, Bert and Phyll Kewish (Tahmero) obtained semen from UK Sh. Ch. Westley Jacob and, in conjunction with Joe Whittall in South Australia, produced puppies from Ch. Tahmero Khalah's Coppa. A bitch from this litter, Cambronze Pippa (AI), gained her title and produced Champion stock for Tahmero. Sue Kowalski (Ambervalley) has also had success with semen from UK Ch. Bethrob Bracken.

More recently, in December 1995, Fred and Beryl Hession leased a bitch from Rosemary Easton (Montego). Montego Maple Syrup produced five dogs and four bitches from Christopher's semen. This was 18 years after his death, and must be considered a milestone for the technique worldwide. Maple Syrup is herself a great grand-daughter of Christopher, being a descendant of Tosca's AI puppy.

BREED DEVELOPMENTS

As mentioned earlier, Golden Retriever Clubs have been formed in New South Wales, Queensland, Victoria, South Australia and Western Australia. In 1995 a National Breed Council was formed, and in 1996 the first 'National' Golden Retriever Club show is scheduled in South Australia. One of the functions of a National Breed Council is to help encourage communication among clubs and breeders around Australia. In a country which takes five hours to cross by air, and where most capital cities are a good full day's drive apart, anything which promotes communication among breeders is a step forward for the future.

Our climate is harsh during the summer months and distances can be long, making travelling and dog showing/trialling difficult. However, few enthusiasts are deterred, and many meet at interstate Championship shows to enjoy their common interest – our beautiful Golden Retrievers.

NEW ZEALAND

The history of the breed in New Zealand is relatively recent with few Goldens being seen until the 1950s, when Wyn Reed of Penkor and Margaret Evans of Vanrose emigrated from the UK and brought their Goldens with them, to establish the early strains of current show stock. In the South Island at around this time, Marguerite Hill-Smith brought three Golden Retriever bitches from England and established her Tanqueny kennels, later importing dogs of basically Camrose breeding. Josh and Joyce Tucker also imported UK dogs for their Lakenheath lines.

A Golden Retriever Club was established in Auckland in 1967 (an earlier Club existed but had been placed in recess some years earlier due to lack of interest), and in later years the Central and the Southern Golden Retriever Clubs were formed to cater regionally for a growing membership. These days, the three clubs have a combined membership of some 665 Golden Retriever enthusiasts and all hold Championship and Open Shows annually,

along with ribbon parades. The Southern Golden Retriever Club is also an affiliated Obedience and Gundog club, holding an Open Obedience Trial and a Championship Field Trial every year.

The showing of Golden Retrievers is a popular activity and the breed generally draws the greatest number of entries at All-Breed shows. At the PAL National Dog Show in 1995 (New Zealand's largest dog show) there was an entry of 142 Golden Retrievers, with Best of Breed being awarded to Ch. Natalia of St Germain, owned by Sandie Milne (Shannongold).

To become a Champion in New Zealand, a dog or bitch must win eight challenge certificates under at least five different judges, with at least one CC being awarded over the age of twelve months. Puppies may be shown from the age of four months and, with recent lines producing slow-maturing Goldens who have 'lasted well', it is not uncommon to see Goldens of up to ten years of age competing regularly at shows. Golden Retrievers these days compete well at Group and Best in Show level with many taking home top awards.

In 1988, the New Zealand Kennel Club introduced the title of Grand Champion. The criteria for this award are fifty New Zealand challenge certificates and three All Breeds Best in Show wins. Golden Retrievers hold third place among the breeds for Grand Champions, with seven (six dogs and one bitch) gaining this title, with an impressive number of Best in Show wins among them.

TOP WINNING DOGS

These seven are well worthy of mention. The six dogs are, Gr. Ch. Amberline Fidele; Gr. Ch. Galway Lad of Monterey (half-brother to Happy Donagh of Monterey, both bred by Ann Morgan of Blenheim); Gr. Ch. and Aust. Ch. Caldicot Swift (the only Golden to win Best in Show at the National Show); Gr. Ch. Shannongold Enterprise (who with Gr. Ch. Amberline Fidele jointly holds the breed record of six All Breeds Best in Shows); Gr. Ch. Charterhall Gaelic Gold; and Gr. Ch. Graveleigh Soaring High QC CDX.

NZ Gr. Ch. Shannongold Enterprise.

WTCH & Ch. Thyme of Graveleigh.

The one bitch is Gr. Ch. Happy Donagh of Monterey QC, owned by David and Margaret Hean of ARANGOLD kennels. As one of the CCs had to be awarded after January 1st 1988, Donagh came out of retirement at ten years of age to win that one CC to take her Grand Champion title, and proceeded to win Best in Show as well. She has produced Champion progeny for Arangold.

IMPORTANT SIRES
Until recent years, the gene pool in New Zealand was small, but more efficient transportation and modern technology have made it more viable to import new lines (generally from Australia and the UK), and

also to import frozen semen. Like Australia, we have no restrictions on the use of frozen semen in New Zealand. This has had the obvious effect of improving the breed overall, and judges from overseas are now hailing many New Zealand Goldens as world-class.

In 1979, Liz Spiers imported Gaylon Celtic Prince (a son of Ch. Camrose Fabius Tarquin) from the UK, who proved to be a very influential sire in the South Island. In later years Ray and Eileen Curry (Makkovik), Esme Russell (Rustledene), Margaret Evans (Vanrose), and Barbara Dick (Charterhall), among others, all imported UK dogs who were to have an effect on the breed.

Margaret Hean (Arangold) was fortunate to obtain an imported son of UK Sh. Ch. Westley Munro of Nortonwood in NZ Ch. Lawnwoods Nocturn, who added further valuable bloodlines.

Esme Russell also, over the years, imported frozen semen from top English dogs and has had a great deal of success with her breeding using this method. Ch. Rustledene Camellia, who is a Sansue Castalian daughter, is one of her successes.

OBEDIENCE
Golden Retrievers in New Zealand compete widely in Obedience and, to date, there are 21 Goldens holding the title of Obedience Champion, three of whom are also Obedience Grand Champions: Ob. Gr. Ch. Croucheau Courtney CDX; Ob. Gr. Ch. and WT Ch. Speyside Charlatan CDX UDX WTX TDX; and his litter brother Ob. Gr. Ch. and Ch. Speyside Chauvinist CDX. To become an Obedience Grand Champion, a dog must win 20 CCs, ten being winning challenges and five being on 295 points or more out of 300 in Test C. The standard of Golden Retrievers in Obedience is very high, and there are many currently working close to their titles.

FIELD TRIALS
Field trialling is not as popular with Golden Retriever enthusiasts as one might expect it to be in New Zealand, and, unlike in the UK, there is no focus on the working ability of the

NZ Gr. Ch. & Aust. Ch. Caldicot Swift.

NZ Gr. Ch. Charterhall Gaelic Gold.

breed. A Golden is not required to prove picking up ability to gain a full Championship title, with each activity having its own titles and levels of achievement.

There are a few keen triallists, however, and there are moves by these people to combine good show stock with working ability to produce the true dual-purpose Golden Retriever. One such person is Miriam Dobson (MOORFIELD) whose Goldens compete successfully in Show and Obedience, as well as being keen Field Trial dogs. Annie Roska (ACHILTY) and Ann Morgan (MONTEREY) imported Holway Eros (imp UK) to inject field trial bloodlines into New Zealand. Annie is also the owner of FT Ch. Marigold of Dalby, the only Golden Retriever in twenty years to earn the title of Field Trial Champion.

WORKING TRIALS
Working Trials and Tracking are attracting a limited number of Goldens, and the title holders are all related. Ruth Eden (GRAVELEIGH) was the first to title a Golden Retriever as Working Trials Champion just a few years ago, with WT Ch. and Ch. Thyme of Graveleigh CDX UDX WDX TDX; and, more recently, her grandchildren, WT Ch. and Ch. Speyside Chenille CDX UDX WDX TDX (owned and handled by Ruth) and Sue Colvin's Gr. Ob. Ch. and WT Ch. Speyside Charlatan CDX UDX WDX TDX, have joined the elite. These three are the only Goldens with Working Trials titles, and all three have also excelled in the Show and/or Obedience fields.

SCANDINAVIA
SWEDEN
Not much is known about the very first Goldens in Sweden, but we do know there were a few imports back in the 1920s and 30s from well-known British kennels like Noranby and Kentford.

It was not until 1950 that the breed really got a foundation through Barthill Fanny, who was imported in whelp to Strelley Starlight and whelped a litter of six pups. At the same time Ch. Stubblesdown Tinker came to Sweden and these dogs, together with Count Leo of Little Compton, did the groundwork during the 1950s.

EARLY BREEDERS
Breed enthusiasts should give thanks to the famous early pioneer breeders in Sweden. Kennels BORGHALLA and HEDETORPET imported the first dogs, and just a few years later kennel APPORT started their winning line with dogs from these lines. In 1958, kennel SANDEMAR was founded, again on the old lines.

At the end of the decade, a Stubblesdown bitch was imported in whelp to a famous field trial dog, and six puppies were born in 1958. Two well-known dogs from this mating were Ch. Apports Larry Jr and Ch. Apports Joy. The first Ch. bitch was a daughter of Larry, Sandemars Azurra.

In the early 1960s, dogs were imported from Stubblesdown and Whamstead and, from Holland, came Ch. Azor v d Kruidberg, of all-English bloodlines. All these made a great impact on the breed. A few years later, the pioneer kennels again wanted to improve our breed and further imports arrived in Sweden. From Denmark came Ch. Wessex Timmy Tinker, of all-Anbria breeding, and, also from Denmark, Goldstones Es, a son of Ch. Honeyat The Viking.

In 1966, Camrose Qualetta came to kennel Apport, and proved a sound brood bitch. In 1969, the outstanding show bitch Ch. Daisy, from Norway, was runner-up Dog of the Year all breeds.

Kennel Hedetorpet imported a dog and a bitch from Stolford, Ch. Stolford Sea Bird and Stolford Larkspur, and the bitch in particular produced a chain of winners for generations. Kennel Sandemar bought the adult Ch. Glennessa Waterbird of Stenbury, Ch. Glennessa Helmsman and Ch. Cabus Clipper, all of whom were well-known.

From Danish and English lines at the end of the 1960s came Dual Ch. Coxy, yet another top-winning dog and a respectable producer for kennel Hedetorpet.

Kennel Sandemar has had tremendous wins on the show scene here since the beginning of the 60s. In 1968, Ch. Glennessa Helmsman was BIS at our prestigious Stockholm Int (our equivalent to Crufts), and, in 1970, Ch. Synspur Iona was runner-up Dog of the Year. At the beginning of the 1970s, two other famous dogs came to Sweden, Ch. Caliph of Yeo and Ch. Glenavis Barman, whose importance as stud dogs was great for generations.

A famous Caliph daughter was Cumulus Emily, who was the dam of Sandemars Viceroy. Another top dog at Sandemar was the Glenavis Barman son, Sandemars Superman. Sandemars Emilio did a lot of winning in the 1980s.

This brief history is a credit to the first breeders of Goldens. Hedetorpet, Apport and Sandemar all made up numerous Champions from the beginning, and are still active, albeit on a much smaller scale. Our sincere thanks go to them for introducing the breed, looking after it so well and giving endless advice to us all.

FAMOUS KENNELS
In the late 60s another three famous kennels were started, kennels Dainty, Knegaren and Dewmist, whose foundation stocks all go back to the early breeders.

DAINTY
Kennel Dainty's foundation bitches came from Apports, and, in 1971, Davern Fergus was

Nor Ch. Stenbury Seamusic (Top winner in her prime, born 1974) by Ch. Camrose Cabus Christopher ex Ch. Nomis Portia of Stenbury. Breeder: Mrs Minter, GB.

imported. He came to be a most valuable stud dog. Later imports such as Ch. Stenbury Sealord and his sister, Ch. Stenbury Seamusic, created more successes. Yet another famous dog was Ch. Alseras Capello, a top winner especially as a veteran. These three were all Christopher progeny.

In the 1980s, Chrisper Caleidoscope and Commander of Nortonwood, both Group or BIS winners, produced more winners.

Dabess Orlando, a son of Ch. Camrose Fabius Tarquin, died as a rather young dog having produced another stud dog in Dainty's Having It All. Kennel Dainty's bitchlines have all been related to the early dogs, and through a combination of the above and various stud dogs, have been very strong, producing a number of winners throughout the years. Artificial insemination has been used successfully, both from Denmark and from England, and Ch. Amirene King Eider of Davern and Ch. Nortonwood Silvanus are behind winners like Dainty's Son of Sky, Dainty's Stormwarning, Dainty's Blues in the Night and Dainty's Right on Cue. One young, but very promising, stud dog is Shanlimore Falcon, who already has produced CC winners for kennel Dainty.

KNEGAREN
Kennel Knegaren started with a bitch from the old lines, out of a Kuldana-imported bitch. At the beginning of the 1970s Ch. Tarquin of Marville, linebred to Ch. Camrose Nicolas of Westley, arrived and one of his most famous progeny was Ch. Knegarens Galalinda. This bitch produced a couple of winners; Ch. Knegarens Issue From Father, by AI from Ch. Davern Figaro, and Ch. Knegarens Kandida.

In 1974, the illustrious Ch. Deremar Donald, a son of Ch. Davern Figaro, made his entrance to Knegaren – a great dog indeed, who was such an outstanding sire that numerous Champions and BIS winners were among his

Knegarens Shine 'n Sparkle (3 CCs) by Ch. Linchael Ravel, ex Knegarens Querida. Breeder & Owner: Karin Eriksson. Kennel: Knegaren.

offspring. Ch. Fanny, a Donald daughter, proved to be a good brood bitch, and was the mother of Ch. Knegarens Like Cousin Jane, Ch. Knegarens Orlane and Knegarens Kathy in Knickers (3CCs). In recent years the Kathy in Knickers daughter, Knegarens Querida, has produced a chain of winners such as Ch. Knegarens Stars 'n Stripes and Knegarens Shine 'n Sparkle.

At the beginning of the 1980s, kennel Knegaren and Dewmist imported two famous stud dogs. These were Styal Samarkand, a brother of Ch. Styal Scott of Glengilde, and Ch. Sansue Golden Arrow, a brother of Ch. Sansue Golden Ruler. Both were sound producers with countless winners to their credit. Arrow, in particular, was campaigned and did a lot of winning, while Samarkand's strength was his many winning offspring.

Stanroph Sweet Sensation came to be an excellent brood bitch at Knegaren, and was the mother of Knegarens Tarantella, who has many awards to her credit. In the mid-90s Sherlock of Glen Shealag came from France to Knegaren, with all-English bloodlines.

DEWMIST
Kennel Dewmist also started off with two Swedish-bred Champion bitches, partly going back to a Camrose bitch imported by kennel Apport.

In 1975 Gyrima Moongleam, a son of Ch. Nortonwood Faunus, was imported and, through a famous daughter, Ch. Sagacious Maid, his lines can still be found. In 1980, Ch. Gyrima Zacharias arrived and produced many winners. When Zacharias mated Ch. Sagacious Maid, an outstanding brood bitch was born, Dewmist Shadow of Your Smile. When she was mated to Ch. Sansue Golden Arrow, she produced four title holders. A daughter, Ch. Dewmist Solitaire, proved herself a lovely brood bitch. Ch. Dewmist Swinging on a Star and Ch. Dewmist Sky is the Limit, plus Ch. Dewmist Sacramento by AI from Holland and Ch. Standfast Angus were a few of her offspring. Another Solitaire daughter is Ch. Shade of Pale, a top brood bitch at Dewmist.

Nor Ch. Styal Sheer Scandal (8 CCs, photgraphed at one year of age) by Ch. Remington Ramsey, ex Styal Sepia. Breeder: Mrs Hinks, GB. Owner: Henric Fryckstrand. Kennel: Dewmist.

Nor Ch. Jobeka Jaguar by Ch. Nortonwood Silvanus, ex Stirchley Sugar Bush of Jobeka. Breeder: Mrs Stokes, GB. Owner: Agneta Cardell. Kennel: Dasty.

Back in the late 1970s, a Christopher daughter was imported. This was Nortonwood Jasamanda, the proud mother of a multiple BIS winner, Ch. Dewmist Chrysander. One of Chrysander's top-winning daughters was Ch. Dewmist Corindabella, top Golden in Sweden in 1994. Ch. Styal Sheer Scandal, born in 1993, was made up easily and already has CC progeny in the ring. A total of 25 Champions, and 200 CC winners have been bred or owned at Dewmist.

OTHER KENNELS
DASTY
In the very south of Sweden, kennel Dasty started its winning line back in 1977 with Westley Prudence. She was out of the outstanding brood bitch, Ch. Westley Victoria. From Prudence, there has been an endless line of winners over the years. One lovely daughter was Dasty Memories of Yeo who, when mated to the aforementioned Ch. Dewmist Chrysander, produced one of the top dogs in Sweden, Int. Ch. Moviestar's Buster Keaton, who did a lot of winning right up to the veteran classes.

Many lovely stud dogs have been imported by kennel Dasty. Standfast Trinity, a son of Ch. Styal Scott of Glengilde, was one. Later came Ch. Jobeka Jaguar (by Ch. Nortonwood Silvanus) and Standfast Louisburg, all three having sired winners. A famous winner is the lovely Dasty Human Touch, a Louisburg daughter with three CCs.

COMBINE
Kennel Combine is yet another kennel which has been successful over the years. Many Champions have been made up. A famous brood bitch was Ch. Deerflite Salome and another was Ch. Sandemars Laughing Doll. In the 1990s, the brother and sister, Stanroph Sailor Man and Ch. Stanroph Sincerely Yours, were imported. Another bitch of interest at Combine has been the English Menna Maid of Gillbryan.

OXUNDA
Since the 1960s, kennel Oxunda has been a

kennel founded on the old Swedish lines. Generations of typy dogs have been bred here. Trebell Argus, an import from the UK, came in the 90s to continue the type, and further winners have been bred.

DREAM MAX
Kennel Dream Max, on the West coast, started in 1973 with a Swedish-bred Ch. dog. A famous son was Ch. Glader, and a few years later came Ch. Spervikbuktens Dream from Norway. These dogs did a lot of winning, and produced many winners for Dream Max. A total of 15 Champions have been bred or owned by this kennel.

The brood bitches were all related to their old stud dogs and to a Mjaerumhogda bitch from Norway. The kennel has long lines of winners, where Ch. Dream Max Have A Dream is behind many famous bitches, such as Ch. Dream Max Never Say Never Again and her daughter Dream Max Licensed To. In 1984, Nortonwood Secreto was imported from England and, with him, a new era began at Dream Max. His progeny have won some 200 CCs. Dream Max Romantic Touch is one of four CC winners in the same litter, and is the mother of the quickly-crowned Ch. Dream Max Christmas Adventure. In 1993 Ch. Blakesley Cromwell came to Dream Max. Here was another top-winning dog, who was made up easily and has won Groups and BIS awards already (top gundog with 10 Groups in 1996). Kennel Dream Max have competed successfully for many years for top Breeder of

the Year in Sweden, all Breeds, and in 1988 they won that highly prestigious award, a great achievement indeed.

GULDKLIMPEN
Another winning kennel is Guldklimpen, who started in the mid-1970s, later bringing in two bitches from Mjaerumhogda in Norway as brood bitches. Ch. Guldklimpens Tarzan was a great winner, and his cousin Ch. Guldklimpens Olga the Comtesse proved the brood bitch of all time with progeny who have won some 40 CCs. Kennel Guldklimpens have won many trophies for Breeder of the Year, and its dogs have won top awards both at shows and trials.

FESTIVAL
Ch. Guldklimpens Olga the Comtesse later came into the ownership of kennel Festival, and more successes followed, with over 20 BOB wins. Olga was mated to Ch. Gyrima Zacharias in 1989 and four daughters won CCs before the age of twelve months. The outstanding winning bitch, Ch. Festival's Prairie Primrose, has kept the flag flying ever since at Festivals, also producing more CC winners and Champions.

CHEERS
Kennel Cheers began in the mid-70s with Swedish bitches, but with an English background. Many lovely bitches have been bred here, and one of the latest stars is Ch. Cheers What's New. Her brother, Ch. Cheers Way of the World, was also made up quickly.

Breeders group from kennel Dream Max. Owners are: Ewa & Kjell Nielsen. Left to right: Nor Ch. Dream Max Christmas Adventure, Nor Ch. Dream Max Never Say Never Again, Dream Max License To, 3 CCs, Nor Ch. Dream Max Ready for You.

ABOVE: Int Nord Ch. Mjaerumhogdas Classic Sound by Ch. Noravon Cornelius, ex Ch. Gitles Natascha. Breeder: Grete Sofie Mjaerum. Owner: Anne Nerell. Kennel: Friendship & Stenbury.

TOP LEFT: Ch. Amirene Larus

LEFT: Nor Ch. Festival's Prairie Primrose by Ch. Gyrima Zacharias, ex Ch. Guldklimpens Olga the Comtesse. Breeder & Owner: Tina Lindeman. Kennel: Festival.

Ch. Shanlimore Baronet is one of the top dogs in Norway. Ch. Knegarens Stars 'n' Stripes, mentioned before, is owned by this kennel and is a lovely stud dog with many winning progeny.

INASSICA
Back in 1974, kennel Inassica was founded on Swedish lines. Ten years later, Ch. Darris Double Agent from England and Ch. Friendship Gaiety Girl of Inassica arrived, both having produced many winners. Two more stud dogs were bought in, Dewmist Secret Service and Sandusky Klammer. At the beginning of the 90s, Stenbury Water Jasmine and Stenbury Water Voyager came to Inassica and have won well.

SOLSTRIMMAN
In the very north of Sweden, an outstanding dual-purpose kennel has been active since 1980. Kennel Solstrimman began with a Swedish Champion bitch, and has had many winning generations from her. A famous imported stud dog was Ch. Cracksavon Crackerjack, and yet another stud was Ch. Amirene Larus – both of these dogs in partnership with kennel Crusade. Another winning dog at Solstrimman was Ch. Dewmist Santinella, who has many winning progeny. Ten Champions have been bred or owned here.

CRUSADE.
Kennel Crusade owned a multiple BIS winner in a son of Ch. Deremar Donald, Ch.

Kimbalee Colonel Peron. Ch. Arbutus Allegro was also owned by Crusade.

LUCRETIA
An outstanding bitch of the 80s was Noravon Lucretia, the dam of numerous winners who were either made up or are behind many winners today. This famous bitch was owned by kennel Lucretia.

FRIENDSHIP & STENBURY
Kennel Friendship owned two great dogs, Ch. Mjaerumhogdas Classic Sound and Ch. Mjaerumhogdas Golden Look. Both were imported from Norway. Classic Sound has been a most valuable stud dog here for a decade, producing countless winners, including Ch. Stenbury Sea Chiefain, the kennel's tenth Champion. Kennel Friendship has made up many Champions for twenty years. The same owner is now a co-owner of the illustrious prefix Stenbury, and a great number of outstanding dogs have arrived here. To mention a few: Ch. Stenbury Waterwingon; Ch. Stenbury Waterwizard; Ch. Stenbury Water Lilac; Ch. Perrimay Fadilla; and Perrimay Hector.

FLOPRYM
In the late 80s, kennel Floprym moved to Sweden from Norway, and has ever since produced top winners from the lovely Ch. Floprym Home Made Hot Do (herself a winner of 20 BOBs and countless BIS). Floprym Lasagne and Ch. Floprym Leonardo are two well-known winners, as is Floprym Ravioli.

GRACELINE
Kennel Graceline is another winning kennel founded in the 1970s on partly-English lines. Famous dogs like Ch. Graceline Enston, Strathern Benjamin and Okey's Explosive Symphony have produced winners.

GOLDSAND
Kennel Goldsand started in the 80s with two outstanding brood bitches from kennel Dainty. They were Dainty's Dream About Music and Dainty's Your Dream. A never-ending line of winners has been bred here ever since.

RESPONS
An outstanding dual-purpose kennel, Respons has won most top awards in the field and in the show ring. Kennel Respons was founded in 1970 with a Swedish bitch, and generations of dual Champions have been bred here. The achievement is great, and many trophies for various awards have been won by this remarkable kennel.

IN SUMMARY
There are so many respectable kennels in Sweden, as the breed has expanded enormously. To mention them all is just not possible, but I hope the above has given an idea of Sweden's enthusiasm for the Golden Retriever.

FINLAND
In the late 1950s the first Goldens appeared in Finland, but it was not until kennel Woodhill imported Ch. Apports Corinna from Sweden in the mid-60s that the breed really got started.

WOODHILL
Kennel Woodhill was one of the pioneer breeders and their successes were great for decades. Whitewater Patricia came from Ireland in 1975. A new line was started through her, and many well-known progeny were born. Ch. Rosemary of Woodhill was a great bitch of that time. Kennel Woodhill has made up numerous Champions over the years, both in the field and at shows. Imports from Sweden and England have combined the best of lines. Artificial insemination from England at the beginning of the 80s produced a litter by Camrose Fidelio of Davern.

REFLECT
One of the top dogs of the 80s was Ch. Noravon Cornelius, a son of Ch. Nortonwood Faunus, owned by kennel Reflect. This kennel enjoyed lots of successes and had several imports from the UK, such as Mytonvale Ceasar and Ch. Thenford Hamish.

ABOVE: Fin Ch. Adelina of Woodhill by Ch. Caliph of Yeo ex Whitewater Patricia. Breeder: Kirsti Wuorimaa. Owner: Eva Liisa Johansson. Kennel: Dinky.

BELOW: Fin Karvin Paloma O'Blanca (Top Golden in 1992 & 94) by Int Ch. Nortonwood Foregoer, ex Ch. Greenglen Golden Gown of Lislone. Owner & Breeder:

ABOVE: Fin Ch. Almeraks Pipers Dream by Ch. Bramhills Pied Piper of Almerak ex Almerak Kandee That is My Girl. Breeder: Mr & Mrs King, GB. Owner: Helena & Heidi Karves. Kennel: Karvin.

BELOW: Fin Ch. & Fin & Swed FT Ch. Fergus of Woodhill by Fin Ch. Chilipepper, ex Pandora of Woodhill. Breeder: Kirsti Wuorimaa. Owner: Anu Kampe.

MAJIK

Kennel Majik imported several bitches from England and, together with Ch. Mjaerumhogdas Your Choice, began a winning line. Many Champions were made up. Dabess Wilberforce was another stud dog here, as was Linchael Corniche. A famous dog is Ch. Majik Johnny B Goode who was Top Golden of the Year and had many successes. A top bitch was Ch. Majik Flower Power and Ch. Majik One Step Ahead was another.

HIEKKAKANKAAN

From Sweden came Ch. Gildas Midnight Sun and Ch. Gildas Touch of Gold. Kennel Hiekkakankaan owned Midnight Sun and

many other top dogs since the beginning of the 1980s, and is still a most prolific kennel. Imports from England and also from kennel Waterloo in Norway have contributed to more successes.

KARVIN

The most outstanding kennel is, however, kennel Karvin which, since the beginning of the 80s, has made up Champions in a never-ending chain – 22 to date. Top stud dogs have been imported from England. Ch. Linchael Ravel, a son of Ch. Camrose Fabius Tarquin, and Ch. Lovehayne Darter, by Sansue Castalian, have done a lot for the breed in Finland. An outstanding brood bitch was Ch.

Greenglen Golden Gown of Lislone, who is behind a long row of winners and eight Champions to date. Imports of great influence have been Gunhills Dalbury, Ch. Almerak Pipers Dream and Ch. Gunhills Summer Day.

One of the top bitches and top Goldens of recent years is Ch. Karvin Paloma Oblanca, who is a daughter of Ch. Nortonwood Foregoer and Ch. Greenglen Golden Gown of Lislone. A spectacular career awaits a young Ch. Lovehayne Darter son owned by kennel Karvin. Gill's Garfield has numerous BOBs and is still only two years of age.

NORWAY
The first Goldens were imported into Norway in the 1940s, but it was not until the 60s that these imports really made an impact on the breed. The first imports of importance came from Camrose, Sansue, Boltby and Cabus.

KARGUL
Camrose Evensky was the foundation of kennel Kargul and has many winning descendants. When mated to Ch. Sansue Sunlover she produced five Champions. Two other outstanding dogs were brother and sister Ch. Kargul Jolack and Ch. Kargul Juno.

ASTOWN & CHRIBAS
A Kargul bitch was the start of kennel Astown which continued to produce many winners over decades. A famous bitch was Ch. Astown Christy, who became the foundation bitch of another top winning kennel, CHRIBAS. Ch. Chribas Crackerjack won many top awards in the 1980s – he was one of Norway's top dogs for nearly a decade. This outstanding kennel has managed to crown numerous Champions over the years. Sansue Royal Seal and Ch. Sansue Viceroy have both proved influential at stud.

Kennel Astown also imported, in the 1970s, the famous Ch. Styal Scimiter, who was a Christopher son. Camrose Hosanna was a top brood bitch.

GITLE
Kennel Gitle had a fantastic start through Ch.

Camrose Tudina in 1966. The bitch was an excellent brood bitch and many Gitle Champions were made up. A particularly good mating was the combination of Ch. Boltby Brigand to Ch. Camrose Tudina. A daughter was mated to another import by Ch. Camrose Nicolas of Westley, Brambledown Harvester. From this famous combination many bitches were made up, and kennel Mjaerumhogda started its career through this line in the beginning of the 70s.

MJAERUMHOGDA
Ch. Camrose Voravey, a top producer of his time, came to Mjaerumhogda at the beginning of the 70s. Few dogs have done so much for the breed as he did. He is behind most of kennel Mjaerumhogda's winning dogs of today. This outstanding kennel has produced well over 50 Champions, which is a fabulous record! Many outstanding dogs were bred here – Ch. Mjaerumhogdas Limelight, Top Golden in Norway for years, Ch. Mjaerumhogdas Crusader, Ch. Mjaerumhogdas Classic Sound and Ch. Mjaerumhogdas Golden Look, to mention just a few.

Ch. Mjaerumhogdas Crusader is especially well renowned as a super stud dog, having sired CC winners and Champions in England during several years living there. One of the top stud dogs and show dogs in Europe is Multi Ch. Standfast Angus. Ch. Ankera Aramis was an imported Crusader son from England who was quickly made up.

Top stud dogs at Mjaerumhogda have been Ch. Likely Lad of Yeo, Ch. Noravon Lucius, Ch. Mjaerumhogdas Magic Man, Janward Dollar and also Ch. Mjaerumhogdas Top Hit. The latter was born as a result of AI from Christopher, some 15 years after the sire's death. The mother of the AI pups was Ch. Linchael Silver Spirit, who has proved to be a good brood bitch. Ch. Nunsbrook Carbon Copy and Gloi Laughter in the Rain are younger stud dogs at Mjaerumhogda.

SPERVIKBUKTEN
Another top winning kennel that no longer is active is kennel Spervikbukten. This kennel

Nor Ch. & Nordic Obed. Ch. Chribas Crackerjack (Top Golden in 1987-88-89) by Ch. Noravon Lucius ex Ch. Astown Christy. Breeder & Owner: Berit & Tore Bondal. Kennel: Chribas.

Nor Ch. Waterloo's Another Yatzy (Top Golden in 1993-94-95) by Ch. Twinkle Ideal at Waterloo ex Waterloo's Ravishing Ricky. Breeder: Torill & Sverre Sand. Owner: Tom & Margareta Berntzen.

was founded in the late 1960s and owned well-known stud dogs like Ch. Cabus Clarion and Anbria Jaslynd Baronet. The first successful AI from Christopher was achieved in 1974. Two attractive and most outstanding dogs were campaigned. These were Ch. Spervikbuktens Philip and Ch. Spervikbuktens Pernille. Another sister was Ch. Spervikbuktens Pebbles, the foundation for kennel ASEBYGARDEN who had many successes in the late 70s and also owned Ch. Camrose Ptarmigan, a famous stud dog. From an AI mating at Asebygarden in the 80s came another famous dog, Ch. Asebygarden Dream Come True.

WATERLOO
Kennel Waterloo has owned or bred 26 Champions, including the great Ch. Mjaerumhogdas Limelight (winner of 44 BOBs), who was the top Golden for many years in the 80s. This highly successful kennel has continued to produce many Champions. Imports like Ch. Trademan of Garbank and Ch. Twinkle Ideal at Waterloo are behind many winners. A remarkable brood bitch was Garbank Giselle, who is the mother of Ch. Waterloos Rock Around the Clock, top dog for many years, who has also been shown on the Continent with great success. Ch. Waterloos Another Yatzi is yet another famous dog, and top dog in Norway in 1993, 94, and 95.

JAKO
On the west coast of Norway, kennel Jako was founded around 1980. Ch. Nortonwood Clarissa has been a fantastic brood bitch and is the dam of many winners. She was by Ch. Nortonwood Checkmate. This kennel also owned Ch. Jamescroft Ryktbarhet and, in later years, the fantastic show dog Ch. Shanlimore Baronet, who has won Groups and BIS awards. This kennel has produced winners right from its start.

A few famous dogs of the 1970s were Ch. Davern Lion Lotcheck, who was a son of Ch. Davern Figaro; Ch. Gyrima Damocles, a Christopher son; and the previously mentioned Ch. Sansue Sunlover, a son of Ch. Camrose Nicolas of Westley.

DENMARK

The first Goldens to appear in Denmark were imported in the late 1950s. The first litter was born in 1958 and became the foundation of a well-known Danish kennel called TAIS. A famous dog of his time was Ch. Philips Tais Flapore.

WESSEX
At the beginning of the 60s, kennel Wessex was founded on Anbria and Camrose dogs. Ch. Camrose Quixote was a renowned stud dog, who did a lot for the breed. Kennel Wessex imported Ch. Anbria Tarlatan, another stud dog of the time, who, together with the

kennel mates Ch. Anbria Joriemour Lisbeth and Anbria Laurel, began a long chain of winners throughout the decade.

During this perod, many sound imports from Camrose, Anbria, Westley and later Sansue, Crouchers and Lacons provided a solid foundation. Later in the decade, two illustrious dogs came to Denmark, Ch. Honeyat the Viking, a son of Ch. Sharland The Scot, and Ch. Byxfield Cedar, a son of Daniel of Westley. Both these stud dogs did a lot for the breed's development in the 1960s. In the 70s came Ch. Lacons Honey Lover and Ch. Crouchers Xavier, two more outstanding stud dogs, and Ch. Gyrima Honest Percy.

TALLYGOLD
Kennel Tallygold, one of the most famous kennels in Denmark, was founded in the 60s. Many outstanding dogs have been produced here, while imports such as Ch. Crouchers Xavier, Ch. Camillo and, in recent years, the

KBHV Mathew by Int. Dk Ch. Crouchers Xavier, ex Tallygold Gentle Gina. Breeder: Ruth Larsen. Owner: Marianne Holm-Hansen. Kennel: Tallygold.

winning brothers Stenbury Waterwizardry and Stenbury Waterwingshot have done a lot for the breed. This kennel also owned the well-known Xavier son, Ch. Mathew, who continued in his winning father's footsteps and also produced winning progeny.

When the outstanding brood bitch Westley Dellajoy was mated to Mathew, she produced yet another lovely bitch, Golden Joy's Polly Peachum, who has kept the line going and is the proud mother of more Tallygold winners, such as Ch. Tallygold Waiting in the Wings, a top dog in the 90s, with numerous awards so far. A famous son was Tallygold Toby Dog. Friendship Classic Tattoo, a Swedish import with mostly English background, was imported in the 90s and is not only winning well, but also producing winners.

RIIS & WOODSTAR
Kennel Riis and kennel Woodstar began in the early 1970s and are still active, producing top dogs. Many imports, both from England and Norway, have contributed to their successes.

Kennel Riis have owned a couple of dogs from the famous Norwegian kennel Waterloo, and in the 90s Ch. Waterloo's Phantom of the Opera came as an adult.

Kennel Woodstar imported, in 1983, the brother and sister Garbank Fieldfare and Fullmarx, sired by Ch. Bethrob Bracken, and both having produced winners. At the end of the 80s Ch. Waterloo's Yankee SOS came to kennel Woodstar, and became another well-known stud dog.

RECO
Nortonwood Telstar, a son of Ch. Nortonwood Checkmate, was imported in 1983 by kennel Reco. This famous stud dog was later joined by Ch. Linchael Star of Africa, who did a lot of winning. Another very well-known stud dog was Lawnwoods Nimrod, by Ch. Westley Munro of Nortonwood.

SHANTEY
Kennel Shantey started with partly Tallygold and Swedish dogs in the 80s. Two famous brood bitches were Zabina and Tallygold

Dk Ch. Shadowfax Amazing Grace by Int Ch. Riis Diago ex Teacher's Passion Echo. Breeder & Owner: Kaj Falk Andreasen. Kennel: Shadowfax.

Hallo Sunshine. This kennel also owned the winning Ch. Wessex Shamrock Shantey.

AMBER BAY

The Swedish import Ch. Goldsand's Dream Conqueror, by Ch. Mjaerumhogdas Classic Sound, and the English import, Ch. Shanlimore Evening Star, are two well-known stud dogs owned by this kennel.

FYLLA

Kennel Fylla seems to be doing very well at both shows and at trials, and is a true dual-purpose kennel. The bitch Fylla's Adele is made up, and more winners are being produced here.

ARTIFICIAL INSEMINATION

AI has been successfully used, from both the UK and Sweden. Since the middle of the 1990s, when the borders were opened to Sweden, further mutual breeding has been in force. For obvious reasons, it is easy for Danish breeders to travel south to the centre of Europe, and a few breeders with ambitions to broaden their horizons have used stud dogs from the Continent.

SOUTH AFRICA
HISTORY

In 1947, the Golden Retriever as a breed was still relatively rare in South Africa. A 'Scottish Retriever' No.5656 belonging to a Jock McPhail was registered in February 1904, but whether this was a Golden Retriever or not is unknown. The first known Golden Retriever to be registered with the Kennel Union of Southern Africa was a dog called Golden Lad, whelped on February 24th 1929, sired by Peter of Quest out of Wendy of Quest (both parents were registered as 'retrievers'). Golden Lad was registered on October 3rd 1929 (KUSA No.34094). The owner is given as A. Treadea of 93 Du Toitís Pan Road, Kimberley.

The 'Quest' line came from M'kuzi, Zululand, and the sires of Wendy and Peter, as well as the one dam, have the 'Dewstraw' affix/prefix. According to the records, 'Dewstraw' appears to be the affix of a Mr Cufton-Blake of Bloemfontein. However, whether or not these Dewstraw dogs were registered is not known. The first Golden to be made up as a breed Champion was Edmund's Pride No. 85083, on November 21st 1949.

THE GOLDEN RETRIEVER CLUB OF THE TRANSVAAL

It was decided to form the Golden Retriever Club of the Transvaal in 1971. The inaugural meeting was held at the Wanderers Club on February 28th 1972, with a nationwide membership of 40. With the late Mike O'Leary as chairman and his wife Carole as secretary, it was all systems go. The first open show was held in 1973, and the first Championship show in 1983. The GRC is still the only Golden Retriever specialist club in South Africa, and it continues to go from strength to strength with a membership of close on 300. The present chairlady is Di Phillipson (Kilifi), and the secretary is Margaret McAra (Macanne).

INFLUENTIAL BREEDERS OF THE 1970s
In the early 1960s Carole O'Leary went into partnership with John MacKay (Summerfold kennels) and they imported Ch. Stubblesdown Jingle of Summerfold FQ. In 1975 he attained Field qualifying status – the first to do so in South Africa. Robert Bischoff moved to Johannesburg from the USA with his 'Lorelei' Goldens. Alex Williamson's (Alexander kennels) imported Ch. Northumbrian Crusader, who made an impact on the breed in South Africa. His other import was Ch. Northumbrian Honey of Alexander. Also a legend in their time in the Transvaal were Maud Sumner's Ollerset Goldens, and, in particular, Bertie and Victoria.

The main breeder in the Cape during this period was Rita Buchanan (Vergezicht kennels), who imported stock from the Janville kennels in the UK. Christine Bowker's Alamount Kenobi also had a part to play in the Cape lines.

The cream of the Goldens were in Natal, where Ruby Newmarch (Buyisa kennels) imported Ch. Stolford Gay Voyager of Buyisa FQ HD00 (Fagin) from Peggy Robertson (Stolford) in the UK. Fagin was the dog that, to this day, must surely stand out as having the most impact on the Golden Retriever breed in South Africa. Fagin was sired by UK Ch. Stolford Happy Lad out of Sh. Ch. Stolford Jasmine, and he was awarded Best in Show at All Breed and Group Championship shows three times. He also held his own at Field Trials. He attained Field Qualifying (FQ) status and won one Retriever Novice Field Trial, and two Certificates of Merit at Open Retriever stakes.

Fagin sired 22 Show Champions, with four Champions coming from one litter. This was Carol O'Leary's Summerfold 'Race Track' litter out of Ch. Summerfold Seringa. The Champion offspring were: the McCormicks' Ft. Ch. & Ch. Summerfold Silverstone (Tamarind), Ch. Summerfold Le Mans (Cleave), the Krugers' Ch. Summerfold Monaco (Byron), and Ch. Summerfold Kyalami (Kenya export). Cleave also went Best in Show at the GRC show.

Other Champions sired by Fagin during this period were: Richard Pienaar's (Cananne) Ch. Kilifi Hi-Lite of Cananne (Gambit) out of Cream Sherry of Kilifi. (Gambit was an All Breeds Best in Show and Group Winner); the late Derek Higgs (Dargledale) Ch. Dargledale Moondust (Moonie), Ch. Dargledale Maestro, Di Phillipson's Ch. Kilifi Gay Lord Taber, out of Cream Sherry. (Taber placed in Field Trials including winning an Open stake); and Ch. Kilifi Alpha FQ (Haig). Haig won a first place in a Novice retriever stake and third place in an Open stake.

Di Phillipson (Kilifi) purchased her first Golden in 1970 – a bitch called Cream Sherry of Kilifi (Tasha), sired by a Zululand dog called Chaka, out of Stolford Polka (a UK import). Di imported Ch. Stolford Moonlight of Kilifi HD00 (Shara) from Peggy Robertson in 1974. Shara was mated to Fagin and produced among others, Haig and litter sister, Ronee Duff's (Lymond) Ch. & Ft. Ch. Kilifi Amber of Lymond. Amber became a Dual Champion at 2 1/2 years old when within a space of eight days she won her last breed ticket and came first in an Open Retriever stake and first in a Retriever Championship stake.

Haig proved his worth in the breed ring and the field and was top GRC stud dog for five years from 1984 to 1988. Haig was mated to the McCormicks' (Sokatumi) Ch. & Ft. Ch. Summerfold Silverstone (Tamarind). This Sokatumi litter of six all went to dual purpose homes: five became Show Champions and two also became Field Trial Champions (Ft. Ch. & Ch. Sokatumi Xugano and Ft. Ch. & Ch. Sokatumi Xaxaba), while litter brother, Ch. Sokatumi Etosha of Kilifi FQ (Tosh) placed in Field Trials and was awarded Best In Show at a GRC Championship show.

When discussing the Natal Goldens, the late Derek Higgs and his Dargledale line come to mind – Ch. Dargledale Moondust; Maestro, Hodette and Melody. Derek used his Goldens as hunting dogs and also showed and field trialled them.

Ch. Kilfi Pasha FQ Hdoo: Top Golden Retriever 1995 (breed shows), Group winner and Reserve Best in Show at Sasolburg Ch. show 1996. Owned by Mrs D.M. Phillipson and Mr. D. Grimbly.

THE MODERN ERA

Peter and Christine Sandford (Redsteps) moved to South Africa in 1980, with their Flatcoated Retrievers. Ch. Redsteps Faustina FQ HD00 (Cider) was the first homebred Golden Retriever bitch they campaigned in their new home. Cider won eight Puppy Groups and two Best Puppy in Show at All breeds shows, and her first Gundog group at the age of ten months.

In 1982 they imported Ch. Shargleam Special Edition of Redsteps HD00 (Rory) from Pat Chapman (Shargleam) in the UK. When bred to Cider, they produced among others Ch. Redsteps Sunblaize HD00 (Blaize), who later went Best in Show at the Golden Retriever Championship (GRC) show. Their second import was Shargleam Wave the Flag of Redsteps (McGreggor), also from Camrose /Nortonwood lines.

Peter and Christine are now among the top Golden Retriever breeders in South Africa, and their vast knowledge and dedication to breeding top-quality dogs has contributed towards the high standard of Goldens we see in the breed ring in South Africa today. Top winning dogs include Ch. Dunmarique Sebastian of Redsteps HD00 (Cameron), multiple Group winner and Best in show at

GRC. Cameron finished his show career with over 50 Best of Breeds to his credit. Ch. Vom Immengrund Asco of Redsteps HD00 (Asco) and his sister Aike have both won Best in Show at the GRC show, plus numerous Groups. All were sired by Special Edition.

Then came Ch. Redsteps Wishfulthinking HD00 (Campbell) who, at the time of writing, has won two Best in Shows at All Breeds Championship shows, plus numerous Groups. Campbell is the son of Asco and both have progeny currently working and winning in the various Field Trial stakes. Asco has also been awarded the trophy for the top stud dog for the last two years (awarded to the male whose progeny wins the most points in the breed ring and the field during the year).

Peter and Christine also won the GRC top show dog trophy with their various dogs from 1988 to 1994. Ch. Redsteps Travelling Man of Charduan was exported to Namibia to Charlene Du Toi, and in 1994 he won Namibian top dog, all breeds.

Di Phillipson's Kilifi line continues to make its mark in the breed ring as well as the field. Her homebred Ch. Kilifi Pasha FQ HD00 (Pasha), sired by Ch. Redsteps Wishfulthinking HD00 out of Ch. Kilifi Magic FQ HD00, and jointly owned by Dave

Grimbly from Zimbabwe, qualified for Junior Dog of the Year in 1994, and in 1995 was the National Golden Retriever at the KUSA National Breed show, went Best in Show at the GRC Championship show and was also the top show Golden for the year.

Margaret and Mike McAra's (Macanne) Ch. Kilifi Pride and Joy of Macanne NHR FQ HD00 (Tess), litter sister to Pasha, was the top show bitch for 1995. Tess has been awarded her first SAHR points in Retriever Field Trials, and has NHR attached to her pedigree name (Novice Hunting Retriever). Ch. Macanne Barry (Dusty), bred by Mike and Margaret, was the GRC top stud dog for three years. Dusty sired, among others, Di Phillipson's Ch. Kilifi Magic FQ HD00, (Millie) and Dave Owen's Kilifi Mystique WHR HD00 (Misty), Helene Kessler's Ch. Sokatumi Ulundi of Gavalat WHR FQ (Crystal), and Ch. Macanne Daydream (Toffee).

Two other dogs making their contribution in the Cape are Thea De Vink's Ch. Buyisa Ivan (Frampton), bred by Ruby Newmarch in Natal, who has been awarded Best in Show at the Cape Gundog Club show, and Helene Kessler's Ch. Klynroc Cobber of Galavat WHR, bred by Gill Ainslie (Klynroc) in Natal, out of Amblaire Commander of Medges (Ben), imported to Natal from the UK by Margaret and Hamish Paterson (Medges).

Other breeders who are making their mark in the breed ring and the field in the Transvaal include: 'Macanne' Mike and Margaret McAra, in Natal, 'Medges' Hamish and Margaret Paterson, and 'Tyweire' Joe and Tessa Kruger, and in the Cape, 'Gavalat' Helene Kessler.

GUIDE DOGS

Christine and Peter Sandford's Rory was used as a sire by the Guide Dog Association on many occasions. They also donated seven puppies from a litter sired by Ch. Vom Immengrund Asco of Redsteps (Asco), out of Ch. Croftamie Queensview of Redsteps (Honey) to the Guide Dog Association of South Africa. This was the first litter where all

Ch. Kifli Magic FQ Hdoo.

members of a litter qualified in over 25 years. Carol O'Leary's UK import Ch. Harsett Minstrel (Mizzy) has also sired guide dog puppies.

FIELD TRIALS

As you can see from this article, a number of breeders in South Africa have been, over the years, very conscious of the division between the show dog and the working dog and have been extremely careful in maintaining the balance when breeding in order to maintain the 'dual purpose' golden retriever (in one animal) whenever possible.

Summerfold Jing-Pip-Jones (owned by Alex Williamson) became the first Golden Retriever to become a Field Trial Champion in South Africa. The second Golden to become a Field Trial Champion was John McCormick's Ft. Ch. & Ch. Summerfold Teak (Jethro), in April 1980. The first Golden Retriever bitch to become a Field Trial Champion was Ronee Duff's Ft. Ch. & Ch. Kilifi Amber of Lymond. Ronee Duff was the first woman to make up a Field Trial Champion in Retriever Trials when she won an Open and a Championship Retriever Stake with Amber.

Ft. Ch. & Ch. Sokatumi Xaxaba holds the record for winning the most Open Retriever Field Trials (14) in South Africa. Second in line with 11 wins is a yellow Labrador Retriever called Sally, owned by Tony Schuil.

The more prominent kennels behind field working golden retrievers in South Africa are still Summerfold, Sokatumi and Kilifi.

In 1994, the Field Trial Liaison Council of the Kennel Union of Southern Africa introduced a new concept into field trialling for Hunting Retrievers known as SAHR (South African Hunting Retriever). This is similar to the NAHRA system in the USA. Retrievers entering Retriever Field Trials in South Africa today are now able to win points towards becoming a Novice Hunter Retriever (NHR), a Working Hunter Retriever (WHR), a Master Hunter Retriever (MHR) and a Grand Master Hunting Retriever (GMHR), as long as they earn over 70 per cent at a particular Field Trial.

A Golden Retriever, Ft. Ch. Pareora Goldilocks GMHR (Georgie Girl), belonging to Jenny Smith, is the first retriever in South Africa since the inception of SAHR to be awarded the highest SAHR title of Grand Master Hunter Retriever. She is also a Field Trial Champion.

CARTING
Ch. & Carting Ch. Kincora Flinders, owned by Judith Buchanan (Kincora), was the first and only Golden to date, in South Africa, to be made up as a Carting Champion.

OBEDIENCE
Casey Jones FQ, owned by Wendy Sanzin (Laird) was the first Golden to win a Qualifying Certificate in Obedience in South Africa. In 1996 the first Obedience Champion to be made up in South Africa was Judith Buchanan's Golden Lucy of Kincora NHR FQ.

16 *HEALTH CARE*

This chapter is intended to give information on the need to maintain your dog in good health. The veterinary surgeon will want to co-operate with you, as the owner of a Golden Retriever, in keeping the animal well for as long a natural life as possible.

Improved diet and preventive vaccinations are contributing to a much longer life for all domestic animals nowadays. Co-operate with your veterinary surgeon by attending for annual booster vaccines, and remember that it is beneficial to allow the dog to be inspected for early signs of disease.

Between visits, you should inspect your dog for any changes in coat condition, breath odour or for any unusual lumps or swellings. The dog's weight should be observed, and it will be helpful to weigh the animal at three-monthly intervals if suitable scales can be found. A grooming routine, followed on a daily basis, will allow the dog to get used to close handling and will also provide the opportunity for the owner to make the sort of regular inspection the veterinary surgeon would like to be made, to spot the earliest signs of illness.

SELECTING VETERINARY CARE
The choice of a veterinarian may be based on accessibility, but some people like to make enquiries among other Golden Retriever owners they meet, before deciding which veterinary practice will have the greatest sympathy to their dog and their needs. Treatment prices will vary, and it is fairly easy to phone around to enquire about the cost of a booster vaccine or the fee for neutering. Facilities in practices are not all the same, and one with 24-hour nursing staff residing on the premises and equipment for emergency surgery will have to charge more than another surgery, which adequately provides for vaccination and other injections, but requires you to go elsewhere for more complicated procedures.

Pet insurance has proved a great incentive for veterinarians to provide additional equipment and persons with specialist knowledge, because the veterinary surgeon is confident that payment will be made for all treatments given to the insured dog. Just as the vet should be chosen to provide the type of health attention needed, the insurance companies' provisions should be compared to find the one with an annual premium that will deliver the most help in times of difficulty. Remember that, in the UK, booster vaccines, routine neutering and some chronic or inherited disorders are not covered by insurance. Many companies do not pay willingly for visits to a dog in your home, nor pay in full for prescription diets that could be part of your dog's treatment.

GENERAL GROOMING AND HYGIENE
Golden Retrievers have relatively easy coats to maintain, but they do require daily grooming, especially when they are moulting. Grooming your dog is an ideal time to inspect the body closely, to look for any unexpected abnormalities and at the general condition.

The sooner a health problem is noticed, the quicker the veterinary adviser can be asked for an opinion, and the better the chance of a full recovery in the case of a progressive disease or a tumour.

Your Golden should be groomed from the earliest age, as the puppy will associate such handling with a pleasurable experience. Procedures will be easier to carry out if this is started early in life. If a dog is used to being handled in this way, it will be far easier for a veterinary surgeon to make an examination, and a visit to the surgery becomes less stressful for the owner as well as the dog. Before you start to groom your Golden Retriever, carry out a thorough physical examination to check for any abnormalities. Always start at the head, as your hands will be cleaner when touching the orifices on the head than after handling the dog's feet and anal region.

EYES: Inspect the eyes first for matter or discharges in the corner. There should be no excessive watering, and the white of the eye should be briefly checked to see that it is not red or discoloured. The surface of the eye should be clear and bright, and the expression one of alertness. There are specific diseases that affect the eyes, so any abnormal signs should be noted and reported to the veterinary surgeon.

EARS: A painful ear can be a very irritating complaint for your dog, so preventing ear problems is important. If there is a noticeable build-up of wax in the ear canal, this can be easily removed by first softening the wax with an ear-cleaning fluid and then wiping gently with cotton wool. The use of cotton wool buds in the ear is discouraged, and all cleaning should be the most gentle possible. There is a range of ear-cleaners suitable for the Golden Retriever, and your veterinary surgeon will advise on the one most appropriate for routine use.

If there is an excessive amount of wax in the ear canal, or if the ear is hot, reddened or swollen, this is an indication of infection or inflammation, and veterinary attention should be sought quickly. Should an infection be left untreated, the dog will scratch the affected ear repeatedly, and often introduce other infections carried on soiled hind toenails. Oozing of fluids and bacteria multiplying in the moist discharges will make the ear much worse, and treatment becomes more difficult.

MOUTH: Check your dog's gums each day for redness or inflammation. This can develop as tartar builds up on the teeth, and food particles get caught at the gum margin. The decaying food will produce breath odour if not removed, and mouth bacteria can result in even worse halitosis. The teeth and gum margins have pain receptors, so any tartar build-up can lead to a disease which puts the dog off food and even causes bad temper.

Canine toothpastes are now available, which can be used to help prevent a build-up of tartar. If the dog's teeth are cleaned regularly, you will avoid a state of dental neglect so advanced that your Golden needs a general anaesthetic for a scale and polish at the veterinarian. Start brushing your dog's teeth at about four months of age, but avoid areas where permanent teeth are about to erupt. At first the puppy will want to play, but, little by little, will become used to having all the teeth cleaned. There may be some resistance at first, but it is far easier to get a puppy used to having teeth cleaned while young and small, rather than waiting until you have a fully-grown dog who objects to the procedure.

Puppies lose their milk teeth between four and six months, and sore gums should be noted at that age. Massaging the skin just below the eye will help when molar teeth are about to erupt. While grooming the older dog, look for signs of abnormality such as mouth warts, excess saliva or white froth at the back of the mouth.

NOSE: Again, remove any discharges, and look for cracking or fissuring. There is little point in worrying about the traditional 'cold wet nose' as a health indicator.

SKIN AND COAT: Examine the whole of your dog's body when grooming. Tell-tale black dirt or white scurf may indicate a parasite infection. Patches of hair loss, redness of skin and abnormal lumps may first be found during grooming. Your Golden Retriever's coat will normally have a slight shine, and oil from the sebaceous glands will provide a waterproofing grease that gives a smooth feel as you run your hand over the hair.

NAILS AND FEET: Nails should be kept short, as over-long nails may splinter painfully, especially in cold weather when the nail is brittle. If the dog is regularly walked on hard surfaces such as concrete, paving stones or rocks, the nails will wear down naturally. Tarmac and grass do little to wear nails down at exercise times. Also, once nails grow too long, they become difficult for the dog to wear down, whatever the surface. As a result, the heel takes more of the weight of the leg and the nails may split, with painful consequences.

Clipping nails is a delicate task. If you cut too short, into the quick, blood will flow and the dog will find it painful. Filing may be safer for the beginner than cutting across the nail with new sharp clippers.

Make a habit of feeling the area between the toes, where tufts of hair attract sticky substances, clay soils may form hard little balls between the toes, and tar or chewing gum can be picked up on a walk. You will notice any cuts or pad injuries while handling your Golden's feet for grooming.

PERINEUM AND GENITAL AREA: Check for swollen anal sacs or unexpected discharges. Segments of tapeworms might be seen near the rectum. A bitch's vulva should not discharge, except when signs of heat are present. The prepuce of a male dog should have no discharge, and the penis should not protrude except if the dog is inadvertently excited during grooming or handling.

GROOMING: Once the first physical examination has been carried out, a grooming routine for your Golden Retriever should be followed. Here is one I recommend:

1. Using your fingertips, massage the coat against the normal backward lay of the hairs. This will loosen dead hairs and encourage the skin to secrete the sebum oil that gives the healthy shine.
2. Use a bristle brush to pick up the hair you have loosened, again working against the lay of the coat.
3. Using a metal-toothed comb, you can now gently remove any knots, combing with the lay of the coat and paying particular attention to the feathering down the hind legs, the tail, and around the neck and ears.
4. Finally, to finish and to bring up the coat, use a bristle brush down the back and limbs. Brush the neck and head, praising the dog or offering a small food reward.

PREVENTIVE CARE – VACCINATION

The use of vaccines to prevent disease is well-established for human as well as animal health. The longer life of the animal, and the comparative rarity of puppy disease and early death, is something that has become taken for granted in the last 40 years. Yet many older people remember ill puppies dying of distemper fits, or left twitching with chorea for the rest of their lives. The appearance of Parvovirus in 1979 was an unpleasant shock to those who thought that veterinary treatment could deal with all puppy diarrhoeas. There were many deaths in puppies under twelve months old until the use of vaccines gave them protection, either through their mother's milk or after the puppy's own body defences became mature enough to respond to a vaccine injected.

Your veterinarian is the best person to advise on the type of vaccines to use and at what ages to give them, since they have a unique knowledge of the type of infection prevalent in a locality and when infection is likely to strike.

An example of this is in the Guide Dogs for the Blind Association's breeding programme where, for many years, early vaccination was given to the six-week-old puppy. No isolation after this early vaccination was needed. This was contrary to general advice given in the 60s and 70s when figures for puppy disease were acceptably low. Later, when Parvovirus infection was widespread in the early 80s, the mortality rate of GDBA puppies was much lower than among breeders who retained puppies in kennels until 12 weeks or older. The temperament of some breeds was suspect due to a longer enforced isolation after vaccination, and proper socialisation did not take place as the new owners of puppies were advised not to take them out until four months of age, after a final Parvovirus booster had been given. This meant that there were no opportunities to mix with people and other dogs until an age when the older puppy had already developed a fear of being handled by strangers, or was suspicious of other dogs met outside the home.

DISTEMPER: This is the classic virus disease which has become very rare where vaccine is used on a regular basis. From time to time, it is seen in larger UK cities where there is a stray or roaming dog population. This may subsequently lead to infection of show or other kennel dogs who do not have a high level of immunity.

The virus has an incubation period of seven to 21 days, and is followed by a rise in temperature, loss of appetite, a cough and, often, diarrhoea. Discharges from the eyes and nose may be watery at first, but often turn into thick mucoid with a green or creamy colour, due to secondary infections. The teeth are affected when a puppy under six months of age is infected by the virus, and enamel defects show as brown marks – they last for life and are known as 'distemper teeth'.

The 'hard pad' strain seen in the 60s is now considered to be nothing more than hyperkeratosis of the nose and footpads that occurs after all distemper infections, although the name is still in use when dog illness is written or talked about. In over half of all dogs affected with Distemper, damage to the

nervous system will manifest itself as fits, chorea (twitching of muscles) or posterior paralysis. Old dogs may develop Encephalitis (ODE), due to latent Distemper virus in the nervous tissue.

The vaccines in use today are generally modified live vaccines, and highly effective in preventing disease. The age for a first injection will partly depend on the maker's instruction sheet, and partly on a knowledge of the amount of protection passed from the mother to the young puppies. Maternally derived immunity (MDI) might block the vaccine in a young puppy, but blood sampling of bitches during their pregnancy is now used as a method of estimating how soon the puppy will respond to vaccine. The use of a first vaccine at six weeks is becoming more widespread, and this allows for the all-important early socialisation period in the puppy's development.

PARVOVIRUS: This is probably the second most important canine virus disease in Europe and, like Distemper, is largely preventable by the correct use of vaccination. The speed with which an infection could spread from kennel to kennel surprised many, but the disease is caused by a very tough virus that can be carried on footwear which has walked though virus-infected faeces. It may then persist for up to a year, untouched by many commonly used kennel disinfectants. The sudden death of puppies, caused by damage to the heart muscle, often just after purchase, is no longer seen, but the gastro-enteritis form of Parvovirus still occurs.

This illness takes the form of repeated vomiting in the first 24 hours, followed by profuse watery diarrhoea, often with a characteristic sour smell and a red-brown colour. The cause of death was often from severe dehydration that accompanied this loss of fluid and, once it was understood that puppies could be treated with intravenous fluids similar to those used in the treatment of human cholera victims, the death rate fell. Fluids by mouth are sufficient in less severe cases, provided they contain the electrolytes that need to be replaced. The traditional mixture of a level teaspoonful of salt and a dessertspoonful of glucose in two pints of water has saved many dogs' lives.

Vaccination of the young puppy is recommended, though the MDI may partially block the effectiveness of the vaccine, as seen with Distemper. A live vaccine at six weeks, followed by a further dose at 12 weeks will protect most puppies. The four-month booster is no longer in common use, but it is now more usual to see Parvovirus in the recently-weaned puppy or the five-month-old puppy, where immunity no longer protects that individual against infection.

HEPATITIS: This disease, produced by an *adenovirus,* is now quite rare, but one form (CAV-2) is often associated with Kennel Cough infection in dogs. After infection, the virus multiplies in the lymphatic system and then sets out to damage the lining of the blood vessels. It was for this reason that the cause of death was liver failure. The name Hepatitis was given because, on post mortem, the dog's liver was seen to be very swollen and engorged with blood. Other organs are also damaged, and about 70 per cent of recovered dogs are found to have kidney damage. The eye damage known as 'blue eye' seen on recovery is not recognised in the Golden Retriever, but was quite common in certain other breeds. Vaccination at six and 12 weeks, using a reliable vaccine that contains the CAV-2 virus, is very effective as a preventive measure against Hepatitis.

LEPTOSPIROSIS: This disease is caused by bacteria, unlike the previous group of viral infections. Protection has to be provided by at least two doses of a killed vaccine, and a 12-monthly repeat dose of this vaccine is essential if the protection is to be maintained. The type of Leptospirosis spread by rats is the most devastating to the dog and frequently results in jaundice then death from kidney and liver failure unless early treatment with antibiotics is available.

The other serotype of leptospira that damages the dog's kidney is seen less often since vaccination and annual boosters have been regularly used. Gundogs and pet Goldens who walk in the country where rats may have contaminated water courses, are especially at risk. Sometimes dogs kept entirely in kennels may be affected if rats cross the exercise yards and leave infected urine for the dog to sniff at or lick up.

KENNEL COUGH: As a troublesome infection that causes a harsh cough originating from the trachea and bronchial tubes, Kennel Cough is now one of the best known canine diseases. Golden Retrievers may become infected in boarding kennels, or perhaps after coming within droplet infection distance of dogs coughing at shows, or in public exercise areas. There are five known viral and bacterial agents that may all, or perhaps two of them at a time, cause Kennel Cough. Vaccination by nose drops of a *Bordetella* vaccine can be offered to provide protection, and is often given just a week before a dog goes into kennels. The normal booster vaccine for dogs contains protection against three of the other known causes.

The disease develops within four to seven days of infection, so it may not be evident until after a dog has left the kennels. The deep harsh cough is often described "as if a bone or something was stuck in the throat." The dog coughs repeatedly. Even with treatment, coughs last for 14 days, but in some dogs the cough carries on as long as six weeks. Infection may then persist in the trachea, and the dog, if a 'carrier', may get subsequent attacks when stressed. This explains why some non-coughing dogs put into board may cause an outbreak of kennel cough. Once a summertime disease, Kennel Cough outbreaks now occur at any time of the year, often after a holiday period when more dogs than usual are boarded.

RABIES: This virus disease is almost unknown to most UK veterinarians, due to a successful quarantine policy that has kept the island free of rabies in dogs and in wildlife such as foxes. The full quarantine period of six months will no longer be considered necessary, and a switch to compulsory vaccination, blood tests and identification for imported animals, is expected in the UK. It has been estimated that 75 per cent of a dog population must be vaccinated at any one time to delay the spread of this disease. The virus disease must always be rigorously controlled in animals because of the devastating effect of one human becoming infected with rabies.

Inactivated rabies vaccine has been available for use in the UK only in dogs intended for export. Elsewhere in the world, both live attenuated vaccines and inactivated vaccines are used on an annual basis.

BOOSTERS: Thanks to the development of effective canine vaccines by the pharmaceutical industry, most of the diseases described above are now uncommon in Europe and North America. The need for an annual booster is essential to keep up a high level of immunity where killed vaccines are used, and with live virus vaccines it probably does no harm to inject repeat doses every year. It is easy to become complacent about the absence of infectious disease in Goldens, and it is false economy to overlook the need for re-vaccination.

PARASITES

INTERNAL PARASITES
ROUNDWORMS: The most common worms in puppies and dogs up to one year of age are *Toxocara* and *Toxascaris*. Puppies with roundworms start to pass worm eggs as early as three weeks, and most when about seven weeks of age. This is the most dangerous time for the environment to be contaminated with eggs, especially for young children who play with the puppies first, then lick their fingers, thus catching Zoonotic Toxocariasis.

Adult dogs also pass roundworms, which may be seen emerging from the rectum of a nursing bitch who develops diarrhoea. Worms may also appear in the vomit if the worm moves forward from the intestine into the

stomach by accident.

Control of worms depends on frequent dosing of young puppies from as early as two weeks of age, repeated every two to three weeks until three months old. To prevent puppies carrying worms, the pregnant bitch can be wormed from the 42nd day of pregnancy with a safe, licensed wormer, such as fenbendazole. The worming treatment can be given daily to the bitch until the second day after all the puppies are born. Routine worming of adults twice a year with a combined tablet for roundworms and tapeworms is a good preventive measure. With young children in the household, even more frequent worm dosing may be advisable to reduce the risk of migrating roundworm larvae in the child, and possible eye damage.

TAPEWORMS: These are not known to kill dogs, but the appearance of a wriggling segment coming through the rectum, or moving on the tail hair, is enough to deter all but the most unsqueamish dog lover. The responsibility of worming dogs regularly reflects the harm that worms can do to other creatures. The biggest threat is from the *Echinococcus* worm that a dog ingests if feeding from raw sheep offal. The worm is only six millimetres long, but several thousand can live in one dog. If a human should swallow a segment of this worm, it may move to the person's liver or lungs, in the same way as it would in the sheep. A major illness would be the unfortunate result, another example of a zoonotic infection.

The most frequently-found tapeworm is *Dipylidium caninum*. It is not a long tapeworm compared with the old-fashioned *Taenia* worms, but when segments break off they may be recognised, as they resemble grains of rice attached to the hairs of the tail. The tapeworm has become more common in dogs and cats since the number of fleas has increased, as the intermediate host of this worm is the flea or the louse. When dogs groom themselves, they attempt to swallow any crawling insect on the skin surface and in this way may become infested with tapeworms even though worming is carried out twice a year. Flea control is just as important as worming in preventing tapeworm infection. Three-monthly dosing with tablets is a good idea, less frequently if the dog is known to be away from sources of re-infection.

The other tapeworms of the *Taenia* species come from dogs eating raw rabbits (*T serialis* or *pisiformis*) or from sheep, cattle or pig offal (*T ovis*, *hydatigena* or *multiceps*).

HOOKWORMS: Hookworms and others are less frequently a cause of trouble in the UK. The hookworm damages the dog's intestine by using its teeth on the lining. *Uncinaria* may be the cause of poor condition and thinness and *Ancylostoma* can be the reason for anaemia and weakness.

HEARTWORMS AND OTHERS

Heartworms are almost unknown in most of the UK, but are a great problem in other countries and states. Bladder worms are only detected when urine samples are examined. They are similar to the Whipworms found in the large intestine and identified when samples are examined after mucoid dysentry affects a dog.

Giardia is a parasite that occurs in dogs in kennels. It should be investigated in dogs with diarrhoea who have come through quarantine. It is a protozoal organism that likes to live in stagnant surface water, and is of especial interest because a similar strain is a cause of dysentry in humans, especially where water-borne infection is blamed for the illness

ECTOPARASITES

External parasites may cause intense irritation and skin diseases from scratching and rubbing. In recent years, the cat flea has become by far the most common ectoparasite of the Golden Retriever, but more traditional sarcoptic mange, lice and ringworm skin infections do appear from time to time.

FLEAS: The flea that hops may never be seen in the Golden's coat, but its presence may be detected by the flea dirt or excreta containing dried blood. Grooming your dog over white paper or a light table top may reveal black bits that have dark red blood stains when moistened. Once the flea dirt is found, a closer inspection of the dog may show fleas running though the coat at skin level. At one time they were more likely to live in the hair down the spine towards the tail head, but now they are found in the shorter hairs of the abdomen or neck. This may be due to the fact that cat fleas are the most commonly found variety in UK dogs. Such fleas prefer a softer hair structure for their 'living space'. All fleas are temporary visitors, who like to feed from the dog by biting to suck blood, but in their development and egg-laying stages they may live freely off the dog thereby escaping some of the anti-parasitic dressing put on their host's coat. Re-infestation then becomes possible, and many flea treatments appear to be ineffective unless the flea in the environment is eliminated at the same time.

There is a wide range of anti-parasitic sprays, washes and baths available, and the Golden Retriever owner may well be confused as to how and when to apply these. There is the further problem that some dogs seem able to carry a few fleas on them with very little discomfort, while others exhibit intense irritation and will bite pieces out of themselves in an attempt to catch a single flea. A cat in the household or crossing the garden may drop flea eggs, and in a warm place they can hatch out and develop into more fleas waiting to jump on to the dog.

Flea eggs and immature larvae may lie dormant for months, waiting to complete their development and become ready to bite. Adult fleas too can live for months off an animal, until they become able to find a host to feed from, so treating the dog is only tackling part of the problem. The kennels or the house must be treated as well. Vacuum-cleaning and easy-to-clean sleeping quarters for the dog help enormously in dealing with a flea infestation, once an environmental spray has been applied. The choice of aerosol spray, medicated bath, tablet by mouth or agent that stops larval development is a wide one, and experience will show which method is most suitable when your particular dog is affected.

LICE: These may be found in the dog's coat, especially a Golden leading more of an outdoor life than the average pet dog. Lice spend their whole life on the dog, and fairly close contact between dogs is necessary to spead these parasites. Large numbers of lice cause intense irritation with hair loss. Biting lice can produce anaemia when they are present in large enough numbers to remove blood continuously, at a rate similar to a bleeding ulcer. Liquid treatments applied as a total bath soak are best. Lice eggs can be transmitted from dog to dog on grooming brushes. The lice and their eggs are visible to the naked eye, and should be spotted during your normal grooming routine.

MANGE MITES: These mites cannot be seen during grooming. If they are suspected, scrapings from the skin surface are sent for examination under the microscope. The two forms of mange, *Sarcoptes* and *Demodex*, can be distinguished in this way, but any bare skin patches of low grade mange infection may at first seem similar when a dog is examined. There are a number of differences in the two forms of mange that I will not enumerate here, but a simple distinction is that sarcoptic mange is very itchy and spreads, while demodectic mange in the older dog usually remains as a scaly, hairless patch and, although an obvious blemish, does not cause a lot of itching. Anti-parasitic baths with pyrethroids or amitraz, and topical applications of organophosphorous washes will have to be repeated, but are usually effective.

TICKS: Ticks are large enough not to be missed, and can be expected in gundogs working where sheep, hedgehogs etc. leave tick eggs about. Applications of pyrethroid or other 'spot' liquids on the neck and rump will keep ticks off a dog for a month. Baths are also effective. Ticks may be removed by first soaking them in vegetable oil, then gently

coaxing and lifting the tick's head away from the dog's skin.

CHEYLETIELLA: These cause surface irritation of dogs and intense itching in humans who happen to get bitten. The so-called 'moving dandruff' show up as white flecks on a Golden Retriever's skin, but may be more difficult to see on a light-coloured dog. Anti-parasitic shampoos will kill the surface feeder, but carrier dogs in kennels may show very few symptoms at all.

MALASEZZIA: This is a yeast-like surface organsim that appears in dogs with low resistance to infection. A patchy coat and dull hair appearance should make a Golden Retriever owner suspect the presence of yeasts in unusually large numbers. Once identified, baths and general hygiene, with improved nutrition, will help your dog to overcome this problem. The yeast will also be found in the ear canal and, if shown to be present on a stained smear in large numbers, the ear should be treated with Miconazole, Nystatin or Thiabendazole.

RINGWORM: Ringworm is found in dogs as a fungal infection of the hairs. The signs of a 'ring' are not always present, and some dogs show quite a violent skin response once infected. Cattle ringworm can be transmitted to country dogs. Ringworm spores can remain in the environment and in old woodwork for a long time. Diagnosis by skin tests is slow but reliable, as the 'Woods' lamp, which uses ultra-violet light, does not identify all types of ringworm. Treatment with anti-fungal washes, or the antibiotic griseofulvin, may be used to eliminate the mycotic infection.

ACCIDENTS AND FIRST AID
The few simple procedures described here do not suggest that there are no other things that can be done as 'first aid', but in most cases the sooner the patient is taken to the veterinary surgery, the better the chance of a full recovery may be. For this reason, splinting broken bones is now out of favour, and more

pain may be caused than if the dog is quickly transported to a place where any shock and pain can be treated professionally. X-rays will better show the nature of a fracture, and what is the best method of treatment.

TRAFFIC ACCIDENTS: Goldens, being large, solid dogs, seldom go underneath vehicles, but they tend to suffer severe chest injuries if hit in front, or pelvic and limb injuries if struck on the side. A dog hit by a car will be distressed and through fright and pain will tend to bite, even when its familiar owners attempt to help. First, assess the injuries, noting any gaping holes and where blood is being lost. Do this before touching the dog's head. Some frightened dogs may try to run away at that point, so a lead or scarf round the neck will help to steady the dog, and a tape muzzle may have to be used before a dog is lifted into a vehicle for transport to the surgery.

A pressure bandage applied to a bleeding area is the best way of staunching blood flow, but improvisation with whatever cloth is to hand is acceptable in a life-saving situation. The dog may be breathing rapidly or gasping with 'air hunger' signs. In this case, the mouth and nostrils should be wiped free of dried blood or saliva to help unblock the airway. If you suspect a spinal injury, slide a board under the dog before picking it up. Otherwise, a blanket is the best way of allowing two or more persons to pick up an injured dog without aggravating the injuries.

CHOKING AND VOMITING: Try to find out the cause of any sudden attack. Grass awns may enter the throat and airways in the summer months, and, at any time of year, a dog playing ball or stick retrieval games may get an obstruction at the back of the throat. Even a fine bamboo cane may become wedged across the upper molar teeth. In the case of one dog, who had been out shooting all day, a length of cane was retrieved from the upper part of the oesophagus the same evening. Poisonous substances cause retching and vomiting in dogs, and thirsty animals have

been known to drink from toilet bowls or lap up bleach and other cleaning substances.

Having initially looked for a foreign body, your first aid measures should be aimed at providing as good an air supply as possible. If there is any blistering or soreness of the lips or tongue, use honey or salad oil to coat the inflamed surfaces. A vomiting dog should be prevented from drinking water and regurgitating it as fast as it is swallowed. Ice cubes left to melt in a dish may be a way of helping the dog, as it will drink the iced water slowly.

COLLAPSE AND UNCONSCIOUSNESS: As in the road accident, assess the dog before touching to determine the cause of the incident, so that appropriate first aid can be given. A dog running in a field on a warm day may have had a circulatory collapse; another dog convulsing may be throwing an epileptic fit; an elderly dog found semi-conscious in the morning after voiding urine and faeces may have had a stroke or vestibular disease. Each condition will need different treatment, but, as a general rule, pull the tongue forward to ensure there is an airway to the lungs, keep the animal cool, and avoid unnecessary noise and commotion. Look for any drugs or poisons the dog may have swallowed, gently feel the left side for gas distending the abdomen, and check the pupils of the eyes and their response to a bright light. The veterinary surgeon will be better able to deal with the situation if a timetable of events, and any contributing factors, can be given in a concise manner.

WASP STINGS: Stings occur more often in late summer. Usually the foot swells rapidly or, if the dog has caught a wasp in its mouth, the side of the face swells up and the eye may become partly shut. Vinegar is a traditional remedy to apply to the sting area. If an antihistamine tablet is available, this can be given to the dog immediately to stop further swelling.

Other biting flies cause swellings on the body, and may be the cause of the 'hot spots' or acute moist eczemas that Goldens can suffer from. Calamine lotions cool the skin but, if licked, calamine causes vomiting.

SHOCK: This occurs to a greater or lesser extent with nearly all accidents. Keep the patient warm, wrapping a blanket, coat or wool garment around the body of the dog. Unless you have reason to think an anaesthetic will be given, or other contraindications exist, offer fluids by mouth in small quantities. Oral rehydration solutions can be obtained from your veterinary surgeon, and a packet should be kept in every emergency first-aid kit. As an alternative, a solution of half a teaspoon of salt and half a teaspoon of bicarbonate of soda dissolved in a litre of water may be given a few dessertspoonfuls at a time.

SKIN DISEASES
PARASITIC SKIN DISEASES: Flea bites may not be obvious, especially in a dense-coated breed. Once a dog becomes sensitised to the proteins injected by the flea when it first bites, any subsequent contact with flea saliva may bring on an itchy rash, even though no live fleas are found on the dog. The various other causes of parasitic skin disease have already been outlined in the section on external parasites.

OTHER PRURITIC SKIN CONDITIONS: Anal sac irritation will cause a dog to nibble at the hair around the tail base, or it may be responsible for a dog licking and nibbling anywhere around the hindquarters. The glands may be so impacted that they cannot be emptied out during the straining necessary to pass faeces. An infected lining of one or both sacs may also be the cause of irritation, and this can often be detected by a fruity odour to the sac's contents, or, at its worst, a smell like rotten meat.

Bacterial dermatoses result from multiplication of skin bacteria such as *Staph. intermedius*. Red blotches and ring-like marks around a central pustule are most clearly seen when the hairless areas of the abdomen are inspected. Skin swabs may be used to identify the bacteria present, and this information can then be used to choose the most appropriate antibiotic for the infection causing the irritation.

HAIR LOSS AND ALOPECIA: A Golden Retriever's coat is normally shed twice a year, but sometimes the growth of new hair is delayed and the coat appears thin, lifeless and, if groomed excessively, bare patches can develop. Investigations into the possibility of thyroid disease may be needed when there is a failure of hair to grow. Other hormonal skin disease may cause symmetrical hair loss on the flanks of a bitch, or bare tail head areas (stud tail) in some dogs. Feminisation of the older male dog will have hair loss as one of the signs of a Sertoli cell tumour. Veterinary advice should be sought.

DIGESTIVE SYSTEM DISORDERS
SICKNESS AND DIARRHOEA: Occasional sickness is not a cause for concern in the younger dog. The dog is adapted to feeding from a wide range of different foods, and part of natural protection against food poisoning is the ability to reject unsuitable foods by returning them from the stomach via reflex vomiting. If there is a yellow coloration to the vomit, it means that the bile from the liver, which normally passes into the small intestine after leaving the bile duct, has for some reason been passed forward to enter the stomach. The bitter bile acids will cause reflex vomiting as soon as they reach the stomach wall, and will be sicked up, together with any food left in the stomach.

Repeated sickness, starting off with recognisable food followed by slime, or food followed by mucus alone, is a more serious sign. It may be associated with obstructions due to a foreign body, or to infection such as Pyometra or Hepatitis. Some outbreaks of diarrhoea will start with food being vomited, as this will stimulate the intestine. As soon as the food enters the small intestine, then the stomach empties itself reflexly, by vomiting any food remaining within the stomach. Sometimes a reversal of the normal flow of food will cause the appearance of a 'faecal' vomit. Diarrhoea is the passage of frequent loose or unformed faeces: it is associated with infections and irritation of the intestine. The rapid transit of food taken in by mouth means that water cannot be absorbed by the large intestine, and soft or runny stools result from the incomplete digestion and water reabsorption. When blood is present, it may appear as streaks from the large intestine. If blackish and foul-smelling, it means that the blood has come from the small intestine and been subjected to some of the digestive fluids. The condition is then known as dysentry.

Chronic diarrhoea is a condition in which the looseness of faeces lasts more than 48 hours. It may be associated with malabsorption, when the lining of the intestine is incapable of absorbing digested food. Alternatively, diseases such as food intolerances, bacterial overgrowth, lymphoid and other tumours may be the cause, or maldigestion, when there is a failure of the digestive juices to break down the food. Other causes include Exocrine Pancreatic Insufficiency (EPI), inflammatory bowel diseases, or any disturbance in gastric or liver function. Investigations by the veterinary surgeon will include blood tests and faecal laboratory examinations. These may be followed by X-rays or endoscope examinations.

The treatment of sickness and diarrhoea involves, firstly, witholding solid food for 24 hours, giving small quantities of replacement fluids as soon as the dog stops vomiting (proprietary electrolyte fluids are probably best), then introducing a highly digestible food in about one third of the normal quantity, fed on the second day of the illness. This amount should be increased slowly, until, by the fourth day, a full ration of food is given again. In the recovery period, fats should be avoided, as well as milk and dairy products, due to the dog's inability to digest lactose.

GASTRIC DILATION: This disease is better-known as Bloat, and 'torsion' can be a problem in any of the larger breeds. It is especially associated with feeding regimes in which a highly digestible food can be swallowed rapidly, combined with the consumption of large quantities of water which contribute to the development of the bloat. Feeding immediately after strenuous exercise has also been blamed. When a dog is fed in the late afternoon or evening, there is the chance of the dog lying down, so that abdominal movement associated with walking or jumping up does not allow for eructation, or the dispersal of gas from the stomach. Greedy feeders who swallow air as they gulp down their food are considered at greatest risk, but this problem does seem associated with flat slab-chest dogs, who have large deep chests and thus loosely suspended stomachs.

The bloated stomach may rotate as a 'torsion' or volvulus, and become a Gastric Dilation and Volvulus condition (known as GDV), which means an acute emergency. The dog needs to be rushed to the veterinary surgery for treatment of shock and for deflation of the stomach. Affected dogs seem uncomfortable, become depressed and look at their flanks with expressions of disbelief. At first, the left side just behind the ribs is the only side to bulge, and tapping with the your fingertips will produce a drum-like resonance over the left rib cage edge, and over the distended abdomen behind. Within a few hours both sides of the abdomen appear distended behind the rib cage, the dog becomes more uncomfortable and lies down a lot as the pain increases. The gas-filled stomach presses on the diaphragm restricting the breathing, the colour of the tongue becomes more purplish and breaths are more frequent and quite shallow. Sometime at this stage, the weight of the enlarging spleen attached to the greater curvature of the gas-filled stomach makes the stomach twist in a clockwise direction. The signs of discomfort become more noticeable as the stomach's exit to the oesophagus is pinched off by a 180-degree rotation. If a stomach tube is passed through the mouth down the oesophagus at this stage, the tube can be pressed down no further than just beyond the entrance level of the oesophagus into the abdomen. No gas will pass back up the tube, even though the stomach is still tight and filled with gas.

Emergency treatment at the veterinary surgery will usually mean setting up an intravenous drip to deal with the shock. Decompression of the stomach will be attempted, possibly first by using the stomach tube as described above, or, probably more successfully, by inserting a wide-bore (18 G needle) canula at the point behind the left rib arch that shows the most distension by gas. The finger should then be kept on the needle hub protruding through the skin, partially to hold it in place as the size of the stomach reduces, and partially to vent the gas out slowly or in 'pulses'. This ensures that the blood in the veins can start to flow towards the heart again, once the abdomen size returns to normal. Frequently, a laparotomy will be necessary to empty the stomach or to provide a means of fixing the stomach to the abdominal wall, so that an adhesion will make it less likely that gas distension will appear again.

CONSTIPATION: This disorder usually occurs either through your Labrador eating too many bones whose chalky residue clogs up the rectum, or, in older male dogs, it may be associated with enlargement of the prostate gland. Treatment with lubricants and enemas should be followed by high-fibre diets. Soluble fibre, as found in oatmeal, is thought to add to the moist faecal bulk and thus retain water from the large intestine lumen, so that the faeces are not bone hard and painful to pass. Allow exercise, or place the dog in the garden 30 minutes after feeding, as this will stimulate the reflexes for normal defecation.

BREEDING AND REPRODUCTION
There are no specific problems in the Golden Retriever breed, and both mating and whelping should proceed with the minimum of trouble (see Chapter Twelve: Breeding Golden Retrievers).

THE OLDER GOLDEN RETRIEVER
GERIATRIC CARE: The Golden is a relatively long-lived breed. Ten to 12 years of age is considered a good age for a working dog, but many Golden Retrievers may live to 15 years, provided they avoid accidents and injuries. The tendency for some dogs to overeat if food is available leads to adiposity and will significantly shorten a dog's life. Some of the oldest dogs are also the leanest, so dietary control helps if you wish your dog to live longer. After about ten years of age, it may be advantageous to divide the daily ration into two small feeds to help absorption and digestion. Any tendency to overweight must be checked, and regular weighing helps to control dietary intake. The older dog will use up less energy in exercise and, if housed for most of the day, fewer calories will be burned up to keep the dog warm. Some reduction in calorie intake is desirable, and there are special diets prepared for the older dog which are higher in fibre and lower in calories than the diet for the younger dog.

Keep a careful watch on the condition of your Golden Retriever's mouth, as breath odour is one of the first signs of dental disease or of decay of food trapped between the gums and 'ledges' of tartar that may have built up on the teeth. Goldens may have cracked teeth from chewing bones earlier in their life, and only in old age does the tooth root become infected, followed by the development of an abscess. The back upper molar teeth are often affected, and an abscess will show as a swelling immediately below the eye if the carnassial tooth has infected roots. Chewing as a form of jaw exercise is one method of keeping teeth healthy, but, when there is a build-up of plaque on the tooth surface, cleaning the teeth using an ultrasonic scaler, followed by a machine polish, is a better way of keeping a healthy mouth.

Monitor the length of your Golden's nails, since less exercise and possible arthritis sometimes lead the older dog to put less weight on the affected leg, so that nail overgrowth occurs. Careful trimming to avoid cutting into the 'quick', or live part of the nail, will help many older Golden Retrievers. Elbows too should be inspected for calluses on their outer side, as dogs who are stiff do not move as often as they might to relieve their body weight on the surface they sleep on. The skin over the outside of the elbow has little padding from fat or muscle and bone lies just underneath, so leathery skin or a callus can easily occur. In extreme cases the callus develops cracks and fissures, and a bacterial infection is set up so that the surface becomes pink and oozing.

URINARY INCONTINENCE: This is one of the problems found in older dogs. Leakage from the bladder, resulting in damp patches on bedding overnight, may be remedied by removing the water bowl after 7pm to prevent evening drinking. Also effective is the possible use of one of the sympathomimetic group of drugs to promote bladder storage. A urine sample should be examined: sometimes mild cystistis and bacteria will be found in the urine, and treatment with an appropriate antibiotic will reduce bladder sensitivity and storage will be better. If large quantities of urine are being voided day and night, then investigation of urine concentrations and blood biochemistry tests is necessary to rule out major disease. Diabetes Insipidus or Mellitus, liver disorders, Cushing's disease and Nephrosis may all be first detected if a dog is incontinent when left shut up indoors. Blood tests are necessary to distinguish many of these conditions in the older Golden Retriever.

17 *BREED ASSOCIATED DISEASES*

A number of diseases which are seen in Golden Retrievers will be dealt with in this chapter, as some are thought to have a genetic basis. Some digestive disorders probably spring from the fact that the Golden is a working dog, bred through generations for retrieving game birds. When kept in a domestic situation, the breed may become more susceptible to diseases related to scavenging and eating whatever becomes available.

Other diseases such as Hereditary Cataract have a strong genetic basis, and can be progressively bred out. The condition can be easily identified in the young dog, so affected animals can be stopped from being used in a breeding programme. There is a lot of inconclusive evidence about some of the conditions described, and the sorts of eye diseases now found in Golden Retrievers (Posterior Pole Subcapsular Cataract and Multifocal Retinal Dysplasia) seem to cause very little disturbance to most working dogs' vision. It is important to recognise all these conditions and, whenever possible, breed from affected dogs only on a limited scale, until the puppies can be examined to see if the condition is more frequent or more severe in the next generation.

INHERITED EYE CONDITIONS

In the USA the control of eye disorders is supervised by CERF, and Diplomates of the Veterinary College of Ophthalmology are the only veterinarians authorised to certify that dogs are free of hereditary eye disease. The situation for eye certification in Europe is more complicated, as there is no one central body to issue a European certificate. The position of certification in countries such as Holland and Sweden is on a par with that of the UK. The UK scheme, administered by the British Veterinary Association and the Kennel Club, is based on certification by veterinary surgeons who have special certificates as eye examiners. In such countries as France and Germany the certification situation is more variable, and panels of eye examiners are often appointed by individual groups of breeders.

LENS DISORDERS

CATARACT (POSTERIOR POLE TYPE): The lens of the eye has a front surface that bends the light to focus it on the retina, and a back surface adjacent to the vitreous jelly which holds the retina in place. The type of cataract most often found in Golden Retrievers, and which also occurs in Labrador Retrievers, usually causes only a minor disturbance in vision. Known as 'pp' (posterior pole) cataract, it produces an opacity affecting the back of the lens at its centre – the part closest to the retina. Due to the multi-layered nature of a lens, the cataract just inside the lens capsule (subcapsular) appears where the lines converge as an inverted letter Y. It seldom causes a total lens opacity, but is not infrequently seen when an ophthalmoscope is used by the veterinary surgeon to inspect the eye. In the guide dog breeding programme, despite attempts to totally eliminate pp cataract from the breeding lines, it is seen in both Golden Retrievers and in Labradors, and equally in first cross matings of the two breeds when working dogs are bred in this way purposely. Parents both clear of pp cataract have produced puppies who develop pp cataracts later in life, so it would seem that a recessive gene with a late-onset factor in some individuals may be responsible.

HEREDITARY CATARACT: Congenital cataract is a cataract seen at birth or soon after the eyes open, and it is a breed problem. A dominant gene for this form of cataract occurs in the Golden Retriever. An opacity of the lens would be seen as a white reflective object in the eye, and a congenital cataract would be found soon after the puppy's eyelids open. The inheritance is by a dominant gene and, fortunately, it is easy to control by stopping the breeding from either parent that has produced one or more affected puppies.

LATE-ONSET CATARACTS: Cataracts that appear in the lens of this breed later in life are less likely to be hereditary. An opacity in the lens may develop at any age, and may be due to an injury to the eye resulting from a blow to the face or a penetrating foreign body, such as a blackthorn. In a metabolic disease such as Diabetes Mellitus, cataracts may form in both eyes. They have a characteristic 'water cleft' appearance. Some toxic substances will damage the lens, while a nutritional deficiency may also result in cataracts. Other conditions affecting the rest of the eye, such as Glaucoma and Uveitis, may develop and cause a cataract as a complication.

RETINA DISORDERS

CENTRAL PROGRESSIVE RETINAL ATROPHY (CPRA): This eye condition is a retinal pigment dystrophy of the epithelium. Unlike the other form of retinal atrophy, this one takes the form of daytime blindness. The centre of the retina, where the cones of light receptors are most closely packed, becomes damaged so the sight deteriorates in the brightest light conditions.

The disease is mainly seen in UK-bred dogs, and both Golden Retrievers and Labrador can suffer from it. Fortunately, this form of eye disorder rarely progresses to total blindness. CPRA is becoming quite rare. Light brown spots on the reflective part of the retina are the characteristics the veterinary surgeon looks for. There is an inherited failure of the retina to get rid of waste products after light falls on its photoreceptor layer. Local antioxidant deficiency and abnormal lipid metabolism are other factors in the profile of this retinal disease. For this reason, it was associated with feeding dogs on tripe diets that are low in Vitamin E, and other protective constituents. When these waste products accumulate to excess, the cell dies and an area of the retina, usually near the centre, also dies and shows brown coloration. Dogs develop blindness only slowly from two to three years of age onwards, but they may have lost a considerable amount of vision by eight years of age before the owner really becomes aware of their partial blindness.

Detailed examination of the retina is made with an ophthalmoscope by a veterinary surgeon, and certification under the Kennel Club/British Veterinary Association scheme can be be made in the UK at eighteen months of age in the Golden Retriever breed. Re-inspection of the eyes every year is recommended, as some dogs do not exhibit CPRA until later in life.

GENERALISED PROGRESSIVE RETINAL ATROPHY (GPRA): This type of eye disease, first described by Parry in 1953 as affecting Irish Setters, was commonly known as night blindness because it was in the dim light near to dusk that affected dogs were most likely to become lost. GPRA was successfully bred out in Irish Setters, as it was inherited through a dominant gene and with the small numbers then present in the breed it was easy to control. Once breeders knew how the disease spread, and they all stopped using affected dogs for mating, the condition became rare in litters of puppies. At the time, it was commonly known as 'PRA' and it was found that other breeds, such as Poodles, might develop a similar PRA. However, this appeared later in life, so was more difficult to breed out. Later, specialists realised that there was yet another sort of PRA, so the term 'Generalised Progressive Retinal Atrophy' (GPRA) was used to describe the first type, in which the photoreceptors of the retina actually degenerate.

The Golden Retriever has a late-onset form of PRA, which may be detected by the ophthalmoscope well before the dog shows any signs of blindness at four to six years of age. There is a gradual degeneration of the photoreceptors that receive the light at the back of the eye, and the blindness develops very slowly. The condition is different from other forms of blindness, as the dog can still constrict the pupils when a bright light is directed at his eye, so there is never a total loss of response to light.

RETINAL DYSPLASIA: When examining eyes for the better-known hereditary diseases, small marks known as 'rosettes' are seen on the highly reflective retina. Sometimes, folds in the retina may also be seen at the back of the eye when ophthalmoscopic examinations are conducted. Some of these folds are seen as fine grey lines that seem to be of little consequence, but sometimes larger areas of brown discoloration are seen against the bright reflective surface of the tapetal fundus – the surface of the retina. Retinal Dysplasia may, later in the disease, display itself as detachments of part or all of the retina, and there may be near-total loss of vision. This detachment is very rare in the Golden Retriever.

MULTIFOCAL RETINAL DYSPLASIA (MRD): The type of Retinal Dysplasia is occasionally seen in Goldens during routine eye inspections with an ophthalmoscope. Folds in the retina, close to the optic disc,

appear as grey streaks but do not affect the dog's sight. Often, as the eyeball grows, these 'stretch marks' tend to become less noticeable. MRD in the Golden Retriever is not inspected for in the current BVA/KC certification scheme, as it has caused no eyesight problem in the breed.

GLAUCOMA
Glaucoma is a condition in which the inside of the eye over-inflates, with fluids causing pressure damage to the retina and the lens, as well as making the cornea opaque. Unless treated early in the disease, a permanent loss of sight may result. A primary glaucoma affecting the Golden Retriever breed is presently under investigation in the British Veterinary Association/Kennel Club scheme.

CORNEAL LIPIDOSIS
This is seen as a white mark obscuring part of the front of the eye, but it seldom causes complete blindness and the dog seems to be able to see through or around the opacity without too much disadvantage. It is usually associated with a high-fat diet which causes the lipid material to pass out of the bloodstream and settle in the layers of the cornea. Corneal lipidosis in Golden Retrievers is also presently under investigation by the British Veterinary Association/Kennel Club scheme.

EYELID DISORDERS

ENTROPION: The condition known as entropion may be an inherited defect of the eyelid structure. It is seen in some Goldens as an in-turning of the eyelids. There may be excessive tear formation, and the overflow of tears is noticeable on the faces of light-coloured dogs. As the eyelashes are pulled on to the eye by a spasm of the eyelid muscle, abrasion of the cornea can result in a corneal ulcer. Once diagnosed, severe cases will need immediate surgery to evert the eyelid edge, while milder cases may be treated with lubricating eye ointments. In a growing dog, the skull conformation alters, so that turning-in of the eyelids may correct itself spontaneously. Small eyes were thought at one time to predispose a dog to entropion. It is true that, if there is a nutritional check or weight loss, the pad of fat behind the eye becomes less thick so that the eyeball sinks more into the skull's orbit. Smallness of the eye may be less noticeable once the nutritional state improves and the eyeball becomes more protruding again.

ECTROPION: This looseness of the eyelids, with undue exposure of the pink lining of the lid, may be an hereditary disease in some breeds with loose skin on the head, but, in the Golden Retriever, ectropion is usually the result of an eyelid injury and is not inherited.

BONE AND JOINT DISEASES WITH HEREDITARY INFLUENCES

HIP DYSPLASIA (HD)
The problem of Hip Dysplasia in the breed has been greatly over-emphasised in some books, but the problem is widespread and can be said to exist in any breed in which more than five per cent of the breed shows recognisable signs. The working guide dog is rarely disadvantaged by HD, as it does not affect the daily life of the dog. Such a dog walks at a slow pace, does not have to jump up and does not do agility work. Any pain or discomfort may be associated in the young dog with rupture of the round ligament of the hip that suddenly allows for subluxation with a short period of pain, or, in the older dog, pain from the disease of osteoarthritis that can develop secondary to an existing Hip Dysplasia.

The disease is not entirely an hereditary one, and environmental factors such as feeding, exercise and the position the young dog is made to sit in, may all be responsible for up to 60 per cent of the occurrence of the Hip Dysplasia changes as seen on X-ray. Fortunately, the extreme views once held by experts, who recommended not breeding from any dog showing any traces of hip dysplasia, have been moderated with time and experience. Some of the matings of 0/0 hip

score dogs have produced litters of puppies with a hip score little better than the breed average of 20. With a hip score range of between 0 and 103 in the UK scheme, there would usually seem little justification for attempting to breed from stock with an above average score. This can be modified when breeding from higher-scoring bitches who may have other characteristics which could be of especial value to the breeder in a programme to seek a particular type of dog.

In the USA, a similar scheme is operated by the Orthopaedic Foundation for Animals (OFA), and a high standard X-ray plate is needed for evaluation by the organisation's radiologists. Established in 1966 as the world's largest all-breed registry, a seven-point scoring system is used for hips ranging from 'excellent' to 'severe dysplasia'. Dogs must be at least two years old to receive a breeding number from the OFA, although preliminary evaluations will be made by the OFA on dogs younger than 24 months, to help breeders choose their future stock. A slightly different approach is taken by the University of Pennysylvania Hip Improvement Programme (PennHIP). Here, two views of the hind limb are required to measure the amount of displacement or 'joint laxity' in the hips. This method of evaluation overcomes the objection that some dogs appear to have very unstable hip joints, but when X-rayed in the extended position they appear to have normal hip structure. The third hip evaluation scheme is operated in the USA by the Institute for Genetic Disease Control in Animals (GDC). Similar open registries of blood lines are used in Norway and Sweden to help breeders select stock for mating. The normal dog can be certified at 12 months of age, and the information is then available on a progeny report held in a database.

GUIDELINES FOR HIP IMPROVEMENT
1) Score all stock using the BVA/KC scheme or similar schemes that are available outside the UK. This necessitates X-rays of all young breeding stock.
2) As far as practical, breed only from stock

with a hip score below the breed average of 20.

3) Follow recommendations about feeding and exercise to avoid undue injury and stress to the growing hip joint.

4) Regularly review all inherited diseases in the dog group (e.g. in a kennels), and enquire about littermates or parents. Expect to get evasive replies when asking others!

ELBOW DYSPLASIA

Another disease with an hereditary basis, osteochondrosis is seen as a major cause of lameness in several large and giant breeds of dogs. The Golden Retriever is likely to suffer from Elbow Osteochondrosis and one or both elbows may be affected, as shown by forelimb lameness in the growing puppy. This lameness is most likely to develop between five and seven months of age. It will not be severe at first, but later one elbow may become so badly affected that the dog cannot fully bend the elbow, and the muscles of the shoulder on that side become thinner, causing an imbalance as the dog walks. A veterinary examination will show that when the elbow is bent up, the dog pulls his foot away because of the pain. The joint may become more distended, and the leg feels thinner than the opposite foreleg, but over half the dogs have OCD in both forelegs affected to a greater or lesser extent. Dogs may show Osteochondrosis of the shoulder joint, and this seems to develop at a slightly younger age than the elbow form, so both shoulder and elbow joints of both legs should be X-rayed to ensure a correct diagnosis. A scoring system for elbows is under development. Screening is at 12 months of age.

An X-ray under general anaesthesia is necessary to view the elbow joints of both legs to show up the signs of osteoarthrosis, secondary to the OCD. Severely-affected parents should not be used in breeding programmes. The rapid bone growth produced by some high-protein diets may make the condition worse, because the bone cartilage grows at too fast a rate to be converted into stronger bone to support a joint.

PANOSTEITIS

This can be a cause of sudden lameness, most often in a foreleg, but sometimes the lameness will alternate from front to back legs. The lameness is sudden and severe, apparently suggesting that a bone has been broken, but the X-ray will show no damage to the bone structure at all. Darker areas in the bone marrow region may be seen in the X-ray plate, and sometimes the periosteal bone appears thickened at the site of pain. It is believed that this is an auto-immune condition, as it does not appear until six months of age, and only infrequently does it cause lameness in the middle-aged or elderly Golden Retriever.

Treatment involves resting the dog for a few days, then giving controlled exercise until the dog walks soundly again. Non-steroidal anti-inflammatory tablets can be given, and severely lame dogs may benefit from corticosteroid injections.

OSTEOARTHRITIS

This condition, which limits joint movement, starts as damage to the cartilage on the joint surface. Additional bone may then be laid down round the edge of the joint, possibly as a result of inflammation and an attempt to support the joint. The disease develops progressively, leading to lameness, pain, the grating feeling known as crepitus and then joint instability. The joint feels thickened from the outside, and there is limited movement when it is bent to stretch it or flex it. If a joint is not moving, then the muscles weaken, or atrophy, so that the leg becomes wasted. X-rays should be taken to assess the degree of new bone building up around the joint. A management plan for the dog can be drawn up, and pain control is the first priority in treatment. Osteoarthritis is particularly associated, in the Golden Retriever breed in old age, with Osteochondrosis of the elbow and with Hip Dysplasia's after-effects.

CRUCIATE LIGAMENT RUPTURE

The stifle, or knee joint, is not robustly constructed and depends on a number of ligaments and on cartilage to hold it together and give free movement. The stifle is used in jumping and for forward propulsion, so overweight dogs who are suddenly asked to perform tasks, even those as simple as jumping out of a car, may land heavily and damage the ligaments.

The cruciate ligaments are those crossing the centre of the stifle joint, and there are two other collateral ligaments that support the sides of the joint. The kneecap, or patella, also has ligaments that run at the front of the joint and these can also fail to support the stifle joint, throwing a greater strain on the two ligaments at the centre. It is usually the front ligament in the centre of the stifle joint – the anterior cruciate ligament – that takes the greatest strain when the dog jumps or turns awkwardly, and this may tear or, at worst, break completely in half. The result is a very lame dog. Often the stifle joint is so unstable that the two bone ends forming the joint can be slid over each other. This instability is used in the 'draw forward' test.

Cruciate rupture usually happens suddenly during extreme exercise and does not improve with enforced rest, as with many other injuries. Heavy dogs the size of Goldens will usually require a surgical operation to repair the torn ligament. There are a number of techniques employed, but most require a ligament implant inserted through or around the joint. Provided the operation is done before arthritic changes develop in the joint surface, the results are very good, since the joint is stabilised again.

OTHER DISORDERS WITH A POSSIBLE INHERITED BASIS

SKIN COMPLAINTS

Many dogs scratch for a variety of reasons. Atopy now seems to be increasingly common in the Golden Retriever breed, perhaps more so since mange has become rare and flea bites have become common. Housing dogs exposes them to house dust mites at an early age, whereas in former times most gundogs were reared in outdoor kennels and frequently spent a lot of their non-working time as an adult, in a kennel. Atopic dogs are those who are genetically predisposed to dermatitis. Often it is the flea bite that first makes the dog itch, but the dog's own genetic make-up causes the irritation to persist and the skin condition worsens.

Some atopic dogs are seen with pink, itchy ears, some excessively lick at their paws which have dark orange saliva-stained hair, while others have pink skin on the abdomen and the perineum. Unfortunately, some dogs may then develop a severe generalised skin disease, and *Staphylococcus intermedius* as a bacterial infection produces a secondary bacterial dermatosis. Ear infections result from atopic ear irritation, and toenails scratching an itchy ear can transfer all sorts of organisms into an ear canal that seems to have a low resistance to infection, with colonies of organisms growing rapidly in the moist, warm ear tube.

Atopy is related to the type of allergic disorder seen in humans as asthma, hayfever and atopic eczema in babies and infants. Such diseases result from allergic response to allergens in the environment such as spores, pollens, moulds, house dust and other dust mites. House dust mites thrive in warm, unventilated houses, feeding on debris including human skin scales or 'dander'. They may well enjoy feeding on dog dander when this is shed in your dog's sleeping or lying area of the house. Fitted carpets are difficult to clean up to their edges, and may require environmental spray applications to control a problem.

Treatment of the atopy may partially correct a situation where a dog 'never stops scratching'. Attention to the sleeping area aimed at removing dust, total eradication of fleas from the house, and feeding a single-protein, low-allergenic diet all help to reduce the scratching threshold. Specific treatments with cortisone drugs provide immediate relief, but the benefit will fade if repeated use of steroids is called for. Alternative treatments for itching include trying to find an antihistamine drug that is effective, and the use of lipid products can be very helpful.

Gamma linoleic acid, one of the constituents of Oil of Evening Primrose, is used in various formulae, but further refining the drug to increase the active constituent DLMG has shown promise in humans, and raises hopes for better veterinary treatments soon.

NERVOUS SYSTEM DISORDERS

SO-CALLED RAGE SYNDROME

Sudden unprovoked attacks are seen in many breeds of dogs and these can often be attributed to some previous incident when a dog has been 'set upon' by another dog. The pain experienced after a fight causes the attacked dog to make sure that it is the first one to bite whenever a dog of similar colour or size appears unexpectedly. Children's games may go too far in teasing a dog and unfortunate consequences may result. In the Cocker Spaniel breed a specific 'rage syndrome' has been studied in which dogs, usually male, make sudden attacks, with barking or snapping, on animals or people that come into close proximity to the Spaniel.

Some male Golden Retrievers have shown excessive male dominanace and, unlike other breeds who curl their lips and lay their ears back before biting, these few Goldens have bitten hands quite severely when correction has been given by handlers or veterinary surgeons. It is not known whether the condition is hereditable, but it does appear in some lines more than others.

It is not correct to discuss this rage syndrome in the same terms as the Golden Cocker Spaniel breed, which has been labelled as having an hereditary nervous disorder. This type of aggression, which apparently appears suddenly and without warning, is reported in the two breeds which are regarded mostly for their softness and reliability. It is possible that these attacks would never happen if the dogs were approached with greater caution.

EPILEPSY OR FITS

There is no known hereditary epilepsy in the breed, but some authors think that the 'rage syndrome' as described above may be a partial brain seizure, where there is a lack of control or 'rage'. This would explain attacks made when a bowl of food is withdrawn from a feeding dog, but in cases where a dog is being caught or handled and biting takes place without warning, it would appear to be a loss of control rather than epilepsy.

DIGESTIVE SYSTEM DISORDERS

BLOAT

Sudden accumulation of gas in the stomach will cause distress and, if left untreated the stomach torsions or twists, resulting in death. Gastric dilation and torsion of the stomach (GDV) can be a problem in any of the larger breeds. It is especially associated with the Giant breeds and Setters, but it may be found in Golden Retrievers as an acute emergency The feeding routine should be such as to avoid hungry dogs swallowing food rapidly, then being left unexercised and unobserved. The GDBA kennel routine is to feed in the morning, before the two work periods during the daytime, so that gas cannot accumulate in the stomach. Any dog with a tendency to Bloat will be seen at the earliest stage of discomfort, and often a silicone-base tablet can be given at this stage to stop bubbles of gas being held in the stomach. Dogs known to 'bloat' can be made to eat more slowly by supervising them and feeding them on their own, with no competition from other dogs stealing their food. The treatment of Gastric Dilation is dealt with in the preceding chapter.

DIARRHOEA FROM BACTERIAL OVERGROWTH

The condition now known as SIBO (Small Intestine Bacterial Overgrowth) is a disorder that may be the cause of persistent diarrhoea, increased appetite and weight loss. The previously-used term BOG was more appropriate to the problem of some dogs suffering from over-frequent defecation. Explained simply, SIBO is a disorder in which too many bacteria for the dog's good health are living in the small intestine. These bacteria take some of the most valuable nutrients out of the food eaten as it passes from the stomach to the small intestine.

Possible causes are defective acid secretion in the stomach juices, slow passage of food through the small intestine, Exocrine Pancreatic Insufficiency (EPI), or defective local immunity of the gut wall to bacteria. Diagnosis has to be confirmed by blood tests, then a month-long course of antibiotics, together with a modified low-fat diet, is usually sufficient to clear the disorder entirely. The diet may be supplemented with Vitamin B and trace elements such as are found in a number of pet health tablets available.

COPROPHAGIA

The eating of faeces is a habit acquired by dogs kept in kennels. Dogs who are adequately supervised at a time when defecation is about to occur will have little opportunity to explore the smells or the taste of recently-voided faeces. The flavouring agents and palatable residues found in faeces after prepared foods have been digested, apparently to a dog's satisfaction, must be blamed for the dog's subsequent nose investigation and ingestion. Efforts to break this behaviour pattern should be adopted. Deterrents such as garlic, paprika and even fresh pineapple have been used to curb a dog's desire to eat faeces. The habit may not be so revolting as first thought, since rabbits use the method of eating faeces from their own rectums as a way of further digesting cellulose for food. Many free-range animals will eat herbivores' faeces left on the ground as a way of obtaining extra Vitamin B.

EXOCRINE PANCREATIC INSUFFICIENCY (EPI)

This is most frequently associated with the German Shepherd breed, but about one third of all cases are found in other breeds and may be found in Goldens. The disease may not show up until middle age as chronic diarrhoea with weight loss, due to a failure of the digestive enzymes in the small intestine. The EPI blood test is used to confirm a diagnosis. Response to treatment, using supplements of digestive enzymes in dried pancreatic extract combined with drugs to lower stomach acidity, has proved to be good. Unfortunately, long-term treatment adds to the expense of medication.

BREEDING AND REPRODUCTION

DYSTOCIA FROM GROSS OVERSIZE OF A PUPPY

There are no specific breeding problems associated with the Golden Retriever breed. Usually, litter numbers are large and the relatively neatly-shaped puppies are delivered by the bitch without human aid. If, for any reason, there are only one or two puppies carried, they will be normally-shaped but will grow relatively too large for the width of the bitch's pelvic canal. This problem may be seen in the older bitch, whelping when partial reproductive failure means fewer eggs are released from the ovary for fertilisation. A single oversized puppy presents the biggest problem of delayed birth. In the case of a five-year-old bitch mated for the first time, she may well develop dystocia with a dead puppy as a result.

DELAYED MATURITY

A few Golden bitches come on heat for the first time later than the norm, which is 10 to 12 months. Most of these slow-to-mature bitches will have their first heat by 18 months of age, and there is no reason why they cannot conceive and carry a normal litter in spite of this later-maturing tendency. Running these bitches with other bitches already on heat can sometimes stimulate reproductive activity. Pheromones or 'smell hormones' may play a part, but some young bitches seem to resist all attempts to get them to breed until the time they are naturally mature. Oestrogen injections have been used successfully in late maturing Goldens to help them breed successfully.

CRYPTORCHIDISM

Before birth, the male dog's testes originate in the abdomen from a site near the kidneys, similar to that occupied by the mature bitch's ovaries. The testes normally descend from within the abdomen through the inguinal canals, and can be felt in the scrotum about 20 days after birth. Export pedigrees for dogs require a statement that both testes are present in the scrotum, and it may be difficult to be certain that both testes can be felt in the scrotum of the very young puppy.

Total absence of the testes (anorchia) is very rare, while monorchidism implies that only one testis has developed. The most usual abnormality is Unilateral Cryptorchidism, when one testis is retained in the abdomen and one can be felt in the scrotum. Unilaterally cryptorchid dogs are fertile, and have mated bitches, but it is a polygenic inherited defect and attempts to breed out the condition should be supported by not using affected dogs for stud. It is considered by some authorities that the litter mates may all carry the same genetic factor for cryptorchidism, so even the litter sisters of affected dogs should not be bred from if it is required to eliminate the condition more thoroughly than at present.

The problem of the testis retained within the abdomen is that, when the testis is in the cooler site of the scrotum, the organ functions better. The higher body temperature within the abdomen seems to stimulate the cells within the testis to produce oestrogens instead of the expected male hormones.

Seroli cell tumours are thirteen times more common in cryptorchid males than in males with normal-sited testes. Other signs of the tumour are a bilateral hair loss in the older dog, a pendulous penis and attraction of other male dogs to the cryptorchid. Anaemia may develop, due to excess oestrogen production depressing the bone marrow. Castration to remove both testes is advised, but occasionally a request is made to leave one testis in the scrotum, and only have the retained intra-abdominal one removed.

OTHER BREED ASSOCIATED CONDITIONS

MYOPATHY DISORDERS
This recently-studied muscle disease has been reported in the USA, UK, France and Australia. The cause of the disease is unknown, but it seems to be transmitted by an autosomal recessive gene. The disease is not fatal, but may appear as a muscle weakness in puppies between the ages of eight weeks and eleven months. The puppies may appear underweight, quite slim and hold the head lower than normal, due to the muscle weakness. The dogs tire easily on exercise and this seems worse in cold weather. A bunny-hopping gait is seen in many affected puppies and should be watched out for.

A similar disease with muscle weakness, and where the legs may show wasting with a plantigrade posture, has been shown to be due to Neospora infection. Infection probably occurs before birth or in the first weeks of the puppy's life. Blood samples can be used to measure the level of antibodies to Neospora, and the dam of any affected puppy should also be tested. Infection may be acquired by eating raw meat products.

MUSCULAR DYSTROPHY
In the USA, a progressive cardiomyopathy associated with x-linked muscular dystrophy was reported in Golden Retrievers. Changes were seen in the heart from six months of age. The condition was described by Moise, and likened to Duchenne cardiomyopathy. It results in progressive skeletal muscle deterioration and occasionally cardiac death.